Herausgeber / Editors
Christoph Thun-Hohenstein
Hartmut Esslinger
Thomas Geisler

D1638349

MADE 4 YOU

/

Design für den Wandel /

Design for Change

HAVERING COLLEGE
LEARNING RESOURCES CENTRE

MAK

VERLAG *für* **MODERNE KUNST**

745.2 AS 174097

MADE 4 YOU

Christoph Thun-Hohenstein
Direktor MAK /
Director, MAK

Designleiter in die Zukunft

A Design Ladder to the Future

Die Ausstellung „MADE 4 YOU" rückt „Design für den Wandel" in den Fokus. Sie richtet sich weder exklusiv an die kleine Gruppe reicher DesignkonsumentInnen noch allgemein an jene restlichen 90 Prozent, denen Design kein bewusstes Anliegen ist, es zum Teil auch gar nicht sein kann. Vielmehr ist jene ständig wachsende Zahl von Menschen angesprochen, die sich bei Konsum- und anderen Entscheidungen in der glücklichen Lage wissen, zwischen verschiedenen Optionen wählen zu können. Exzellentes Design muss so überzeugend sein, dass möglichst viele die richtige Wahl treffen. „Richtig" bedeutet: im Sinne einer positiven gesellschaftlichen Weiterentwicklung, insbesondere im Interesse der Umwelt.

Exzellentes Design hat demnach viel mit Verantwortung zu tun, in gestalterischer Hinsicht – als Verpflichtung gegenüber der angestrebten Funktionsweise – wie auch inhaltlich. Jede Gesellschaft ist letztlich nur so fortschrittlich wie ihr schwächstes Glied – je nachhaltiger Design Verantwortung erwirken kann, umso eher nützt dies jenen, die in prekären Umständen leben, ebenso wie künftigen Generationen, die sich noch kein Gehör verschaffen können. Exzellentes Design ist also in der Lage, einen positiven gesellschaftlichen Wandel voranzutreiben. Und die Besten haben das Zeug, andere mitzuziehen.

„Nachhaltig" zählt mittlerweile leider zu den verbrauchtesten Begriffen der Sprache von Politik, Wirtschaft und zunehmend auch Kultur. An diesem Umstand lässt sich nicht zuletzt ablesen, welchen grundsätzlich willkommenen Bewusstseinswandel die seit Jahrzehnten geführten Debatten über Sustainable Development, nachhaltige Entwicklung, eingeleitet haben. Zugleich besteht mehr denn je die Gefahr, dass durch eine inflationäre Verwendung des Begriffes die Potenziale, die ein nachhaltiger Ressourceneinsatz birgt, an der Oberfläche politischer Korrektheit verkümmern und die wahren Dimensionen des Problems verschleiert bleiben. Ähnlich strapaziert erscheint spätestens seit Barack Obama der Begriff des „Change". Und doch eignet sich kein Wort besser dafür, den umfassenden Anspruch positiver Veränderung prägnant auf den Punkt zu bringen, geht es doch nicht um kleine, partielle Korrekturen, sondern um einen unumkehrbaren allgemeinen Wertewandel, der durch breite Akzeptanz eine grundlegende Verbesserung der Wirkungsweisen menschlicher Zivilisation herbeiführen soll.

Es wäre eine Illusion zu glauben, dass sich die für einen nachhaltigen positiven Wandel notwendige breite Akzeptanz allein durch Design erreichen ließe. Ebenso unwahrscheinlich ist aber, dass sie ohne den punktgenauen Einsatz

The exhibition "MADE 4 YOU" puts the spotlight on the idea of "design for change." It is aimed neither exclusively at the small group of wealthy design consumers, nor generally at the other 90 percent to whom design is not and partly cannot be of conscious concern. Rather, it is conceived to address the steadily growing number of people who, in their decisions as consumers and otherwise, are in the happy situation of being able to choose between different options. Excellent design must be so convincing that it motivates as many people as possible to make the right choice. Here, "right" means: in the interest of society's positive further development, especially with regard to environmental issues.

Excellent design, then, has much to do with responsibility, both in terms of giving shape to things—as an obligation toward their intended functions—and in terms of content. Ultimately, every society is only as progressive as its weakest member—and the more lasting design's impact on responsibility is, the more benefit it provides to those who live in precarious circumstances as well as to future generations that cannot yet make their voices heard. Excellent design, therefore, is in a position to drive positive societal change. And the best designs have the capacity to act as a motivating force.

By now, "sustainable" has unfortunately become one of the most overused terms in the languages of politics, business, and—increasingly—culture. One of the things indicated by this is the generally welcome shift of consciousness that decades-long debates over sustainable development have succeeded in catalyzing. At the same time, however, there is a greater danger than ever before that the inflationary use of this term could allow the potential inherent in the sustainable use of resources to wilt on the altar of political correctness while the true dimensions of the issue remain hidden. The word "change," at the latest since the ascendance of Barack Obama, has been looking similarly the worse for wear. But even so, no other word is better able to concisely express the comprehensive desire for positive transformation: not minor, partial corrections, but rather an irreversible shift in values that, on the basis of broad acceptance, can effect a fundamental improvement in how human civilization functions.

It would be illusory to believe that design alone could bring about the broad acceptance that is a prerequisite for lasting positive change. But it is just as improbable that such change would be even remotely possible without design's targeted deployment. The function of design is currently experiencing a radical transformation: alongside functionality and aesthetics, the project of designing new products is also subject to the requirement that it contribute toward a better society. In light of this, one can currently discern two, even three fundamentally different design worlds: First, the ever more traditional-looking, up-market "lifestyle design" that is celebrated especially by the home living industry in countless magazines devoted to the topic. Second, design as wannabe art: limited

von Design überhaupt möglich wäre. Die Funktion von Design ist gegenwärtig einem radikalen Wandel unterworfen: Neben Funktionstüchtigkeit und Ästhetik tritt bei der Gestaltung neuer Produkte die Anforderung, eine bessere Gesellschaft zu schaffen. Dementsprechend lassen sich zurzeit zwei, ja sogar drei grundverschiedene Designwelten ausmachen: Erstens das zunehmend traditionell wirkende gehobene Lifestyle-Design, wie es insbesondere im Bereich des Wohnens in unzähligen einschlägigen Magazinen zelebriert wird. Zweitens Design als verhinderte Kunst: Durch limitierte Sammlungseditionen wird nach dem Beispiel des Kunstmarktes eine Verknappung der von den berühmtesten DesignerInnen gestalteten Produkte erreicht. Und drittens die angesprochene neue inhaltliche Ausrichtung von Design auf ein Ziel, das da lautet: „to make a better society". In diesem Bereich bringt Design maßgebliche Beiträge zur Ermöglichung von Innovationen in den verschiedensten Lebensbereichen – wie zum Beispiel Mobilität, Gesundheitswesen, Bildung, Kultur, Sport und Freizeit – hervor; besonders erwünscht sind durch Design bewirkte soziale Innovationen, also etwa spielerische Kommunikation der unterschiedlichsten Generationen oder effektivere Integration von gesellschaftlichen Minderheiten.

Damit soll freilich nicht der Anschein erweckt werden, dass nur diese neue Kategorie von Design künftig Beachtung verdient. Im besten Fall könnte sogar von einer limitierten Designedition eines Stars der Zunft Signalwirkung in Richtung einer nachhaltigen Veränderung ausgehen. Auch traditionelles Lifestyle-Design kann und soll Beiträge für einen positiven Wandel leisten – zum Beispiel durch Verwendung vollständig recyclebarer Materialien – und idealerweise irgendwann im neuen Designverständnis aufgehen. Unter Gesichtspunkten der Nachhaltigkeit erfahren neuerdings auch hochwertige Gebrauchsgegenstände des Kunstgewerbes durch ihren umfassenden Qualitätsanspruch eine Neubewertung gegenüber Billigware und Wegwerfprodukten. Formalästhetisch bleibt abzuwarten, ob sich die zahlreichen Ansätze einer Rückbesinnung auf die einfache Form zu jener Gestaltungsmaxime verdichten, die nachhaltigem „Design for Change" am überzeugendsten entspricht.

Die im vergangenen Jahrzehnt in Dänemark und Schweden entwickelte Designleiter bietet ein Modell für die Messung des Einsatzes von Design in der Wirtschaft. Unterschieden werden vier Stufen der Designreife von Unternehmen: Die unterste Stufe besteht im Non-Design, also in der Nichtanwendung von Design. Zur nächsthöheren Stufe zählen Unternehmen, die Design als Behübschung, als bloßes Styling einsetzen – ob sie nun Designprofis heranziehen oder nicht. Die dritte Stufe bezieht sich auf Design als Prozess: Hier werden DesignerInnen bereits in einem frühen Stadium der Produktentwicklung eingesetzt, um in einem multidisziplinären Prozess und in engem Zusammenwirken mit den Arbeitsebenen des betreffenden Unternehmens auf die Bedürfnisse der NutzerInnen zugeschnittene Produktlösungen zu erarbeiten. Die vierte und höchste Stufe der Designleiter hat Design als Strategie zum Gegenstand: „Die DesignerInnen arbeiten mit dem Management zusammen, um einen innovativen Ansatz für alle oder besonders wichtige Teile der Geschäftsgrundlage zu übernehmen. Der Designprozess kombiniert die Vision der Firma mit ihrer zukünftigen Rolle in der Wertschöpfungskette und bleibt nicht auf Produkte

collector's editions that take up the example of the art market by ensuring the scarcity of products by the best-known designers. And third, the aforementioned reorientation of design's purpose toward the objective of "creating a better society." In this segment, design makes crucial contributions toward facilitating innovation in a wide variety of areas—such as mobility, health care, education, culture, sports, and leisure. Particularly desirable are the social innovations effected by design, such as enjoyable intergenerational communication or more effective social inclusion of minorities.

This is not, of course, to say that only this category of design deserves to be given attention in the future. In the best of all worlds, even a limited designer edition by a star of the craft could have a signaling effect that supports sustainable change. Traditional lifestyle-oriented design, as well, can and should make contributions toward a positive shift—for example by employing fully recyclable materials—and, ideally, merge into the new understanding of design at some point. In terms of sustainability, high-quality, artisan-made utilitarian items have also begun enjoying increased favor relative to cheap and throw-away products. In terms of formal aesthetics, it remains to be seen whether the numerous moves back toward simple forms may yet coalesce into that maxim of design that most convincingly corresponds to sustainable "design for change."

The "design ladder" developed over the past decade in Denmark and Sweden offers a model for evaluating the use of design in the business world. The ladder measures companies' design maturity, distinguishing between four steps: The lowest level is that of "non-design," or design's not being utilized at all. The next step is populated by companies that employ design as decoration, as mere styling—regardless of whether actual design professionals are involved. The third step signifies an understanding of design as a process: here, designers are present even in the early stages of product development, contributing to a multidisciplinary process in close collaboration with the companies' various levels of activity, a process of generating product solutions adapted to users' needs. The fourth and topmost level of the "design ladder" identifies design as a strategy: "The designers cooperate with the management to take on an innovative approach for all or the major sectors that form the basis of the business. The design process is not just limited to products, but combines the vision of the company with its future role in the value-creation chain," reads the study "The Austrian Design Ladder," published in 2006 by "departure," the creative agency of the City of Vienna.

As valuable as the design ladder model may be for the statistical measurement of businesses' use of design, the neutrality of its contents seems quite mundane: it starts from the assumption that design is a value purely unto itself. Without a doubt, successful design can make the world a more beautiful place, but it is just as well-suited to being used as a perfect instrument of manipulation in the hands of individuals with less-than-laudable motives. The present-day world is an all-pervading gesamtkunstwerk of consumption, and design plays a decisive role in this phenomenon's dominance. The question of why—for what purpose—new products, services and concepts are designed, must not only be permitted, it must in fact be mandatory. Therefore, the design ladder must be invested with content—and particularly its highest rung, "design as strategy," must also be employed strategically: as a driving force of positive change. But a design ladder oriented toward such goals must not be limited to the business world—it must also promote the sustainable employment of "design for change" by politics and society in the broadest possible sense, including the arts and culture.

beschränkt", so die 2006 von departure, der Kreativagentur der Stadt Wien, veröffentlichte Studie „Die österreichische Designleiter".

So wertvoll das Designleitermodell für die statistische Messung des Designeinsatzes durch Wirtschaftsunternehmen sein mag, so ernüchternd ist seine inhaltliche Neutralität: Es gibt vor, Design wäre ein Wert für sich, ja purer Selbstzweck. Zweifelsohne kann gelungenes Design die Welt verschönern, das aber ebenso gekonnt als perfektes Manipulationsinstrumentarium in Händen zwielichtiger Zeitgenossen. Die Welt von heute ist ein alles durchdringendes Gesamtkunstwerk des Konsums, an dessen Durchschlagskraft Design maßgeblichen Anteil hat. Die Frage, wofür – zu welchem Zweck – neue Produkte, Dienstleistungen, Konzepte gestaltet werden, muss nicht nur erlaubt sein, sondern ist zwingend geboten. Daher gilt es die Designleiter inhaltlich aufzuladen und insbesondere deren höchste Stufe, „Design als Strategie", auch strategisch einzusetzen: als treibende Kraft positiver Veränderung. Eine solchermaßen zielorientierte Designleiter darf sich aber nicht auf die Wirtschaft beschränken – sie muss auch den nachhaltigen Einsatz von „Design for Change" durch Politik und Gesellschaft im weitesten Sinn einschließlich Kunst und Kultur thematisieren.

Politisch korrekte Überzeugungsarbeit ist wichtig. Breite Teile der Bevölkerung werden jedoch erst dann kundig und mündig handelnd Verantwortung übernehmen, wenn der „Fun Factor" stimmt. Design stellt das ideale künstlerische Werkzeug dar, um Spaß und Freude an der Verantwortung für nachhaltigen Wandel zu vermitteln. In meiner Zeit bei departure wurde dafür der Slogan „Irresistibly responsible" geprägt – besser wurde bis heute vermutlich nicht auf den Punkt gebracht, worum es hier geht.

Das MAK, vor rund 150 Jahren als Österreichisches Museum für Kunst und Industrie gegründet, will in der zweiten Dekade des 21. Jahrhunderts im Einklang mit einem zeitgemäßen Verständnis angewandter Kunst konkreten Nutzen für den Alltag erbringen. Die von Hartmut Esslinger und Thomas Geisler kuratierte Ausstellung, die den Anlass für den vorliegenden Katalog bildet, thematisiert das erfolgreiche Zusammenwirken exzellenter Unternehmen und Designschaffender. Sie setzt damit einen entscheidenden Schritt zur Neupositionierung des MAK im Designbereich, die dem Experiment auf der einen Seite und der positiven gesellschaftlichen Durchschlagskraft von Design auf der anderen in gleicher Weise verpflichtet ist. Letztlich hat Design – „MADE 4 YOU" – immer dem Menschen zu dienen, dies aber unter Bedachtnahme auf ökologische, soziale und kulturelle Nachhaltigkeit.

Politically correct persuasion is important. But broad swaths of the populace will only begin to assume responsibility based on literacy and agency when the "fun factor" is properly included. Design represents the ideal artistic tool with which to communicate the fun to be had and the joy to be found in assuming responsibility for sustainable change. During my tenure at departure, the slogan "irresistibly responsible" was coined for this idea—and since then, probably no better expression has been found with which to sum up what this is all about.

The MAK, founded around 150 years ago as the Austrian Museum of Art and Industry, seeks, in the second decade of the 21st century, to provide concrete utility for everyday life in harmony with a contemporary understanding of applied art. This exhibition curated by Hartmut Esslinger and Thomas Geisler, for which the present catalogue has been produced, centers on the successful interaction of excellent companies and working designers. It thus takes a decisive step toward repositioning the MAK's design focus such that equal justice is done to experimentation and to design's ability to affect society in a positive way. Ultimately, design—"MADE 4 YOU"—must always serve human beings, but with consideration for ecological, social, and cultural sustainability.

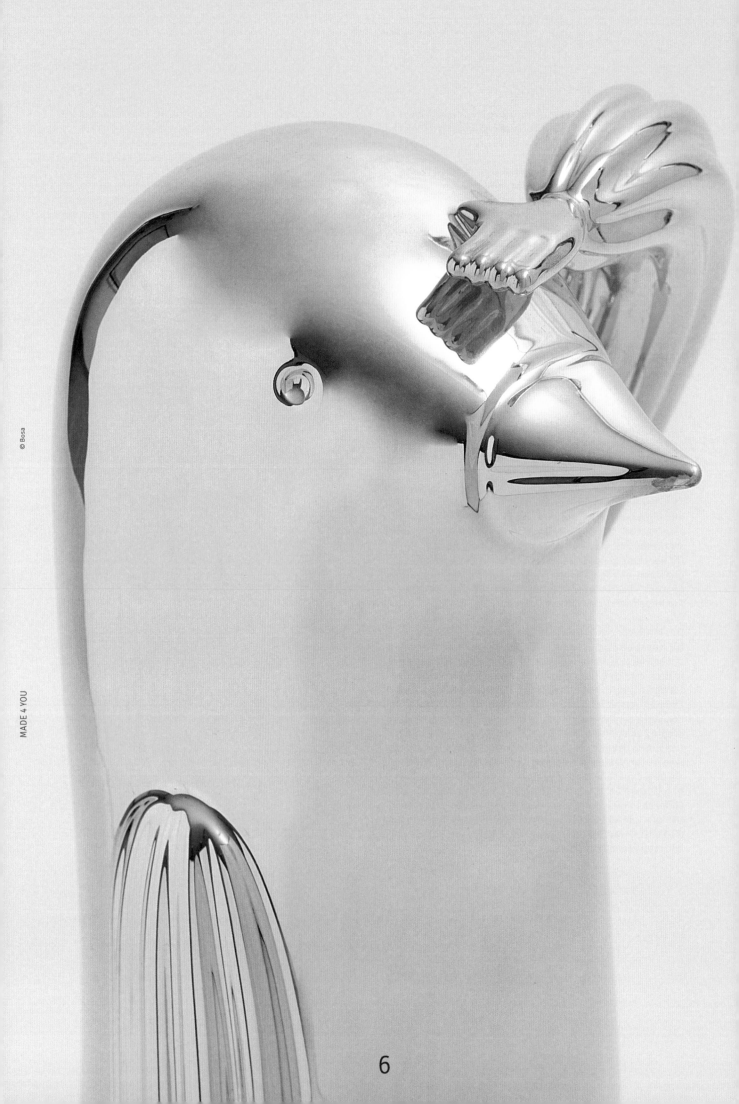

© Bosa

Thomas Geisler
MAK-Kustode Design /
MAK Curator, Design

Looking Forward

Looking Forward

Als im Spätsommer 2011 der Entschluss zur Ausstellung „MADE 4 YOU. Design für den Wandel" gefasst wurde, hatte sie zwar noch keinen Titel, dafür aber ein ambitioniertes Ziel: Für diese erste programmatische Designschau unter neuer MAK-Direktion sollte binnen weniger Monate die Neuorientierung im Industriedesign des 21. Jahrhunderts herausgearbeitet werden: Ist diese Designsparte überhaupt noch zeitgemäß, wo einerseits schon lange von der „postindustriellen Gesellschaft" die Rede ist und andererseits manche Medien, da die Digitalisierung vieles abgelöst hat, von einer „Dritten Industriellen Revolution"[1] berichten? Seit seiner Gründung vor fast 150 Jahren, damals als k. k. Museum für Kunst und Industrie, kommt das MAK seinem Auftrag nach, sich mit künstlerischer Kreativität und seiner wirtschaftlichen Verwertung konstruktiv auseinanderzusetzen[2]. Was erst später als angewandte Kunst bezeichnet wurde, umfasst auch die facettenreiche Disziplin Design, unter der sich von handwerklich gefertigten Einzelstücken über serielle Massenware bis hin zu virtuellen Anwendungen, Serviceleistungen und ganzen Prozessen vieles subsumieren lässt. Wie also kann man den aktuellen Paradigmenwechsel industrieller Produktion und Konsumkultur – und um diese sollte es in der Ausstellung gehen – an einem Ort aufzeigen, der nicht allein Designmuseum ist?

Das bereits angebrochene Millennium hält große soziale, ökologische und ökonomische Herausforderungen bereit – für jeden Einzelnen und für die Gemeinschaft. Design als kreativer Prozess und Katalysator für Transformation spielt seit jeher eine Schlüsselrolle in der Weiterentwicklung unserer Zivilisation. So gesehen ist die aktuelle Auseinandersetzung mit Design als treibender Kraft des Wandels in dieser Ausstellung, aber auch darüber hinaus, eine relative, leben wir doch in ständiger Veränderung. So wie damals, in der Gründungszeit des Museums, die zunehmende Industrialisierung den Lebens- und Arbeitsalltag revolutionierte und nachhaltig veränderte, führt heute die weitreichende Digitalisierung in allen Bereichen zu Umbrüchen im Privaten und Öffentlichen, löst diese Dimensionen räumlich und zeitlich auf und stellt sich an, den Menschen in seiner Intelligenz zu kopieren, ja ihm sogar unter die Haut zu gehen. „When technology goes nano, the human body will become the product", stand kürzlich in der „New York Times" unter dem Titel „The Bionic Bond" im Zusammenhang mit einem Projekt zu lesen, das Stardesigner Philippe Starck angeblich mit Apple durchführt. Ob wir KonsumentInnen uns auf ein Zukunftsszenario wie dieses freuen oder nicht: Fortschritt ist unaufhaltsam.

When, in the late summer of 2011, we decided to mount the exhibition "MADE 4 YOU. Design for Change," we had not yet chosen the title but we had an ambitious goal: For the first programmatic design presentation by the MAK under a new director, the task was to develop a presentation encapsulating the reorientation of industrial design taking place in the 21st century, and to do so within just a few months. The question to be answered was: Is this field of design still in any way relevant to an era in which, on the one hand, the "postindustrial society" is old hat and, on the other hand, some media even speak of a "third industrial revolution" in view of the fact that digitization has superseded many things that came before it?[1] Since its establishment nearly 150 years ago as the Imperial and Royal Museum of Art and Industry, the MAK has been fulfilling its mission of dealing constructively with artistic creativity and its use in the economic sense.[2] The field that only later would come to be known as applied arts also encompasses the multifaceted discipline of design, under which much can be subsumed, from individually handmade products through mass-produced items to virtual applications, services, and entire processes. How, then, is one to shed light on the current paradigm shift in industrial production and consumer culture—this being the chosen subject of the exhibition—at a venue that is not solely a design museum?

The millennium currently underway holds major social, environmental, and economic challenges in store, both for each individual and for society at large. Design, as a creative process and as a catalyst of transformation, has always been a key factor in the development of our civilization. In this sense, the focus on design as a driving force of change, in the context of the present exhibition and beyond it, is a relative one, for we live within a process of continual transformation. During the period of the museum's founding, everyday life and work were revolutionized and lastingly transformed by increasing industrialization; similarly, today, broad-based digitization in all fields is bringing about sea changes in private and public life, dissolving their spatial and temporal parameters and seemingly aiming to copy human beings in terms of their intelligence even as it holds them in its thrall. "When technology goes nano, the human body will become the product," a recent New York Times article, "The Bionic Bond," stated in connection with a project that star designer Philippe Starck is reportedly working on together with Apple. Regardless of whether or not we, as consumers, would actually look forward to such a scenario: progress continues relentlessly.

Verblüffend, mit welch rasanter Geschwindigkeit dieser im digitalen Zeitalter vonstattengeht. Die bestimmende Politik der Geschwindigkeit als Zeichen von Macht und Reichtum kann jedoch, wie der französische Philosoph, Urbanist und Medienkritiker Paul Virilio bereits in den späten 1970er-Jahren befand, die Gesellschaft auch lähmen – ein Phänomen, das er als „Dromologischen Stillstand" bezeichnete und unter anderem am Beispiel der zunehmenden Zahl an Autos pro Haushalt erklärte: Die Verdichtung von Verkehr hat Staus zur Folge, die angestrebte Mobilität verlangsamt sich[3]. Abgesehen von den ökologischen Folgen wie dem CO_2-Ausstoß und der Verschwendung unwiederbringlicher Ressourcen beschäftigt sich die Infrastruktur- und Technologieforschung in den Ländern des Nordens erst jetzt mit der Behebung dieses Wohlstandseffekts. Fortschritt und Stillstand sind also ebenso untrennbar miteinander verknüpft wie Ursache und Wirkung.

Auf die Notwendigkeit einer kritischen Betrachtung beider Seiten der Medaille des Fortschritts weist uns Virilio auch in seinem Buch „Die Universität des Desasters" hin, in dem er für eine globale Risikoforschung zur Verhinderung kommender Megakatastrophen plädiert[4]. Man muss kein fundierter Skeptiker wie Virilio sein, um Störfälle wie Tschernobyl, Fukushima oder andere nicht atomare, jedoch durch den menschlichen Fortschrittswillen und Forschungsdrang verursachte Katastrophen zu hinterfragen. Wir leben in der ständigen Ambivalenz, unsere Zivilisation – und das nicht erst seit der Aufklärung – voranzutreiben, letztlich aber auch die Konsequenzen in Kauf nehmen zu müssen, Kriege und ihre Folgen mit eingeschlossen. Ein einfaches „Zurück zur Natur", wie es teilweise Fortschrittskritiker fordern, ist nicht möglich. Es ist vielmehr eine Illusion, die der Negierung von rund 200.000 Jahren Menschheitsgeschichte gleichkommt. Die Erzeugung und Beherrschung des Feuers stellt eine der wichtigsten Kulturtechniken in der Entwicklungsgeschichte des Menschen dar. Ähnlicher Einfluss kommt der zunehmenden Digitalisierung unseres Alltags zu. Das „Spiel mit dem Feuer" kennt keine Grenzen, die Verschmelzung von künstlicher und biologischer Intelligenz ist letztlich nur eine Frage der Zeit, der Verantwortung und der Moral einer Gesellschaft.

Doch wir haben Warnsysteme, die uns instinktiv schützen, indem sie uns letztlich Korrekturen vornehmen lassen. So erleben wir derzeit nicht nur einen noch nie dagewesenen technologischen Innovationsschub, sondern auch eine sozial und ökologisch motivierte Ära der Kalibrierung. Wir beginnen uns intensiv mit den nachhaltigen negativen Auswirkungen des 20. und letztlich auch des 19. Jahrhunderts seit der Industrialisierung zu beschäftigen und stellen fest, dass viele der verfestigten Systeme – von der Produktion bis hin zur Verteilung – in Zukunft nicht tragbar sind, zumindest nicht für alle, und weiterhin auf Kosten limitierter natürlicher Ressourcen gehen. Immer lauter und unüberhörbarer ertönt der Ruf nach einem „positiven Wandel". Infrage gestellt gehören dabei auch die Bequemlichkeiten nördlichen Lebensstandards, findet hier doch eine Kalibrierung zwischen Nord und Süd statt. Angesichts maroder Staatshaushalte und Finanzkrisen sind aber auch in den sogenannten Industrienationen viele aus der „Komfortzone" gefallen.

It is amazing with what speed the digital age is moving forward. However, as the French philosopher, urbanist, and media critic Paul Virilio found as early as the 1970s, speed as the determining logic of technological society—a phenomenon he referred to as "dromology"—can also cripple the society in which it serves as an expression of power and wealth. One of the examples he used to explain this concept was the increasing number of cars per household: the increase in vehicle traffic density entails traffic jams, slowing down the desired mobility.[3] Apart from the attention being paid to ecological consequences such as CO_2 emissions and the squandering of non-renewable resources, research in infrastructure and technology being done in the Global North is only just beginning to focus on how to repair this side effect of wealth. Progress and stasis, then, are linked with each another just as inseparably as are cause and effect.

Virilio, in his book "The University of Disaster," also points out to us the necessity of critically examining both sides of the coin when thinking of progress, calling for global risk research to prevent coming mega-catastrophes.[4] One need not be an established skeptic like Virilio to critically question accidents such as Chernobyl and Fukushima, or other disasters that, although non-nuclear, were nevertheless caused by human beings' will to progress and urge to research. Since well before the Enlightenment, we have lived with the constant ambivalence of advancing our civilization but ultimately having to accept the negative effects of doing so, including wars and their consequences. A simple "back to nature," as some critics of progress demand, is not possible. This is an illusion that is tantamount to the negation of some 200,000 years of human history. The ability to produce and control fire represents one of the most important cultural technologies in the history of humankind's development. The increasing digitization of our everyday life is having a similar impact. This form of "playing with fire" knows no boundaries, and the melding of artificial and biological intelligence is ultimately just a question of time—and of a society's sense of responsibility and morality.

But we do have warning systems on the instinctive level that ultimately protect us by producing the urge to take corrective measures. We are currently experiencing not only a phase of technological innovation the likes of which has never been seen, but also a socially and ecologically motivated era of calibration. We are beginning to look closely at the long-term negative effects of the 20th century and ultimately of the entire period since the industrialization of the 19th century, and we are in the process of ascertaining that many of the presently entrenched systems—from production to distribution—will not be feasible in the future, at least not for everybody, and that they will continue only at the expense of limited natural resources. The call for a "positive change" is growing ever louder and ever more difficult to ignore. Also to be questioned are the comforts of Northern standards of living, since a calibration is currently taking place here between the Global North and the Global South. In light of bankrupt governments and financial crises, however, even the so-called industrialized nations have witnessed large numbers of people dropping out of the "comfort zone."

„Vielleicht lernen wir aus Katastrophen am meisten", schrieb der austroamerikanische Designer, Autor und Kritiker Victor J. Papanek in einer Überarbeitung seines bereits 1971 erschienenen, nicht unumstrittenen Buchbestsellers „Design for the Real World. Human Ecology and Social Change" [5]. Er bezog sich auf die wachsende Arbeitslosigkeit in der Automobilindustrie, auf diverse Ölkrisen und verheerende Naturkatastrophen in den USA. Rund 40 Jahre und länger melden sich also bereits kritische Stimmen – auch im Design – über die Konsum- und Produktionskultur nördlicher Prägung zu Wort. Die Designhistorikerin Penny Sparke zählt Papaneks Schriften zur, wie sie es nennt, „alarmierenden Literatur", deren Ursprung sie bereits in den frühen 1930er-Jahren zu sehen meint. [6] Papanek selbst stellte später seine Originalpublikation in Bezug zu Alvin Tofflers Fortschrittskritik „Future Shock" (1972) und Fritz Schumachers dezentraler Ökonomietheorie „Small is Beautiful" (1973). Auf der Suche nach alternativen Gesellschaftsmodellen und Lebensstilen begründeten und unterstützten die Genannten seit den 1960er-Jahren mit ihren Theorien und praktischen Anleitungen eine Bewegung der Gegenkultur und Konsumkritik. Den 1968 erstmals erschienenen „Whole Earth Catalog" von Stewart Brand, eine systematisch bewertete Zusammenstellung von Produktempfehlungen und Informationen für ein nachhaltiges und autonomeres Leben, bezeichnete Apple-Gründer Steve Jobs, damals selbst Anhänger dieser Gegenkultur, viel später gar als Vorläufer von Suchmaschinen im Web [7]. Welchen Einfluss Brands Katalog gerade auch auf die Entstehung der PC-Industrie im Silicon Valley hatte, lässt sich in Walter Isaacsons Biografie über Jobs nachlesen [8]. Am Beispiel der Apple-Story kann auch nachvollzogen werden, wie sich Gegenkultur in Mainstream verwandeln lässt. Dies gibt all jenen Mut, die noch heute mit alternativen Start-ups gegen Windmühlen kämpfen. Andererseits ist Apples kommerzielle Erfolgsgeschichte aber auch von den zuvor beschriebenen Ambivalenzen geprägt. Dass die Preispolitik im globalen Markt auf Kosten der Arbeitsbedingungen geht, ist nur ein Teil der Kehrseite von Virilios Fortschrittsmedaille.

Das Design des noch jungen 21. Jahrhunderts hat bereits seine eigenen „alarmierenden" Stimmen und kann auf eine sich formierende Bewegung des Wandels verweisen. Auf der Suche nach alternativen und gesellschaftsrelevanten Gestaltungsfeldern erfreuen sich die einst radikalen Thesen Papaneks und seiner Zeitgenossen zunehmender Aktualität. Die erste, von Krisen geschüttelte Dekade des neuen Millenniums ließ das Interesse wachsen: Die Ereignisse um 9/11 finden im Designdiskurs ebenso Niederschlag wie die latente Wirtschaftskrise, die sich, gekoppelt an politische und gesellschaftliche Umbrüche, in einer kritischeren und verantwortungsvolleren Haltung im Design widerspiegelt. Menschliche und natürliche Katastrophen werden zu Auslösern und Handlungsfeldern für den humanitären Einsatz von „Designern ohne Grenzen" und anderen Designaktivisten. Darüber hinaus bezeugen zahlreiche Mission Statements von Designinstitutionen oder Vorworte von Ausstellungskatalogen wie diesem die Suche nach einem Wandel zum Positiven [9]. Es scheint, die Welt, auch jene des Designs, sei in Alarmbereitschaft und bereit für eine Kalibrierung bestehender Systeme.

"Maybe we learn best from disasters," writes Austro-American designer, author, and critic Victor J. Papanek in a revised edition of his bestselling book "Design for the Real World. Human Ecology and Social Change," which was subject to a certain degree of controversy in the wake of its initial publication in 1971. [5] He was referring to the increase in unemployed automotive industry workers as well as to various oil crises and horrendous natural disasters in the USA since the 1970s. Thus, in the past 40 years or more, critical voices have been raised—among them those of designers—regarding the culture of consumption and production in the Global North. Design historian Penny Sparke includes Papanek's writings in a category which she calls "alarmist literature," the origins of which she places in the early 1930s. [6] Papanek himself later placed his original publication in the context of both Alvin Toffler's critique of progress "Future Shock" (1972) and Fritz Schumacher's decentralized theory of economics "Small is Beautiful" (1973). In their search for alternative societal models and lifestyles, the aforementioned writers spent the period from the 1960s onward establishing and/or supporting a countercultural and consumption-critical movement featuring various theories and practical prescriptions. Apple founder Steve Jobs, at that time himself an adherent of this counterculture, characterized Stewart Brand's "Whole Earth Catalog," first published in 1968—a systematically evaluated compilation of product recommendations and information for a sustainable and more autonomous way of life—as the forerunner of Web search engines. [7] The impact that Brand's catalog had especially on the nascence of the PC industry in Silicon Valley is described in Walter Isaacson's biography of Jobs. [8] The example of the Apple story also lets us trace the process by which counterculture can be turned into something mainstream. This can serve to encourage all those who are still battling windmills with alternative startups today. On the other hand, Apple's story of commercial success is also marked by the ambivalences described above. The fact that price policies in a globalized market act to the detriment of working conditions is just one part of the flip side of Virilio's progress coin.

The design field of the still-young 21st century has already developed its own "alarmist" voices and can now boast a nascent movement of transformation. Amidst the search for alternative and societally relevant creative outlets, the once-radical theses of Papanek and his contemporaries are gaining in topicality and acceptance. The first, crisis-rocked decade of the new millennium has occasioned growing interest: the events of 9/11 impacted the design discourse and so did the latent economic crisis, which, coupled with political and social upheavals, has contributed to a more critical and responsible attitude in the field of design. Human and natural disasters have become catalysts and fields of action for the humanitarian missions of "designers without borders" and other design activists. Furthermore, numerous mission statements of design institutions, and forewords to exhibition catalogues, such as this one, testify to the search for a positive turnaround. [9] It seems as if the whole world, including the world of design, were on high alert and ready to undertake a recalibration of existing systems.

Vorwort /
Preface

Die Kraft von Design. Aus diesem Grund hat das MAK einen der weltweit einflussreichsten Designer und Denker dazu eingeladen, gemeinsam zukunftsweisende Beispiele aus Industrie und Forschung zu erkunden. Hartmut Esslinger, der Gründer von frog design, brachte dabei seine jahrzehntelange Erfahrung als Kreativberater der weltgrößten Konzerne, als erfolgreicher Designstratege und Unternehmer sowie als inspirierender Mentor kuratorisch ein. Bereits in seiner 2009 erschienenen Publikation „Schwungrat"[10] findet sich Esslingers kritische Betrachtung der Entwicklungen in der Industrie- und Produktionskultur der letzten Dekaden. Sie floss nun ebenso in die Arbeit an der Ausstellung ein wie sein Optimismus hinsichtlich der positiven Wirkung unternehmerischen Denkens und Handelns – vor allem im Zusammenspiel von Kreation und Produktion. „Design forward"[11] heißt sein jüngstes Buch, das nahezu zeitgleich mit dieser Ausstellung erscheint und gleichsam ein Manifest für die verändernde Kraft von Strategischem Design ist. Den schier überwältigenden Herausforderungen des 21. Jahrhunderts können wir uns nur mit gemeinsam entwickelten strategischen Ansätzen stellen, wollen wir ganzheitliche und nachhaltige Lösungen erzielen. Laut Esslinger muss die dafür nötige Kreativität in Entscheidungsprozessen auf höchster Managementebene gleichwertig Beachtung finden. Dies setzt aber auch ein neues Selbstverständnis der DesignerInnen voraus, die sich nicht in künstlerische Selbstverwirklichung flüchten, sondern als kompetente Kreativunternehmer in der rational und zahlengesteuerten Geschäftswelt selbstbewusst positionieren. Die humanistische Verantwortung der DesignerInnen besteht darin, menschliche Bedürfnisse und Träume mit neuen Möglichkeiten und Inspirationen aus Wissenschaft und Forschung zu verbinden, um mitunter neue Geschäftsmodelle hervorzubringen. In dieser Schlüsselfunktion und ausgestattet mit der Macht ihrer kreativ-künstlerischen wie analytischen und kommunikativen Methoden haben sie die Möglichkeit, bedeutsame und clever einsetzbare physische wie virtuelle Objekte zu erschaffen, um im schonenden Umgang mit den begrenzten Ressourcen dieses Planeten neue geistige und kulturelle Werte zu schaffen. „Gutes Design" bedeutet unter diesem Gesichtspunkt, bessere Produkte, Mechanismen oder Software-Anwendungen zu gestalten, die eine inspirierende, auf den Menschen bezogene Erfahrung schaffen. Ethisches Verhalten gepaart mit höchster Qualität dieses Schaffensaktes kreiert bedeutsame soziale, ökologische und kulturelle Innovationen, die selbst zu einem markenbildenden Statement werden.

Die Ausstellung „MADE 4 YOU. Design für den Wandel" ist eine umfassende Auseinandersetzung mit Designinnovationen von Weltklasse-Unternehmen, die von A wie Amazon bis Z wie Zumtobel reichen, sowie mit zukunftsweisenden Studien der jungen Designgeneration. Die mit Hartmut Esslinger entwickelte Ausstellung ermöglicht aber mehr als bloß als ein Design-Erleben – sie zeigt die Bedeutung von Design als zentrale Komponente gesellschaftlicher und technologischer Umbrüche im 21. Jahrhundert auf und schafft Bewusstsein für seine Rolle als treibende Kraft des positiven Wandels. Über einen rein geschmacksbildenden und formalästhetischen Diskurs hinaus stellt sich das MAK mit „MADE 4 YOU" beinahe 150 Jahre nach seiner Gründung einer für die Identität des Hauses und seine zukünftige Vermittlungsarbeit wichtigen Auseinandersetzung mit der Rolle von Design, dem als angewandte Kunst wie als wirtschaftlicher Motor Bedeutung zukommt. Vor dem Hintergrund der schon selbstverständlich gewordenen Omnipräsenz von Design im Alltag verweist die für ein breites Publikum konzipierte Schau auf die soziale, ökologische und kulturelle Wirkung von Design.

The Power of Design. For this reason, the MAK invited one of the world's most influential designers and thinkers to explore, with the museum, pioneering examples from industry and the research field. For this curatorial task, frog design founder Hartmut Esslinger brought to bear his decades of experience as a creative consultant to the world's largest corporations, as a successful design strategist and businessman, and as an inspiring mentor. Esslinger's 2009 book "A Fine Line"[10] already contains his critical assessment of the past decade's developments in the culture of industry and production. In his work for this exhibition, he has applied the views expressed there combined with his optimism regarding the positive influence of entrepreneurial thought and action—above all in cases where creation and production interact. "Design forward"[11] is the title of his most recent book, the publication of which is taking place almost simultaneously with this exhibition; it amounts to a manifesto in favor of the transformative power of Strategic Design. If holistic and sustainable solutions are what we are after, then it is imperative that we favor collaboratively developed strategic approaches toward dealing with the well-nigh overwhelming challenges of the 21st century. According to Esslinger, the creativity that is so essential here must be equally present and valued in decision-making processes at the highest level. But this presupposes a new self-conception on the part of designers, who must not take refuge in artistic self-fulfillment but rather position themselves self-assuredly as capable creative entrepreneurs within the rationality and number governed world of business. The humanistic responsibility of designers consists in linking human needs and dreams with new possibilities and inspirations from science and research, giving birth to new business models in the process. In this key role, and equipped with the power of methods that are creative and artistic as well as analytic and communicative, designers are in a position to create meaningful and ingeniously practical physical and virtual objects in order to generate new intellectual and cultural values while making sparing use of our planet's limited resources. Accordingly, "good design" means creating better products, mechanisms, and software applications with all this in mind, bringing things into the world that make for an inspiring and unequivocally human experience. In this creative act, the marriage of ethical behavior with superlative quality brings forth meaningful social, ecological, and cultural innovations that become brand-founding statements in their own right.

The exhibition "MADE 4 YOU. Design for Change" is a comprehensive examination of design innovations by world-class companies from A as in Amazon to Z as in Zumtobel as well as of trailblazing studies by designers of the young, up-and-coming generation. But this presentation, as developed together with Hartmut Esslinger, makes possible more than just an experience of design—it also demonstrates the significance of design as a central component in societal and technological sea changes of the 21st century, giving rise to a consciousness of design's role as a driving force of positive change. Beyond a purely taste-forming and formal aesthetic discourse, the MAK, with "MADE 4 YOU," takes on an examination of the important role of design both as applied art and as an economic motor. For the MAK, founded nearly 150 years ago, this project is significant in terms of both the identity of the museum and its future educational work. Against the backdrop of the already accepted omnipresence of design in everyday life, this exhibition, conceived with a broad audience in mind, highlights the social, ecological, and cultural effects of design.

10

Ein Unternehmen der Zukunft. Anhand von über 80 Projektbeispielen aus global agierenden Designagenturen und Unternehmen werden intelligente und zukunftsweisende Entwicklungen aufgezeigt. Gebündelt in die sechs Alltagsthemen „Mobilität", „Digitale Konvergenz", „Leben & Freizeit", „Leben & Arbeit" sowie „Gesundheit" und „Überleben" geht die Ausstellung den Fragen nach: Wie bewegen wir uns in Zukunft fort? Wie smart sind Technologien von morgen? Was bereitet uns weiterhin Freude? Was erleichtert uns Arbeit und Alltag? Wie schaffen wir Gesundheitssysteme für alle? Was sichert unser (Über-)Leben?

Der Besuch der Ausstellung gestaltet sich als Werksbesuchs eines „Unternehmens der Zukunft", gegliedert in drei Zonen:

Die L o b b y führt anhand von Hartmut Esslingers früher Zusammenarbeit mit Apple in das Strategische Design ein. Dieser Eingangs- und Aufenthaltsbereich versammelt zudem aktuelle Perspektiven von Wissenschaft, Forschung und Wirtschaft in Bezug auf die großen Fragestellungen der Ausstellung. Die Stimmen der dabei zu Wort kommenden ExpertInnen sind auch im vorliegenden Katalog den jeweiligen Themenbereichen vorangestellt.

Das L a b o r zeigt im Zentrum der Ausstellung ein breites Spektrum vielversprechender Ansätze von DesignstudentInnen und -absolventInnen der Universität für angewandte Kunst in Wien, an der Hartmut Esslinger von 2006 bis 2011 als Professor für Industriedesign (ID2) zum einflussreichen Mentor einer neuen Generation von DesignerInnen wurde. Gemeinsam mit ihnen erforschte er eine Vielzahl von Handlungsfeldern des Designs für den Wandel. „Discover, Design & Define" – „Entdecken, Entwerfen & Präzisieren" – wurde für seine Schützlinge, die aus aller Welt gekommen waren, um bei Esslinger zu studieren, so etwas wie ein Mantra bei der Gestaltung ihrer Ideen für die Zukunft. Dieser Bereich gibt den Blick auf Esslingers investigative Zusammenarbeit mit seinen StudentInnen, AssistentInnen und TutorInnen frei. Bei aller Vorausschau fanden stets auch das „Real World"-Szenario und tatsächliche unternehmerische Potenziale Berücksichtigung. Der Einblick in dieses Labor der Zukunft umfasst Modelle und Multimediapräsentationen von rund 30 Projekten, die bereits internationale Aufmerksamkeit erregt oder renommierte Preise gewonnen haben. Die Dynamik des Labors wird verstärkt durch die temporäre Bespielung mit Workshops, die über die gesamte Dauer der Ausstellung in Kooperation mit departure, der Kreativagentur der Stadt Wien, stattfinden. So sind das Institute of Design Research Vienna (IDRV) und das Institut für Entrepreneurship und Innovation der Wirtschaftsuniversität Wien – beide hier im Katalog auch mit Beiträgen vertreten – dazu eingeladen, Impulse aus der Ausstellung in die lokale Kreativszene und die Wirtschaft zu tragen. Das Labor steht exemplarisch für viele Forschungseinrichtungen an universitären und außeruniversitären Instituten, aber auch in den Unternehmen und Designstudios selbst – denn nur durch Interaktion und Interdisziplinarität sowie durch eine gemeinsame Innovationskultur lassen sich die komplexen Aufgabenstellungen des 21. Jahrhunderts bewerkstelligen.

The Enterprise of the Future. Intelligent and pioneering developments are identified on the basis of over 80 examples of projects by globally active design agencies and companies. Grouped into the six everyday themes of "Mobility," "Digital Convergence," "Life & Fun," "Life & Work," "Health," and "Survival," the exhibition seeks possible answers to the following questions: How will we move from place to place in the future? How smart are the technologies of tomorrow? What will we continue to enjoy? What can make work and everyday life easier for us? How can we create health care systems for all? What guarantees our existence and survival?

A visit to this exhibition takes the shape of a visit to the factory of an "enterprise of the future", divided into three zones:

The L o b b y uses Hartmut Esslinger's earlier collaboration with Apple to introduce the topic of Strategic Design. This entrance and lounge area presents current perspectives from science, research, and economics with regard to the major questions posed by the exhibition. The opinions of experts that have been included here also introduce the respective thematic areas in the present catalogue.

The central L a b o r a t o r y introduces a broad range of promising approaches developed by design students and graduates of the University of Applied Arts Vienna, where Hartmut Esslinger became the influential mentor of a new generation of designers during his tenure as a professor of industrial design (ID2) from 2006 to 2011. Together with them, he explored numerous fields of activity relevant to the theme of "Design for Change." For his students, who came from all over the world to study with him, the concept "Discover, Design & Define" became something of a mantra in developing their ideas for the future. This area acts as a window on Esslinger's investigative collaboration with his students, assistants, and tutors. Their work, for all its forward-looking élan, never lost sight of real-world scenarios and actual business potentials. The exhibits in this laboratory of the future include models and multimedia presentations of around 30 projects that have already attracted international attention and/or won famous awards. The dynamic atmosphere of the Laboratory is being reinforced by holding temporary workshops there throughout the exhibition in cooperation with departure, the creative agency of the City of Vienna. In this context, the Institute of Design Research Vienna (IDRV) and the Institute for Entrepreneurship and Innovation of the Vienna University of Economics and Business—both of which are represented in this catalogue with written contributions—have been invited to communicate impulses gleaned from this exhibition to the local creative scene and business circles. The Laboratory is intended to exemplify the numerous research organizations at universities and non-university institutions, as well as the way in which such activities are pursued in business enterprises and design studios—for only through interaction and interdisciplinarity, as well as through a culture of mutual innovation, will it be possible to master the complex tasks of the 21st century.

Vorwort /
Preface

Die F a b r i k gewährt Einblick in die Umsetzung durch die Designprofis – mittels State-of-the-Art-Produkten und -Dienstleistungen, die entweder schon auf dem Markt sind oder auf ihre Einführung hin entwickelt werden. Die Auswahl dieser Beispiele folgte einem Ziel: zu veranschaulichen, dass Design, wenn es die Bedürfnisse der KonsumentInnen befriedigt und sich einem positiven Wandel verschreibt, auch wirtschaftlich erfolgreich sein kann. Natürlich vermag diese Auswahl nur eine exemplarische zu sein, sie verweist in den jeweiligen Themenbereichen aber doch auf branchenführende Best-Practise-Beispiele. Als kuratorische Filter dienten neben der Vision eines gesellschaftlichen und nachhaltigen Wandels für die Zukunft auch der Markterfolg sowie die Betrachtung der gesamten Wertschöpfungskette von der Idee über das Design und die Herstellung bis zum Gebrauch. Auf Basis dieser Filter wurden mit den eingeladenen Designagenturen und Firmen die Ausstellungsbeiträge erarbeitet. Die präsentierten Entwurfszeichnungen, Prototypen, Serienprodukte, digitalen Applikationen oder Filmbeiträge geben Auskunft über Absicht, Idee und Konzept, ebenso wie über den Entwicklungsprozess, über Herstellung oder Anwendung.

Die Gestaltung der Ausstellung und das visuelle Erscheinungsbild, entwickelt vom jungen Wiener Designstudio Vandasye, folgen der Idee und Ästhetik des industriellen Entwurfs unter den geänderten Vorzeichen des Wandels. So griffen Georg Schnitzer und Peter Umgeher, MAK Designer-in-Residence 2012, auf Bestehendes zurück, fügten hinzu, was später wieder Verwendung finden oder in einen Kreislauf zurückgeführt werden kann, setzten Ressourcen schonend ein. Typografisch orientierten sie sich an der Anwendungsfreundlichkeit von Google-Fonts für alle heute üblichen Formate von Print über digitale Medien bis hin zu Smart-Applikationen. Das Farbkonzept greift auf die Kalibrierung im Druckprozess zurück und verweist auf die eingangs erwähnte Neuorientierung und Kalibrierung in der Designindustrie, wie sie derzeit mit Blick auf die Zukunft stattfindet.

Die Einbettung dieser Ausstellung in einen erweiterten Zusammenhang globaler Betrachtung geschieht über die beiden Gastbeiträge von Katarina V. Posch und Barry M. Katz in diesem begleitenden Katalog. Beide Kenner der Designwelt diesseits und jenseits des Atlantiks, sprich: Nordamerikas und Europas, schlagen eine Brücke zwischen den in der Ausstellung mit Beispielen stark vertretenen, aber unternehmerisch wie kulturell verschiedenen Kontinenten. Posch geht auf die kulturellen Aspekte des Wandels als designimplizite Konstante ein und nimmt einen Vergleich der beiden Kontinente in Erweiterung um Japan – einen historisch und strategisch wichtigen Partner in globalen Veränderungsprozessen ebenso wie im Design – vor. Katz' erfahrener Einblick in die Mechanismen der Innovationsschmieden im Silicon Valley, das seit den 1980er- Jahren Hartmut Esslingers Wirkungsumfeld ist, eröffnet wiederum ein anderes Verständnis vom Wandel wirtschaftlicher Prägung, in dem Kreativität zum wichtigen Kapital für die Zukunft wird.

The F a c t o r y offers insights into how design professionals actually implement the approaches they have developed—with examples of state-of-the-art products and services that are either already on the market or being developed for market launch. The selection of these examples was made with one goal in mind: to make clear that design that satisfies consumer needs and is devoted to positive change can also enjoy economic success. This selection can only include a few examples, of course, but among these are representatives of industry-leading best practices in their respective thematic areas. Alongside the vision of a societally based and lasting transformation for the future, additional curatorial filters were the criterion of market success and the examination of the entire value added chain, from the idea to the design and its production and, finally, its actual use. It was on the basis of these filters that exhibition contributions were developed together with the invited design agencies and companies. The design drawings, prototypes, mass-produced products, digital applications, and films on exhibit provides information about intents, ideas, and concepts, as well as about development processes, production, and uses.

The design of this exhibition and its visual appearance, developed by the young Viennese design duo Vandasye, follows the idea and aesthetics of industrial design as affected by the context of change. In their concept, Georg Schnitzer and Peter Umgeher (the 2012 MAK Designers in Residence) employed existing ideas, added elements that could be used again later, returned to the cycle as it were, and generally made sparing use of resources. Typographically, they oriented themselves on the user-friendliness of the fonts used by Google for all of today's common formats ranging from print to digital media and smart applications. The color concept has recourse to the calibration used in the printing process—a reference to the aforementioned future-oriented reorientation and recalibration currently taking place in the design industry.

This exhibition has been contextualized within the expanded framework of global perspectives by two guest contributions, written by Katarina V. Posch and Barry M. Katz, in this accompanying catalogue. Both these experts on the design world, from this and the other side of the Atlantic—that is to say, from Europe and from North America—create a bridge between these two economically and culturally different continents, which are both represented strongly among the various exhibits. Posch, looks at the cultural aspects of change as a design-implicit constant and conducts a comparison of the two continents augmented by Japan, a historically and strategically important partner both in processes of global change and in the field of design. On the other hand, Katz's experienced insight into the mechanisms of the innovation centers of Silicon Valley, which has been Hartmut Esslinger's chief place of activity since the 1980s, opens up another understanding of change as it relates to business, in which creativity is becoming a type of capital that is important for the future.

MADE 4 YOU

← **Hopebird**
Keramik für Bosa, 2012
Design: Jaime Hayon

Hopebird
Ceramic for Bosa, 2012
Design: Jaime Hayon

© Bosa

Das von mir gewählte Maskottchen für dieses Ausstellungsprojekt, Jaime Hayons „Hopebird", hat nicht nur die Hoffnung auf eine zeitgerechte Fertigstellung von „MADE 4 YOU" beflügelt, sondern steht in gewisser Weise mit seiner Symbolkraft auch für jene optimistische Haltung, die dieser Ausstellung und ihren Verantwortlichen zugrunde liegt: Keine Zukunft ohne Hoffnung. Die Herausforderungen des 21. Jahrhunderts scheinen manchmal erdrückend – umso mehr brauchen wir vorausschauende Optimisten vom Schlag eines Hartmut Esslinger, um der Zukunft eine für alle lebenswerte Gestalt zu geben.

The mascot that I chose for this exhibition project, Jaime Hayon's Hopebird, not only gave wings to the hope that we would complete this catalogue in time for the exhibition, but in a certain way also symbolizes the optimistic attitude underlying this exhibition and those responsible for it: There can be no future without hope. The challenges of the 21st century sometimes seem oppressive—which is why we are all the more in need of forward-looking optimists of the likes of Hartmut Esslinger, so that the future can be shaped in such a way as to give everyone a life worth living.

[1] Paul Markillie, „A third industrial revolution", in: Manufacturing and Innovation. The Economist, Special Report, London 2012

[2] Peter Noever (Hg.), Kunst und Industrie. Die Anfänge des Museums für angewandte Kunst in Wien, Ostfildern-Ruit 2000

[3] Paul Virilio, Vitesse et politique, Paris 1977 (dt. Paul Virilio, Geschwindigkeit und Politik, Berlin 1980)

[4] Paul Virilio, L'université du désastre, Paris 2007 (dt. Paul Virilio, Die Universität des Desasters, Wien 2008)

[5] Victor Papanek, Design for the Real World. Human Ecology and Social Change, New York 1971 (dt. Victor Papanek, Design für die reale Welt: Anleitungen für eine humane Ökologie und sozialen Wandel, Wien 2008)

[6] Penny Sparke, An Introduction to Design and Culture in the Twentieth Century, London 1986

[7] „,You've got to find what you love', Jobs says", in: Stanford Report, 14. Juni 2005, http://news.stanford.edu/news/2005/june15/jobs-061505.html (23.5.2012)

[8] Walter Isaacson, Steve Jobs: A Biography, Chicago 2011 (dt. Walter Isaacson, Steve Jobs: Die autorisierte Biografie des Apple-Gründers, München 2011)

[9] Martina Fineder, Thomas Geisler, „,Design Clinic' – Can design heal the world? Scrutinising Victor Papanek's impact on today's design agenda", Konferenzbeitrag zu „Design Activism and Social Change", Barcelona, 2011, http://www.historiadeldisseny.org/congres/ (23.5.2012)

[10] Hartmut Esslinger, A Fine Line. How Design Strategies are Shaping the Future of Business, San Francisco 2009 (dt. Hartmut Esslinger, Schwungrat. Wie Design-Strategien die Zukunft der Wirtschaft gestalten, Weinheim 2009)

[11] Hartmut Esslinger, Design forward, Stuttgart 2012

[1] Paul Markillie, "A third industrial revolution," in: Manufacturing and Innovation. The Economist, Special Report, London 2012

[2] Peter Noever (ed.), Kunst und Industrie. Die Anfänge des Museums für angewandte Kunst in Wien, Ostfildern–Ruit 2000

[3] Paul Virilio, Vitesse et politique, Paris 1977

[4] Paul Virilio, L'université du désastre, Paris 2007

[5] Victor Papanek, Design for the Real World. Human Ecology and Social Change, New York 1971

[6] Penny Sparke, An Introduction to Design and Culture in the Twentieth Century, London 1986

[7] "'You've got to find what you love,' Jobs says," in: Stanford Report, June 14, 2005, http://news.stanford.edu/news/2005/june15/jobs-061505.html (23 May 2012)

[8] Walter Isaacson, Steve Jobs: A Biography, Chicago 2011

[9] Martina Fineder, Thomas Geisler, "'Design Clinic' – Can design heal the world? Scrutinising Victor Papanek's impact on today's design agenda," conference contribution on "Design Activism and Social Change," Barcelona, 2011, http://www.historiadeldisseny.org/congres/ (23 May 2012)

[10] Hartmut Esslinger, A Fine Line. How Design Strategies are Shaping the Future of Business, San Francisco 2009

[11] Hartmut Esslinger, Design forward, Stuttgart 2012

Vorwort /
Preface

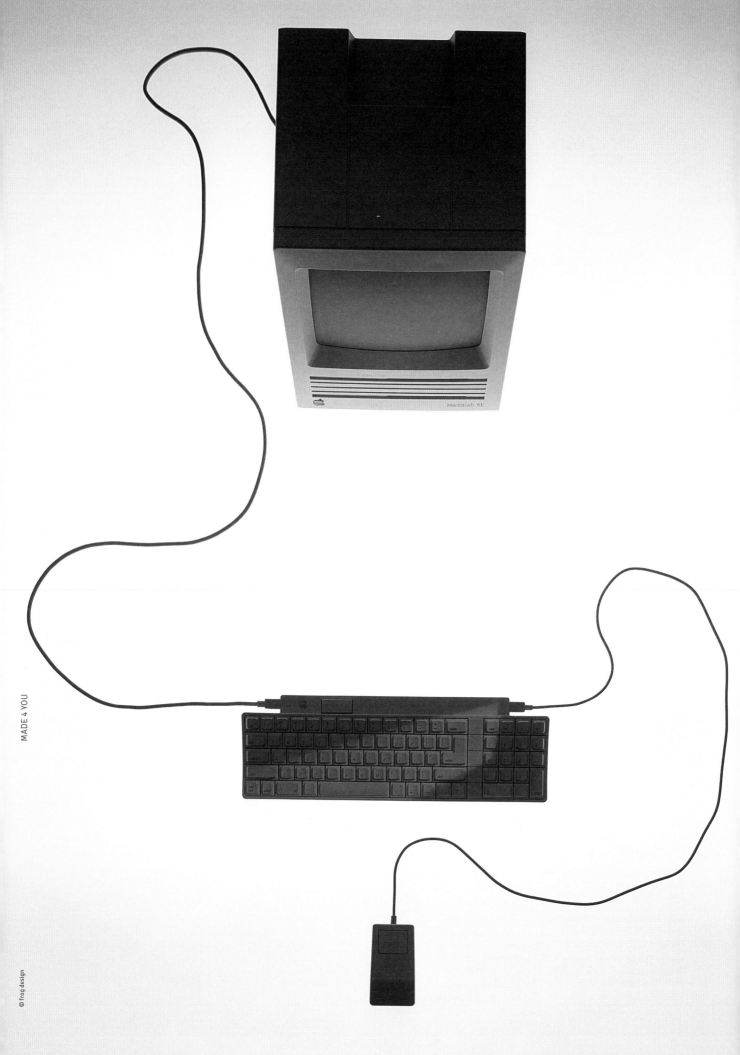

MADE 4 YOU

© frog design

Hartmut Esslinger
Gastkurator /
Guest Curator

Strategisches Design

Strategic Design

Obschon eine junge und dynamische Profession, hat Strategisches Design bereits einen weiten Weg hinter sich – jenen von individualistisch und künstlerisch verstandener Kreativität zu einer Problemlösungsdisziplin, die konzeptuelle Vision und kompetente Umsetzung verlangt. Im Bündnis von Wirtschaft und Design ist Strategisches Design zu einem respektierten Partner mit großem Einfluss geworden. Es war kein leichter Weg dorthin; nun aber lassen sich die rapid steigende Anerkennung dieser Macht und die Notwendigkeit erkennen, sie in Bahnen zu lenken. Ein erster Schritt in diese Richtung ist mit einem gefestigten Verständnis der unabdingbaren Rolle von Design bei der Gestaltung eines innovationsgetriebenen Geschäftsmodells gegeben. Allerdings bedarf es auch einer Neubewertung dieses Geschäftsmodells, seiner Entwicklung sowie einer stärkeren Berücksichtigung der Beteiligten (ebenso wie einer weiter gefassten Definition, wer diese Beteiligten sind oder sein sollen). Insbesondere werde ich das Argument vertreten, dass es ein neues Geschäftsmodell braucht, und zwar eines, das a) KonsumentInnen gleichermaßen als Individuen ansieht, deren komplexe Bedürfnisse durch Konsum nur teilweise zu befriedigen sind, wie als Mitglieder größerer Gemeinschaften mit komplizierten wechselseitigen Abhängigkeiten, und das b) die heute unterrepräsentierten Gruppen ebenso berücksichtigt wie c) die Gesellschaften von morgen, sprich: jene Generationen von Individuen und Gruppen, die auf uns folgen werden und die in hohem Maße von unseren heutigen Entscheidungen und Verhaltensweisen abhängig sind. Ich möchte dieses Geschäftsmodell als nachhaltigkeitsgetriebenes bezeichnen – und meine, dass sich DesignerInnen aufgrund ihrer Rolle hervorragend dafür eignen, seine Verwirklichung in Angriff zu nehmen.

<u>KonsumentInnen mit komplexen Bedürfnissen als voneinander abhängige Mitglieder einer größeren Gemeinschaft</u>. Im größeren Kontext der Kreativität ist Design das lebende Bindeglied zwischen unseren menschlichen Zielen und Bedürfnissen einerseits und der materiellen Kultur andererseits, die uns hilft, diese zu erfüllen. DesignerInnen und ihre Geschäftspartner haben die schier einzigartige Möglichkeit, eine Umgebung zu schaffen, die nicht nur lebenswert und nachhaltig ist, sondern auch Spaß macht und kulturell bereichert. Unsere dingliche Umwelt ist von Menschen gemacht – jede ihrer Komponenten wird erzeugt, verkauft, benützt, weggeworfen, recycelt und (hoffentlich) wiederverwendet. Jedes einzelne Element hat einen Prozess durchlaufen, in dem menschliche Ideen in Entwürfen Niederschlag finden und aus diesen wiederum physische und virtuelle Dinge hergestellt werden. Um eine materielle Kultur hervorzubringen, die uns Auftrieb gibt und stützt, müssen wir stets wachsam für die Möglichkeiten – und manchmal für die gefährlichen Versuchungen – unserer Geschäftsmodelle, unserer Strategien, Werkzeuge, Verfahren und Fabriken bleiben.

← Apple Macintosh SE,
<u>Minimal Keyboard & Mouse 2, 1984</u>
Design: Hartmut Esslinger / frog design

Strategic Design as a young and very dynamic profession has come a long way from individualistic "artsy" creativity to a problem-solving discipline requiring conceptual vision and competent implementation. It has become a respected partner with true power in the business/design alliance. This process hasn't been easy but what's new is the rapidly growing recognition of this power and the need for cultivating it. An initial step toward achieving that goal is a firm understanding of the vital role of design in shaping an innovation-driven business model. What is required next, however, is a reassessment of the innovation-driven business model, its evolution, and to more broadly consider the needs of its various stakeholders (as well as a broader definition of who the stakeholders are, or should be). Specifically, I will argue that a new business model is needed; one that considers a) consumers as individuals with a complex set of needs that consumption of products only partially satisfies and as members of a larger community with complex interdependencies, b) today's underrepresented communities, and c) tomorrow's communities, i.e., the generations of individuals and communities that will follow our own and which depend critically on our current decisions and behaviors. I will refer to this evolved business model as the sustainability-driven business model—a model that I believe designers are especially well suited and positioned to address.

<u>Consumers with complex needs as members of a larger, interdependent community.</u> In the larger context of creativity, design is the living link between our human goals and needs and the material culture that helps to fulfill them. Designers and their business partners have an almost unparalleled opportunity to build an environment that's not only livable and sustainable, but also fun and culturally inspiring. Our material culture is man-made—every component of it is manufactured, sold, used, discarded, re-cycled, and (hopefully) re-used. Every individual element of it has passed through a process in which human ideas are shaped into designs, and designs are manufactured into physical and virtual matter. To build a material culture that uplifts and sustains us, we have to remain ever alert to the opportunities—and sometimes dangerous temptations—of our business models, our strategies, our tools, our processes, and our factories.

The holistic challenge for Strategic Design is to create physical and virtual objects which are useful art, and inspire spiritual values by as few atoms and bits as possible. In my view, design is our modern-day continuation of "technical" functionality converted into human-historic and metaphysical symbolism. When designers create a new and better object, a mechanism, a software application or a more inspiring, human-centric experience, this becomes a "branding symbol" through meaningful innovation, good quality, and ethical behaviors. People recognize the resulting visual symbols as a cultural expression of humanized technology and not just a fashion statement. It must advance our industrial culture by providing sustainable innovation, cultural identity and consistency so as to create emotional

MADE 4 YOU

Die ganzheitliche Herausforderung für Strategisches Design besteht darin, physische und virtuelle Objekte zu kreieren, die Gebrauchskunst sind, und mit so wenigen Atomen und Teilchen wie möglich ideelle Werte zu schaffen. Meiner Ansicht nach ist Design die moderne, mit der Symbolik von Menschheitsgeschichte und Metaphysik aufgeladene Variante „technischer" Funktionalität. Wenn DesignerInnen ein neues und besseres Objekt, einen Apparat, eine Softwareanwendung oder ein anregendes, auf den Menschen gerichtetes Erlebnis entwerfen, wird daraus durch sinnvolle Innovation, hohe Qualität und ethisches Verhalten ein Markenzeichen. Die Menschen erkennen in den daraus resultierenden visuellen Symbolen kulturelle Ausdrucksformen einer humanisierten Technik und nicht bloß ein modisches Statement. Design muss unsere Industriekultur voranbringen, indem es für nachhaltige Innovation, kulturelle Identität und Konsistenz sorgt und emotionale wie soziale Zugehörigkeit entstehen lässt. Sollen Produkte und ihr Gebrauch kulturell relevant, ökonomisch gewinnbringend, politisch nützlich und ökologisch nachhaltig sein, so kommt DesignerInnen die Verantwortung zu, menschliche Bedürfnisse und Träume mit neuen Möglichkeiten und Anregungen aus Wissenschaft, Technik und Wirtschaft in Einklang zu bringen.

Die unterrepräsentierten Gruppen von heute. In Kombination mit der durch Exzesse der Finanzwelt, verschwenderische Überproduktion und Kulturkolonialismus ausgelösten gegenwärtigen Krise stellt die Beschleunigung der Globalisierung vor gewaltige Herausforderungen, schafft aber auch neue Möglichkeiten. Gefragt sind DesignerInnen, die ebenso talentiert wie fähig sind, neue Trends zu setzen und mitzuprägen, die zur Eindämmung des Outsourcings in Niedriglohnländer und zu einer Abkehr von der derzeitigen Überproduktion unpraktischer und generischer Produkte führen. DesignerInnen müssen auch neue „Home-Sourcing"-Konzepte erfinden, indem sie lokale und Kulturen der Menschen vor Ort aufgreifen. Um in der rationalen Welt der Wirtschaft auf gleicher Augenhöhe agierend Respekt zu genießen und Erfolg zu haben, müssen DesignerInnen selbst zu KreativunternehmerInnen oder -managerInnen werden. Letztendlich hat Design jedoch über kommerziell-funktionale Maßstäbe hinauszuwachsen und nach immerwährender kultureller Bedeutung zu streben.

Als Kreativstratege und als Unternehmer bin ich optimistisch: Dieses neue Wirtschaftsparadigma wird lebendigeren, schöneren und emotional befriedigenderen Produkten Auftrieb verleihen. Eine ansprechendere Produktkultur wird tatsächlich Teil einer erfolgreichen grünen Strategie sein. Und das wird für a l l e Länder und Kulturen auf der Erde gelten. Die Humanisierung der Industrien in Europa und den USA wird mit der Entwicklung und Umsetzung eines ökologischen Ideals einhergehen, das uns dazu befähigt, ärmere Länder zu industrialisieren, ohne deren Identität und Kultur zu zerstören. Ein in China designtes, produziertes, verkauftes, benütztes und recyceltes Mobilgerät wird nicht mehr mit einem in modularer Produktion in Zentralafrika, den baltischen Staaten oder Brasilien gefertigten Produkt konkurrieren müssen. Dank dieses neuen Wirtschaftsparadigmas werden wir alle lokal einkaufen und damit stärker in den gesamten Lebenszyklus, in die Kosten-Nutzen-Analysen unserer Verbrauchgüter eingebunden sein.

and social belonging. Designers have a responsibility to connect and coordinate human needs and dreams with new opportunities and inspirations from science, technology, and business in order for products and their usage to be culturally relevant, economically productive, politically beneficial, and ecologically sustainable.

Today's underrepresented communities. The acceleration of globalization—including the current crisis caused by financial excesses, wasteful overproduction and cultural colonialism—is posing both huge challenges and offering new opportunities. It requires designers that are both talented and competent to influence and define new trends with regard to mastering outsourcing to "lower cost" economies and reversing the current excesses of overproducing generic and hard-to-use products. Designers also need to invent new concepts for "home sourcing" by converting local and tribal cultures into beneficial concepts. To succeed as competent and respected "executive partners" in the rational world of business, designers must become creative entrepreneurs or creative executives themselves. However, ultimately, design must rise above commercial-functional benchmarks and aspire to near-eternal cultural relevance.

As a creative strategist and entrepreneur, I am optimistic that this new business paradigm will also promote livelier, lovelier, and more emotionally fulfilling products and a more appealing product culture will actually be part of a winning green strategy. And this will be true for a l l countries and cultures on Earth. Humanizing our industries in Europe and the United States involves developing and implementing an ecological ideal. It will enable us to industrialize poorer countries without destroying those country's identity and culture. A mobile device, designed, produced, sold, used, and recycled in China will not have to compete with one provided by a modular production model in Central Africa, the Baltics or Brazil. It will enable all of us to buy locally and therefore be more closely engaged in the full life cycle, the profits and costs, of our consumable goods.

Tomorrow's communities. Design, like marketing, still is mostly about driving mass consumption, and anything produced on a mass scale contributes to pollution and global warming. That makes designers and their business clients systemic players in an economic model that has a profound effect on the environment—with significant implications for tomorrow's communities. The more items we send flying off the production line, according to traditional business reasoning, the better our chances for economic success. But now, we've realized that the traditional indicators of economic success might not have been giving us the whole story. We've seen the powerful influence of design on the business model, and how strong leadership shapes and implements creative, innovation-driven strategies to achieve more sustainable profitability. We also have to understand that design's role in building sustainability extends well beyond the profits of individual enterprises.

All of those "cheap" goods that have been churned out have proven themselves to be much too expensive culturally, socially, and environmentally—in fact, they're killing us—and "green thinking" finally has taken hold as a mainstream political and economic issue. Today, governments around

Die Gesellschaften von morgen. Wie beim Marketing geht es auch beim Design hauptsächlich darum, den Massenkonsum anzutreiben. Jegliche Massenproduktion trägt aber zu Umweltverschmutzung und Erderwärmung bei. Dadurch machen sich DesignerInnen und ihre Kunden zu Mitspielern eines Wirtschaftsmodells, das tiefgreifende Auswirkungen auf die Umwelt und auf künftige Generationen hat. Je mehr Stücke vom Fließband laufen, umso größer sind nach dem herkömmlichen wirtschaftlichen Denken die Chancen auf ökonomischen Erfolg. Nun haben wir jedoch erkannt, dass die traditionellen Indikatoren für wirtschaftlichen Erfolg nur eine Seite der Medaille abbilden. Wir haben gesehen, welchen bedeutenden Einfluss Design auf das Geschäftsmodell hat, wie starkes Leadership kreative, innovationsgetriebene Strategien entwirft und umsetzt, um zu nachhaltigerer Profitabilität zu kommen. Wir müssen auch begreifen, dass, wenn es um Nachhaltigkeit geht, die Rolle von Design weit darüber hinausreicht, einzelnen Unternehmen Gewinne zu verschaffen.

All die „billige" Massenware hat sich als zu teuer erwiesen, in kultureller, sozialer und ökologischer Hinsicht ... Genau genommen bringt sie uns um. „Grünes Denken" ist in Politik und Wirtschaft zum Mainstream geworden. Heute bündeln Regierungen auf der ganzen Welt ihre Kräfte; sie gestehen ein, dass die gedankenlose Umweltzerstörung ein enormes, von Menschenhand geschaffenes Problem zur Folge hatte. Nun bleibt nur zu hoffen, dass unser menschlicher Intellekt und unser Einfallsreichtum der Herausforderung, dieses Problem in Griff zu bekommen und unseren Planeten zu retten, gewachsen sind. Die steigende Zahl an Menschen, die einen Ökokapitalismus propagieren, übt sich nicht im „Gutmenschentum". Vom Selbsterhaltungstrieb gelenkt, fordert die Bewegung einen raschen Kurswechsel in puncto Produktion und Konsum. Jedenfalls müssen wir ein intelligenteres und umweltverträglicheres Modell von Produktion, operativer Produkt-Unterstützung und Recycling erdenken und entwerfen. Unsere Lösungen können sich nicht in gutem Produktdesign erschöpfen.

Lagern wir die Herstellung der von uns entworfenen Produkte irgendwohin aus, so entziehen wir uns damit nicht unserer Verantwortung für die Umweltverschmutzung und andere negative Folgen, die aus der Produktion resultieren – ebenso wenig wie wir das Müllproblem lösen können, indem wir unseren Abfall in Nachbars Garten kippen. „Aus den Augen, aus dem Sinn" – nach diesem Paradigma dürfen verantwortungsvolle BürgerInnen einer Industriegesellschaft nicht mehr handeln. Wir haben die ethische Verpflichtung, für eine bessere Welt zu kämpfen. Wissenschaft und Wirtschaft müssen ein Gewissen entwickeln, das stärker auf den Menschen hin ausgerichtet ist: indem wir unsere Ziele dahingehend überdenken, dass unsere wirtschaftlichen Bemühungen Resultate zeitigen müssen, die sich gut ausmachen – für uns, für unsere Familien und Freunde, für Nachbarn und Gemeinschaften, für Menschen auf der ganzen Welt. Richten wir uns auf wesentliche – zweifelsohne hoch gesteckte – Ziele wie soziale Verantwortlichkeit und Ressourcenschonung, wird dies dazu beitragen, der Zerstörung des Planeten Einhalt zu gebieten. Noch einmal: Wir müssen ein intelligenteres und umweltverträglicheres Modell für Produktkreisläufe erdenken und gestalten.

the world are joining forces, admitting that our thoughtless destruction of the earth's environment has created an immense—and man-made—problem. Now, we can only hope that our human intellect and ingenuity will be up to the task of solving that problem and saving our planet. The growing movement toward eco-capitalism isn't an exercise in "dogoodism." It's driven by self-preservation, and it demands a rapid change of course in our approach to production and consumption. In any case, we need to envision and design a more intelligent and ecological industrial model of production, product support, and recycling. And our solutions can't stop with good product designs.

Outsourcing our designs to be produced elsewhere doesn't eliminate our responsibility for the pollution and other negative outcomes of that production, just as we can't take care of our own trash problem by tossing it in our neighbor's yard. The "out of sight, out of mind" paradigm must shift, if we want to be responsible industrial citizens. I believe we have an ethical obligation to strive for a better world. We have to create a more human-centric conscience in science and business by rethinking our objectives in such ways, that our business efforts must create results that look good to ourselves, our families and friends, our neighbors and communities—and to people all over the world. Essential and quite challenging objectives, such as social accountability and conservation will help to reverse the destruction of the planet. Again: We need to envision and design a more intelligent and ecological industrial model of production, product support, and recycling.

What is needed next? Traditionally, ecology hasn't rated high in the value perception of many. That's changing, of course, for many of the reasons I've written about in my book "A Fine Line"[1]. Bio-fuels are beginning to liberate us from Big Oil, and solar and wind energy technologies are making inroads into the traditional coal-fired and nuclear energy sector. The Internet is unraveling the old telecommunications companies' hold on customers. And, as we've learned, more companies are adopting sustainable strategic goals and building business models based on long-term vision and ongoing innovation. Or in other words: the old-fashioned monopolies are falling, creative endeavors are rising. One of our most powerful methods for achieving that shift is to reshape the industrial process. Designers, with the help of their business partners, have a strategic opportunity to affect the early stage of the PLM system (Product Lifecycle Management). In fact, we m u s t define the strategy in that early stage if we want it to be effective. By changing the industrial process model from one designed to support mass efficiency to one designed to promote socially and environmentally responsive innovation—for example, by incorporating ecological competence and waste reduction or elimination into our process model—we can both increase the value of a company and improve its sales.

This important shift requires a change in the way companies work, and in the way they interact and collaborate with their customers. We have to innovate business models so that customers join executives, employees and owners/ shareholders on equal footing as competent "caretakers" of businesses and the world they serve. Designers, whose work

© Hartmut Esslinger

↑ **Studie für die Apple Macintosh Workbench, 1983**
Design: Hartmut Esslinger / frog design

Study of Apple Macintosh Workbench, 1983
Design: Hartmut Esslinger / frog design

Modelle für den „Snow White"-
Wettbewerb für Apple und Folge-
projekte aus der Zusammenarbeit
von Hartmut Esslinger / frog design
mit Steve Jobs

Models for Apple's "Snow White"-
competition and subsequent projects
designed by Hartmut Esslinger /
frog design in collaboration with
Steve Jobs

→ **Apple //c System & Drucker, 1983**
Design: Hartmut Esslinger /
frog design

Apple //c System & Printer, 1983
Design: Hartmut Esslinger /
frog design

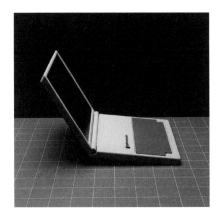

↑ Studie für den Apple Macintosh Laptop, 1982
Design: Hartmut Esslinger / frog design

Study of Apple Macintosh Laptop, 1982
Design: Hartmut Esslinger / frog design

© Hartmut Esslinger

↑ Studie für das Apple Macintosh Tablet, 1983
Design: Hartmut Esslinger / frog design

Study of Apple Macintosh Tablet, 1983
Design: Hartmut Esslinger / frog design

↑ Studie für den Apple MacSlate, 1985
Design: Hartmut Esslinger / frog design,
Susan Kare (Interface)

Study of Apple MacSlate, 1985
Design: Hartmut Esslinger / frog design,
Susan Kare (Interface)

Vorwort /
Preface

↑ Studie für das Apple Phone, 1985
Design: Hartmut Esslinger / frog design

Study of Apple Phone, 1985
Design: Hartmut Esslinger / frog design

↑ Studie für den Apple Baby Macintosh, 1985
Design: Hartmut Esslinger / frog design

Study of Apple Baby Macintosh, 1985
Design: Hartmut Esslinger / frog design

Was kommt als nächstes? Umweltbewusstsein nimmt im Wertekanon vieler Menschen keinen Top-Rang ein. Daran ändert sich gerade etwas – aus vielerlei Gründen, die ich auch in meinem Buch „A Fine Line"[1] schildere: Dank Biotreibstoffen beginnen wir uns von „Big Oil", der Dominanz der Öl- und Gas-Multis, zu befreien. Solar- und Windenergietechnologien preschen in Richtung der traditionellen Energiesektoren wie Kohle und Atomkraft vor. Das Internet löst die Umklammerung, mit der die Telekommunikationsfirmen ihre KundInnen bis dato fest im Griff hatten. Mehr Firmen setzen sich, wie wir gesehen haben, nachhaltige strategische Ziele und entwickeln Geschäftsmodelle, die sich auf langfristige Sichtweisen und stete Innovation stützen. Mit anderen Worten: Die Monopole alten Zuschnitts fallen, kreative Unternehmungen bekommen Aufwind. Dieser Wandel lässt sich mittels Umgestaltung des Industrieprozesses am wirkungsvollsten bewerkstelligen. Unterstützt von ihren Geschäftspartnern haben DesignerInnen die Möglichkeit, schon in der Frühphase strategischen Einfluss auf das System des PLM, des Produktlebenszyklusmanagements, zu nehmen. Wollen wir, dass diese Strategie Wirkung zeitigt, m ü s s e n wir sie in Wahrheit schon in diesem frühen Stadium definieren. Ändern wir die Ausrichtung der industriellen Produktion von der Massenfertigung zu sozial und ökologisch verträglicher Innovation – etwa durch Einbindung ökologischer Kompetenz und Abfallreduktion oder -vermeidung in unser Prozessmodell –, können wir zugleich den Firmenwert steigern und die Umsätze erhöhen.

Diese bedeutsame Verschiebung geht mit einem Wandel der Art und Weise einher, wie Firmen arbeiten und wie sie mit ihren Kunden interagieren. Wir müssen Geschäftsmodelle dahingehend ändern, dass KundInnen auf Augenhöhe mit ManagerInnen, Angestellten und EigentümerInnen bzw. AktionärInnen Verantwortung für Unternehmen und die Welt tragen, der diese dienen. DesignerInnen, die an der Schnittstelle zwischen Menschen und Wissenschaft, Technik und Wirtschaft arbeiten, haben die Möglichkeit und die Verpflichtung, die treibenden Kräfte der neuen grünen Ökonomie zu beeinflussen und an vorderster Front dieser Bewegung zu stehen.

Angesichts der Größe der Herausforderungen kann keine Disziplin – auch Design nicht – im Alleingang die Aufgabe übernehmen, Industrie und Wirtschaft zu „begrünen". Dies hob auch Alix Rule, Studentin der Politikwissenschaften in Oxford, in ihrem mit „Die Revolution wird nicht designt"[2] übertitelten Eintrag im Blog „In These Times" hervor. Um die „hässlicheren sozioökonomischen und ökologischen Folgen des Wachstums" in Griff zu bekommen, müssten wir, so Rule, ungeachtet des von DesignerInnen zum Ausdruck gebrachten Optimismus mehr tun als nur „zuzupacken". Das industrielle System sei einfach zu komplex, zu viele hätten ihre Hände im Spiel. Der Kreislauf aus Produktion, Nutzung und Recycling sei „begrenzt", sprich: Nichts verschwindet einfach. Bewährte Systeme wie Strom- und Verkehrsnetze lassen sich nicht kurzerhand ausmustern – vielmehr müssen wir sie organisch, stufenweise umformen. Wir mussten schon miterleben, wie Egoismus, Eigeninteressen und beschränkte Fähigkeiten der Spitzen von Wirtschaft, Wissenschaft, Politik und Industrie engagierte

forms the interface between humans and science, technology and business, have the obligation and opportunity to shape the drivers of the new "green" economy, and to be on the front lines of that effort.

Given the size of the challenges, no single discipline—even design—can single-handedly take on the task of "greening" industry and business. Alix Rule, a student of politics at Oxford underscored this point in her "In These Times" blog entry titled "The Revolution Will Not Be Designed."[2] Rule noted that, in spite of the optimism expressed by designers, we need more than a "can-do attitude" to address "the nastier socioeconomic and environmental corollaries of growth." The industrial system just is too complex, with too many different players. The cycle of production, usage, and recycling is "finite," meaning nothing will just disappear, and we can't just discard established systems, such as our electric grid or transportation networks. Instead, we have to transform them organically, in stages. We've already looked at how egotism, special interests, and limited competencies among the world's leaders in business, science, politics, and industry have fractioned efforts toward environmental progress, and limited progress with narrowly defined motivations and goals. Nevertheless, designers have the tools to grasp a unique opportunity to drive the development of sustainable products by virtue of our role in the early stages of the product lifecycle process.

How does design partner with marketing? Like Alix Rule, I admire the progressivism behind much of the current generation of design thinking. But I also know she's right when she says that the belief that design can save the world without a "coherent set of ideas" represents a type of progressivism that is "naïve, at best." Sustainability driven design, at its core, is not about the "next new thing" but about "the next better thing," and many designers find this goal very boring and limiting. That's why designers must rely on strong alliances with market leaders to devise sustainable strategies that will succeed in the world as it is, while helping to shape the world as we want it to be. For all of these reasons, evolving our industrial processes is going to require a much deeper understanding of our potential. There are many great opportunities how we can apply technologies, or products, or practices that are currently available or can be easily adapted from existing models and practices—both in regards to innovating design methods as well as creating new business models and processes. Naturally, there is some radical change required and a lot work to be done. New ideas and concepts for the "greening and humanizing industry and business" are critical elements for developing and achieving sustainable strategies that are driven by a more environmentally- and economically-driven vision of a better future.

Bewegungen für den ökologischen Fortschritt gespalten, diesen mit eng gesteckten Zielen gebremst haben. Nichtsdestoweniger haben DesignerInnen dank der Rolle, die sie im Anfangsstadium des Produktlebenszyklus einnehmen, die Möglichkeit und das Werkzeug in der Hand, die Entwicklung nachhaltiger Produkte voranzutreiben.

Wie arbeiten Design und Marketing zusammen? Wie Alix Rule bewundere ich die Fortschrittlichkeit vieler Design-DenkerInnen von heute. Aber ich teile auch ihre Ansicht, dass der Glaube, Design könne die Welt retten, ohne ein „zusammenhängendes Ideengebäude" einer „bestenfalls naiven" Fortschrittsgläubigkeit gleichkommt. Bei Design, das auf Nachhaltigkeit ausgerichtet ist, geht es im Kern nicht um das nächste neue Ding, sondern um das nächste bessere Ding – was viele DesignerInnen als langweilig und einschränkend empfinden. Um nachhaltige Strategien zu entwickeln, die in der Welt, wie sie ist, Erfolg haben, und gleichzeitig dazu beitragen, die Welt so zu gestalten, wie wir sie uns wünschen, müssen DesignerInnen daher auf starke Allianzen mit Marktführern setzen. Aus all diesen Gründen wird es für die Weiterentwicklung industrieller Prozesse ein viel tieferes Verständnis unseres Potenzials brauchen. Im Hinblick auf innovative Designmethoden, als auch was die Entwicklung neuer Geschäftsmodelle und -prozesse betrifft, stehen heute viele großartige Möglichkeiten offen, bereits verfügbare oder anhand existierender Modelle oder Verfahren adaptierbare Technologien, Produkte oder Methoden anzuwenden. Natürlich setzt das einen radikalen Wandel voraus, viel Arbeit bleibt noch zu tun. Neue Ideen und Konzepte für eine „grünere und menschengerechtere Industrie und Wirtschaft" sind entscheidende Elemente, wenn es darum geht, nachhaltige Strategien zu entwickeln, hinter denen eine ökologie- wie ökonomiegelenkte Vision einer besseren Zukunft steht.

© Dietmar Henneka

Vorwort /
Preface

↑ NeXT Cube, 1986
Design: Hartmut Esslinger /
frog design

[1] Hartmut Esslinger, A Fine Line. How Design Strategies are Shaping the Future of Business, San Francisco 2009 (dt.: Hartmut Esslinger, Schwungrat. Wie Design-Strategien die Zukunft der Wirtschaft gestalten, Weinheim 2009)

[2] Alix Rule, „The Revolution Will Not Be Designed", 11. Januar 2008, in: In These Times, Blog, http://www.inthesetimes.com/article/3464/the_revolution_will_not_be_designed/ (23.5.2012)

[1] Hartmut Esslinger, A Fine Line. How Design Strategies are Shaping the Future of Business, San Francisco 2009

[2] Alix Rule, "The Revolution Will Not Be Designed," 11. Januar 2008, in: In These Times, Blog, http://www.inthesetimes.com/article/3464/the_revolution_will_not_be_designed/ (23 May 2012)

Kontext / Context

MADE 4 YOU

Katarina V. Posch

Welten im Wandel, Wandel im Design

Die Bedeutung von Veränderung im Design in Europa, den USA und in Japan

Changing Worlds, Changing Design

The Meaning of Change as Observed in the Creation of Design in Europe, the USA, and Japan

Wandel scheint im Design unvermeidlich. Man erwartet, dass sich Autos und Bekleidung mit jeder neuen Saison verändern; die Handy- und die Computerindustrie blühen und gedeihen, weil die Kunden nach den jeweils aktuellsten Modellen lechzen. Innovatives Lampen- und Möbeldesign begeistert die Besucher heftig beklatschter internationaler Designmessen. Parallel dazu gibt es einen Markt für ähnliche, aber ältere Modelle – Klassiker, Sammlerstücke oder einfach zeitloses Design.

Wandel kann auch überraschen. Von Architektur erwartet man, dass sie eine längere Lebensspanne aufweist als Objekte. Und doch variiert das Tempo der Bautätigkeit in verschiedenen Weltteilen drastisch. Europa scheint den Begriff „Immobilie" im eigentlichen Wortsinn der „Unbeweglichkeit" am ernstesten zu nehmen; in den USA tendiert man dazu, die nächste Generation beim Bauen außer Acht zu lassen. Zwar mag es historische Bauwerke geben, der Denkmalschutzgedanke ist aber schwach ausgeprägt. Japan, der Industriegigant im Fernen Osten, hat das geringste Interesse daran, Gebäude für eine jahrhundertelange Nutzung zu erhalten. Dort verdient die Bauindustrie gut daran, Klein- und Großstadtlandschaften in einem Zustand ständiger Metamorphose zu halten, und verändert so stetig das Gesicht des Landes.

Im Vergleich über Kulturgrenzen hinweg betrifft der Wandel demnach nicht alle Objekte gleichermaßen schnell und aus den gleichen Gründen. Design ist die Sprache der Massen; als solche ist es der direkteste Ausdruck von Kultur. Kulturen wiederum spiegeln sich in ihren jeweiligen Märkten wider – durch Design als „DNS einer Industriegesellschaft".[1] Freilich wird Design nicht, wie Marx meinte, einseitig vom Markt diktiert, sondern stellt, mehr im Sinne der Gedanken Pierre Bourdieus, eher wechselseitige Kommunikation zwischen Angebot und Nachfrage dar. Designer und Hersteller müssen sich auf die Nachfrage einstellen; gleichzeitig sollen neue Produkte regelmäßig Anstoß zu Änderungen des Geschmacks geben. Die Konsumenten von heute sind mündig[2] und wollen geschmacklich herausgefordert werden. Das führt dazu, dass sie mit dem Markt wachsen und die Märkte sich wiederum anpassen.[3]

Europa, die USA und Japan sind nach wie vor jene drei Märkte mit dem weltweit höchsten Bruttoinlandsprodukt. Allerdings haben unterschiedliche Entwicklungen in der politischen, Religions- und Kulturgeschichte dieser Länder Interesse an Produkten von jeweils anderem ästhetischen, funktionalen und symbolischen Wert hervorgerufen. Ihre Märkte, die von vergleichbarer Wirtschaftskraft sind, bieten ein interessantes Feld für einen Kulturvergleich. Die Zeiten, in denen man versuchte, einen globalen Geschmack zu konstruieren, sind passé, sogar im Lichte des Onlinehandels.[4] Heutzutage berücksichtigen internationale Warenlieferanten unterschiedliche Gruppen auf dem Markt. Global agierende „Tastemaker" haben ein feines Gespür für lokale Konsumenten.

Change in design seems inevitable. Cars and clothing are expected to be strikingly different when the new season comes around; the cell phone and computer industries thrive on their customers' craving for the newest versions. Innovative lamp and furniture design excite visitors at internationally acclaimed trade shows. At the same time, there is a market of similar, but aged objects such as vintage, collectibles, or simply timelessly approved designs.

Change can surprise, too. Architecture is expected to have a longer lifespan than objects. And yet, the pace of new construction varies dramatically in different corners of the world. Europe seems to take the meaning of the term "immobilia" the most seriously, while the US has a tendency to build without the next generation in mind. Historic buildings may still exist, but the concept of preservation is weak. Japan, the industrial giant in the Far East, has the least interest in preserving buildings for secular use. There, the regular turnover of construction leaves town and cityscapes in a state of constant metamorphosis, regularly changing their entire faces.

Hence, when compared across culture lines, change does not affect all objects at the same speed and for the same reasons. Design is the language of the masses; as such, it is the most direct expression of any culture. In turn, cultures are reflected by their respective markets—through design as the "DNA of an industrial society."[1] However, design is not one-sidedly dictated by the market, as Marx has suggested, but rather the result of a constant intercommunication between supply and demand, more in the line of Pierre Bourdieu's ideas. Designers and producers have to be attuned to the demands; at the same time, new products are supposed to stimulate a regular change of taste. Today's consumers are mature,[2] and expect to be challenged in their tastes. As a result, they grow with the market, and the markets adapt in turn.[3]

Europe, the U.S. and Japan are still three markets of the highest GDP worldwide. However, different developments in their political, religious and cultural histories have brought forth interests in products of varying aesthetic, functional and symbolic values. Similar in economic power, their markets offer an interesting palette for a cultural comparison. Times of attempted construction of global taste are passé, even in the light of online trade.[4] Today's international suppliers take different market groups into account. So-called "tastemakers" are global people with a fine-tuned ear for local consumers.

Aesthetic changes may occur for various reasons. Classical beauty as derived from the arts may have some influence, since "exposure to a fine piece of sculpture is likely to create in a person awareness of the excellent lines of a thermos jug or a lamp, and vice versa. Thus, when a good design is mass-produced, its influence is tremendous."[5] Yet, aesthetic value per se differs from culture to culture. A distorted teacup would be discarded in European

25

Ästhetischer Wandel passiert aus verschiedenen Gründen. Klassische Schönheit, wie sie sich aus der Kunst herleiten lässt, mag einigen Einfluss haben, da „die Begegnung mit einer schönen Skulptur mit einiger Wahrscheinlichkeit dazu führen wird, in einem Menschen das Bewusstsein für die vortrefflichen Linien einer Thermoskanne oder Lampe zu wecken und umgekehrt. Daher ist, wenn gutes Design in Massen produziert wird, sein Einfluss ungeheuer".[5] Und doch unterscheidet sich ästhetischer Wert als solcher von Kultur zu Kultur. Eine leicht verformte Teetasse würde in einer europäischen Produktion ausgesondert. Dieselbe Tasse könnte freilich in Japan zu einem geschätzten Kleinod werden. Schönheit liegt im Auge des Betrachters, und ästhetische Veränderungen werden eher individuell denn kollektiv wahrgenommen.

Funktionale Veränderungen im Design scheinen eher rational verstehbar. Neue Technologie bringt üblicherweise eine ganze Reihe von neuen Geräten und neuen Verhaltensweisen mit sich: Elektrizität und die allmähliche Beleuchtung des halben Erdballs erlaubten, dass sich menschliche Aktivitäten in die Nacht verlagerten. Die aus dem Bau von Autos und Eisenbahnen resultierende Möglichkeit, dass jedermann reisen und pendeln kann, sowie Handys und die ununterbrochene Erreichbarkeit der Gesellschaft sind weitere überzeugende Beispiele.

Symbolwert – ob bewusst oder unbewusst als solcher wahrgenommen – wird für gewöhnlich über allen anderen Faktoren stehen. Trotz Energiekrise und der drohenden Zerstörung der Erdatmosphäre ist das SUV immer noch das wichtigste identitätsstiftende Symbol Amerikas. Die Europäer sind stolz auf ihr Zuhause und sehen darin ihre Persönlichkeit widergespiegelt, ungeachtet ihrer in Massenproduktion gefertigten Möbel von Ikea und Co. Japanische Konsumenten bestehen auf aufwendigen Verpackungen, trotz höherer Kosten und Materialverschwendung. Kulturen transportieren eine Fülle symbolischer Bedeutungen, und deren Assoziationen wiegen tendenziell schwerer als funktionale und ästhetische Anliegen.

So unterschiedlich er sich auch in Bezug auf Kultur, Disziplin, Tempo und Bedeutung darstellen mag: Wandel passiert. In Europa vollzieht er sich selten geradlinig. In einer Kultur, die Tradition und Geschichte hochhält, muss das Neue mit dem Althergebrachten konkurrieren. Doch es gibt sie im europäischen Design, die Veränderungen, und am interessantesten sind jene auf häuslichem Gebiet, in der Sphäre des Privaten, wo die Entwicklung in Richtung einer effizienteren Materialnutzung und Bauweise Haushaltsgeräte leistbarer machte. Ästhetisch allerdings scheint der Weg zu akzeptierten Änderungen entlang historischer Pfade zu mäandern. Ein Umweg über die Vergangenheit – unter Rückgriff auf bestehende Assoziationen und akzeptierte Konventionen – ist hilfreich bei der Einführung neuer Ideen.

Die Wiener Werkstätte, die an der Wende zum 20. Jahrhundert zumindest in ästhetischer Hinsicht eine moderne gestalterische Sprache entwickelte, verband die Arbeitsgrundsätze der britischen Arts-and-Crafts-Bewegung[6], die wiederum mittelalterliche Handwerkskunst neu belebte, mit der stilistischen Einfachheit des Biedermeier, das damals bereits 50 Jahre aus der Mode war.[7] ABB. 1

Der Schwerpunkt, den man in den Entwürfen des Art Nouveau auf asymmetrische Gestaltung legte, wäre ohne dessen Vorgängerin, das bei der konservativen und prätentiösen Bourgeoisie des Zweiten französischen Empire beliebte Neorokoko, nicht möglich gewesen.[8] Le Corbusiers Studium der klassischen griechischen Architektur und seine Bewunderung dafür fanden in seiner Villa Savoye (1929–1931) Niederschlag.[9]

production. The same cup may become a highly prized treasure in Japan, though. Beauty lies in the eyes of the beholder, and aesthetic changes are perceived individually rather than collectively.

Functional changes in design seem to be more rationally comprehensible: new technology usually brings a succession of changed devices and changed behavior in its wake—electric power and the successive illumination of half the globe allowed human activities to shift well into nighttime; other potent examples are train and car design and the consequent possibility to travel and commuting for everyone, or cell phones and society's unbreakable connectivity.

Symbolic value, whether consciously or unconsciously perceived as such, tends to ultimately trump all other factors. The SUV is still America's most important symbol of identity, despite energy crises and threats of the destruction to the global atmosphere. Europeans cherish their homes as expressions of their personality, regardless of their mass produced furniture by IKEA & Co. Japanese consumers continue to insist on elaborate packaging, despite elevated costs and wasteful materials. Cultures carry a vast array of symbolic meanings, and their associations tend to outweigh functional and aesthetic concerns.

However different in culture, discipline, pace, or meaning: Change happens. Change in Europe hardly happens in a straight forward manner. In a culture that prizes tradition and history, the new has to compete with the incumbent. However, changes happen in European design, and most interesting are those in the domestic field. In the private sphere, the evolution toward a more efficient use of materials and construction resulted in making household goods more affordable. In aesthetic terms, however, the path to accepted changes seems to meander along historic pastures. A detour through the past—using existing associations and accepted conventions—is instrumental to introduce new ideas.

The Wiener Werkstätte, which at least aesthetically developed a modern visual language at the turn to the 20th century, combined the work principles of the British Arts and Crafts Movement[6], which in turn revived medieval handicraft, with the austerity of the Biedermeier style, by then more than 50 years out of fashion.[7] FIG. 1

The focus on asymmetric layout of French Art Nouveau designs would hardly have happened without its predecessor, the Rococo Revival Style, fashionable within the conservative and pretentious bourgeoisie of France's Second Empire.[8] Le Corbusier's adoration and study of Greek classical architecture translated smoothly in his Villa Savoye (1929–1931).[9]

Charlotte Perriand's masterpieces, which were produced while she was responsible for Le Corbusier's domestic furnishings,[10] enjoy our lasting appreciation. Though being a convinced Modernist, she was also a virtuoso on the keyboard of bourgeois connotations. The famous chaise longue was clad in linen canvas and leather to allude to the aesthetics—and the cachet—of an Hermès handbag.[11] FIG. 2

Scandinavian Modern would not exist without Swedish Neoclassical style; Italian Radical Design built upon historic sampling—however—ironically twisted. Double-coding[12] allowed connoisseurship of historic icons to turn into playful yet sophisticated new forms, whose connotations lured the clientele into a warm and cozy feeling of familiarity. The transformation of classical design vocabulary into a different voice is commonplace in today's European design. FIG. 3

© Thomas Dix/Vitra Design Museum
© VBK Wien / Vienna und / and VG Bild-Kunst, Bonn 2012 für Le Corbusier, Pierre Jeanneret, Charlotte Perriand

↑ ABB. 1
Teeservice für Mileva Roller, 1907/1908
Design: Josef Hoffmann / Wiener Werkstätte

FIG. 1
Tea set for Mileva Roller, 1907/1908
Design: Josef Hoffmann / Wiener Werkstätte

↑ ABB. 2
Chaise Longue B 306, 1928
Design: Le Corbusier, Pierre Jeanneret,
Charlotte Perriand

FIG. 2
Chaise Longue B 306, 1928
Design: Le Corbusier, Pierre Jeanneret,
Charlotte Perriand

Die Meisterwerke von Charlotte Perriand – entstanden in jener Zeit, da sie für Le Corbusiers Inneneinrichtungen verantwortlich zeichnete [10] – genießen anhaltende Wertschätzung. Obwohl überzeugte Modernistin, spielte sie auch virtuos auf der Klaviatur bürgerlicher Assoziationen. Die berühmte Chaiselongue war mit Leinen und Leder bezogen – eine Anspielung auf die Ästhetik, und das Prestige, einer Handtasche von Hermès. [11] ABB. 2

Die skandinavische Moderne würde ohne die schwedische Neoklassik nicht existieren; das italienische Radical Design baute auf historischen Anleihen auf, wie ironisch gebrochen diese auch immer gewesen sein mögen. Durch Doppelkodierung [12] konnte die Kenntnis historischer Ikonen ihren Ausdruck in spielerischen und doch raffinierten neuen Formen finden, deren Konnotationen ihre Klientel verführten, indem sie ein warmes Gefühl von Vertrautheit hervorriefen. Klassisches Designvokabular in eine andere Stimmlage zu transponieren ist im europäischen Design von heute alltäglich. ABB. 3

Wenn es um das häusliche Umfeld geht, vollzieht sich Wandel im europäischen Design oftmals über einen Umweg, der in die Vergangenheit führt. Auch in den USA wird Innovation diesbezüglich nicht gerade groß geschrieben. [13] Anders als europäische Wohnungen kann die häusliche Sphäre in den USA aber kaum als Schaukasten der Identität der Eigentümer gelten. [14] Bestenfalls unterliegt sie demselben Maßstab wie der Arbeitsplatz, an dem Veränderungen mehr im Dienste der Effizienz als des persönlichen Ausdrucks vollzogen werden: „In den Vereinigten Staaten, [...] ist es die Gruppe der aktiv mit der Hausarbeit befassten Frauen, die das arbeitssparende und verbesserte moderne Gerät am meisten anspricht. Zeit und Mühe der Hausfrau müssen auf jeden Fall gespart werden. Sie sollte daher bestrebt sein, alle diese Haushaltsgeräte zu kaufen und zu benutzen, die Kraft und Zeit sparen und sie von der Mühsal im Haushalt befreien." [15]

Die Änderungen, denen Gerät und Arbeitsplatz in Funktion und Ästhetik unterworfen waren, dehnten sich letztendlich auf die ganze Welt aus. Überrascht es, dass eine Nation, deren Unabhängigkeitserklärung aus der Feder eines Erfinders stammt, dieses Erbe bis zum heutigen Tage fortführt? [16] Die folgende Industrialisierung setzte sich in den USA viel leichter durch als in Europa. Auf beiden Seiten des Atlantiks wurden die ersten industriell

Changes to European design happen in the domestic realm frequently via a loop back into the past. As for the private domain, innovation is not high on the American citizen's agenda. [13] Contrary to European homes, the domestic sphere in the US can hardly be considered as a showcase for their owners' identity. [14] At best, it is measured by the same scale as work places, where changes are made for the sake of efficiency rather than personal expression: "In the United States, ... It is to this class of women who are actively concerned in the work of the home that the labor-saver and improved modern tool most appeal. The homemaker's time and effort are worth conserving by every means. She should therefore be eager to buy and use all the household tools which will save her strength and time and liberate her from household drudgery." [15]

Functions and aesthetics of tools and work spaces have undergone changes that eventually spread around the world. Is it any surprise that a nation whose Declaration of Independence stems from the pen of an inventor continues the legacy into the present day? [16] The eventual industrialization flourished at much greater ease in the U.S. than its counterpart in Europe. On both sides of the Atlantic Ocean, the first wave of industrial products—such as pottery, furniture, ironware—was designed for and used by the emerging middle class. They took pride in their possessions, which represented a new social status of wealth. However, past imagery and visual connotation eased the introduction of novel technology and usage to a potential market. [17] A good example of this is Wedgwood who applied classical shapes and motifs on his pottery created from cutting edge material and production techniques. Similarly in furniture design, even early Thonet bentwood chairs did not show off their novel technology; aesthetically, they did not stray far from the appearance of a Biedermeier chair, en vogue during the 1830s and 40s. By mid-19th century, rising lamentation in Europe over poor quality of industrial products was actually over the loss of the good old days. Industrial products lost their appeal to the educated bourgeoisie in Europe, and on the one hand, their interest changed toward hand crafted objects, which were sold to a wealthy upper middle class (Arts & Crafts Movement). Such handcrafted objects recalled the uniqueness of a work of fine art, an appeal that resonated long into the 20th century. [18] On the other hand, industrial products came on the market that overtly imitated styles from pre-industrial periods. These were cheaper, and thus widely sought after by a middle and petit bourgeoisie.

© Moooi

MADE 4 YOU

erzeugten Produkte – Steingut, Möbel, Eisenwaren – für die aufstrebende Mittelklasse entworfen. Sie war stolz auf ihren Besitz, der einen neuen gesellschaftlichen Status, nämlich Wohlstand, repräsentierte. Zugegebenermaßen erleichterten die Bildsprache der Vergangenheit und die visuellen Konnotationen die Einführung und Nutzung neuer Technologien auf einem potenziellen Markt.[17] Ein gutes Beispiel dafür ist Wedgwood, das klassische Formen und Motive für sein mit neuesten Materialien und Produktionstechniken erzeugtes Geschirr verwendete. Ähnlich war es im Möbeldesign: Selbst die frühen Thonet-Bugholzstühle ließen die neuartige Technologie dahinter nicht erkennen und unterschieden sich ästhetisch nur wenig von den Biedermeierstühlen, die in den 1830er- und 1840er-Jahren en vogue gewesen waren. Das bis zur Mitte des 19. Jahrhunderts anschwellende Lamento über die schlechte Qualität von Industrieerzeugnissen galt in Wahrheit dem Verlust der guten alten Zeit. Industrieerzeugnisse verloren für das gebildete Bürgertum ihren Reiz. Deren Interesse galt nun einerseits handgefertigten Objekten, die in der betuchten oberen Mittelschicht großen Absatz fanden (Arts-and-Crafts-Bewegung). Solche handgemachten Objekte hielten die Erinnerung an einzigartige Kunstwerke aufrecht – eine Eigenschaft, die bis weit ins 20. Jahrhundert ihren Reiz bewahrte.[18] Andererseits kamen industriell gefertigte Erzeugnisse auf den Markt, die ganz unverhohlen Stilformen aus vorindustrieller Zeit imitierten. Diese waren billiger und daher bei Mittelschicht und Kleinbürgertum sehr begehrt. Obwohl sie unterschiedliche Gesellschaftsschichten ansprachen, spielten beide Produkttypen auf einen vorbürgerlichen Lebensstil an. Einzelstücken wie massenproduzierten Waren haftete jenes aristokratische Flair an, von dem die gesamte Bourgeoisie träumte. Die eigentliche Funktion der Produkte wurde völlig außer Acht gelassen, was bisweilen absurde Formen annahm: So erlebten Krinoline und massive Meublements in den 1860er-Jahren eine Renaissance, obwohl sie für die kleinen, engen Wohnungen des 19. Jahrhunderts viel zu groß dimensioniert waren. Das führte schließlich dazu, dass spätviktorianische Räume mit Nippes vollgestopft wurden, die weder der Zeit entsprachen noch ihren Zweck erfüllten. Alles und jedes war in einem Nostalgiestil gestaltet, der vergangene Zeiten heraufbeschwor und verklärte. Ob Neubarock, Neorenaissance, Neugotik oder irgendein Mischmasch historisierender Stile – die Assoziation mit dem vergangenen Glanz eines anderen Standes war das Um und Auf.

Amerikanische Industrielle des 19. Jahrhunderts mussten auf kein historisches Erbe Rücksicht nehmen, das den industriellen Fortschritt womöglich aufgehalten hätte – sie konnten Entwicklungen viel schneller vorantreiben. Wie die Unternehmer erkannten sie rasch die Bedeutung der Massenproduktion: Wer Massenware am Fließband produzierte, konnte sie günstig anbieten und machte so ein Vermögen. In einer Gesellschaft mit „nomadischen Wurzeln" muss stets alles in Bewegung bleiben: Aus Rohstoffen werden Produkte erzeugt, ein kaufmännischer Schritt folgt auf den anderen, und schließlich werden riesige Entfernungen zurückgelegt, um das Produkt an den Mann zu bringen. Dinge anzupacken ist das Geheimnis des Erfolgs. „Wer rastet, der rostet" – permanent „busy" zu sein ist eine der höchsten Tugenden der amerikanischen Kultur.

Der Businessman ist der amerikanische Aristokrat. Das Smartphone ist das Zepter, und Bluetooth die Krone. Während Europa ein Ort symbolhafter Schätze ist, ist Amerika eine Kultur emblematischer Funktionalität. Im Lichte des amerikanischen Widerstands gegen den europäischen Begriff von Funktionalismus in den 1920er- und 1930er-Jahren mag das überraschen. Allerdings ist die Bedeutung von Funktionalität unterschiedlich. Die junge

↑ ABB. 3
Blow Away, Vase für Moooi, 2010
Design: Front

FIG. 3
Blow Away, vase for Moooi, 2010
Design: Front

Though used by different sectors of society, both results alluded to a pre-middle-class way of life. Both the unique and the mass-produced objects implied the aristocratic lifestyle that the entire bourgeoisie dreamed about. Function was disregarded to the point of absurdity—the crinoline and massive cabinetry made their comeback in the 1860s, for example, but 19th century apartments were too small and narrow to provide the necessary room for their dimensions. As a result, late Victorian interiors were cluttered and stuffed with possessions that did not fit the times or the times' needs. Everything was designed in a revival style evoking and celebrating idealized times gone by. Whether it was neo-Baroque, neo-Renaissance, neo-Gothic, or just a hotchpotch of historicizing styles, the connotation of the past glory of a different class was everything.

American industrialists of the 19th century could move forward at a much quicker pace as there was no historic heritage that needed to be considered, potentially holding back industrial progress. Industrialists and entrepreneurs understood the importance of mass-production. Whoever churned out a multitude of identical items could offer them at an affordable price and made a fortune. The paramount function in a society that has "nomadic roots" is motion—to turn material into products, to get from one mercantile step to the next, and to bridge vast distances to sell. To get things done is the insignia of success. He/she who keeps busy and never rests turning equity around is king.

The businessman is the American aristocrat. The scepter is the smart phone, and the crown is the Bluetooth. While Europe is a place of symbolic treasures, America is a culture of emblematic functionality. This may be surprising in the light of the American resistance to the European notion of functionalism of the 1920s and 30s. However, the meaning of functionality is a different one. The young generation of European Modernists waged war against any sort of connotations. Symbolic allusions to a feudal past were seen as the shackles that were responsible for the stagna-

Generation europäischer Modernisten sagte jedweder Art von Konnotation den Kampf an. Symbolische Anklänge an eine feudale Vergangenheit galten als Fesseln, die für die Stagnation der europäischen Kultur und Gesellschaft bis ins frühe 20. Jahrhundert hinein verantwortlich gemacht wurden. Marinetti stand mit seinem Futuristischen Manifest[19] und der Forderung nach Zerstörung jedes mit Konnotationen befrachteten Kulturguts nicht allein da. Museen, Bibliotheken und akademische Institutionen wurden mit Friedhöfen verglichen und als verweiblicht und verweichlicht abgekanzelt. In ganz Europa forderten radikale modernistische Bewegungen eine tatkräftige, ja gewaltsame Beseitigung „alter" Werte. Was auf politischem Terrain in das grauenhafte Blutvergießen des Ersten Weltkrieges mündete, führte auf dem Gebiet des Designs zur Idee eines nahezu chirurgischen Reduktionismus: „Die Zivilisationen drängen vorwärts. Sie verlassen das Zeitalter des Bauern, des Kriegers und des Priesters, um zu dem zu gelangen, was man Kultur nennt. Kultur ist das Ergebnis eines Ausleseprozesses. Auslesen heißt ausscheiden, ausräumen, verringern, das Wesentlich nackt und klar herausbringen."[20]

Vom spitzzüngigen Kulturkritiker Adolf Loos[21] ermutigt, fasste Le Corbusier in seinem pseudoevolutionären Plädoyer das europäische modernistische Denken zusammen: Wandel wurde schlicht mit Beseitigung und Eliminierung gleichgesetzt, was gefährlich nahe an Verstümmelung und Auflösung herankam, kurz gesagt: Wandel wurde als negativer Prozess betrieben. Umgekehrt war der Ruf nach radikaler Unterdrückung jeder Konnotation das letzte Hindernis auf dem Weg zu einer neuen Beschaffenheit von Design, das bar jeder emotionalen Bindung sein sollte. Europäische Modernisten versuchten Objekte zu gestalten, deren Ästhetik die Funktion m i t t e i l t e : Ein Stahlrohrstuhl wurde entworfen, um darauf zu sitzen, und so sieht er auch aus – wie ein Teil von Corbusiers „Wohnmaschine"[22]. Effizienz passte allerdings besser in die Berufswelt, wie die erfolgreiche amerikanische Anwendung verdeutlicht: Möbel aus Stahl in standardisierten Formen und Maßen machten einen Arbeitsplatz wahrhaft funktionstüchtig. Frühe Remington-Schreibmaschinen mochten wenig modern ausgesehen haben, doch ihre Massenproduktion von 1875 an führte zu einer Steigerung der Effektivität von Unternehmen im ganzen Land.

Der amerikanische Geschäftsmann ist jedoch Pragmatiker. Nur weil etwas ausgeklügelt ist, muss es nicht unbedingt ankommen oder Erfolg haben. „Der Mann, der mit Ideen handelt, die seiner Zeit voraus sind, ist zur Vergessenheit bestimmt, nicht zum Erfolg. Erfolg stellt sich am häufigsten bei jenen ein, die lang überfällige Innovationen perfektionieren."[23]

Man muss nicht ausdrücklich darauf hinweisen, dass das europäische modernistische Design mit seinem utopischen Anspruch kaum Erfolg hatte. Die Bedrohung durch das Naziregime war nicht der einzige Grund dafür, dass sich das Bauhaus auflöste; mit Erzeugnissen, deren Gestaltung auf einem ureigenen Funktionsgedanken[24] fußte, gelang es nicht, den Markt zu überzeugen, zumal in einer Gesellschaft, deren Träume und Aspirationen im Gefolge des verheerenden Ersten Weltkrieges weitgehend auf der Strecke geblieben waren. Anstatt sich allzu sehr auf die Konnotationen der Vergangenheit zu verlassen, versuchten die europäischen Modernisten den Sprung in eine doch zu entlegene Zukunft. Auf dem amerikanischen Markt hingegen sind Risiken in vernünftigem Rahmen einkalkuliert. Bei geringer ästhetischer und emotionaler Produktbindung ist Marktfähigkeit die treibende Kraft der Innovation.

tion of European culture and society up to the early 20th century. Marinetti's Futurist Manifesto[19] was not alone in demanding the destruction of any cultural asset with connotations. Museums, libraries and academic institutions were compared to cemeteries and belittled as feminine and weak. Radical Modernist movements all over Europe called for a vigorous, even violent removal of "old" values. What led to the horrific bloodshed of WWI in political terms also led to the idea of almost surgical reductionism in the field of design: "Civilizations advance. They pass through the age of the peasant, the soldier and the priest and attain what is rightly called culture. Culture is the flowering of the effort to select. Selection means rejection, pruning, cleansing; the clear and the naked emergence of the Essential."[20]

Emboldened by the disgruntled cultural critic Adolf Loos[21], Le Corbusier's pseudo-evolutionary plea for reduction sums up European Modernist thought: change was simply equated with removal and elimination, coming dangerously close to the notion of mutilation and discrimination—in short, change was pursued as a negative process. Inversely, the call for a radical suppression of connotation was the ultimate roadblock to a new state of design, which was supposed to be divorced from emotional attachment. European Modernists tried to design objects whose aesthetics s p o k e of function: a tubular steel chair is designed to be sat on, and it looks just like that—like a part of Le Corbusier's "machine for living."[22] Efficiency was better suited for the professional world, as American successful application shows: Steelcase furniture with standardized shapes and dimensions made a workplace truly efficient. Early Remington typewriters may not have looked very modern, but their mass production from 1875 onward made businesses all over the country effective.

The American businessman however is pragmatic. Just because something is ingenious doesn't mean it will catch on or succeed. "The man who deals in ideas that are ahead of his time is destined for oblivion, not success. Success most often goes to those who perfect innovations that are long overdue."[23]

Needless to say European Modern design proved unsuccessful with their utopian approach. The Bauhaus did not close solely because of the threat of the Nazi government; having its products designed to fulfill "the nature of the object"[24] alone failed to convince a market within a society that had lost most of its dreams and aspirations in the wake of the devastating WWI. Instead of depending too heavily on connotations of the past, European Modernists tried to leap into a too distant future. In the U.S. market, risks are more acceptable, but within reason. Since the aesthetic and emotional attachment levels are low, marketability is the driving force behind innovation.

The history of industrialization in the U.S. is full of success stories based on the improvement of existing ideas: Neither Isaac Singer nor Henry Ford invented their merchandize; they developed existing prototypes and adapted them to both the American usage and market. Singer integrated the Colt triggering mechanism into the sewing machine. As a crucial tool in the land of the Second Amendment,[25] weapon parts were already in mass production and therefore cheap. FIG. 4 Ford took the idea of the conveyer belt from Chicago's slaughterhouses. By applying the then new business theories of Frederick Taylor to their practices, American industrialists maximized the production steps in their plants. Combining innovative ideas with a product that already existed helped change American society: Singer's sewing machines allowed millions of women to make a living through home industries. Ford's Model T

© Ann Ronan/Heritage Images/Scala, Florence

© The Museum of Modern Art/Scala, Florence

MADE 4 YOU

Die Geschichte der Industrialisierung in den USA ist voll von Erfolgsstorys, die auf der Verbesserung existierender Ideen basieren: Weder Isaac Singer noch Henry Ford hatten erfunden, was sie verkauften; beide entwickelten existierende Prototypen weiter und adaptierten sie für den Markt und die Nutzung in Amerika. Singer baute den Abzugsmechanismus des Colts in die Nähmaschine ein. Als unverzichtbares Gut in einem Land, in dem das Recht auf den Besitz und das Tragen von Waffen in der Verfassung verbrieft ist,[25] wurden Waffenbauteile bereits günstig in Massenproduktion erzeugt. ABB. 4 Ford übernahm die Idee des Förderbandes von den Chicagoer Schlachthäusern. Indem sie die damals neuen Grundsätze der Betriebsführung von Frederick Taylor auf ihre Verfahren anwandten, optimierten amerikanische Industrielle die Produktionsschritte in ihren Fabriken. Die Kombination von innovativen Ideen und bereits existierenden Produkten trug zur Veränderung der amerikanischen Gesellschaft bei: Singers Nähmaschinen ermöglichten es Millionen Frauen, sich mit Heimarbeit den Lebensunterhalt zu verdienen. Das Modell T von Ford bediente den Bedarf der amerikanischen Landbevölkerung nach einem leistbaren, robusten und verlässlichen Transportmittel, mit dem sich die weiten Entfernungen in dem riesigen Land überwinden ließen. ABB. 5 Beide, Singer wie Ford, gaben die verbesserten Versionen zum Nutzen ihrer Kunden weiter, freilich nicht ohne großen persönlichen Profit daraus zu schlagen. Der Wandel war somit verantwortlich für die Steigerung von Funktionalität und Einkommen.

Die Industrie lebt von effizienter Kommunikation und Mobilität – auf beiden Gebieten ist Amerika herausragend. Damit brachte die US-Fahrzeugindustrie diese Dienste auch erfolgreich an ihre Kunden: Ford verhalf der amerikanischen Mittelschicht zur Mobilität; bereits 1928 besaß einer von fünf Amerikanern ein Auto. Chrysler, General Motors und andere aufstrebende Mitbewerber gaben ihren Fahrzeugen dazu noch eine symbolische Botschaft mit auf den Weg: jene der Geschwindigkeit, wie sie von den stromlinienförmigen Karosserien der 1930er-Jahre bis zu den Heckflossen der Fünfziger versinnbildlicht wurde. ABB. 6 Keines dieser Merkmale hatte tatsächlich Auswirkungen auf die Geschwindigkeit der Wagen, ließen diese jedoch so aussehen, als könnten sie mit 180 Sachen dahinrasen. Den Wandel vom Nutzfahrzeug zum stylischen Flitzer leitete 1927 die Ernennung Harley Earls zum Leiter der neugeschaffenen „Art and Colour Section" bei General Motors ein. Wenig überraschend wurde diese erste Designabteilung eines Autoherstellers auch zur Geburtsstätte der geplanten Obsoleszenz[26] – Designwandel zur Belebung des Absatzes. Bis heute wird das Auto als Symbol amerikanischer Identität hoch gehalten; die solcherart beschworenen Konnotationen orientieren sich nicht, wie es in Europa der Fall wäre, an Vergangenem, sondern utopisch – an der „Welt von morgen"[27].

Merkur, der geflügelte Gott des Handels und Überbringer von Botschaften, ist der Schutzheilige der amerikanischen Lebensart. Er nimmt die Rolle eines Vermittlers ein – so wie Telefon, Radio, Fernsehen und Internet. Die Medien der postindustriellen Ökonomie, das sind einander gleichende Erfolgsgeschichten made in USA. Die Effizienz, die Singer und Ford durch Produktionssteigerung erzielten, maximierten Alexander Graham Bell, Bill Gates und Steve Jobs durch Kommunikation, bei der Geschwindigkeit und Mobilität den Ausschlag geben – noch jemand ohne iPad, bitte?

In der amerikanischen Kultur betrifft der Wandel demnach mehr das Medium als den Inhalt. Kommunikationsmedien sind, was traditionelle Konnotationen anbelangt, relativ neutral, da ihnen die historischen Anknüpfungspunkte fehlen. Nur wenige Anklänge an

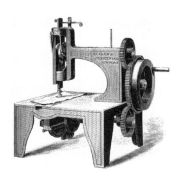

→ ABB. 4
**Isaac Merrit Singers
erste Nähmaschine,
patentiert 1851**

FIG. 4
Isaac Merrit Singer's
first sewing machine,
patented in 1851

→ ABB. 5
Ford Modell T, 1913

FIG. 5
Ford Model T, 1913

served the needs of the American rural population for an affordable, sturdy, and reliable means of transportation to bridge extensive distances in the vast country. FIG. 5 Both Singer and Ford passed on the adapted and improved function of their devices to the benefit of their customers and to great personal profit. Thus, changes were responsible for more efficient functionality and a higher income.

Industry thrives on efficient communication and mobility, which both are fields of American excellence. On top of that, the American transportation industry marketed these services successfully to their clients: Ford allowed middle class America to be mobile. By 1928, one in five Americans owned a car. Chrysler, General Motors, and other emerging competitors added a symbolic message to their vehicles: the message of speed, as visualized in streamlined car bodies the 1930s up to the tailfins of the 1950s. FIG. 6 None of these features had any real effect on the car's speed, but they looked like they would race at 100 miles an hour. The change from utilitarian vehicle to a stylish one was marked by Harley Earl's employment at General Motors to head the newly established "Art and Colour Section" in 1927. Not surprisingly, this very first design department of any automotive company became the birthplace of planned obsolescence[26]—change in design for the sake of stimulating sales. The car is still held in highest esteem as symbol of American identity today; the connotations evoked in these cases are not geared toward past notions, as they would be in Europe, but utopian—toward the "World of tomorrow."[27]

Mercury, the winged god of messages and trade is the patron saint of the American life. His role is that of a mediator, as is that of the telephone, the radio, TV, and the Internet. The media of the post-industrial economy are synonymous success stories made in USA. The efficiency that Singer and Ford created via increased production, Alexander Graham Bell, Bill Gates and Steve Jobs maximized via communication, where speed and mobility is paramount–iPad, anyone?

traditionellen Gebrauch oder Bedeutung bremsen Innovationen. So konnte die Verbesserung der Verbindung des Einzelnen mit der Welt relativ ungehindert ablaufen. Handschriftliche Briefe wurden von maschinengeschriebenen abgelöst; Fernschreiber und Fax beschleunigten deren Zustellung. Interessanterweise veränderte die schnellste Form der Kommunikation via Internet und SMS sogar die Sprache der Kommunikation. ABB. 7 Es war daher ein Leichtes, das Neue zu akzeptieren – nicht nur in den Vereinigten Staaten, sondern auch in Europa und anderen Regionen mit großem historischen Gepäck.

Wenn Ästhetik den Gebrauch erleichtert, ist sie auch bei amerikanischen Produkten gern gesehen. Die Firma Apple griff darauf zurück, um die Aufmerksamkeit potenzieller Kunden von den langweiligen Produkten der Konkurrenz auf die eigenen zu lenken – von Hartmut Esslingers ersten Designs in den 1980er-Jahren bis zu Jonathan Ives frischem Look der 1990er- und der Nullerjahre. Ästhetik wird hier als Mittlerin zwischen Mensch und Handlung eingesetzt, wie Roland Barthes es so gut beschrieb. [28] Zu einer Zeit, als Le Corbusier daranging, die Menschen in sterilen, in Massenproduktion hergestellten und übereinandergestapelten Betonboxen unterzubringen[29], hob Henry Dreyfuss, einer der großen amerikanischen Designer, die wohltuend katalytische Wirkung eines richtig gedeckten Tisches auf die Verdauung, eines gut gestalteten Arbeitsplatzes auf die Effizienz und guter Sitzungssäle auf politische Entscheidungen hervor. [30] Das klare Erscheinungsbild heutiger Computer und Handys schließt den Kreis dieser Geschichte. Simple Formen, glänzende Materialien, minimalistische Funktionen: All das ist nicht willkürlich gewählt, sondern soll bereits suggerieren, wofür diese Geräte stehen – einen mühelosen Betrieb. Nicht umsonst rangieren elektronische Kommunikationsgeräte und ihre Programme ganz oben auf der Skala der Identitätskonnotationen der amerikanischen Kultur: Sie vermögen die Effizienz der Menschen zu ändern. Der entscheidende Punkt ist: Sie helfen dem Benutzer, in der Wirtschaft und im Leben besser zu funktionieren.

Letztendlich gelangten die USA nicht alleine durch Produktion und Industrie zu ihrem Reichtum. Sie waren nur die Saat für ein weitaus größeres geschäftliches Unterfangen: Die Verschiebung von Vermögenswerten aus Industrie und Transport an die Börse vervielfachte den Reichtum der Aktionäre. Ein Land, dessen Reichtum letztendlich durch den Stock Exchange entsteht, trägt die Bedeutung des Wandels in jeder Faser seiner Kultur. Dass Dinge permanent in Bewegung sind, ist Alpha und Omega der amerikanischen Wirtschaft. Das Alpha steht für den Ursprung: ein Land zu sein, das von Siedlern entwickelt, von Revolutionären zur Nation geformt, durch Handel mit Gütern und Geld zur Wirtschaftsmacht wurde. Das Omega oder das Resultat ist eine vollständig entwickelte Nation mit eigenen gesellschaftlichen Regeln, eine Demokratie seit mehr als 250 Jahren und das reichste Land der Welt. All das wurde durch das Umackern des Bodens, den Umsturz eines Regierungssystems, den Übergang von Rädern zu Maschinen und den Umschlag von Zahlenwerten erreicht. Angetrieben wird diese Kette des Erfolgs von einer zukunftsorientierten Einstellung zum Wandel.

„Das Gesetz des Wandels, das der Leitfaden des Lebens ist, ist auch das Gesetz, das die Schönheit regiert." (Kakuzo Okakura)[31] Wandel war seit jeher Teil der japanischen Lebensweise. Durch bewegliche Wände und Raumteiler veränderbare Wohnräume, temporäre Möbel und zusammenklappbare Gegenstände erlauben die optimale Nutzung von Objekten und Räumen je nach Bedarf. Wandelbare aktuelle Designs führen die Funktionen traditioneller

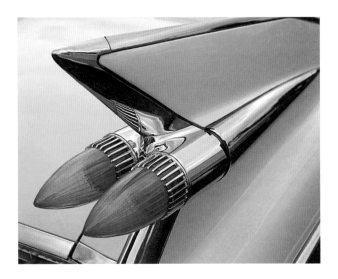

© L Green

↑ ABB. 6
Cadillac-Heckflossen, 1950er

FIG. 6
Cadillac tailfins, 1950s

Thus in American culture change affects the medium much more than the content. Media are relatively neutral in the realm of traditional connotations, as these devices lack historic points of reference. Few allusions to traditional use or meaning hold innovation back. The improvement of one's connectedness to the world went relatively unhindered. Handwritten letters turned into machine-typed ones; telex and fax increased the speed of their delivery. It is interesting to note that the fastest way of communication via the ether through internet and text messages even changed the language of communication. FIG. 7 The acceptance of the new therefore was easy, not only in the U.S., but also in Europe and other regions with historic baggage to defend.

If aesthetics help the ease of use, it will be embraced by American products as well. The Apple Company applied this strategy to steal potential clients' attention from their competitors' boring looking products—from Hartmut Esslinger's first designs in the 1980s to Jonathan Ives's fresh looks of the 1990s and 2000s. Aesthetics comes thus to be used as a mediator between man and action, as Roland Barthes defined it so well. [28] At a time when Le Corbusier tried to house people in sterile, mass-produced concrete boxes stacked upon each other,[29] Henry Dreyfuss, one of the great American designers, emphasized the catalytic benefits of a well-set table for digestion, a well-designed workplace for efficiency, and good assembly halls for political decisions. [30] The slick look of today's computers and cell phones bring this history full circle: simple shapes in shiny materials with minimalistic functional tools are not gratuitous, rather they are meant to suggest a possible smoothness of operation, which these devices stand for. Thus, electronic communication devices and their programs rank highest on the scale of connotation to identity in American culture because of the ability of changing people's efficacy. The focal point is the improvement of the user's ability to function in business and life.

Lastly, the U.S. did not gain its riches through production and industry alone. This was but the seed for a far greater business venture. The transference to the stock market of fortunes earned in industry and transportation multiplied the stockholders' wealth. A country whose ultimate wealth is a result of the stock-exchange carries the importance of change in every fiber of its culture. Things changing hands is the alpha and omega of American economy. The alpha is the origin: being a country developed by settlers, turned into a nation by revolutionaries, becoming an

Kontext /
Context

© Apple Inc.

MADE 4 YOU

Futons, Fächer und Sonnenschirme fort. ABB. 8 Im japanischen Design ist „das Prinzip des steten Wandels der Gestalt entlang der Zeitachse gleichbedeutend mit dem Gesetz der Natur". [32] Das mag seine Wurzeln in den beiden religiösen Hauptlehren, Buddhismus und Shintō, haben. Im Buddhismus dreht sich alles um Vergänglichkeit und Bewusstseinswandel. Es geht um die Erhöhung der Bewusstseinsebene bis hin zur Selbstauflösung. Da nichts von Dauer ist und sein soll [33] – wozu dann am Bestehenden festhalten? Shintoismus, eine animistische Weltanschauung, versucht die Natur mit ihren zyklischen Abläufen in sich einzubeziehen: „Kontinuität innerhalb des Wandels zu bewahren ist ein typisch japanisches Muster. Vielleicht lässt sich die besondere Stellung des Wandels innerhalb der Kontinuität im japanischen Denken durch die Beziehung zum ununterbrochenen, subtilen Zyklus des Jahreszeitenwechsels erklären, der das japanische Bewusstsein tief geprägt hat." [34]

Diese spirituellen Weltsichten sind beide immens wichtig für die Bewältigung von Naturkatastrophen, wie etwa regelmäßig auftretenden Erdbeben, Wirbelstürmen, Feuersbrünsten und Überflutungen. Häuser, Dörfer und Städte durchleben in regelmäßigen Abständen Zerstörung und Wiederauferstehung und passen sich dabei veränderten sozialen Bedingungen an. [35] Die Bewegung der Metabolisten unter den japanischen Architekten der 1960er-Jahre münzte dieses Prinzip ständigen Wandels in Architekturtheorie und -praxis um. [36] Der ikonische Nakagin Capsule Tower mit Raumzellen zum Anfügen sollte wie ein Baumstamm mit erneuerbarem Blattwerk funktionieren. Was wie eine funktionale Idee wirkt, scheint in der buddhistisch-shintoistischen Akzeptanz des Wandels als Teil des Lebens zu wurzeln: „Schönheit bleibt in jedem Moment im Einklang mit den Umständen bestehen; das sorgsam aufgebaute Werk wird in einem sich unaufhörlich selbst erneuernden Kanon der Schönheit verzehrt, während es zugleich Geschichte und Jahreszeiten durchwächst." [37]

Die japanische Kultur ist vorsichtig. Zwar ist Wandel ein selbstverständlicher Teil des Lebens, überstürzt wird aber nichts. Wahrscheinlich wäre es angemessener, in Japan von M e t a m o r p h o s e statt von W a n d e l zu sprechen. Die japanische Designgeschichte kennt keine abrupten Brüche. Verschiedene über die Jahrtausende entstandene visuelle Sprachen bestehen in scheinbarem Widerspruch nebeneinander. Freilich sind sie alle Teil eines breiten Spektrums von Lebenskulturen innerhalb eines präzisen Entwicklungssystems. Anders als in Europa oder Amerika, wo Originalität geschätzt wird, basiert in der japanischen Erziehung jederlei Wachstum oder Entwicklung darauf, sich die jeweils führenden Kompetenzen bis hin zur Imitation anzueignen. Der Auszubildende – Student, Lehrling, Jungdesigner – muss die Verfahrens-, Gestaltungs- und Handlungsweisen seines Sensei [39] akribisch nachahmen. Das erste Ziel besteht darin, diese Fertigkeiten zu verinnerlichen und sich vollständig zu eigen zu machen. [40] Freilich hört der schöpferische Prozess hier nicht auf: Das Resultat soll die Qualitäten des Vorgängers, noch viel mehr aber die sukzessiven Verbesserungen durch die Hand des Nachfolgers erkennen lassen. Das ist es, was Zeami, der japanische Shakespeare des Nō-Theaters, das „lebendige Nō" oder die Fähigkeit nennt, seine Kunst auf die Schultern der Vorgänger zu stellen und ihr zu neuer Blüte zu verhelfen. Die Vergangenheit wird als Quelle akzeptiert, doch ohne den Funken zeitgenössischer Lebendigkeit würde die hoch verfeinerte Virtuosität eine leere und bedeutungslose Hülle bleiben. Selbst auf diesem Niveau von Kunstfertigkeit verharren schöpferische Ausdrucksformen und Gestaltungen nicht unverändert. Das japanische Denken kennt die Vorstellung dauerhafter Perfektion nicht. Während der europäische Modernist dem Phantom

↑ ABB. 7
Apple iPad, 2010

FIG. 7
Apple iPad, 2010

economic power by trade of goods and money. The omega, or the result, is a fully developed nation with its own societal rules, a democracy for more than 250 years, and the richest country in the world. All of this by turning over soil, a governmental system, wheels in machines, and numeric values. This chain of success is fueled by a forward looking attitude toward change.

"That law of change which is the guiding thread of life is also the law which governs beauty." (Kakuzo Okakura) [31] Change has always been part of Japanese lifestyle. Adaptable living spaces created through mobile walls and partitions, temporary furnishings, and folding objects allow optimized use of objects and space as needed in the very moment. Convertible contemporary designs perpetuate the function of traditional futons, folding fans, and umbrellas. FIG. 8

In Japanese design "the principle of the constant change of Gestalt on the axis of time is tantamount to the law of nature." [32] This may be rooted in both main religious beliefs, Buddhism and Shinto. Buddhism itself revolves around the transience and the transformation of consciousness. The elevation of one's consciousness to the level of dissolution is the name of the game. If all things are, and are supposed to be, impermanent, [33] why hold on to the existing? Shinto is an animistic view of the world, and tries to incorporate nature with its cyclic run: "Preserving continuity within the course of change is a typically Japanese pattern. Perhaps it is possible to explain the special place of change within continuity in Japanese thinking by its relation to the uninterrupted, subtle cycle of seasonal change, which has deeply affected the Japanese consciousness." [34]

Both of these spiritual worldviews are crucial to cope with natural disasters, such as regularly occurring earthquakes, typhoons, fires and floods. Japan is sadly, a shaken country of unstable living conditions. Houses, villages, and towns are undergoing destruction and resurrection in regular intervals, and thereby adapt to changed social conditions. [35] The Metabolist movements among Japanese architects in the 1960s had turned this very principle of constant transformation into a theory and practice of architecture. [36] The iconic Nakagin Capsule Hotel with attachable room-cells was meant to function like a tree trunk with renewable foliage. What looks like just a functional idea appears to have roots in Buddhist and Shinto's acceptance of change as part of life: "Beauty is sustained in each instant in accordance with circumstance; the work that has been carefully built up is consumed within a constantly self-renewing canon of beauty, with its weaving in and out of both history and the seasons." [37]

Japanese culture is cautious. Though change is an unquestioned part of life, there is no rush into it. It is probably more appropri-

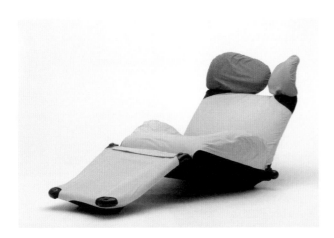

↑ ABB. 8
Wink Chair, Liegesessel, 1980
Design: Toshiyuki Kita

↑ FIG. 8
Wink Chair, 1980
Design: Toshiyuki Kita

der absoluten Lösung in zeitlosem Design nachgejagt sein mag, ist fortlaufende Verwandlung in Japan ein Faktor, der für Theatervorstellungen gleichermaßen gilt wie für Industriedesign.

Ausgefeilte Herstellungsverfahren erlauben heute eine stufenweise, wenngleich rasch erfolgende Änderung ein- und desselben Produkts: „Es wird zu ständigen, fortlaufenden Verbesserungen ermutigt und nicht zu radikalen Lösungen."[41] Adaptionen werden erzielt, indem man den Mittelweg zwischen den ersten beiden Lösungen auf einer Liste oder mehrerer Varianten wählt. Das soll schroffe Stilbrüche vermeiden helfen und für Kontinuität in der Produktentwicklung sorgen.[42] Diese Herangehensweise erinnert nicht nur an die religiöse und gesellschaftliche Einstellung zu schrittweisem Wandel, sie verbessert überdies die Konkurrenzfähigkeit auf dem Markt.

Japan hat traditionellerweise Unterstützung und Inspiration bei anderen Kulturen gesucht.[43] Als gelehrige Leser der konfuzianischen Klassiker, die das hierarchische Verhältnis zwischen Lehrer und Schüler betonen, sind die Japaner eifrig bestrebt, von jenen zu lernen, die sie als Meister auf ihrem jeweiligen Gebiet anerkennen.[44] Schließlich hat sich Japan der modernen Weltgemeinschaft mit ihrem grenzenlosen Kommunikationsfluss zwischen den Staaten angeschlossen und seinen Nutzen daraus gezogen. Das Gesundheits- und Verwaltungssystem hat seine Wurzeln im deutschen Kaiserreich, feines Gebäck und Sonnenschirme mit weißer Spitze erinnern an das Frankreich impressionistischer Gemälde, Baseball wurde zum Nationalsport und die schottische Weise „Auld Lang Syne" kündigt im ganzen Land die Schließung öffentlicher Gebäude an.[45] Immer noch wahrnehmbare Spuren dessen stürzen den heutigen Besucher Japans ob dieser seltsam anmutenden Verlagerung von Kulturgütern in Verwirrung.

Jede Begegnung führte zur Übernahme ausgewählter Elemente in die einheimische Kultur. Die stufenweise Abstraktion ausländischer Ideen erlaubt es, sie in das Bestehende einzufügen und „durch Synthese und Adaption etwas Neues und Überlegenes zu schaffen".[46] Im späten 19. Jahrhundert war der Anblick eines japanischen Gentlemans in Kimono und Melone nichts Ungewöhnliches. Im Laufe eines Jahrhunderts machte das anfängliche Liebäugeln mit exotischen Accessoires der Verschmelzung von Ideen Platz. Aus in West und Ost fest verwurzelter Haute Couture und Prêt-à-porter wurden Meisterwerke japanischen Modedesigns, wie man sie seit den 1970er-Jahren kennt.[47] Modeschöpfer wie Issey Miyake, Rei Kawakubo und Yohji Yamamoto feierten

ate to call c h a n g e in Japan t r a n s f o r m a t i o n. There are no abrupt breaks in its history of design. A variety of visual languages that were produced over the millennia may coexist in seeming contradiction. However, they are all part of a broader range of living culture within a concise system of development. Unlike Europe or America where originality is applauded, the Japanese education bases any kind of growth and development on the adoption of the current best skills to the point of absorption.[38] The trainee—the student, the apprentice, the junior designer—has to copy meticulously his sensei's[39] way of doing, designing and making. The first goal is to internalize these skills and make them one's own.[40] However, the process of creation does not stop there: the final result is supposed to show the qualities of the predecessor's skills and, what is more, improvement by the follower's original touch. This is what Zeami, the "Japanese Shakespeare" of Noh Plays, called the "living Noh", or the artistry that steps upon the shoulders of one's elders to blossom anew. The past is accepted as the source; but without the spark of contemporary life the highly polished virtuosity on its own would remain a hollow and meaningless shell.

Even at this elevated level of artistry, creative expressions and designs do not remain stable. The idea of lasting perfection does not exist in Japanese thinking. While the European Modernist may have chased the phantom of the perfect solution of timeless design, in Japan, continuing transformation is a factor that applies to theatrical performances as much as to industrial design. Contemporary sophisticated manufacturing methods allow gradual but rapid changes of the same products. "Constant, incremental improvement, is encouraged instead of radical solutions."[41] Adaptations tend to be achieved by finding the middle ground between the first two solutions on the list or out of variants. This is meant to avoid harsh breaks in style, and thus to provide a continuity of product development.[42] Not only does this approach echo the religious and societal attitude toward gradual transformation, it enhances competitiveness in the market.

Japan has traditionally sought for assistance and inspiration from other cultures.[43] As devoted students of the Confucian classics, which emphasize the hierarchical relationship between teacher and pupil, the Japanese people eagerly take lessons from those whom they acknowledge as masters in their fields.[44] Eventually Japan joined the modern world community with its borderless flow of cross-national communication and made good use of it. The medical and bureaucratic system have their roots in Imperial Germany, pastry and white laced parasols recall the France of Impressionist paintings, baseball became a national sport, not only in America, and the tune "Auld Lang Syne" from Scotland rings in the closure of public places nationwide[45]. Still perceivable traces thereof leave today's visitor puzzled about this rather strange displacement of cultural entities.

Each encounter led to the absorption of selected entities into the native culture. The successive abstraction of foreign ideas allows them to blend into the existing fabric, "creating something new and superior through synthesis and adaptation."[46] It was not unusual in the late 19th century to see a Japanese gentleman dressed in a kimono and bowler hat. In the course of one century, the flirtation with exotic accessories shifted toward a fusion of ideas. Couture and prêt-a-porter clothes firmly rooted in East and West turned into the masterpieces of Japanese fashion design that have appeared since the 1970s.[47] Fashion designers such as Issey Miyake, Rei Kawakubo and Yohji Yamamoto succeeded on the world stage with original designs as a result of absorption of such "Japanization."[48]

Kontext /
Context

33

© The Museum of Modern Art/Scala, Florence

MADE 4 YOU

internationale Erfolge mit Originalentwürfen, die das Ergebnis dieser absorbierenden „Japanisierung"⁴⁸ waren.

Interessanterweise vollziehen sich Wandel und Verwandlung weder entlang einer linearen Zeitachse noch in einem dualistischen System des Entweder-Oder. Die japanische Kultur vermag mehrere Systeme gleichzeitig hochzuhalten und zu leben, dabei aus Bezügen zu verschiedenen Epochen der Vergangenheit und aus einer Vielzahl von Inspirationen zu schöpfen. So übernahm die japanische Kultur nicht nur das Schriftsystem von China und vermengte es mit dem eigenen syllabischen Alphabet und lateinischen Lettern aus dem Westen; Japan hieß auch den Buddhismus und das von ausländischen Missionaren eingeführte Christentum willkommen und fügte diese Glaubenslehren dem bestehenden Shintoismus hinzu. Tempura – frittierte Speisen, die ursprünglich von portugiesischen Seeleuten nach Japan gebracht worden waren – isst man mit den aus Korea übernommenen Stäbchen. Die Annäherung an westliches Industriedesign geschah im 20. Jahrhundert auf eine ähnlich integrative Weise: Man interessierte sich gleichermaßen für den europäischen wie für den amerikanischen Modernismus. Die eingeladenen europäischen Designberater Bruno Taut und Charlotte Perriand gehörten beide nicht zur Speerspitze des radikalen Modernismus. Allerdings legten sie die Saat für ein Design des integrativen Funktionalismus. Die amerikanische Mid-Century Moderne, die zeitgemäße Einfachheit mit Komfort und Anklängen an ein prononciertes Mittelklassemilieu mischte, eignete sich sehr gut als weitere Inspirationsquelle modernen japanischen Designs. Von den Anfängen der Industrie bis in unsere Tage lassen sich Beispiele für unglaublich integrative Entwürfe finden: Sori Yanagi, einer der ersten professionellen Industriedesigner in Japan, durchschlug den gordischen Knoten der drei ineinander verwobenen Kulturen. Yanagi, Sohn eines der ersten Verfechter der Bewahrung der traditionellen japanischen Kultur, Soetsu Yanagi, und Assistent Charlotte Perriands während ihres Aufenthalts in Japan, brachte schließlich ein Design hervor, das die amerikanische Technik der Sperrholzverformung mit der typisch europäischen Anspielung auf die Vergangenheit und dem japanischen Respekt vor der visuellen Sprache altehrwürdiger Sakralentwürfe verband: den Butterfly-Hocker. Auch Nendos Cabbage Chair aus dem 21. Jahrhundert zeichnet eine mehrfache Abstammung aus: Er ist aus Papier, das Issey Miyake benutzte, um seine berühmten „Pleats" zu plissieren; die aufgeschnittene Papierrolle bedarf noch der endgültigen Formung durch den, der darauf Platz nimmt. Durch den Gebrauch verändert sich die Struktur, was aus dem Objekt einen einzigartigen persönlichen Gegenstand macht. Die Verwendung von wegwerfbarem Material erinnert dabei an die amerikanische Kultur, die Plissiertechnik stammt aus Europa, und die Veränderung zur organisch gewachsenen Unvollkommenheit als Zeichen für den Lauf des Lebens ist ganz und gar japanisch. ABB. 10

Andere Designfirmen überbrückten die kulturelle Kluft durch Adaption technischer Erfindungen. Basierend auf der japanischen Idee der Miniaturisierung – man denke nur an Bonsai – kamen die kleinen Proportionen der Fahrzeugentwürfe von Honda und Co. aus wirtschaftlichen Gründen in Europa und Amerika gut an. Miniaturisierte Elektronik war aus verschiedenen Gründen erfolgreich: Das Transistorradio TR 55 von Sony aus dem Jahr 1955 machte aus einem scheinbar nutzlosen Produkt der US-Militärindustrie den Meilenstein einer neuen Ära: Es läutete die weltweite Kultur tragbarer Eletronikgeräte ein. Sein Nachfolger, der Walkman, fand aus vielerlei kulturellen Motiven Anklang: Im schnelllebigen American Way of Life ermöglichte er Doubletasking – Musik zu hören, während man etwas anderes tut, bei dem

↑ ABB. 9
Butterfly Stool, 1956
Design: Sori Yanagi

FIG. 9
Butterfly Stool, 1956
Design: Sori Yanagi

Interestingly, change and transformation neither occur on a linear timeline, nor in a dualistic system of either/or. The Japanese culture manages to value and live multiple systems at the same time, drawing from references to various periods in the past and from a multitude of inspirations. As a result, Japanese culture not only adopted the writing system from China, mixing it eventually with their own syllabic alphabet and Roman letters from the Western world, Japan also welcomed Buddhism and Christianity from foreign missionaries adding these belief systems to the existing one, Shinto. Tempura, fried foods actually brought by 16th century Portuguese visitors to Japanese shores, are eaten with chopsticks, once introduced from Korea. The approach toward Western industrial design in the 20th century happened in a similarly inclusive way: there was interest in both European and American Modernisms. The invited European design consultants Bruno Taut and Charlotte Perriand were not quite at the forefront of radical Modernism. However, they left the seeds for a design of inclusive functionalism. The American mid-century modern way of blending modern simplicity with comfort and allusions to a distinct middle class environment was well suited as another inspiration for a modern Japanese design. Examples of incredible integrative designs span from early industry to our days: Sori Yanagi, one of the earliest professional industrial designers in Japan successfully cut the Gordian knot of the three entangled cultures. Brought up by one of the earliest advocates of preserving traditional Japanese culture, Soetsu Yanagi, and assistant to Charlotte Perriand during her stay in Japan, Sori Yanagi eventually brought forth a design that integrates the American technology of molding plywood, the European way of alluding to things past, and the Japanese respect of their ancestry's visual language of sacred design: the Butterfly Stool. FIG. 9

© Masayuki Hayashi

© Sony Corporation

↑ **ABB. 11**
Sony Walkman TPS-L2, 1979

FIG. 11
Sony Walkman TPS-L2, 1979

↑ **ABB. 10**
Cabbage Chair, 2008
Design: Nendo

FIG. 10
Cabbage Chair, 2008
Design: Nendo

Nendo's Cabbage Chair of the 21ˢᵗ century is of similar multiple parentage: made of the paper that Issey Miyake used to pleat his famous Pleats, the cut-open roll of paper needs the finishing touch through the sitter. The usage eventually damages the structure and changes the generic into a uniquely personal object. The use of disposable material recalls American culture, the technology of pleating is European, and the change to imperfection as a sign of life's course is utterly Japanese. FIG. 10

Other design companies bridged the culture gap by adapting tech-nological inventions. Based on the Japanese idea of miniaturizing scale—think of Bonsai—the small proportions of transportation designs by Honda and Co. caught on in both Europe and America for economic reasons. Miniaturized electronics succeeded for different reasons: Sony's transistor radio TR 55 from 1955 trans-formed a seemingly useless product of the US army industry into a milestone of a new era. It rang in the worldwide culture of mobile electronic devices. Its successor, the Walkman, was accepted for multiple cultural effects: in the American speedy way of life, it allows double tasking—listening to music while doing something else, mostly as an activity in motion. [49] FIG. 11 In the crowded Japanese world, though, listening devices create a bubble of privacy amidst thousands of people. This personal space is not only the effect but also part of the device. The user steps into the sound bubble and thus shares physically the device's properties.

As a result, not only one's master has to be matched/absorbed/surpassed; the subject matter is approached in a similar inclusive way: "There is the Master's saying: 'Of the pine-tree learn from the pine-tree. Of the bamboo learn from the bamboo.' By this the Master meant that one should free oneself from subjective arbitrariness. There are those who indulge in interpreting freely in their own manner what is meant by the word 'learn', resulting in 'not-learning' after all. To 'learn' means here to have the existential experience in which a poet first penetrates into, and identifies himself with, a thing, and in which as 'the first and faintest stir of the inner reality' (bi) emerges from the thing, it activates the cre-ative emotion of the poet (as an instantaneous sensation), which becomes crystallized on the spot into a poetic expression." [50] Transformation thus is sought through subject a n d object, by in-tegration and absorption into the creative's fabric. The encircling sources of influence eventually zoom onto both designer and user. The self changes and becomes part of the design.

Design undergoes change in all three cultures. Interestingly, associations are the most powerful tool to withhold and to support change in European cultures. European ideas of the future are borne out of historical connotation. In economic and emotional

man zumeist in Bewegung ist. [49] In der übervölkerten japanischen Welt wiederum schaffen Geräte mit Kopfhörern eine Sphäre der Privatheit inmitten tausender Menschen. Der Benutzer taucht in die Klangwolke ein und wird gleichsam Teil des Geräts. ABB. 11

Somit geht es nicht nur um das Nachahmen/Verinnerlichen/Über-treffen des Meisters; dem Gegenstand nähert man sich in ähnlich assimilatorischer Weise: „Es gibt einen Ausspruch des Meisters: ‚Über die Kiefer lerne von der Kiefer, über den Bambus lerne vom Bambus!' Das besagt: ‚Befreie dich von deiner subjektiven Willkür!' Nun gibt es einige, die dieses ‚Lerne!' auf ihre eigene, bequeme Weise interpretieren und am Ende gar nichts lernen. ‚Lernen' bedeutet hier, dass man ganz in eine Sache hineinschlüpft und mit ihr eins wird und dass die geringste innere Regung (bi), die von der Sache ausgeht, das schöpferische Empfinden des Dichters spontan aktiviert, was dann unmittelbar in ein Gedicht umgesetzt wird." [50] Verwandlung wird somit vermittels Subjekt u n d Objekt angestrebt, durch Integration und strukturelle Übernahme des Kreativen. Die umkreisenden Einflüsse fokussieren letztendlich sowohl auf den Designer als auch auf den Benutzer. Das Ich verändert sich und wird Teil des Designs.

Design unterliegt in allen drei Kulturen einem Wandel. Interes-santerweise sind in europäischen Kulturen Assoziationen das wirkungsvollste Mittel, um Wandel zu hemmen oder zu fördern. Europäische Vorstellungen von der Zukunft entspringen histo-rischen Konnotationen. Ökonomisch und emotional verbinden die Europäer Erfolg mit einem Bild von Gesetztheit und Stabilität. Ein rollender Stein setzt kein Moos an, also sollte er besser zu Ruhe kommen. Die amerikanische Zukunftsprojektion ist eine von andauerndem Fortschritt – von Wachstum und Entwicklung. Geld auf der Bank zu haben ist das Ziel europäischen Ehrgeizes, Geld zu haben, um damit noch mehr Geld zu machen, jenes des amerikanischen Unternehmers. Die Basis für den Erfolg dieses Systems sind zwei ineinandergreifende Prämissen: eine begrenzte emotionale Bindung an Vergangenheit und Gegenwart sowie die

Offenheit für und die Ausrichtung am Neuen, Riskanten, Unbekannten. Der Amerikaner schaut nach vorne – in eine Zukunft, die hell strahlende Verheißung eines besseren Lebens ist. Der Wandel dient hier als effiziente und willkommene Methode. Und die Methode ist wiederum das, was zählt. Wandel und Innovation finden in den USA auf der Ebene der Funktion statt. Im Gegensatz dazu integriert Japan den Wandel mit jeder Faser in seine Kultur. Darin, dass die Aufgliederung in Ästhetik, Funktion und Konnotation nicht in gleicher Weise Anwendung findet, unterscheidet sich Japan in gestalterischer Hinsicht vom Westen. Im ästhetischen Wert kann die Funktion eines Objekts liegen; und der Begriffsinhalt kann eins sein mit seiner ästhetischen Erscheinung. Alle drei sind miteinander verwoben und existieren, weil sie in sich ständig verändernden Beziehungen zueinander stehen.

Das Neue reicht dem Alten die Hände, und gemeinsam umtanzen sie das Design. Das Neue steht nicht im Widerspruch zum Alten, sondern ist relativ. Wandel wird im Geflecht von Schöpfung, Leben und Mensch begrüßt, ohne dass man die Vergangenheit aus den Augen verliert oder gar ablegt. Wenn Wandel sich in der europäischen Kultur durch den Rückgriff auf die Konnotationen vergangenen Ruhms vollzieht und in der amerikanischen durch die Vorwärtsbewegung hin zu einer verlockenden Zukunft, dann ist Japan in eine Spirale des Wandels gehüllt, die das Universum umschließt.

Wandel passiert – auf viele atemberaubend interessante Weisen.

terms, the European understanding of success is an image of settlement and stability. A rolling stone gathers no moss, so it eventually better comes to rest. The American projection of the future is that of continuing progress—of growth and development. Having money in the bank is a goal of European ambitions. Having money to make more money is the goal of the American entrepreneur. Two interlocked premises are the basis of such a system's success: limited emotional attachment to the past and present, and openness to and focus on the new, the risky, the unknown. The American is forward-looking; the future is a bright and shining promise of a better life. Change is an efficient and welcome method. And the method is what counts. Function is the place of change and innovation in the USA. Japan, by contrast, integrates change in every fiber of its culture. What is different from Western creation is that the division in aesthetic, function and connotation does not apply in the same way. Aesthetic value may be an object's function; and connotation may be one with its aesthetic appearance. All three are intertwined and exist because they are in constant shifting relations to each other.

The new is holding hands with the old, and together they dance around the focus of design. The new is not in contradiction with the old, but is relative. Change is welcomed into the fabric of creation, life, and the human being itself, without losing track of, let alone abandoning, the past. If change happens in European culture through a step back to the connotations of past glory, in American culture through forward motion toward an appealing future, then Japan is enveloped in a spiral of changes which comprises the universe.

Change happens: in a breathtakingly interesting variety of ways.

[1] Deyan Sudjic, The Language of Things, Understanding the World of Desirable Objects, New York 2009, S. 44

[2] Rachel Bowlby, Carried Away, The Invention of Modern Shopping, New York 2001, S. 7

[3] Adrian Forty, Objects of Desire, Design and Society since 1750, London 1986, S. 8

[4] Ungeachtet der Tatsache, dass die gleichen Ladenketten und Markennamen in Tokio, New York und Wien vertreten zu sein scheinen, unterscheiden sich ihre Waren üblicherweise von Kontinent zu Kontinent, manchmal sogar von Land zu Land.

[5] Henry Dreyfuss, Designing for People, New York 1955, S. 82

[6] Faksimile des Arbeitsprogramms der Wiener Werkstaette (1905), in: Der Preis der Schönheit. Zum 100. Geburtstag der Wiener Werkstätte (Ausst. Kat.), Wien 2004

[7] Maria Reissberger, Peter Haiko, „Alles ist einfach und glatt", in: Moderne Vergangenheit 1800–1900 (Ausst. Kat.), Wien 1981, S. 13ff.

[8] Interessanterweise ist Nancy im Osten Frankreichs nicht nur Ausgangspunkt des Art Nouveau, sondern auch ein Hauptzentrum der Rokokoarchitektur.

[9] Le Corbusier, Vers une architecture, Paris 1923

[10] Charlotte Perriand, Une vie de création, Paris 1998, S. 31

[11] Dies., S. 33

[12] Charles Jencks, The Language of Postmodern Architecture, New York 1977

[13] Amerikanische Modedesigner haben sich nicht mit bahnbrechenden Erfindungen hervorgetan: Die Businessbekleidung hat sich seit den 1950er-Jahren kaum verändert, und selbst die einst revolutionären Jeans sind gut und gern 150 Jahre alt. Das typische Vorstadtheim ähnelt einem neokolonialen Gebäude aus dem 19. Jahrhundert, ist oft auch entsprechend möbliert und verströmt das Flair der guten alten Zeit – vom „Cottage-Look" bis zum amerikanischen Neo-Empire. Die Einrichtung besteht aus Massenware von der Stange oder ist von professionellen Innenausstattern entworfen.

[14] The American Style: Colonial Revival and the Modern Metropolis, hg. v. Donald Albrecht, New York 2011

[15] Christine Frederick, Household Engineering: Scientific Management in the Home, Chicago 1920, S. 104f.

[1] Deyan Sudjic, The Language of Things: Understanding the World of Desirable Objects, New York 2009, p. 44

[2] Rachel Bowlby, Carried Away: The Invention of Modern Shopping, New York 2001, p. 7

[3] Adrian Forty, Objects of Desire: Design and Society since 1750, London 1986, p. 8

[4] Despite the fact that the same chain stores and brand names seem to be available in Tokyo, New York and Vienna alike, their merchandise usually differs from continent to continent, sometimes even from country to country.

[5] Henry Dreyfuss, Designing for People, New York 1964, p. 82

[6] Facsimile of the Wiener Werkstätte Working Program (1905), in: Yearning for Beauty. The Wiener Werkstätte and the Stoclet House (exhib. cat.), Vienna–Ostfildern-Ruit 2006

[7] Maria Reissberger, Peter Haiko, "Alles ist einfach und glatt," in: Moderne Vergangenheit 1800–1900 (exhib. cat.), Vienna 1981, p. 13ff.

[8] Interestingly, Nancy in Eastern France is not only the hotbed of the French Art Nouveau style, but also one of the major centers of Rococo architecture.

[9] Le Corbusier, Vers une architecture, Paris 1923

[10] Charlotte Perriand, Une vie de création, Paris 1998, p. 31

[11] Ibid., p. 33

[12] Charles Jencks, The Language of Postmodern Architecture, New York 1977

[13] American fashion designers have not excelled in groundbreaking inventions; business outfits have hardly changed since the 1950s, and even the once revolutionary blue jeans are well over 150 years old. The typical suburban home resembles a neocolonial building of the late 19th century and tends to be furnished accordingly, spreading the flair of the good old days—from the "cottage look" to an outright American Empire Revival style. Interiors often consist of mass produced cookie-cutter furnishings or is designed by a professional interior designer.

[14] The American Style: Colonial Revival and the Modern Metropolis, ed. by Donald Albrecht, New York 2011

[15] Christine Frederick, Household Engineering: Scientific Management in the Home, Chicago 1920, p. 104f.

[16] Der Politiker Thomas Jefferson beschäftigte sich nebenher mit der Verbesserung zahlloser Geräte, die die schwere Landarbeit des 18. Jahrhunderts erleichtern sollten: einem Pflug mit verbesserter schollenwendender Schar, einer Dreschmaschine mit einem Aufsatz zum Hanfbrechen und einer neuen zeitsparenden Maschine zum Walken von Wolle. Vgl. Silvio A. Bedini: „Godfather of American Invention", in: The Smithsonian Book of Invention, New York 1978, S. 83

[17] Adrian Forty, Objects of Desire, Design and Society since 1750, London–New York 1986, S. 11ff.

[18] Walter Benjamin, „Das Kunstwerk im Zeitalter seiner technischen Reproduzierbarkeit" (3., autorisierte letzte Fassung 1939), in: ders., Gesammelte Schriften, Bd. I, Werkausgabe Bd. 2, hg. v. Rolf Tiedemann u. Hermann Schweppenhäuser, Frankfurt am Main 1980, S. 471–508

[19] Filippo Tommaso Marinetti, „Manifeste du futurisme", in: Le Figaro, Paris, 20. Februar 1909

[20] Le Corbusier, Ausblick auf eine Architektur, Berlin 1963, S. 109

[21] Adolf Loos, „Ornament und Verbrechen" (1908), in: ders., Gesammelte Schriften, hg. v. Adolf Opel, Wien 2010

[22] Le Corbusier, Vers une architecture, Paris 1923, S. 83

[23] Harold C. Livesay, American Made, Men Who Shaped the American Economy, Boston, Toronto, 1979, S. 141

[24] Walter Gropius, „Grundsätze der Bauhausproduktion", in: Walter Gropius, László Moholy-Nagy (Hg.), Neue Arbeiten der Bauhauswerkstatt (Bauhausbücher 7), München 1925, S. 5–8

[25] Der 2. Zusatzartikel zur Verfassung der Vereinigten Staaten ist Bestandteil des Grundrechtekatalogs, der sogenannten Bill of Rights, und garantiert das Recht der Bürger, Waffen zu besitzen und zu tragen. Die zehn Artikel umfassende Bill of Rights wurde vom Kongress beschlossen und trat nach der Ratifizierung durch elf Bundesstaaten am 15. Dezember 1791 in Kraft.

[26] Stephen Bayley, Harley Earl, New York 1990, S. 57

[27] Motto der New Yorker Weltausstellung 1939

[28] Roland Barthes, „Semantics of the Object" (1964), in: ders., The Semiotic Challenge, übers. v. Richard Howard, Berkeley–Los Angeles 1994, S. 181

[29] Unité d'Habitation, Marseille, 1947–1952. Von Le Corbusier zusammen mit dem Maler und Architekten Nadir Afonso entwickeltes Gestaltungsprinzip im Wohnbau. Das Konzept bildete die Grundlage für mehrere große Wohnbauten dieses Namens, die er in ganz Europa entwarf.

[30] Siehe Anm. 5, S. 88f.

[31] Kakuzo Okakura, The Ideals of the East (1904), Rutland, Vermont, 1970, S. 178

[32] Yoshinobu Ashihara, The Hidden Order. Tokyo Through the Twentieth Century, Tokio 1989, S. 19

[33] Leonard Koren, Wabi-Sabi for Artists, Designers, Poets & Philosophers, Berkeley 1994

[34] Kisho Kurokawa, Rediscovering Japanese Space, New York 1988, S. 24

[35] Edward Seidenstricker, Low City, High City, New York 1983, S. 11

[36] Siehe Anm. 34, S. 13

[37] Kenji Ekuan, The Aesthetics of the Japanese Lunchbox, Cambridge, Mass., 2002, S. 51

[38] Thomas W. Cutler, A Grammar of Japanese Ornament and Design, London 1880, S. 34

[39] Wörtlich „der früher Geborene"

[40] Shuichi Kato, Japan, Spirit & Form, Rutland, Vermont, 1994, S. 24

[41] John Heskett, „The Growth of Industrial Design in Japan", in: Japan 2000, hg. v. John Zukowsky, München–New York 1998

[42] Kunio Shibuya, „Modern Product Design in Japan", in: Proceedings of the Seventh International Symposium on Japan Today, Kopenhagen, 23.–25. Oktober 1986, Tokio 1986, S. 117

[43] Im Laufe seiner Geschichte kam Japan mit den klassischen Kulturen Asiens (China, Korea) sowie mit verschiedenen westlichen Kulturen in Berührung – aus religiösen (Spanier, Portugiesen), wirtschaftlichen (Holländer, Amerikaner) und kulturellen Gründen.

[44] Basil Chamberlain Hall, Japanese Things (1905), Rutland, Vermont, 1994, S. 8

[45] Das Volkslied „Auld Lang Syne" wird in Amerika traditionellerweise zum Jahreswechsel um Mitternacht gesungen. In Schottland allerdings, wo das Lied herstammt, wird es auch zur „Burns Night" am 25. Januar im Gedenken an den großen Dichter und Schriftsteller Robert Burns gesungen.

[46] Siehe Anm. 34, S. 24

[47] Leonard Koren, New Fashion Japan, Tokio o. J. [1984]

[48] Siehe Anm. 40, S. 45

[49] Paul du Gay, Stuart Hall, Linda James u. a., Doing Cultural Studies, The Story of the Sony Walkman, London–Thousand Oaks, Kalif., 1997, S. 15

[50] Toshihiko u. Toyo Isutzu, Die Theorie des Schönen in Japan, Köln 1988, S. 207

[16] The politician Thomas Jefferson moonlighted to improve a number of items that made the hard labor of the late 18th century easier: a more effective soil-turning plow, a threshing machine with a hemp-break attachment and a new time-saving machine for the fulling of wool. Cf. Silvio A. Bedini, "Godfather of American Invention," in: The Smithsonian Book of Invention, New York 1978, p. 83

[17] Adrian Forty, Objects of Desire: Design and Society since 1750, London–New York 1986, p. 11ff.

[18] Walter Benjamin, The Work of Art in the Age of Mechanical Reproduction, London 2008 (dt. Das Kunstwerk im Zeitalter seiner Reproduzierbarkeit, 1939)

[19] Filippo Tommaso Marinetti, "Manifeste du futurisme," in: Le Figaro, 20 February 1909

[20] Le Corbusier, Towards a New Architecture, trans. Frederick Etchells, New York 1986, p. 138

[21] Adolf Loos, "Ornament and Crime," in: Ornament and Crime: Selected Essays, trans. Michael Mitchell, Riverside, Calif., 1998

[22] Le Corbusier, Vers une architecture, Paris 1923, p. 83

[23] Harold C. Livesay, American Made: Men Who Shaped the American Economy, Boston, Toronto, 1979, p. 141

[24] Walter Gropius, "Bauhaus Dessau: Principles of Bauhaus Production" (1925), in: Architecture and Design 1890–1939, ed. by Tim and Charlotte Benton with Dennis Sharp, New York 1975, p. 148

[25] The Second Amendment to the United States Constitution is the part of the Bill of Rights and protects the right of the people to keep and bear arms. It was adopted on 15 December 1791, along with the rest of the Bill of Rights.

[26] Stephen Bayley, Harley Earl, New York 1990, p. 57

[27] Motto of the 1939 World's Fair in New York

[28] Roland Barthes, "Semantics of the Object" (1964), in: The Semiotic Challenge, trans. Richard Howard, Berkeley–Los Angeles 1994, p. 181

[29] Unité d'Habitation, Marseille (1947–1952). Residential housing design principle developed by Le Corbusier, with the collaboration of painter-architect Nadir Afonso. The concept formed the basis of several housing developments designed by him throughout Europe with this name.

[30] See note 5, p. 88f.

[31] Kakuzo Okakura, The Ideals of the East, Rutland, Vt., 1970, p. 178

[32] Yoshinobu Ashihara, The Hidden Order: Tokyo Through the Twentieth Century, Tokyo 1989, p. 19

[33] Leonard Koren, Wabi-Sabi for Artists, Designers, Poets & Philosophers, Berkeley, Calif., 1994

[34] Kisho Kurokawa, Rediscovering Japanese Space, New York 1988, p. 24

[35] Edward Seidenstricker, Low City, High City, New York 1983, p. 11

[36] See note 34, p. 13

[37] Kenji Ekuan, The Aesthetics of the Japanese Lunchbox, Cambridge, Mass., 2002, p. 51

[38] Thomas W. Cutler, A Grammar of Japanese Ornament and Design, London 1880, p. 34

[39] Literally: "the one born earlier"

[40] Shuichi Kato, Japan: Spirit & Form, Rutland, Vt., 1994, p. 24

[41] John Heskett, "The Growth of Industrial Design in Japan," in: Japan 2000, ed. by John Zukowsky, Munich–New York 1998

[42] Kunio Shibuya, "Modern Product Design in Japan," in: Proceedings of the Seventh International Symposium on Japan Today, 23–25 October, Tokyo 1986, p. 117

[43] In the course of its history, Japan was exposed to classical Asian cultures (China and Korea) as well as to the Western cultures—for religious (Spanish, Portuguese), economic (Dutch, American), and cultural reasons.

[44] Basil Chamberlain Hall, Japanese Things (1905), Rutland, Vt., 1994, p. 8

[45] The song "Auld Lang Syne" is traditionally sung by most Americans on the stroke of midnight of each New Year's Eve. However, in Scotland where the tune originates, it is also sung on Burns Night, 25 January, in commemoration of the famous poet and writer Robert Burns.

[46] See note 34, p. 24

[47] Leonard Koren, New Fashion Japan, Tokyo 1984

[48] See note 40, p. 45

[49] Paul du Gay, Stuart Hall, Linda James, Hugh Mackay and Keith Negus, Doing Cultural Studies: The Story of the Sony Walkman, London–Thousand Oaks, Calif., 1997, p. 15

[50] Toshihiko and Toyo Isutzu, The Theory of Beauty in the Classical Aesthetics of Japan, The Hague 1981, p. 162f.

Kontext /
Context

Barry M. Katz

Das Missing Link

Silicon Valley: Design als Schlüssel der Veränderung

The Missing Link

Silicon Valley: Design as the Key to Change

Vor 30 Jahren wäre in jeder Auflistung der tonangebenden Zentren des Designs die gleiche Handvoll Metropolen aufgeschienen: Mailand, London, New York, Tokio, vielleicht ein paar mehr. Hätte Kalifornien überhaupt Erwähnung gefunden (was unwahrscheinlich ist), dann im Zusammenhang mit dem seit Mitte des Jahrhunderts nachklingenden Modernismus Charles und Ray Eames' oder den psychedelischen Plakaten, die eine treue Fangemeinde zu einem Grateful-Dead-Konzert lockten. „Kalifornisches Design" beschwor einen Lebensstil herauf, der an Sonnentage am Strand und die Eskapaden einer verblassenden Gegenkultur denken ließ.

Wenn Kalifornien in der internationalen Designgemeinde eine Randstellung einnahm, dann lag Nordkalifornien an deren äußerster Peripherie. Anders als Los Angeles 500 Kilometer weiter südlich hatte die Gegend um die Bucht von San Francisco keine Unterhaltungsindustrie, die Kreative und Designer hätte ernähren können, kein Hollywood und kein Disneyland. Während aber Südkalifornien durch Wiener Modernisten, unter ihnen Richard Neutra, Rudolph Schindler und Victor Gruen, geprägt wurde, beschränkte sich der europäische Einfluss in Nordkalifornien auf die englische Arts-and-Crafts-Bewegung mit ihrem zwiespältigen Vermächtnis als Vorläuferin des Modernismus und gleichermaßen letzter gescheiterter Protest dagegen. Auf der Landkarte des Designs war die nordkalifornische Bay Area nicht eingezeichnet.

Umso bemerkenswerter, dass im kalifornischen Silicon Valley heute vermutlich mehr DesignerInnen arbeiten als irgendwo sonst auf der Welt. Die Produkte, die hier in den vergangenen 30 Jahren konzipiert, designt und gelauncht wurden, bestimmen ganze Industrien: der Taschenrechner HP-35, die Spielkonsole Atari 2600, der Macintosh-Computer, Adobe-Photoshop, der Operationsroboter Da Vinci, um nur einige leuchtende Beispiele zu nennen. Von weitreichenderer Bedeutung ist allerdings, wie neue Produkte und Branchen dem Design neue Betätigungsfelder eröffneten, die inzwischen anerkannte Gebiete in der praktischen Berufslandschaft darstellen. Wie ist es dazu gekommen, und was sagt das über Design als treibende Kraft des Wandels aus? Welche Aspekte dieser einzigartigen Erfahrung haben über die Grenzen Kaliforniens hinaus Bedeutung, und welche Lehren ließen sich daraus ziehen?

Der Schlüssel zum Verständnis der Designkultur des Silicon Valley liegt darin, dass sie sich nicht auf ein Produkt oder eine Reihe talentierter und unternehmerisch denkender Einzelpersonen reduzieren lässt. Vielmehr entwickelte sich Design als Teil eines größeren Ökosystems, das 60 Jahre für seine Entstehung brauchte und wie jede komplexe organische Struktur viele voneinander abhängige Elemente umfasst: natürlich die Technologiefirmen, aber auch ein dichtes Netzwerk aus firmeneigenen Forschungslabors und staatlich finanzierten Denkfabriken, eine Risikokapitalbranche, die kontinuierlich in die Region investiert,

Thirty years ago, any survey of the leading design centers would have identified a small number of world capitals: Milan, London, New York, Tokyo, and possibly a very few others. If California were even mentioned (which would have been unlikely), it would have been in the context of the lingering mid-century modernism of Charles and Ray Eames or the psychedelic posters summoning the faithful to a Grateful Dead concert. "California Design" conjured a lifestyle suggesting sunny days at the beach and the antics of a fading counterculture.

If California occupied a marginal position in the global design community, then Northern California was on the margins of the margins: Unlike Los Angeles, 500 km to the south, the San Francisco Bay Area had no entertainment industry to support a community of creative artists and designers, no Hollywood, and no Disneyland. And where Southern California had absorbed the influence of Viennese modernists including Richard Neutra, Rudolph Schindler, and Victor Gruen, the most palpable European influence in Northern California was the English Arts and Crafts movement, with its ambiguous legacy as both the progenitor of the modern movement and the last, failed protest against it. In terms of design, at least, the Bay Area of Northern California was on nobody's map.

It is all the more remarkable, then, that there are, arguably, more design professionals working in northern California's Silicon Valley today than anywhere else in the world. Products were conceived, designed, and launched in Silicon Valley during the last 30 years that have define whole industries: the HP-35 calculator, the Atari 2600 game console, the Macintosh computer, Adobe Photoshop, the da Vinci surgical robot, the iPod—to name only a few of the most obvious. Of even more far-reaching significance, however, is the manner in which new products and new industries inspired whole new fields of design that are now recognized parts of the landscape of professional practice. How did this happen, and what does it say about design as an agent of change? Which aspects of this singular experience are relevant beyond the shores of California, and what lessons might be learned?

The key to understanding the design culture of Silicon Valley is that it cannot be reduced to an inventory of products or a roster of talented and entrepreneurial individuals. Rather, design evolved as part of a larger ecosystem that has been in formation for 60 years and is, like any complex ecology, of many interdependent parts: the technology companies most obviously, but also a dense network of corporate research labs and government-funded think tanks; a venture capital industry that has injected a continuing flow of investment dollars into the region; professional service firms with expertise in patent, trademark, and intellectual property law; publishing and high-tech marketing; a cluster of research universities, state colleges, and private art institutes and design schools that have served both as a recruiting ground for new talent and a

professionelle Dienstleister mit profundem Wissen über Patent-, Marken- und Urheberrecht, Publizistik und Hightech-Marketing, einen Cluster von forschenden Universitäten, staatlichen Colleges und privaten Kunstinstituten sowie Designschulen, die gleichermaßen als Rekrutierungsbecken für Talente wie als Übungsgelände für die Umsetzung von Konzepten dienen, die einem Markttest noch nicht standhalten, und schließlich Immobilienmoguln mit besonderem Verständnis für die rasche Realisierung von Bauvorhaben und eine variable Raumkonzeption, wie sie aufstrebende Firmen benötigen. Zu dem Anfang der 1980er-Jahre einsetzenden dramatischen Zuwachs an unabhängigen Design-Beratungsunternehmen hätte es nicht kommen können, wären diese Voraussetzungen nicht gegeben gewesen. Umgekehrt haben DesignerInnen eine zentrale Rolle dabei gespielt, Ideen aus den Forschungslabors zu marktfähigen Produkten zu machen. Da man aber, wenn es um Design geht, vielfach nur an von schillernden Persönlichkeiten ersonnene technische Spielereien und sonstigen Firlefanz denkt, ist seine Rolle missverstanden und falsch dargestellt worden. Ich schlage daher vor, von Design als dem Missing Link im komplexen Innovationsökosystem des Silicon Valley zu sprechen.

„Das Tal der Herzensfreude". Ende des Zweiten Weltkriegs war das nordkalifornische Santa Clara Valley noch nicht für seine Risikokapitalgeber und Dotcom-Milliardäre bekannt, vielmehr diente es wohlhabenden Leuten aus San Francisco als Wochenendparadies. Einige wenige heimische Unternehmen – insbesondere IBM – hatten in der Gegend um San Jose Forschungs- und Produktionsbetriebe angesiedelt, und ein paar einheimische Firmen nutzten das angenehme Klima, um sich in Landwirtschaft, Elektronik oder Rüstung zu etablieren. Das waren allerdings Ausnahmen. Lange bevor das Googleplex in die Bucht hineinragte und die Firmenzentralen von Cisco, Yahoo!, eBay, Oracle und Genentech über die Hügelausläufer ragten, wurde die Landschaftsstimmung von einem lokalen Poeten eingefangen, der diesen duftenden Landstrich in rhapsodischem Überschwang als „das Tal der Herzensfreude" beschrieb.

Der Wandel kam im Gefolge des Zweiten Weltkriegs. Frederick W. Terman, Dekan der Schule für Ingenieurswesen der Stanford University, war nach einer Zeit als Direktor des im Krieg eingerichteten Funkforschungslabors der Universität Harvard an die Westküste zurückgekehrt – entschlossen, sich einen Anteil von dem Bundesbudget zu holen, das eben in Richtung der für den Kalten Krieg wichtigen Forschung umgeleitet werden sollte. Terman rekrutierte Leute, die in den Gebieten Halbleiter, Mikrowellenelektronik und Aeronautik tätig waren, und entwickelte die Idee einer – wie es heute hieße – „Sonderwirtschaftszone", um den Wissenstransfer zwischen Industrie und universitärer Forschung zu optimieren. Er ermutigte Studenten, ihre Ideen aus dem Hörsaal auf den Markt zu bringen, und nährte eine Kultur universitären Unternehmertums, die sich von Hewlett und Packard bis zu Larry Page und Sergey Brin von Google ungebrochen gehalten hat.

Binnen eines Jahrzehnts nahm die Infrastruktur des „Silicon Valley" Gestalt an, doch es sollten noch viele Jahre vergehen, ehe dort DesignerInnen in nennenswerter Zahl beschäftigt wurden. Das lag größtenteils am Wesen der neuen Technologiebranchen, deren Produkte fast ausschließlich von Ingenieuren für Ingenieure entwickelt wurden. Zwar spiegelt das „Design" eines Raketenlenksystems bei Lockheed, eines integrierten Schaltkreises bei Intel oder National Semiconductor sowie eines Heißluft-Windkanals im Ames Research Center der NASA auch den Willen zur Gestaltung wider, doch ist dieser von einer ganz anderen Art als der

place for the exploration of concepts that may not yet be ready to be tested in the market; and even real estate tycoons with a particular understanding of the rapid construction and flexible spaces required by emerging companies. The dramatic growth of the independent design consultancies that began in the early 1980s would not have happened without these predisposing factors, but the reverse is also true: designers have played a vital role in moving ideas from laboratory science to market-ready products. Because "design" has been thought of mainly as gadgets and gizmos conceived by colorful individuals, its role has been misunderstood and misrepresented. It is in this regard that I propose to speak of design as "the missing link" in Silicon Valley's complex ecosystem of innovation.

"The Valley of Heart's Delight". At the end of World War II, Northern California's Santa Clara Valley was still better known as a weekend retreat for wealthy San Franciscans than for its venture capitalists and dotcom billionaires. A few national companies—IBM, most notably—had located research or manufacturing facilities in the area around San Jose, and a few homegrown firms took advantage of the pleasant climate to establish a presence in agriculture, electronics, or defense. They, however, were the exceptions: Long before the Googleplex jutted into the bay, and the corporate headquarters of Cisco, Yahoo!, eBay, Oracle, and Genentech rose above the foothills, the spirit of the place was captured by a local poet who had written rhapsodically of this fragrant strip of land as "the Valley of Heart's Delight."

Change came in the aftermath of World War II. Frederick W. Terman, the dean of the School of Engineering at Stanford University, had returned to the West Coast following a period as the director of the wartime Radio Research Lab at Harvard University, determined to capture a share of the federal budget that was about to be redirected toward Cold War research. Terman recruited heavily in areas such as semiconductors, microwave electronics, and aeronautics, and conceived the idea of what might today be called a "special economic zone" to facilitate the transfer of knowledge between industry and academia. He encouraged students to take their ideas out of the classroom and into the market, nurturing a culture of academic entrepreneurialism that has stretched unbroken from Hewlett and Packard to Google's Larry Page and Sergey Brin.

Within a decade, the infrastructure of "Silicon Valley" had begun to take shape, but it would be many years before designers would be employed there in appreciable numbers. This is largely due to the nature of the new technology industries, whose products were, in almost every case, developed by engineering professionals and intended for use by other engineers. The "design" of a missile guidance system at Lockheed, an integrated circuit at Intel or National Semiconductor, or a high-temperature wind tunnel at NASA's Ames Research Center reflects choices, but these are of a quite different nature than the choices made by the designer of an airport signage system or a piece of office furniture. It was not until the products of Silicon Valley's technology companies began to pass from the professional to the wider consumer market that designers—and their clients—began to take notice.

This happened gradually and without fanfare. In 1951, with considerable reluctance, Hewlett-Packard added its first professionally trained industrial designer to its 250-person workforce in Palo Alto. For the first couple of years, Carl Clement worked mainly as a draftsman, and only gradually was allowed to try his hand at improving the appearance of HP's oscilloscopes, electronic counters, and signal generators. By the mid-fifties, an internal corporate design group had begun to form, but it was regarded with utmost

des Designers eines Flughafenleitsystems oder eines Möbelstücks. Erst als die Produkte der Technologiefirmen des Silicon Valley nicht mehr nur Spezialisten, sondern KonsumentInnen kauften, wurden DesignerInnen – und deren Kunden – auf den neuen Markt aufmerksam.

Das geschah schrittweise und ohne großes Tamtam. 1951, nach beträchtlichem Zögern, erweiterte Hewlett-Packard seine 250-Mann-Belegschaft in Palo Alto um einen ausgebildeten Industriedesigner. Die ersten paar Jahre arbeitete Carl Clement ausschließlich als Zeichner, nach und nach durfte er sich schließlich an der Verbesserung der Oszilloskope, elektronischen Zählwerke und Signalgeber von HP versuchen. Bis Mitte der Fünfzigerjahre entstand eine interne „Corporate Design"-Abteilung, die innerhalb der in hohem Maße technikbestimmten Unternehmenskultur aber mit größtem Argwohn betrachtet wurde. Als etwa Allen Inhelder, frischgebackener Absolvent des Art Center College of Design in Los Angeles, bei einem Vorstellungsgespräch seine Mappe mit Airbrush-Arbeiten zeigte, antwortete ihm David Packard selbst: „Sehr hübsch, aber so was machen wir hier nicht."[1] Die erste Generation von DesignerInnen bei HP kämpfte darum zu beweisen, dass es möglich ist, Effizienz, Bedienbarkeit und Sicherheit von hoch technischen Produkten noch zu verbessern. Bis man jedoch mehr von ihnen erwartete, als nach Wegen zu suchen, Elektronik in Blechbehältnisse zu packen, sollten viele Jahre vergehen. ABB. 1

Auch einige andere Technologiefirmen beschäftigten IndustriedesignerInnen und GrafikerInnen – in symbolischer Zahl und als Anhängsel von Produktions-, Marketing- oder Kommunikationsabteilungen. Unter ihnen war die – nach den Initialen ihres Gründers Alexander M. Poniatoff benannte – Ampex Corporation, die ursprünglich kleine Elektromotoren für das Militär herstellte. Nach Kriegsende versammelte Poniatoff ein Team von talentierten Maschinenbauern und Elektroingenieuren, die ihre Aufmerksamkeit der Magnettonaufzeichnung zuwandten und bis 1947 einen funktionierenden Prototyp des 200A bauten – jenes Apparates, von dem letztendlich die moderne Audio-, Video- und Datenaufzeichnungsindustrie ihren Ausgang nahm. Es war eine brillante Innovation. Der Chefingenieur Harold Lindsay soll ein wahrer Perfektionist in Bezug auf die mechanischen und visuellen Details gewesen sein. Innerhalb eines Jahrzehnts gelang es Ampex, die gesamte Aufzeichnungsindustrie zu dominieren. Erst dann richtete die Firma eine eigenständige Designabteilung ein, in der eine neue Generation von Industrie- und Grafikdesignern arbeitete. ABB. 2

Die dritte Firma, die bei der Entstehung einer professionellen Designkultur eine Rolle spielte, war IBM. Schon 1956 errichtete IBM in San Jose eine eigene Fabrik für den Bau des revolutionären 305 RAMAC (Random Access Method for Accounting and Control), des im Wesentlichen ersten kommerziellen Großcomputers. Zum Team gehörte eine rudimentäre Schar an Industriedesignern, die sich vor allem der heiklen Frage der Gestaltung der Mainframe-Schränke widmeten. Allerdings war dies das Jahr, in dem IBM sein gefeiertes Corporate-Design-Programm unter der Leitung von Eliot Noyes startete, dessen weltweit gültige Designstandards die regionalen Bemühungen in Kalifornien bald in den Schatten stellten. „Wir können keinen Westküstenstil einführen", verfügte der für Datenverarbeitungsprodukte zuständige Manager von der IBM-Zentrale in New York aus.[2] ABB. 3

Trotz des ambitionierten Anfangs war das Häufchen professioneller DesignerInnen bei Hewlett-Packard, Ampex und IBM – im Vergleich zum phänomenalen Wachstum der Halbleiterindustrie in den Sechziger- und Siebzigerjahren – bloß die Fußnote einer

suspicion within the supremely engineering-driven culture of the company. When Allen Inhelder, a recent graduate of the Art Center College of Design in Los Angeles, presented his airbrushed portfolio at a job interview, David Packard himself responded, "It's very nice, but we don't do that here."[1] HP's first generation of designers struggled to prove that through their thoughtful intervention it was possible to improve the efficiency, operability, and safety of even highly technical products, but it would be many years before they were asked to do more than find efficient ways of packaging electronics in sheet metal enclosures. FIG. 1

A few other technology companies employed industrial and graphic designers—in token numbers and mainly as adjuncts to manufacturing, marketing, or corporate communications departments. Among them was the Ampex Corporation—named for the initials of its founder, Alexander M. Poniatoff—which had its origins making small electric motors for the military. At the end of the war, Poniatoff assembled a team of talented mechanical and electrical engineers who turned their attention to magnetic sound recording, and by 1947 they had built a working prototype of the 200A, the machine that effectively launched the modern audio, video, and data recording industry. It was a brilliant innovation, and the chief engineer, Harold Lindsay, was by all accounts a perfectionist in terms of both visual and mechanical detail. It was not for another decade, however, by which time Ampex dominated the entire recording industry, that the company created a formal design department, staffed not with electrical engineers but with a new generation of industrial and graphic designers. FIG. 2

The third company to play a role in the formation of a professional design culture was IBM, which in 1956 had created a dedicated facility in San Jose to build the 305 RAMAC, the revolutionary Random Access Method for Accounting and Control machine—essentially the first commercial mainframe computer. The team included an embryonic industrial design group that attended to many subtle features of the external cabinetry. That was the year, however, in which IBM had launched its celebrated Corporate Design Program under the direction of Eliot Noyes, whose global design standards soon eclipsed the regional program in California: "We can't have a West Coast style," decreed the manager for data processing products from IBM's corporate headquarters in New York.[2] FIG. 3

Although it was a promising beginning, in comparison with the phenomenal growth of the semiconductor industry during the 1960s and '70s, the smattering of design professionals at Hewlett-Packard, Ampex, and IBM was a footnote to a footnote in Silicon Valley history. The acknowledged centers of design in the United States remained tied to the traditional manufacturing regions around New York, Chicago, and the Midwest, and as one designer discovered, having made the impulsive decision to relocate from Ohio to the Bay Area in 1964, "any sensible person could have told you that, geographically, this was a really dumb place to establish an industrial design practice."[3]

Almost without exception, the work of the Bay Area's corporate design offices was directed toward technical products whose "end users" (had such a concept existed at the time) were engineers, machine operators, or highly skilled technical professionals. Products such as audio oscillators, gas analyzers, and industrial lasers won recognition at industry trade shows for their clean lines and uncluttered surfaces, but they were remote from most people's lived experience and unlikely to attract the attention of a larger public. The few occasions uponwhich the technology giants ventured out into the world of consumer product development ended mainly

© Allen Inhelder

© Stanford University Libraries,
Special Collections Dept.

© Computer History Museum

MADE 4 YOU

Fußnote in der Geschichte des Silicon Valley. Die anerkannten Designzentren in den Vereinigten Staaten blieben an die traditionellen Industrieregionen um New York, Chicago und im Mittelwesten gebunden. Wie ein Designer feststellte, der 1964 die spontane Entscheidung getroffen hatte, von Ohio in die Bay Area umzuziehen, „hätte jeder vernünftige Mensch einem sagen können, dass das geografisch ein wirklich blöder Ort dafür war, sich als Industriedesigner niederzulassen"[3].

Die Arbeit der firmeneigenen Designbüros in der Bay Area war fast ausnahmslos auf technische Produkte ausgerichtet, deren „Endverbraucher" (wenn es den Begriff damals schon gegeben hätte) sich aus Ingenieuren, Maschinenführern oder anderen hoch qualifizierten Technikern zusammensetzten. Produkte wie Tonfrequenzgeneratoren, Gasanalysatoren und Industrielaser erfuhren wegen ihrer klaren Linien und aufgeräumten Oberflächen Anerkennung auf Branchenmessen, fanden aber kaum Eingang in das Alltagsleben und waren wenig dazu angetan, die Aufmerksamkeit einer breiteren Öffentlichkeit auf sich zu ziehen. Wagten sich die Technologiegiganten bisweilen in die Welt der Produktentwicklung für den Konsumentenmarkt vor, endete dies meist im Desaster: 1972 kündigte die mächtige Intel Corporation die Armbanduhr Microma an, die sich als 15-Millionen-Dollar-Abschreibposten erwies: „Wir gingen ins Uhrengeschäft, weil wir Uhren als technisches Produkt sahen und das Gefühl hatten, dass wir wussten, wie man an technische Fragen herangeht", meinte der Vorstandvorsitzende Robert Noyce. „Aber dann stellte es sich als Schmuckgeschäft heraus, und von Schmuck verstanden wir gar nichts."[4] Kaum besser erging es Hewlett-Packard einige Jahre später mit der HP-012-Rechner-Uhr – ein Wunder an miniaturisierter Technik, aber ästhetisch und ergonomisch eine Monströsität. ABB. 4

Erfolg hatte nur ein einziges Produkt, und das als die Ausnahme, die die Regel bestätigt: 1973 stellte Hewlett-Packard den HP-35 vor, den ersten elektronischen Taschenrechner. Dieses bahnbrechende Produkt sollte zur Quelle der Inspiration für zahllose spätere DesignerInnen (einschließlich Steven „Steve" Jobs) werden, zum Teil wegen der radikalen Umkehrung des normalen Entwicklungsverfahrens bei HP: Normalerweise stellte damals die Technikabteilung das elektromechanische Werk eines Geräts fertig und reichte es dann ans Design weiter, um es in ein passendes Gehäuse packen und mit dem Firmenlogo auf einer Metallplatte versehen zu lassen. Im Falle des HP-35 wurde diese Abfolge auf den Kopf gestellt: William Hewlett selbst gab die Maße für das Produkt vor, und die Industriedesigngruppe der Firma legte die Form fest, noch ehe irgendeiner der technischen Prozesse auch nur begonnen hatte. Trotz des enormen Markterfolgs war der HP-35 ausdrücklich für Techniker im Außendienst gedacht; bei einem Preis von 395 Dollar – mehr als 2.000 heutigen Dollar – war nicht davon auszugehen, dass der Rechner an Schulen oder beim Lebensmittelhändler zum Einsatz kommen würde. ABB. 5

Ironischerweise war es ein – von konsumentenfreundlichem Produktdesign so weit wie nur irgend möglich entferntes – wissenschaftliches Forschungslabor, das jene Entwicklungen in Gang brachte, die das Silicon Valley zur Welthauptstadt des Designs machen sollten. Mitte der 1960er-Jahre gründete Douglas Engelbart, ein Elektroingenieur am Stanford Research Institute (heute das SRI International), mit Mitteln der Advanced Research Projects Agency, der Finanzierungsagentur des US-Verteidigungsministeriums, das Augmentation Research Center. Engelbart hatte nicht die Vision, eine Maschine zu bauen, sondern er wollte Werkzeuge schaffen, mit deren Hilfe „WissensarbeiterInnen" verschiedener Büros kooperieren und sich austauschen können,

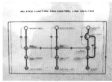

↑ ABB. 1
„Related Function and
Control Link Analysis"
von Allen Inhelder

FIG. 1
Allen Inhelder's
"Related Function and
Control Link Analysis"

← ABB. 2
Der Ingenieur als Designer:
Harold Lindsay mit dem Ampex 200A, 1947

FIG. 2
The engineer as designer:
Harold Lindsay with the Ampex 200A, 1947

↑ ABB. 3
IBM 305 RAMAC mit Zentralprozessor,
Kartenlesegerät und Drucker, 1956

FIG. 3
IBM 305 RAMAC with central processor,
card reader and printer, 1956

in disaster: In 1972, the mighty Intel Corporation announced the Microma wristwatch, which proved to be a $15 million write-off: "We went into the watch business because we saw it as a technical problem and we felt we knew how to solve technical problems," stated chairman Robert Noyce. "But it turned into a jewelry business and we didn't know anything about jewelry."[4] Hewlett-Packard fared no better, a few years later, with the HP-01 watch-calculator, a marvel of technical miniaturization and an aesthetic and ergonomic monstrosity. FIG. 4

Only one product succeeded, but in a manner that merely serves to show that the exception proves the rule. In 1973, Hewlett-Packard introduced the HP-35, the first hand-held electronic calculator. It was a groundbreaking product and would inspire countless later designers (including Steven "Steve" Jobs), in part because of a radical reversal of HP's normal process. Normally, in those days, the "Engineering Department" would complete the electro-mechanical workings of a device and then hand it over to "Design" to be packaged in a suitable enclosure and branded with a metal faceplate bearing the company's logo. In case of the HP-35, this sequence was turned on its head: William Hewlett himself had specified the dimensions of the product, and the corporate industrial design group created the

overall form factor before any of the technical processes had even begun. Despite its enormous market success, however, the HP-35 was explicitly intended for use in the field by technical professionals; at $395—more than $2000 in today's dollars—there was never any thought that it would be carried to school or to the grocery store. FIG. 5

Ironically, it was a science-based research laboratory—about as far removed as one could get from consumer-oriented product design—that set in motion the developments that would transform Silicon Valley into the design capital of the world. In the mid-1960s, Douglas Engelbart, an electrical engineer at the Stanford Research Institute (now SRI International) set up the Augmentation Research Center with funding from the Advanced Research Projects Agency, the funding arm of the U.S. Department of Defense. Engelbart's vision was not to build a machine, but to devise collaborative tools that would leverage the intellectual power of white-collar "knowledge workers" by allowing them to collaborate even if they happened to be working independently at different times and in different locations. In a famous presentation in 1968, Engelbart demonstrated to an audience of computer scientists in San Francisco that it is possible to manipulate "objects" on the screen of a computer through the use of a handheld "X-Y position indicator" (today we call it a "mouse"), while connected by a coaxial cable to his lab 50 kilometers away in Menlo Park. The unmistakable implication was that the computer might someday be thought of as an interactive information and communications medium and not simply an expensive calculating machine.

The story of Engelbart's ambitious research program has been told many times. What has not been told is the role of design in the revolution that would transform the nature of work itself. In the mid-1960s, Douglas Engelbart formed a partnership with Robert Propst, the visionary director of the Research Division of the Herman Miller Corporation in Michigan. Propst, who preferred to describe himself not as a furniture designer but as "a researcher studying large problems in a changing world," had been working on the flexible, modular Action Office for Herman Miller. Working in partnership with Engelbart, Propst's team, led by industrial designer Jack Kelley, created the physical tools that, for the first time, enabled a computer operator to interact with the "oNLine System (NLS)" in real time. Their collaboration of designer and engineer prefigured the development of the personal computer and the modular workstation—the two most profound innovations in the history of the modern office. FIG. 6

The other point at which design—as a specific professional practice and not simply a generic term for "planning and making"—figured in the birth of the personal computer industry took place only a few miles away, where a core team from Engelbart's lab relocated to the Xerox Corporation's Palo Alto Research Center (PARC). Charged with inventing "the office of the future," the PARC researchers built the first networked personal computer with an interactive graphical user interface, the so-called Alto. Although the Alto was primarily the work of scientists and engineers, the researchers at PARC also drew upon the professional services of one of the very few independent design consultancies that had formed in the region. Having left Hewlett-Packard, Carl Clement founded Clement DesignLabs—so named to appeal to the technology-driven practice of the region rather than the atelier culture of the European designer—in 1967. Once the basic architecture of the Alto was complete, PARC engaged DesignLabs to develop the outer form and physical interface of the system that would evolve, over the course of the coming decade, into the personal computer. FIG. 7

© Computer History Museum

→ ABB. 4
Werbeanzeige für die Intel Microma LCD-Armbanduhr, 1975
Design: George Thiess, Willy Crabtree

FIG. 4
Advertisement for the Intel Microma LCD watch, 1975
Design: George Thiess, Willy Crabtree

→ ABB. 5
Der erste elektronische Taschenrechner HP 35, 1973

FIG. 5
The first electronic hand-held electronic calculator HP 35, 1972

selbst wenn sie zu unterschiedlichen Zeiten an unterschiedlichen Orten arbeiten. In einer berühmt gewordenen Präsentation im Jahre 1968 demonstrierte Engelbart einem Publikum von ComputerwissenschaftlerInnen, dass es möglich sei, „Objekte" auf einem Computerbildschirm durch Benutzung eines „XY-Positionsindikators" (heute sagen wir „Maus" dazu) zu manipulieren, während er über ein Koaxialkabel mit seinem 50 Kilometer entfernten Labor verbunden war. Die unmissverständliche Implikation: Eines Tages könnte der Computer als interaktives Informations- und Kommunikationsmedium verstanden werden und nicht einfach als teure Rechenmaschine.

Die Geschichte von Engelbarts ehrgeizigem Forschungsprogramm ist schon viele Male erzählt worden. Nicht erzählt wurde, welche Rolle Design bei dieser Revolution spielte, die die Natur der Arbeit schlechthin veränderte. Mitte der Sechzigerjahre ging Douglas Engelbart eine Partnerschaft mit Robert Propst, dem visionären Direktor der Forschungsabteilung der Herman Miller Corporation in Michigan, ein. Propst, der es vorzog, sich nicht als Möbeldesigner zu bezeichnen, sondern als „Forscher, der umfangreiche Probleme in einer sich wandelnden Welt studiert", hatte für seine Firma an einem flexiblen modularen „Action Office" gearbeitet. In partnerschaftlicher Zusammenarbeit mit Engelbart schuf Propsts Team, angeführt vom Industriedesigner Jack Kelley, die physischen Werkzeuge, die einen Computeranwender erstmals in die Lage versetzten, in Echtzeit mit dem „oNLine System (NLS)" zu interagieren. Die Zusammenarbeit von Designer und Ingenieur deutete bereits auf die Entwicklung von PC und modularer Workstation, den beiden tiefgreifendsten Neuerungen in der Geschichte des modernen Büros, hin. ABB. 6

Und noch ein weiteres Mal trat Design – als spezifische professionelle Praxis und nicht einfach als Allgemeinbegriff für „Planen und Machen" – bei der Geburt der PC-Industrie in Erscheinung. Nur wenige Meilen entfernt übersiedelte ein Kernteam aus Engelbarts Labor ins Palo Alto Research Center (PARC) der Xerox Corporation. Mit der Erfindung des „Büros der Zukunft" beauftragt, bauten die PARC-ForscherInnen den ersten vernetzten Personal Computer mit interaktiver grafischer Benutzeroberfläche, den sogenannten Alto. Obwohl dieser primär das Werk von WissenschaftlerInnen und Ingenieuren war, nahmen die ForscherInnen auch die professionellen Dienste einer der wenigen unabhängigen Designberatungen in Anspruch, die in der Region entstanden waren. Nach seinem Weggang von Hewlett Packard hatte Carl Clement 1967 die Clement DesignLabs gegründet; der Name nahm auf die in der Region übliche Praxis Bezug, sich eher an der Technik als an der Atelierkultur europäischer Designer zu orientieren. Sobald die Basisarchitektur des Alto fertig war, engagierte PARC die DesignLabs, um die äußere Form und die physische Schnittstelle des Systems zu entwickeln. Im Laufe des kommenden Jahrzehnts sollte daraus der Personal Computer entstehen. ABB. 7

Design spielte bei der hard- und softwarebestimmten Arbeit dieser Labors eine vernachlässigbare Rolle: Die 500-Dollar-Mäuse wurden von einem lokalen Maschinenbauer, Jack Hawley, hergestellt, und das Gehäuse für den Alto war eine simple Verpackung, bei der auf Benutzerfreundlichkeit, Ergonomie oder Produktästhetik wenig geachtet wurde. Genau genommen könnte man sagen, dass der Computer weit mehr zur Gestaltung des Berufsbildes „Design" beitrug als Design zur Gestaltung des Computers. Evident wird das im Fall von Atari, gegründet 1972 von zwei Ampex-Ingenieuren. Verzeichnete das Unternehmen nach der Markteinführung von Pong, dem ersten kommerziell erfolgreichen Videospiel, rasantes Wachstum, so waren in den Anfangsjahren ein und dieselben Mitarbeiter noch für alles verantwortlich gewesen, vom Konzept bis zur Ausführung; „SpieledesignerInnen" gab es nicht. Ein Entwickler erinnert sich: „Man hatte die Idee, schrieb das Programm, kreierte die Grafik, machte die Soundeffekte, ging auf die Jagd nach Programmfehlern, testete das Spiel an Jugendlichen, überarbeitete es, bis man zufrieden war, und schrieb einen Entwurf für das Handbuch."[5] Als Computer leistungsfähiger und die Spiele komplexer wurden, erhielt das Design zusehends eine eigenständige Funktion, und „Spieledesigner" wurde ein anerkannter Beruf. Mit anderen Worten: Spiele produzierten DesignerInnen – nicht umgekehrt. ABB. 8

„Silicon Valley, USA". Mitte der 1970er-Jahre – etwa zu jener Zeit, als ein Lokaljournalist den Begriff „Silicon Valley, USA" für die Halbinsel südlich von San Francisco prägte – war ansatzweise ein Netzwerk von DesignerInnen im Entstehen, um die Nachfrage von Hewlett Packard, Raychem, Spectra Physics und anderen hoch spezialisierten Hightech-Firmen zu bedienen.

Noch war die Designgemeinde des Silicon Valley sehr klein, und es schien nicht einmal klar, in welchem Verhältnis sie zum Design im Allgemeinen stand. Im Gegensatz zur florierenden Designszene in New York, Chicago und Los Angeles zeigten sich in der San Franciscoer Niederlassung der Industrial Design Society of America gerade einmal neun Büros vertreten, die sich in ihrer Arbeit wenig von jenen im Rest des Landes unterschieden. Das größte, GVO, hatte sich eine prestigeträchtige Kundenliste erarbeitet. Ehrgeiziges Ziel aber war es, als den großen Designfirmen im Osten – „dem Land von Loewy, Bel Geddes, Dreyfuss and Teague", wie ein Neuankömmling es formulierte – ebenbürtig anerkannt zu werden und weniger als Initiator von etwas Neuem und Einzigar-

© Jack Kelley

← ABB. 6
Doug Engelbart (links) und Jack Kelley testen eine All-in-one-Konsole.

FIG. 6
Doug Engelbart (l.) and Jack Kelley testing "all-in-one" console.

CLEMENT DESIGNLABS ASSEMBLY SHOP

© Carl Clement

← ABB. 7
Montage des Xerox Alto Computers in den Clement DesignLabs, um 1970

FIG. 7
Assembly of the Xerox Alto computer in the Clement DesignLabs, around 1970

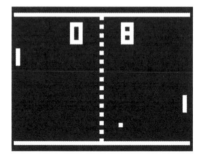

© flickr/Forrest Olinger

← ABB. 8
Atari Pong, erstes kommerzielles Videospiel (Screenshot), 1972

FIG. 8
Atari Pong, first commercial video game (screen shot), 1972

Design played a negligible role in the hardware and software driven work of these labs: the $500 mouse pointers commissioned by the scientists at Xerox PARC were built by a local mechanical engineer, Jack Hawley, and the housing for the Alto was a straightforward packaging job that owed little to user testing, ergonomics, or product aesthetics. In fact, it could be argued that the computer contributed far more to shaping the design profession than design did to shaping the computer. This is clearly evident in the case of Atari, founded in 1972 by a pair of Ampex engineers and—following the introduction of Pong, the first commercially-successful video game—reportedly the fastest-growing company in the world. In the early years, there were no "game designers" at Atari; the same individual was responsible for everything from concept to execution. As one early developer recalled, "You had the idea, wrote the program, created the graphics, did the sound effects, chased down bugs, tested the game on kids, revised it until you were satisfied, and wrote a draft of the game manual."[5] As computers became more powerful and games more complex, "design" became an increasingly distinct function, and "game designer" became a recognized professional field: in other words, games produced designers, not the other way round. FIG. 8

tigem zu gelten. Bei anderen wie Inova and Interform meinte man, es fehle an technischer Expertise, um erfolgreich mit Hightech-Kunden zusammenzuarbeiten.

Bis zum Ende des Jahrzehnts freilich mehrten sich aus politischen, kulturellen und technologischen Gründen die Anzeichen, dass sich das Selbstbild des Designs im Silicon Valley zu verändern begann. Während die weltweite Designszene weiterhin von Promistylisten dominiert wurde, waren die DesignerInnen, die innerhalb der Technologieindustrie des Silicon Valley arbeiteten, dabei, ihre eigene Stimme zu finden. Wie einer der damals Neuen es formulierte: „Die Designpraxis in Kalifornien erfordert es, dass wir in allen gestalterischen Fertigkeiten versiert sind und uns zusätzlich noch mit Maschinenbau, menschlichen Faktoren, Produktplanung (und) einer Vielzahl von Fertigungstechniken auskennen, was ein Designer aus dem Osten wahrscheinlich als unter seiner Würde erachten würde."[6]

Beflügelt von dem Gefühl, eine neue Welle ausgelöst zu haben, machte eine Gruppe von jungen IndustriedesignerInnen aus der Bay Area 1978 den Vorschlag, das landesweite Jahrestreffen der wichtigsten Berufsorganisation IDSA auszurichten. Ende September kamen DesignerInnen aus dem ganzen Land und der ganzen Welt drei Tage lang im idyllisch gelegenen Asilomar Conference Center am Rand der Bucht von Monterey zusammen und lauschten einer Reihe von Rednern, von denen viele bis dahin nie vor einer Zuhörerschaft von Designern aufgetreten waren. Sie präsentierten eine Vision des Planeten am Rande des öko-logischen Kollapses, eines kulturellen Lebens, das sich blindem Konsumismus ergeben hatte, und einer Designprofession, die eher Mitverursacher der dräuenden Krise denn Urheber eines Wandels zum Besseren war: „Wir haben uns vorgenommen, etwas Erder-schütterndes, das Denken Aufrüttelndes, Bewusstseinweckendes zu schaffen", erklärte einer der Organisatoren.[7]

Das nationale Vorstandsgremium sah die Sache freilich an-ders: Die Designer-AktivistInnen in Nordkalifornien litten an „offensichtlichem jugendlichen Mangel an Respekt", befand der Präsident der nationalen Organisation und beklagte weiters, dass die Bay Area zum „Epizentrum der Unzufriedenheit in der IDSA"[8] geworden sei. Es war dies in vielerlei Hinsicht ein bestimmender Moment für eine Designgemeinde, die drauf und dran war, eine regionale Identität herauszubilden. Während deren AktivistInnen früher lautstark Anerkennung eingefordert hatten, taten sie nun die gesamte nationale Organisation als engstirnig, selbstbezogen und irrelevant ab. Dabei handelte es sich allerdings nicht einfach um einen Fall von gegenkulturellem Protest und politischem Dissens, denn in dem hoch aufgeladenen Biotop des Silicon Valley nahmen allmählich atemberaubende technologische Entwick-lungen Gestalt an, die alle Regeln neu schreiben sollten.

Ende der Siebzigerjahre wurden die Produkte aus Forschung und Entwicklung im Silicon Valley auch außerhalb der Labormilieus von SRI, Xerox PARC und Stanford nachgefragt und drängten auf den Verbrauchermarkt – das war der Punkt, an dem DesignerInnen die Möglichkeit bekamen, ihren besonderen Mehrwert beizusteu-ern. Selbst ein eingetragenes IDSA-Mitglied hat zum Design eines Halbleiterchips wenig beizutragen; geht es allerdings darum, das Aussehen des Desktop-Computers, Telefons oder der Spiel-konsole festzulegen, in die der Chip eingebaut wird, dann ist für den Designer weitaus mehr zu tun, als sich auf die ohnehin in die Jahre gekommene Formel von „Form und Funktion" zu verlegen. Wenn die technische Leistungsfähigkeit von Konkurrenzprodukten ähnlich ist und die dahinterstehende Technik so klein wird, dass

"Silicon Valley, USA". By the mid-1970s—from about the time that a local journalist began to refer to the peninsula south of San Francisco as "Silicon Valley, U.S.A."—an embryonic network of designers was forming to meet the demands of Hewlett-Packard, Raychem, Spectra Physics, and other highly specialized high-tech companies.

The Silicon Valley design community was still very small, and it was not even clear how it related to the larger profession. In contrast to the flourishing design scene in New York, Chicago, and Los Angeles, in 1974 there were exactly nine offices represented in the San Francisco Bay chapter of the Industrial Design Society of America, and there was little to distinguish their work from what might be found anywhere else in the country. The largest of them, the GVO consultancy, had won for itself a list of marquee clients, but GVO's stated aspiration was to be recognized as an equal to the great consultancies of the east—"the land of Loewy, Bel Geddes, Dreyfuss and Teague," as one new arrival put it—rather than as the pioneer of something new and unique. Others, such as Inova and Interform, found that they lacked the technical expertise to work effectively with high-tech clients.

By the end of the decade, however, for reasons of politics, culture, and technology, there were signs that this was starting to change. Whereas the mainstream of the profession remained dominated by celebrity stylists, designers working within the technology industries of Silicon Valley were finding their own voice. As one recent arrival put it, "The design practice in California demands that we [be] proficient in all of our design skills as well as in the additional skills of mechanical engineering, human factors, product planning, [and] a multitude of manufacturing techniques that the eastern designer would probably consider beneath his dignity."[6]

In 1978, emboldened by the feeling that they were part of a new wave, a group of young Bay Area industrial designers submitted a proposal to host the national meeting of the IDSA, the main professional organization. Over the course of three days at the end of September, designers from around the country and around the world descended upon the idyllic Asilomar Conference Center on the edge of the Monterey Bay. They heard a litany of speak-ers, many of whom had never appeared before an audience of designers, present a vision of a planet on the edge of ecological collapse, a cultural life given over to mindless consumerism, and a design profession that was more often complicit in the gathering crisis than an agent of positive change: "We were of a mind that we wanted to create something earth-shattering, mind-blowing, con-sciousness-raising," declared one of the organizers.[7] The national governing body saw things differently, however: The designer-activists in northern California suffer "the apparent disrespect of youth," noted the president of the national organization, who went on to complain that the Bay Area had emerged as "the epicenter of IDSA discontent."[8]

It was, in many respects, a defining moment for a design community that was beginning to forge a collective regional identity. Where they had previously clamored for recognition, activists now came to dismiss the national organization itself as parochial, self-absorbed, and irrelevant. It was not simply a case of countercultural protest and political dissent, however, for in the supercharged environment of Silicon Valley, dramatic new developments were taking shape in technology and science that would rewrite all of the rules.

By the end of the 1970s, there were signs that the products of Silicon Valley research and development were starting to spill out of

Kontext /
Context

45

sie beinahe unsichtbar ist, gerät Produktdifferenzierung zur Überlebensfrage. Die Dienstleistung von DesignerInnen gewann mit einem Mal eine größere Bedeutung, es ging nicht mehr um das einfache Hinzufügen von Styling- und Funktionselementen. Die Grenzen des Berufs begannen sich aufzulösen, und neue Formationen nahmen Gestalt an.

Diese in Fluss geratene Situation begünstigte eine neue Art von BeraterInnen, ModellbauerInnen und MischpraktikerInnen, viele von ihnen AbsolventInnen des Produktdesign-Studienprogramms in Stanford, bei dem Ingenieurswesen in einem Ausmaß in die Ausbildung einfloss, das für ein Industriedesignstudium unüblich war. „Gestalten Sie von innen nach außen", lehrte der Stanford-Professor Robert McKim, „dann drehen Sie's um und gestalten von außen nach innen." Ein Beispiel für diesen neuen Typus von Designer-Ingenieur, der antrat, häufig vorhandene Probleme in der Elektronikindustrie zu lösen, ist Bill Dresselhaus. Seine Ausbildung zum Chemieingenieur und Produktdesigner befähigte ihn, als Berater für Technologiefirmen wie Hewlett-Packard ebenso zu arbeiten wie für Start-up-Unternehmen der aufstrebenden Computerindustrie, insbesondere für die junge Firma Apple Computer, in der er für das Design des Lisa-Computers verantwortlich zeichnete. Dresselhaus teilte sich eine Zeit lang ein Studio mit einem weiteren Stanford-Absolventen, Jerry Manock. Nachdem er einige Jahre mit einem subalternen Ingenieursjob bei Hewlett-Packard und Spectra Physics zugebracht hatte, mietete Manock ein winziges Büro in der Innenstadt von Palo Alto und eröffnete – mit einer Reverenz an Buckminster Fullers Vision einer „umfassenden antizipatorischen Designwissenschaft" – die Einmannfirma Manock Comprehensive Design.

Im Januar 1977 erhielt Manock einen Anruf des 21-jährigen Steve Jobs, der ihn zu einer Zusammenkunft des Homebrew Computing Club beorderte. Das heute legendäre Treffen begeisterter ComputeramateurInnen fand jeden Monat im Auditorium des Stanford Linear Accelerator Center statt, um Programmiertipps auszutauschen und selbst gebastelte Schaltplatinen vorzuführen. Jobs bat Manock, ein Gehäuse für die zweite Version des Computers zu entwerfen, den er und sein Partner Steve Wozniak im April auf der Computermesse West Coast Computer Faire zu präsentieren beabsichtigten. Vernünftigerweise verlangte Manock Bezahlung im Voraus. Im Laufe der nächsten drei Wochen lieferte er eine Reihe von technischen Zeichnungen eines kompakten keilförmigen Gehäuses, das imstande war, die von Wozniaks Kontrollerplatine abgestrahlte Wärme abzuleiten, und eine interne Stromquelle sowie eine abgeschrägte Tastatur in unaufdringlichem Beige integrierte. Der ungeheuer erfolgreiche Apple II wurde vollständig zusammengebaut ausgeliefert und war der erste Personal Computer dieser Art. Einen PC nicht mehr als Bausatz mit rechteckiger Blechkiste zu verkaufen war eine entscheidende Designneuerung. Sie gründete auf Jobs' Überzeugung, dass auf jeden Hardware-Fan, der sich seinen eigenen Computer zusammenbauen wollte, tausend Software-Fans kamen, die ihren Computer einfach aus dem Karton nehmen, anstecken und damit zu spielen anfangen wollten. ABB. 9

Die neuen Ingenieur-DesignerInnen im Silicon Valley – Leute wie Jerry Manock und Bill Dresselhaus – hatten bald mehr Arbeit, als sie bewältigen konnten, und leiteten Projekte großzügig an andere Firmen weiter, die sich in der Region ansiedelten. In der gleichen Straße wie Manock Comprehensive war ein Stück weiter in einem Obergeschoß das überfüllte Studio von Hovey-Kelley Design untergebracht, gegründet von einer Gruppe gleichgesinnter Freunde aus dem Produktdesign-Studienprogramm in

the laboratory environments of SRI, Xerox PARC, and Stanford and toward the broader consumer market—the point at which designers are in a position to add their peculiar form of value. A card-carrying member of the IDSA has little to add to the design of a chip; when it comes to determining the character of the desktop computer, the telephone, or the game console in which that chip is embedded, however, the designer is in a position to do far more than simply apply the aging formula of "form and function." On the contrary, where the technical performance of competing products is similar, and the enabling technology is invisibly small, product differentiation becomes a matter of life and death, and the services of designers came to be seen as something more than simply the adding of styling and affordances. The boundaries of the profession seemed to be dissolving, and new formations were taking shape.

This fluid situation favored a new breed of consultants, model makers, and hybrid practitioners, many of them graduates of Stanford's Product Design program, whose training often included a level of engineering that was unusual in industrial design education: "Design from the inside out," instructed Stanford Professor Robert McKim, "then turn it around and design from the outside in." Bill Dresselhaus is an example of this new type of designer-engineer who stepped forward to solve problems common to the electronics industry. His training in chemical engineering as well as in product design enabled him to work as a consultant to technology companies such as Hewlett-Packard as well as startups in the emerging personal computer industry, most notably the young Apple Computer, where he was responsible for the industrial design of the Lisa computer. For a time, Dresselhaus shared studio space with another Stanford graduate, Jerry Manock. After a period working in a low-level engineering job at Hewlett-Packard and Spectra Physics, he rented a tiny office in downtown Palo Alto and—with a nod toward Buckminster Fuller's vision of a "comprehensive anticipatory design science"—opened the one-person firm of Manock Comprehensive Design.

In January, 1977, Manock received a call from the 21-year old Steve Jobs, summoning him to a meeting of the Homebrew Computing Club, a now-legendary gathering of amateur computer enthusiasts who gathered every month in the auditorium of the Stanford Linear Accelerator Center to share programming tips and show off their homemade circuit boards. Jobs asked Manock to design an enclosure for the second version of the computer he and his partner, Steve Wozniak, intended to present at the West Coast Computer Faire in April. Sensibly, Manock demanded to be paid in advance, and over the next three weeks developed a set of mechanical drawings for a compact, wedge-shaped case capable of dissipating the heat given off by Wozniak's circuit board, accommodating an internal power supply, and presenting to the user an angled, integral keyboard in an unobtrusive beige color. The hugely successful Apple II came fully assembled and was the first personal computer to be sold in anything other than a rectangular sheet metal box—a critical design innovation grounded in Jobs' conviction that for every hardware enthusiast who wished to assemble his own computer, there were a thousand software enthusiasts who simply wanted to take it out of the box, plug it in, and begin to play with it. FIG. 9

Silicon Valley's new breed of engineer-designers—people such as Jerry Manock and Bill Dresselhaus—soon had more work than they could handle and were generous in recommending projects to other firms that had begun to populate the region. Just up the street from Manock Comprehensive was the cramped, upstairs studio of Hovey-Kelley Design, formed by a group of like-minded friends from the Stanford Product Design program. When Jobs approached them to

46

Stanford. Als Jobs mit dem Wunsch an sie herantrat, aus der PARC-Maus von Xerox ein Zwanzigdollargerät zu machen, das von jedermann bedient werden konnte, sagten sie bereitwillig zu, wenngleich keiner von ihnen eine Vorstellung von der Funktion einer „Maus" hatte. Die Episode spiegelt das damalige Zeitgefühl wider: Die DesignerInnen verließen sich eher auf Instinkt und Intuition als auf rigide Methoden. Frei von derartigen Zwängen entwickelten sie Konzepte, kauften Material für den Bau eines Prototyps im Künstlerbedarfsladen um die Ecke und erfanden aus dem Stegreif Testverfahren, die in jedem Sinn neu für die Welt waren: „Wäre ich damals in New York gewesen", meinte Mitbegründer David Kelley, „hätte ich nur einen weiteren Abfalleimer entworfen."[9]

Die zumeist in Amerika geborenen DesignerInnen, die sich Ende der 1970er-Jahre im Silicon Valley sammelten, hatten Ausbildungen als Elektroingenieure oder Maschinenbauer, in Informatik oder Produktdesign; viele hatten die Studienrichtung Industriedesign an der San Jose State University, am Art Center College of Design in Los Angeles oder an einigen anderen Ausbildungsstätten absolviert, die Designstudien anboten. Während sie einen hohen Standard an technischem Know-how in ihre Berufspraxis einbrachten, waren sie in anderen Bereichen wenig erfahren und schenkten Ideen, die unter DesignerInnen anderswo auf der Welt kursierten, keine Beachtung. In den Anfangsjahren mochte das ein Vorteil gewesen sein, da es sie befähigte, an neue Probleme ohne vorgefasste Annahmen heranzugehen. Mit der Zeit allerdings führte dieses Inseldasein häufig zu uninspirierten Formen, die sich mehr nach den Bedürfnissen der „an der Quelle" des Endproduktes arbeitetenden Ingenieure richteten als nach jenen der KundInnen, also der KäuferInnen und EndverbraucherInnen.

Einigen DesignerInnen an der Westküste wurde ihre Isolation nach und nach bewusst. Manche erweiterten ihren Horizont über die englische Zeitschrift „Design", die deutsche „Form" und die italienische „Domus"; andere bewunderten die Produkte von Siemens, Porsche und Olivetti. Mitte der Siebzigerjahre begannen zwei unternehmungslustige Designer aus der Bay Area, James Ferris und Peter Lowe, Pilgerreisen zu organisieren, die ihre provinziellen KollegInnen in die berühmten Studios von London, Paris, Stuttgart und Mailand führten. Sie trafen dort auf eine europäische Designtradition, die mehr als ein Jahrhundert zurückreichte und deren führende Vertreter – Giugiaro, Bellini, Rams – eine Formensprache entwickelt hatten, die elaborierter war als alles, was sich in den USA finden ließ. Die Europäer ihrerseits arbeiteten hauptsächlich in traditionellen Produktfeldern – Autostyling, Beleuchtung, Interieurs –, die vertraut und etabliert waren, was die Palette an bahnbrechenden Innovationen sehr beschränkte.[10] Zur gleichen Zeit, da die Amerikaner in Europa nach Inspiration suchten, begann eine kleine Gruppe europäischer DesignerInnen zu entdecken, welche Möglichkeiten die neuen Technologien und Industrien boten, die im amerikanischen Westen erblüht waren.

Gezeitenwechsel. Der erste europäische Forschungsreisende, der in die Neue Welt Segel setzte, war Bill Moggridge, Gründer der anerkannten Londoner Firma Moggridge Associates. Als Industriedesigner machte sich Moggridge zunehmend Sorgen über den Trend von der Industrie- hin zur Dienstleistungsgesellschaft im Vereinigten Königreich und begann, sich nach Betätigungsfeldern im Ausland umzusehen. Am verheißungsvollsten schien die Gegend entlang der Route 128 in Massachusetts, von den Forschergemeinden von Harvard und vom MIT mit neuen Ideen versorgte Heimat etablierter Minicomputerfirmen wie Digital Equipment Corporation und Data General. Moggridge entschied sich allerdings,

transform the Xerox PARC mouse into a $20 appliance that anyone could use, they readily accepted, even though none of them had any idea of what a "mouse" was or how someone might use it. This was the climate of the time, however: operating more on instinct and intuition than on any sort of rigorous design methodology, they proceeded to define the concept, purchase prototyping materials from the neighborhood art supply store, and invent ad hoc procedures to test it that were in every sense new to the world: "If I had been in New York," commented co-founder David Kelley, "I would have been designing another wastebasket."[9]

The mostly American-born designers who were gathering in Silicon Valley in the late 1970s were trained in electrical and mechanical engineering, computer science, or product design; many were graduates of the industrial design programs at San Jose State University, the Art Center College of Design in Los Angeles, or a few other places with design curricula. Although they brought to their practice a high level of technical ingenuity, they tended to be not very worldly in their outlook and were generally inattentive to ideas circulating among designers in other parts of the world. This may have been a real asset in the early years, as it enabled them to approach brand new problems without prior assumptions. Over time, however, this insularity resulted in forms that were often uninspired and responsive more to the requirements of the engineers working "upstream" of the final product than to the "downstream" world of clients, customers, and end users.

A few west coast designers were becoming aware of their isolation. Some were already leafing through the pages of the English "Design", the German "Form", and the Italian "Domus"; others had come to admire the products of Siemens, Porsche, and Olivetti. In the mid-1970s, two enterprising Bay Area designers, James Ferris and Peter Lowe, began to organize pilgrimages that brought their provincial American colleagues to the famous studios of London, Paris, Stuttgart, and Milan. What they encountered was a European design tradition that stretched back over a century and whose leading practitioners—Giugiaro, Bellini, Rams—had internalized a more sophisticated language of form than anything that could be found in the USA. The Europeans, for their part, worked mainly on traditional product categories—automotive styling, lighting, interiors—that were familiar and very well established, which limited the possibilities of truly unprecedented innovation.[10] At the same moment that Americans were beginning to look to Europe for inspiration, then, a small number of European designers were starting to sniff out the opportunities presented by the new technologies and new industries that were blossoming in the American West.

Sea Change. The first European explorer to set sail for the New World was Bill Moggridge, founder of the respected firm Moggridge Associates of London. As an industrial designer, Moggridge had become concerned over the drift of the UK from a manufacturing to a service economy, and had begun to look for opportunities abroad. Most promising seemed to be the region around Route 128 in Massachusetts, home to established minicomputer companies including Digital Equipment Corporation and Data General, and fed by the research communities of Harvard and MIT. Moggridge decided to take a chance on the West, however, and in 1979 he announced to his clients that the company would soon be opening a branch office, ID Two, in California: "We have chosen the Bay Area of San Francisco for its electronic technology and hope that this will enable us to transfer technical knowledge to our UK office."[11] As so often happens, however, the colony soon overtook the imperial capital. In contrast to old Britain—beset by restive trade unions, declining productivity, factory closures, and low profit margins—Silicon Valley

47

sein Glück im Westen zu versuchen, und kündigte seinen Kunden 1979 an, in Kürze eine Filiale, ID Two, in Kalifornien zu eröffnen. „Wir haben uns die Bay Area von San Francisco wegen der dortigen Elektroniktechnologie ausgesucht und hoffen, dass uns das einen Transfer von technischem Wissen zu unserem Büro in Großbritannien ermöglichen wird."[11] Wie so oft allerdings überholte die Kolonie bald die imperiale Hauptstadt.

Im Gegensatz zum alten England, das im Konflik mit Gewerkschaften lag, mit nachlassender Produktivität, Fabriksschließungen und niedrigen Gewinnmargen kämpfte, erschien das Silicon Valley Moggridge als ein Land der unbegrenzten Möglichkeiten. Während die europäische Designkultur elitär und hierarchisch war, fand er sich in Kalifornien in „Informationsnetzwerke" eingebettet, an „unsichtbaren Universitäten" inskribiert und genoss eine in diesem Ausmaß nicht gekannte Zusammenarbeit zwischen Industrie und akademischer Welt, zwischen einzelnen Leuten konkurrierender Firmen, ja sogar zwischen den konkurrierenden Firmen selbst.[12] Neben einigen ambitionierten Unternehmen, die mit dem „Eurostil" experimentierten, öffnete sich ein weiter Raum zwischen der Tradition verfeinerten europäischen Designs und der Kühnheit amerikanischer Innovation, der großteils unbeackert war. „Hier konnte man auf einem leeren Blatt Papier arbeiten, anstatt wie sonst auf einem bereits mit Vorläuferprodukten, Herstellungsausrüstung und Vertriebskanälen beschriebenen."[13]

Das „leere Blatt Papier", das Moggridge vorfand, blieb tatsächlich länger leer, als er erwartet hatte, doch begann er schrittweise, sich unter den etablierten Firmen des Silicon Valley und den Hightech-Start-ups eine Klientel aufzubauen. Am bemerkenswertesten darunter war zweifelsohne GRiD Systems, eine Firma, die John Ellenby gegründet hatte, vormals Wissenschaftler bei Xerox. Er hatte das PARC frustriert verlassen, nachdem es ihm nicht gelungen war, das Firmenmanagement davon zu überzeugen, ernsthaft ins Computergeschäft einzusteigen. Als der Mainframe eben erst auf die Dimensionen des Desktop-Computers geschrumpft war, dachte Ellenby bereits daran, einen Computer zu bauen, der klein genug war, dass ihn ein Geschäftsmann in ein Meeting mitnehmen konnte, ein Soldat in den Kampf oder ein Astronaut ins All. Er engagierte ID Two, um das Konzept zu 2-D-Darstellungen und einem 3-D-Modell weiterzuentwickeln, die es GRiD ermöglichten, sich einen ersten Schwung Risikokapital zu sichern, um dann den GRiD Compass (1982) zu entwerfen und zu bauen – den ersten Laptop-Computer. ABB. 10

Einige Merkmale dieser Geschichte bezeugen den ungewöhnlichen Charakter des Designprozesses im Silicon Valley; sie sollten sich auch für die Zukunft als prägend erweisen. Erstens gab es für das Konzept eines „Laptop-Computers" – bei dem ein an Scharnieren befestigter Bildschirm sich als Deckel über die Tastatur klappen ließ und eine kompakte durchgehende Oberfläche bildete – keine Vorläufer und ergo keine Anhaltspunkte, wie die technischen Herausforderungen zu meistern sind. Daher war auch der Businessplan, auf dem er beruhte, ein neuer. Seit den 1930er-Jahren waren DesignerInnen in den USA typischerweise engagiert worden, um alten Produkten neue Formen zu geben; hier aber ging es um eine völlig neue Produktkategorie, für die keine Modelle existierten, an denen man sich anhalten konnte. (Neben zahllosen Auszeichnungen erhielt der GRiD Compass nicht weniger als 43 Patente zugesprochen).

Zweitens erkannte der Auftraggeber, dass eine derart radikale Innovation eine radikal neue Arbeitsweise erforderte:

seemed to Moggridge to be a land of unprecedented opportunity. Where the European design culture was elitist and hierarchical, in California he found himself embedded in "information networks," enrolled in "invisible colleges," and enjoying an unheard-of level of cooperation between industry and academia, between individuals working for competitive companies, and sometimes between competing companies themselves.[12] Apart from a few ambitious firms that were experimenting with "Eurostil," however, the space between the refined tradition of European design and the boldness of American innovation remained largely unexplored. "Here was a blank sheet of paper to work on, instead of the usual one already covered with product precedents, manufacturing equipment, and distribution channels."[13]

The "blank sheet of paper" Moggridge encountered actually remained blank for longer than he had expected, but gradually he began to build a clientele among Silicon Valley's established firms and high-tech startups. The most notable of these was undoubtedly GRiD Systems, a company launched by John Ellenby, a Xerox scientist who had left PARC in frustration after failing to persuade corporate management to move seriously into the computer business. Just as the mainframe had shrunk to the dimensions of a desktop, Ellenby proposed to build a computer small enough to be carried by a businessman into a meeting, a soldier into combat, or an astronaut into space. He hired ID Two to develop the concept into 2-D renderings and a 3-D model that enabled GRiD to secure a first round of venture funding, and ultimately to design and build the GRiD Compass (1982), the first laptop computer. FIG. 10

Several features of this story speak to the unusual character of the design process and to its future in Silicon Valley. First, the concept of a "laptop computer"—one in which the hinged screen folded down over the keyboard to form a compact, unbroken surface—was unprecedented, as were the technical challenges in creating it and the business plan that would sustain it. Since the 1930s, designers in the USA had typically been hired to give new form to old products, but here was an entirely new product c a t e g o r y with no precedents to consult (in addition to countless honors, the GRiD Compass would be awarded no less than 43 patents).

Second, the client recognized that a radical innovation of this sort required a radically innovative way of working: A master designer in the European tradition might create a form and hand it off to the client to be realized without further involvement; conversely, an American corporate design group would typically be given the technical components of a product and instructed to enclose them in a suitable box. Ellenby, by contrast, insisted that the designer be part of the team at the outset and participate in all of its deliberations throughout the entire process: "We did this to provide the physical constraints within which the design team would work and to ensure that human factors and mechanical design were appropriate for the unique integrated product design we were undertaking."[14]

Finally, it must be noted that the GRiD Compass, the competing WorkSlate tablet computer designed by Moggridge's colleague, Mike Nuttall, for Convergent Technology, and a very small number of other products from that era, had a massive impact upon a generation of young American designers who had been struggling to formulate a new design language: sleek, restrained, devoid of gratuitous styling gestures, and black. The founders of many of the consultancies that would give Silicon Valley its identity acknowledged the influence of the first generation of expatriate European designers in freeing them from a slavish subordination to engineering, on the one hand, or the arbitrariness of superficial styling, on the other.

Ein Generaldesigner europäischen Zuschnitts konnte eine Form kreieren und sie ohne weiteres Zutun dem Kunden zur Realisierung überlassen; umgekehrt würde eine amerikanische Designergruppe typischerweise die technischen Komponenten eines Produkts nebst der Anweisung erhalten, sie in einer passenden Kiste unterzubringen. Im Gegensatz dazu bestand Ellenby darauf, dass der Designer von Anfang an Teil des Teams und während des gesamten Prozesses an allen Überlegungen beteiligt war: „Damit wollten wir die physischen Beschränkungen vorgeben, innerhalb deren das Designteam arbeiten würde, und sicherstellen, dass die menschlichen Faktoren und das mechanische Design dem einzigartigen integrierten Produkt angemessen waren, an das wir uns wagten."[14]

Sowohl der GRiD Compass als auch das Konkurrenzprodukt – der von Moggridges Kollegen Mike Nutall für Convergent Technology entworfene Tablet-Computer WorkSlate – und eine kleine Zahl anderer Produkte aus dieser Zeit übten eine massive Wirkung auf eine ganze Generation von jungen amerikanischen DesignerInnen aus, die darum kämpften, eine neue Designsprache zu formulieren: schnittig, reduziert, ohne überflüssiges Styling und schwarz. Die Gründer vieler Firmen, die für das Silicon Valley identitätsstiftend wurden, ließen sich von den aus Europa kommenden Designern dahingehend beeinflussen, dass sie sie einerseits aus der sklavischen Unterordnung unter die Ingenieurstechnik befreiten und andererseits dem bis dahin beliebigen Styling der Oberflächen mehr Beachtung einräumten. Während der GRiD Compass und der Convergent WorkSlate hauptsächlich innerhalb der Designcommunity selbst bewundert wurden, sollten sich die Produkte von Apple Computer – „Der Computer für uns andere" – als Motor des Gezeitenwechsel erweisen, der das Silicon Valley mit seinem kleinen Kader von Technikneuerern in eine der Designmetropolen transformierte. Design kam, wie gesagt, im Silicon Valley nicht in einem Karton mit dem Etikett „Apple Computer" an – aber Apple war mit Sicherheit die treibende Kraft hinter dem Aufstieg zum Design-Mekka. IDEO, frog design und Lunar können ihren Erfolg auf Projekte für Apple und auf die Standards zurückführen, die dieser fordernde Kunde durchsetzte. Steven Jobs' Designversessenheit wurde von seinen Kritikern als Ausflucht für seinen Mangel an Technikkenntnissen bezeichnet, während seine Bewunderer darin den Beweis für seine Hingabe an die umfassende Nutzerfreundlichkeit sahen. Für welche Sichtweise man sich auch entscheidet, es lässt sich kaum bestreiten, dass Jobs einen Wandel bewirkte.

Das Schlüsselmoment war die Entscheidung von Apple, den Schwerpunkt vom Zusammenbau von Hardware auf die Arbeit mit Software zu verschieben; das wiederum eröffnete ein breites Spektrum von Designfragen, die bis heute relevant sind. Wie Jobs im Gespräch mit dem Autor erläuterte: „Wir dachten, wenn wir einen Computer machen können, den die Leute nicht zusammenbauen müssen, könnten wir viel mehr verkaufen – und wir hatten recht. Also wollten wir den Apple II in ein Gehäuse stecken, das eine mehr humanistische Sichtweise widerspiegelte. Sobald wir einen Weg fanden, das zu tun, lautete die nächste Frage: Wie soll er aussehen? Was soll er ausdrücken? Wie soll er funktionieren? Diese simple Entscheidung brachte uns auf einen Weg, auf dem wir jeden Aspekt der Nutzererfahrung auf eine Art und Weise durchdenken mussten, die neu für die Branche war."[15]

Nachdem der bereits erwähnte Designer Jerry Manock begonnen hatte, als externer Auftragnehmer am Apple II zu arbeiten, stellte er fest, dass er mehr und mehr Zeit bei seinem neuen Kunden verbrachte. 1979 fügte er sich ins Unvermeidliche, schloss seine

Whereas the GRiD Compass and the Convergent WorkSlate were mainly admired within the design community itself, the products of Apple Computer—"the computer for the rest of us"—would prove to be the driver of the sea change that transformed Silicon Valley from a narrow cadre of technology innovators to, arguably, the design capital of the world. Design, as we have shown, did not arrive in Silicon Valley in a box labeled "Apple Computer," but Apple was surely the principal force in its rise to prominence: IDEO, frog design, and Lunar can all trace their success to the projects done for Apple and to the standards this exacting client imposed. Steven Jobs' obsession with design has been cited by his critics as an excuse for his lack of technical expertise and by his admirers as proof of his commitment to a seamless user experience. Whatever perspective one chooses to adopt, there can be little argument that the effect was transformative.

The key moment was Apple's decision to shift the focus from assembling the hardware to working with the software; this, in turn, opened the door to a huge range of design issues that continues to this day. As Jobs explained in conversation with the author, "We thought that if we could make a computer that people didn't have to assemble, we could sell a lot more—and we were right. So we wanted to put the Apple II in a housing that would reflect more of a humanistic point of view. Once we found a way to do that, then the next question was, what should it look like? What should it express? How should it work? That simple decision led us down the path of having to think through every aspect of the user experience in a way that was new to the industry."[15]

Having begun work on the Apple II as an outside contractor, Jerry Manock found himself spending an increasing amount of time with his new client. In 1979 he finally bowed to the inevitable, closed his private consulting practice, and joined Apple, where, as Corporate Manager of Product Design, he oversaw the design of the epoch-making Macintosh computer. Despite the unparalleled success of the Mac, however, Manock perceived a larger task, which was to create "a new unified appearance for the '80s."[16] This goal lay beyond the scope of the informal Design Guild he had assembled, so in 1982 he proposed that Apple undertake a global search for a world-class design consultant. A small delegation consisting of Manock, his design partner Terry Oyama, and a fellow designer, Rob Gemmell from Apple's printer division, set out for the Continent, where they interviewed some of the grandees of European design, including Mario Bellini and Ettore Sottsass in Italy, Roger Tallon in Paris, and Dieter Rams in Frankfurt. They ultimately narrowed the field to the British firm BIB, and Esslinger Design in the Black Forest village of Altensteig in Germany, and over a period of nine months, each of them developed a series of prototypes. The so-called "Snow White" competition, named for Apple's seven divisions, was decisively won by Esslinger, who welcomed the opportunity to relocate to California. Fortified by an unprecedented $2 million retainer, Esslinger began shipping precision shop equipment from the Federal Republic of Germany to the new offices of frog design in Campbell, at the southern end of Silicon Valley. "Everything seemed possible," he reflected, "if only the connection between meaningful innovation, ease of use, and elegant design could be demonstrated."[17] FIG. 11

Over the next three years, frog design evolved the "Snow White" concept—compact, mathematically proportioned units; unpainted grey-white ABS finish; elegant Univers typography; zero-draft tooling to eliminate the dated chamfers of the Apple II and discourage cheap knockoffs; iconic line grids to facilitate venting—into a corporate design language intended to unify Apple's family of computers, printers, and peripherals. The internal politics were intense, but by

© ddp images/AP Photo/Sal Veder

eigene Beratungsfirma und ging ganz zu Apple, wo er als leitender Produktdesign-Manager das Design des epochemachenden Macintosh-Computers beaufsichtigte. Trotz des noch nie dagewesenen Erfolgs des Mac sah Manock eine größere Aufgabe vor sich, die darin bestand, „ein neues einheitliches Erscheinungsbild für die Achtzigerjahre"[16] zu kreieren. Dieses Ziel lag jenseits des Horizonts der Gilde informeller DesignerInnen, die er um sich versammelt hatte; so schlug er 1982 vor, dass Apple sich international auf die Suche nach einem Weltklasse-Designer begeben solle. Eine Delegation aus Manock selbst, seinem Designpartner Terry Oyama und einem weiteren Kollegen, Rob Gemmell von der Druckerabteilung bei Apple, brach in Richtung Europa auf, wo man Gespräche mit einigen der Granden des europäischen Designs, darunter Mario Bellini und Ettore Sottsass in Italien, Roger Tallon in Paris und Dieter Rams in Frankfurt, führte. Schließlich wurde die Auswahl auf die britische Firma BIB und Esslinger Design im deutschen Schwarzwaldstädtchen Altensteig eingeengt, und über einen Zeitraum von neun Monaten entwickelten beide eine Reihe von Prototypen. Den sogenannten „Schneewittchen"-Wettbewerb – so benannt wegen der sieben Abteilungen bei Apple – entschied Hartmut Esslinger klar für sich. Sofort ergriff er die Gelegenheit, nach Kalifornien zu übersiedeln, und begann, ausgestattet mit dem erstaunlich hohen Vorschuss von zwei Millionen Dollar, Präzisionsgerät aus Deutschland für die neuen Büros von frog design in Campbell am Südende des Silicon Valley zu verschiffen. „Alles schien möglich", erinnerte er sich, „wenn sich nur eine Verbindung von sinnvoller Innovation, leichter Benutzbarkeit und elegantem Design demonstrieren ließ."[17] ABB. 11

Die nächsten drei Jahre hindurch entwickelte frog design das „Snow White"-Konzept – kompakte, mathematisch proportionierte Einheiten, ungefärbte grauweiße ABS-Gehäuse, elegante Univers-Schriftzüge, Guss ohne Formschrägen, um die veralteten Schrägkanten des Apple II zu beseitigen und billigen Nachbauten keine Chance zu geben, ikonische Raster von Lüftungsschlitzen – zu einer Corporate-Design-Sprache weiter, die auf Vereinheitlichung der Apple-Produktfamilie von Computern, Druckern und Peripheriegeräten ausgerichtet war. Der interne Machtkampf war heftig, aber bis Steve Jobs aus dem Amt gedrängt wurde und die Beziehung zu Apple abzukühlen begann, hatte frog design sich bereits einen Ruf als eine der führenden Designfirmen des Silicon Valley aufgebaut.

Die Ankunft von Bill Moggridge, von Hartmut Esslinger und ihrer jeweiligen Gefolgschaft signalisierte den Beginn der Globalisierung des Designs im Silicon Valley; ein amerikanischer Designer erinnert sich, die ersten Anzeichen der Invasion aus Europa mit einem Gefühl der Verwirrung beobachtet zu haben: „Warum kommen diese Typen h i e r her? Was haben die in Silicon Valley gesehen und wir nicht?"[18] Der transatlantische kulturelle Austausch erwies sich als wirkmächtig, und so wuchsen im Laufe der 1980er-Jahre die unabhängigen Designfirmen rapide und entwickelten sich, um den Herausforderungen von neuen Computertechnologien, Software und Internet gewachsen zu sein. frog design legte seinen deutschen Akzent ab, verbreiterte seine Kundenbasis und brachte Esslingers Formel „Form follows emotion" bald schon im Silicon Valley und über dieses hinaus zur Anwendung. 1991 tat Moggridges ID Two sich wieder mit Mike Nuttalls Matrix Design zusammen (nachdem sie sich einige Jahre zuvor in aller Freundschaft getrennt hatten, um mit konkurrierenden Kunden zu arbeiten) und fusionierte in der Folge mit der amerikanischen Firma David Kelley Design zu IDEO, das heute mehr als 500 Angestellte hat und Büros in Europa, Asien und quer durch Nordamerika unterhält. Lunar Design, eine der ersten Partnerschaften im Silicon Valley,

© Bill Moggridge

MADE 4 YOU

↑ **ABB. 10**
Entwurfszeichnung für den Laptop-Computer
GRiD Compass, 1982
Design: Bill Moggridge / ID Two

FIG. 10
Drawing of the laptop computer GRiD Compass, 1982
Design: Bill Moggridge / ID Two

the time Steve Jobs was ousted and the relationship with Apple had begun to chill, frog design had established its reputation as one of the preeminent Silicon Valley consultancies.

The arrival of Bill Moggridge and Hartmut Esslinger, with their respective retinues, signaled the beginning of the globalization of Silicon Valley design; one American hopeful recalls observing the first signs of the European invasion with a sense of bewilderment: "Why are these guys coming h e r e ? What did they see in Silicon Valley that we did not?"[18] The transatlantic cultural interchange proved potent, and over the course of the 1980s the independent consultancies grew rapidly and evolved to meet the challenges of the new computer technologies, software, and the Web. frog design shed its German accent, expanded its client base, and was soon applying Esslinger's formula that "form follows emotion" both within Silicon Valley and beyond. In 1991, Moggridge's ID Two reunited with Mike Nuttall's Matrix Design (they had separated amicably a few years earlier to pursue work with competing clients) and merged with the American firm David Kelley Design to form IDEO, which now has in excess of 500 employees and maintains offices in Europe, Asia, and across

© frog design

← ABB. 9
**Steve Jobs (links), John Sculley und Steve Wozniak
stellen den neuen Apple //c vor, 1984.**

FIG. 9
Steve Jobs (left), John Sculley and Steve Wozniak
unveil the new Apple //c, 1984.

← ABB. 11
**Modelle für den „Snow
White"-Wettbewerb und
Folgeprojekte für Apple,
1982–1983
Design: Hartmut Esslinger /
frog design**

FIG. 11
Models for the "Snow White"
competition and follow-up
projects for Apple, 1982–1983
Design: Hartmut Esslinger /
frog design

die mit AutoCAD-Software arbeiteten und Ingenieurswesen und Design miteinander verbanden, wuchs sich nach zaghaften Anfängen in einer verlassenen Hubschrauberfabrik zu einer der angesehensten Firmen der Region aus. Sie alle gründeten Ableger im Ausland, beginnend in Japan, und bildeten einen Teil der Start-up-Kultur im Valley; Dutzende Firmen leiten sich von IDEO, frog design und Lunar her.

Interaktionsdesign. Wichtiger allerdings als bloße Zahlen ist die Verbreiterung des Berufsfelds selbst, die sich in der Bay Area zutrug. Nachdem Apple vorgeführt hatte, dass die äußere Hülle des Computers ein lohnens-wertes Objekt designerischer Aufmerksamkeit war, wandte sich die Community zunehmend den Problemen von Schnittstellen und Interaktivität zu. Und obwohl sie aufgerufen war, spezifische Probleme extrem dynamischer Technologiebranchen zu lösen, waren die Werkzeuge, Techniken und Methoden anfangs nicht so grundlegend anders als jene, die man anderswo erwartet hätte. „Die Tatsache, dass es sich um eine neue Produktkategorie handelte, machte nicht viel Unterschied", bemerkte ein Industriedesigner. „Genauso wie man an einem Fernseher, Radio oder Kühlschrank arbeitet, beginnt man mit einer Pappschachtel voller Teile."[19] Mit der Zeit wurde allerdings klar, dass das Design einer neuen Generation softwarebetriebener Produkte eine viel größer Bandbreite an Fertigkeiten erforderte als einfach die Fähigkeit, physische Formen zu manipulieren. Das belegte auch Bill Moggrides Erfahrung mit dem GRiD-Compass-Laptop-Computer: Sobald er mit einem funktionierenden Prototyp zu experimentieren begann, stellte er fest, dass „fast alle subjektiven Qualitäten, die mir am wichtigsten waren, in den Interaktionen mit der Software lagen, nicht mit dem physischen Design … Meine Frustrationen und Belohnungen lagen in diesem virtuellen Raum."[20] Mitte der 1980er-Jahre begannen er und sein Kollege Bill Verplank von einer neuen Disziplin, „Interaktionsdesign", zu sprechen; bis Mitte der Neunzigerjahre hatte Terry Winograd vom Stanford Computer Science Department einen Aufruf publiziert, „Design in die Software zu bringen".[21] Der Kreis weitete sich aus.

North America. Lunar Design, one of the first of the Silicon Valley partnerships to begin working with AutoCAD software and to combine engineering and design, grew from tentative beginnings in an abandoned helicopter factory to become one of the most respected firms in the region. All of them planted colonies overseas, starting in Japan, and they themselves were not immune to the startup culture of the Valley; the number of firms that can trace their origins to IDEO, frog design, and Lunar can be counted in the dozens.

Designing for Interaction. More important than mere numbers, however, is the broadening of the field of professional practice itself that has taken place in the Bay Area. Once Apple had demonstrated that the exterior shell of the computer was a legitimate object of the designer's attention, the community turned increasingly to problems of interface and interaction. Initially, although they had been called upon to solve problems specific to the extremely dynamic technology industries, their tools, techniques, and methodologies did not differ markedly from the practices one might have expected to find elsewhere: "The fact that it was a new product category did not make that much difference," observed one industrial designer. "Just like working on a TV, a radio, or a refrigerator, you start with a cardboard box full of components."[19] In time, however, it became clear that the design of the new generation of software-driven products required a much wider range of skills than simply the ability to manipulate physical forms. Bill Moggridge's experience with the GRiD Compass laptop computer is a case in point: Once he began to experiment with a working prototype, Moggridge made a discovery: "Almost all of the subjective qualities that mattered most to me were in the interactions with the software, not with the physical design My frustrations and rewards were in this virtual space."[20] In the mid-1980s, he and his colleague Bill Verplank began to speak of a new discipline, "Interaction Design"; by the mid-1990s, Terry Winograd of the Stanford Computer Science Department had issued a call for "bringing design to software".[21] The perimeter continued to expand.

The task, then, was to approach digital artifacts with the same degree of discipline that industrial designers had brought to kitchen appliances and office furniture a generation earlier. To do so, the consultancies needed once again to change their work practices and expand their field of expertise. Having added competency in mechanical and electrical engineering to their staffs, the consultancies began to draw upon the professional expertise of the social and behavioral sciences, initially in a research capacity, but increasingly as part of multidisciplinary project teams. To enable a person to operate a toaster or a power drill, the industrial designer must provide clear physical affordances. However, to design a photocopy machine with an interactive display panel and dozens, if not hundreds, of possible functions, it is necessary to situate operator and product within a contextual "environment of use", and this requires a rigorous ethnographic methodology as well as an understanding of cognitive, behavioral, and socio-cultural patterns.

The Cognitive and Instructional Science Group at PARC, founded by John Seely Brown in 1978, was probably the first Silicon Valley organization to involve social scientists in a sustained program of design research. In a famous documentary video, PARC anthropologist Lucy Suchman demonstrated that even Alan Newell, one of the founders of the field of artificial intelligence, was stumped by the challenge of producing a two-sided copy on one of Xerox's new, superbly engineered but horribly designed machines. Clearly, the problem was not one of technical competence but rather, as Suchman argued, "mundane difficulties of sense-making characteristic of any unfamiliar object".[22]

Kontext /
Context

51

Die Aufgabe bestand darin, an digitale Geräte mit derselben Disziplin heranzugehen, die DesignerInnen eine Generation zuvor für Küchengeräte und Büromöbel aufgewandt hatten. Dazu mussten die Firmen ein weiteres Mal ihre Arbeitspraktiken ändern und ihr Fachwissen erweitern. Nachdem ihre MitarbeiterInnen schon über Maschinenbau- und Elektroningenieurskompetenzen verfügten, begannen die Firmen nun, auf das Know-how der Sozial- und Verhaltenswissenschaften zurückzugreifen. Anfangs noch Forschungsinstanz, wurden sie zunehmend Teil multidisziplinärer Projektteams. Damit ein Nutzer einen Toaster oder eine Bohrmaschine bedienen kann, muss der Industriedesigner physische Bedienelemente mit klarem Angebot vorsehen. Um einen Kopierer mit interaktivem Display und Dutzenden, wenn nicht Hunderten möglicher Funktionen zu entwerfen, ist es notwendig, das Produkt und den, der es bedient, in eine kontextuelle „Nutzungsumgebung" zu stellen. Das aber erfordert eine strenge ethnografische Methodik sowie Verständnis für kognitive, soziokulturelle und sonstige Verhaltensmuster.

Die von John Seely Brown 1978 begründete Cognitive and Instructional Science Group am PARC war wahrscheinlich die erste Organisation im Silicon Valley, die SozialwissenschaftlerInnen an einem fortlaufenden Design-Forschungsprogramm beteiligte. In einem berühmten Dokumentarvideo zeigte die PARC-Anthropologin Lucy Suchman, wie sogar Alan Newell, einer der Begründer des Fachgebiets Künstliche Intelligenz, ratlos vor einer der technisch hervorragenden, aber benutzerunfreundlich gestalteten neuen Maschine von Xerox stand, um eine beidseitige Kopie zu machen. Das Problem bestand offensichtlich nicht in technischem Unvermögen, sondern, wie Suchman meinte, in den „alltäglichen Schwierigkeiten, sich zurechtzufinden, wie sie bei jedem nicht vertrauten Objekt typisch sind". [22]

Diese Übung in angewandter Ethnografie erregte die Aufmerksamkeit von Arnold Wasserman, dem für Corporate Industrial Design und Human Factors zuständigen Manager in der Xerox-Zentrale in Rochester, New York. Wasserman – alarmiert von der Tatsache, dass Xerox über einen Zeitraum von fünf Jahren schwindelerregende 50 Prozent seines Marktanteils an günstige Einzelfunktionskopierer aus Japan verloren hatte – verbrachte daraufhin mehr Zeit in Palo Alto. Wassermans Werdegang war stark von Designgeschichte und Designtheorie geprägt. Er glaubte, dass ein neuer konzeptueller Rahmen Erfolg bringen könnte, wo bisheriges Industriedesign versagt hatte. Die ForscherInnen am PARC wiederum waren hocherfreut, dass jemand „von der Firma" sie endlich ernst nahm. In Zusammenarbeit mit John Rheinfrank von der anerkannten Firma FitchRichardsonSmith in Ohio, mit PARC und in der Folge auch mit Moggridges ID Two leitete Wasserman, was zu einem legendären multidisziplinären Designforschungsprogramm werden sollte. Es war darauf ausgerichtet, nicht bloß einen neuen Kopierer zu gestalten, sondern die Zukunft von Dokumentverarbeitung und Informationsmanagement zu kartieren.

Während der ersten Programmphase führte das Team ausgedehnte ethnomethodologische Forschungen über das Nutzerverhalten durch – von SekretärInnen über BüroleiterInnen bis zu ServicetechnikerInnen, die häufig angefordert wurden, um etwas so Simples wie einen Papierstau oder eine leere Tonerpatrone zu „reparieren". Die zweite, 1986 beginnende Phase führte die vorgeschlagene Xerox-Innovationsstrategie von der Gegenwart in die Zukunft. Mit Blick auf die kommenden 15 Jahre schuf das Team Prototypen von Flachbildschirm-Workstations zur Dokumenterstellung, die es künftigen Nutzern gestatten würden, Seiten mit

This exercise in applied ethnography caught the attention of Arnold Wasserman, Manager of Corporate Industrial Design and Human Factors at Xerox headquarters in Rochester, New York, who began to spend increasing amounts of time in Palo Alto. Wasserman had watched with alarm as Xerox lost a staggering 50 percent of its market share over a five-year period to inexpensive, single-function copiers from Japan. With a background heavily informed by design history and design theory, Wasserman believed that a new conceptual framework might succeed where industrial design had failed. The research staff at PARC, for their part, were delighted that somebody from "corporate" was finally taking them seriously. Working together with John Rheinfrank of the respected Fitch Richardson Smith consultancy in Ohio, PARC, and subsequently Moggridge's ID Two, Wasserman oversaw what would become an iconic program of multidisciplinary design research intended not simply to design a new copy machine but to chart the future of document handling and information management.

During the first phase of the program, the team conducted extensive ethnomethodological research into user behaviors—from secretaries to office managers to service technicians, who were often summoned to "repair" something as simple as a paper jam or an empty toner cartridge. The second phase, which began in 1986, carried the proposed Xerox Innovation Strategy from the present into the future. With a focus on the next 15 years, the team created prototypes of a flat-screen document creation workstation that would allow future users to lay out pages with complete graphical fidelity; word processing and networking software that integrated text and audio and allowed for instant access to remote collaborators; and a cluster of information management tools, both physical and digital, intended to extend the reach of the office worker from the flat plane of the screen into three-dimensional, virtual space. Substantively, the effect of this long-term program was to shift the emphasis "from the machine side to the user's side of the user-machine interface". [23] More generally, it signaled a shift in the orientation of the design community from problem-solving in the present to envisioning the future, a reorientation the effects of which would reverberate throughout Silicon Valley and the world.

Although the shifting balance from classical product design to strategic consulting has been dramatic, it is in some respects a logical outgrowth of the digital revolution that has emanated from California's Silicon Valley. The computer, as described by the visionary Alan Kay, represents a whole new product type and calls for a new way of thinking: "It is the first metamedium, and as such it has degrees of freedom for representation and expression never before encountered and as yet barely investigated." [24] Not surprisingly, these early investigations produced some spectacular failures: Atari Labs was abruptly closed in the midst of pioneering experiments in multimedia; frox, Hartmut Esslinger's ambitious attempt to develop an integrated, customizable, and fully integrated digital entertainment system, drove frog design to the brink of bankruptcy; Interval Research Corporation, the multidisciplinary think tank created to explore the intersection of technology, popular culture, and the emergent culture of the Internet, was a brilliant $300 million write-off for its funder, Microsoft co-founder Paul Allen. But as it has become increasingly clear that technology is the first, not the last, stage in breakthrough innovation, the role of designers has only grown and they have moved closer and closer to the coveted "phase zero": from problem-solving at the end of a project to the conceptual phase in which problems are defined at the start.

totaler grafischer Genauigkeit zu gestalten, weiters Textverarbeitungs- und Netzwerksoftware, die Text und Ton integrierten und unmittelbaren Zugang für räumlich entfernte Mitarbeiter ermöglichten, außerdem ein Bündel von physischen wie digitalen Informationsmanagement-Werkzeugen, die dafür gedacht waren, die Reichweite des Büroarbeiters von der flachen Ebene des Bildschirms in den dreidimensionalen virtuellen Raum zu vergrößern. Im Wesentlichen bestand die Wirkung dieses langfristigen Programms darin, das Hauptgewicht von „der Maschinenseite zur Nutzerseite der Nutzer-Maschine-Schnittstelle"[23] zu verschieben. Allgemeiner gesagt signalisierte es eine Verschiebung der Orientierung der Design-Community vom Lösen gegenwärtiger Probleme zur visionären Gestaltung der Zukunft – eine Neuorientierung, deren Auswirkungen im Silicon Valley und in der ganzen Welt widerhallten.

Die Gewichtsverschiebung vom klassischen Produktdesign zur strategischen Beratung ist dramatisch, wenngleich in mancherlei Hinsicht logische Folge der digitalen Revolution, die vom kalifornischen Silicon Valley ihren Ausgang nahm. Der Computer, wie ihn der Visionär Alan Kay beschreibt, repräsentiert einen völlig neuen Produkttyp und verlangt nach einem neuen Denken: „Er ist das erste Metamedium und bietet als solches Grade von Freiheit für Darstellung und Ausdruck, wie sie nie zuvor angetroffen und bis dato kaum untersucht wurden."[24] Wenig überraschend brachten diese frühen Untersuchungen auch einige spektakuläre Fehlschläge: Atari Labs wurde während bahnbrechender Multimedia-Experimente abrupt geschlossen; frox, Hartmut Esslingers ehrgeiziger Versuch, ein individualisierbares, voll integriertes Unterhaltungssystem zu entwickeln, brachte frog design an den Rand des Konkurses; die Interval Research Corporation, ein multidisziplinärer Thinktank, der die Überschneidungen von Technologie, Populärkultur und aufkommender Internetkultur erforschen sollte, war ein fulminanter 300-Millionen-Dollar-Reinfall für seinen Finanzier, den Microsoft-Mitbegründer Paul Allen. Während sich zusehends herauskristallisierte, dass Technologie das erste, nicht das letzte Stadium des Innovationsdurchbruchs darstellt, ist die Rolle des Designs stetig gewachsen. DesignerInnen kamen der angepeilten „Phase null" zusehends näher: von der Problemlösung am Ende eines Projekts zur konzeptuellen Phase, in der die Probleme überhaupt erst definiert werden.

Das Missing Link. Aus einer kleinen Gruppe von Pionieren wurde ein vitales Element im komplexen Ökosystem der Innovation – die Designfirmen des Silicon Valley ergänzten das „Missing Link", das den Menschen Ideen auf greifbare, erlebbare Weise vermittelt. Auf diesem Weg entwickelten sie technische Kompetenzen und Geschäftsmodelle, die es ihnen gestatteten, mit Start-up-Firmen ebenso zu arbeiten wie mit Konzernen auf der „Fortune 500"-Liste, mit staatlichen Behörden und NGOs und querbeet in jeder nur vorstellbaren Branche: medizinische Instrumente, Kinderspielzeug, Konsumentenelektronik, Fluglinien und Hotels, um nur einige zu nennen. Im letzten Jahrzehnt haben sie sich ans Design, nicht bloß die Entwicklung von Software gewagt; Autofirmen sind en masse im Silicon Valley eingefallen, da sie mehr und mehr verstanden haben, dass Autos nicht die alleinige Domäne von Karosseriestylisten und „Automobildesignern" sind; Ökotech, Cleantech und Biotech sind die neuen Hoffnungsgebiete für DesignerInnen, die natürlich auch eine zentrale Rolle bei der Gestaltung des Web 2.0 gespielt haben. Entsprechend symbolträchtig war es, als Facebook unlängst von einem alten, von Hewlett-Packard angemieteten Industriegebäude auf einen sich weit erstreckenden Campus übersiedelte, der früher die Firmenzentrale von Sun Microsystems war. Eine „Produktdesignerin"

The Missing Link. From modest beginnings, the design firms of Silicon Valley have emerged as a vital component of a complex ecosystem of innovation—they form the "missing link" that connects ideas to people in tangible, experiential ways. Along the way, they developed technical competencies and business models that allowed them to work with venture startups as well as with Fortune 500 corporations, government agencies and NGOs, and across every imaginable industry: medical instruments, children's toys, consumer electronics, airlines and hotels, to name only a few. In the last decade they have ventured into the design, and not just the development, of software; the automotive industry has begun to arrive in Silicon Valley in force, as it is increasingly understood that cars are not the exclusive domain of auto body stylists and "transportation designers;" green-tech, clean-tech, and biotech are new frontiers for designers, and they have of course played a central role in defining the nature of Web 2.0. In a move fraught with symbolic significance, Facebook recently moved from an old industrial building leased from Hewlett-Packard to a sprawling campus that served as the former headquarters of Sun Microsystems. A "product designer" at Facebook may have little in common with her ancestor in companies that built oscilloscopes or servers, but she still speaks about a "shipping product"—even if that product is nothing more than a stream of electrons. FIG. 12

The latest—but undoubtedly not the last—development in Silicon Valley is the turn from classical product design to strategic consulting and social entrepreneurship. Whereas clients used to ask designers "How should things look?," increasingly they are asking them "What should we do?." In response, some practitioners have begun referring to themselves not as designers but as "design thinkers," to signal the idea that the skills of the designer can be applied far beyond what has traditionally been supposed: not just to the plenitude of consumer gadgets, but to the management of innovation itself; not the packaging of sugary snacks to children, but addressing the epidemic of pediatric obesity in the United States; not simply marketing products to the developing world, but participating in programs for the alleviation of extreme poverty in Colombia, understanding the cultural dynamics of mobile phone use in Afghanistan, or incentivizing entrepreneurs in Kenya to create businesses around the delivery of clean drinking water. And the corollary is obvious: It is not necessary to b e a designer in order to t h i n k like one.

Jane Fulton Suri was among the first of the human factors to be employed in a Silicon Valley design firm. Initially she was lucky to get two days out of a project budget, but as she proved her worth, she and her fellow social scientists became full-blown members of design teams everywhere: "We joined earlier and earlier in the process," she observed, "and were given bigger and bigger questions."[25]

This insight can, in fact, be applied to the whole sixty-year history of Silicon Valley design, which can be thought of as the campaign by designers to "join earlier and earlier in the process" and to be "given bigger and bigger questions." In the first phase, designers struggled to establish that they had a contribution to make; if they were given a hearing at all, it was often to perform menial tasks— "panel-and-hinge jobs," in the jargon of the trade—in an indistinct netherworld between engineering and marketing. As Silicon Valley technology companies continued their relentless march from the professional to the consumer market, from hardware to software, and from traditional economics to the Web, the importance of understanding and accommodating the needs of a larger user population became critical. Human-centered design remains central to the practice of Silicon Valley, but as new product categories have come into existence, physical ergonomics has been augmented by entirely

© facebook

MADE 4 YOU

bei Facebook mag mit ihren Vorläufern in Firmen, die Oszilloskope
oder Server bauten, wenig gemein haben, aber sie spricht immer
noch von „Produktauslieferung" – auch wenn dieses Produkt nicht
mehr ist als ein Elektronenstrom. ABB. 12

Die neueste, aber gewiss nicht die letzte Entwicklung im Silicon
Valley ist die Wende vom klassischen Produktdesign zum strategischen Consulting und zu sozialem Unternehmertum. Während
AuftraggeberInnen früher von DesignerInnen wissen wollten:
„Wie sollen Dinge aussehen?", fragen sie heute zunehmend: „Was
sollen wir tun?" Als Reaktion darauf haben einige Praktiker ange-
fangen, sich selbst nicht mehr als Designer, sondern als Design-
denker zu bezeichnen, um zu signalisieren, dass die Fähigkeiten
eines Designers weit über alles traditionellerweise Vermutete
hinaus Anwendung finden können: nicht nur bei der Unzahl von
Geräten für VerbraucherInnen, sondern im Innovationsmanage-
ment selbst; nicht beim Verpacken überzuckerter Snacks, sondern
bei der Bekämpfung der epidemischen Fettleibigkeit von Kindern
in den USA; nicht nur bei der simplen Vermarktung von Produkten
für die Dritte Welt, sondern bei der Teilnahme an Programmen zur
Bekämpfung extremer Armut in Kolumbien, dem Verständnis der
kulturellen Dynamik der Verwendung von Handys in Afghanistan
oder dabei, UnternehmerInnen in Kenia Anreize zur Gründung
von Geschäften rund um die Lieferung von frischem Trinkwasser
zu geben. Die Schlussfolgerung liegt auf der Hand: Man muss kein
Designer s e i n , um wie einer zu d e n k e n.

Jane Fulton Suri war eine der ersten ArbeitswissenschaftlerInnen,
die bei einer Designfirma im Silicon Valley angestellt wurden.
Anfangs musste sie froh sein, wenn von einem Projektbudget
zwei Tage für sie abfielen. Als sie jedoch unter Beweis stellte, wie
wertvoll ihre Arbeit war, wurden sie und ihre KollegInnen aus den
Sozialwissenschaften vollwertige Mitglieder von Designteams:
„Wir wurden immer früher im Prozess beigezogen", stellte sie fest,
„und mit immer größeren Fragen betraut."[25]

Genau genommen lässt sich die gesamte 60-jährige Entwicklung des Designs im Silicon Valley als Erfolgsgeschichte der
DesignerInnen lesen. Es ist ihnen gelungen, „immer früher im
Prozess beigezogen" und „mit immer größeren Fragen betraut" zu
werden. In der ersten Phase mussten sie beweisen, dass sie etwas
beizutragen hatten; wenn man ihnen überhaupt Gehör schenkte,
dann meist in Fragen von untergeordneter Bedeutung. Sie wurden
mit minderen Aufgaben – im Branchenjargon „Schalter-und-
Scharnier-Jobs" – in der Zwischenwelt von Maschinenbau und
Marketing betraut. Als die Technologiefirmen des Silicon Valley in
einem unaufhaltsamen Vormarsch aus dem reinen Markt für Fach-
leute auf den für Konsumenten zustrebten, ihre Handlungsfelder
von der Hard- auf die Software, von der traditionellen Wirtschaft
auf das Web ausweiteten, wurden Verständnis und Bedienung der
Bedürfnisse einer größeren Nutzerpopulation von elementarer
Bedeutung. Menschenzentriertes Design steht auch weiterhin im
Mittelpunkt der Praxis des Silicon Valley. Immer neue Produktka-
tegorien machten es notwendig, die Grundsätze der Ergonomie auf
immer mehr Bereiche anzuwenden und sich schließlich auch dem
Verständnis von Menschen (und Gruppen) im virtuellen Raum zu
widmen. Daraus entstanden neue Disziplinen: Interaction Design,
Experience Design, Usability Design und ein Dutzend weiterer,
die man sich vor zehn Jahren noch nicht einmal hätte vorstellen
können. Im Kern geht es beim Design im Silicon Valley also um
die Erfindung nicht nur neuer Produkte, sondern neuer Kombina-
tionen von Fähigkeiten, neuer Formen der Zusammenarbeit und
sogar neuer Designfelder, entsprechend den Bedürfnissen eines
fortwährend sich entwickelnden Ökosystems der Innovation.

← ABB. 12
"Like"-Button auf facebook, 2012

FIG. 12
"Like" button on facebook, 2012

new fields dedicated to the understanding of the behaviors of people
(and groups) in virtual space: Interaction Design, Experience Design,
Usability Design, and a dozen others that could scarcely be imagined
a decade ago. The essence of Silicon Valley design, then, is the
invention not just of new products, but of new skill combinations,
new collaborative practices, and even new fields of design to meet
the needs of a constantly evolving ecosystem of innovation.

[1] Interview with Allen Inhelder:
Portola Valley, CA (18 August 2011)

[2] "The IBM Design Program", from a
confidential presentation made by
C.C. Hollister (June, 1973), graciously provided by Ms. Stacy Castillo, IBM
Corporate Archives

[3] Budd Steinhilber, Looking Back,
vol. II, p. 76 (unpublished manu-
script, cited with the permission of
the author)

[4] Noyce is quoted in Michael S.
Malone, The Big Score: The Billion
Dollar Story of Silicon Valley, New
York 1985, pp. 68, 152

[5] Warren Robinett, "Adventure as a
Video Game", in: Katie Salen and
Eric Zimmerman, The Game Design
Reader, Cambridge, 2006, p. 692

[6] Darrell Staley, IDSA News 8
(October 1977), p. 2

[7] Memorandum (n.a.,n.d., but most
likely Marnie Jones in the immediate
aftermath of the conference); papers
of Marnie Jones

[8] This and the following quotes are
from Carroll Gantz, "My 50 Years
with the IDSA" (unpublished: 2011),
passim, cited with the permission of
the author

[9] Conversation with the author, Computer History Museum, Mountain
View, California (July 11, 2011)

[10] There were obvious and important
exceptions, many sponsored by
Olivetti: the Elea computer system
designed by Sottsass in 1959 and the
Divisumma calculator, designed by
Bellini in 1973. By the 1970s many
European consultancies were working on the edges of the computer
and telecommunications industries.

[11] "Bill Moggridge Associates
Industrial Designers," promotional
brochure (undated, but 1979): in the
author's collection

[12] Bill Moggridge, "The Lessons of
Silicon Valley," Design 371 (November 1979), pp. 50–52

[13] Bill Moggridge, quoted in "The
Compass Computer: The Design
Challenges Behind the Innovation" in:
Innovation: The Journal of the Indus-
trial Designers Society of America
(Winter 1983), pp. 4–8

[14] John Ellenby, quoted in "The
Compass Computer: The Design
Challenges Behind the Innovation" in:
Innovation: The Journal of the Indus-
trial Designers Society of America
(Winter 1983), pp. 4–8

[15] Steve Jobs, interview with the
author Cupertino: (November 11,
1998)

[16] "Product Development: A
Designer's Viewpoint," Apple Product
Design Guild, Jerry Manock, ed. (17
March, 1983); papers of Jerrold C.
Manock, graciously provided to the
author

[17] Hartmut Esslinger, Inside frog
design, unpublished ms. cited with
the permission of the author

[18] Peter Lowe, interview with the author:
Healdsburg, California (December 15,
2010)

[19] Mike Nuttall, referencing his work
with Bill Moggridge on the GRiD
Compass, in conversation with the
author: Portola Valley, California
(March 13, 2011)

[20] Bill Moggridge, submission for
the Prince Philip Designers Prize,
courtesy of Bill Moggridge

[21] Terry Winograd, ed., Bringing Design
to Software, New York 1996

[22] Lucy Suchman, "Work Practice
and Technology: A Retrospective,"
in: Margaret Szymanski and Jack
Whalen, eds., Making Work Visible:
Ethnographically Grounded Case
Studies of Work Practice, Cambridge
2011, p. 27

[23] John J. Rheinfrank, William R.
Hartman, and Arnold Wasserman,
"Design for Usability: Crafting a
Strategy for the Design of a New
Generation of Xerox Copiers," in:
Paul S. Adler and Terry A. Winograd,
eds., Usability: Turning Technology
into Tools, Oxford-New York 1992, p. 35

[24] Alan Kay, "Computer Software," in:
Scientific American, vol. 251, no. 3
(September 1984), p. 59

[25] Jane Fulton Suri: interview with
the author: Palo Alto (January 23,
2012)

55

[1] Interview mit Allen Inhelder, Portola Valley, Kalif. (18. August 2011)

[2] „The IBM Design Program", aus einer vertraulichen Präsentation von C.C. Hollister (Juni 1973), dankenswerterweise zur Verfügung gestellt von Stacy Castillo, IBM Corporate Archives

[3] Budd Steinhilber, Looking Back, Bd. II, S. 76 (unpubliziertes Mansukript, zitiert mit Genehmigung des Autors)

[4] Noyce, zit. in: Michael S. Malone, The Big Score: The Billion Dollar Story of Silicon Valley, New York 1985, S. 68, 152

[5] Warren Robinett, „Adventure as a Video Game", in: Katie Salen u. Eric Zimmerman, The Game Design Reader, Cambridge, Mass., 2006, S. 692

[6] Darrell Staley, IDSA News 8 (Oktober 1977), S. 2

[7] Memorandum (o.V., o.D., höchstwahrscheinlich aber Marnie Jones unmittelbar nach der Konferenz), Unterlagen von Marnie Jones

[8] Dieses und die folgenden Zitate aus Carroll Gantz, My 50 Years with the IDSA, unpubliziert, 2011, passim, zitiert mit Genehmigung des Autors

[9] Gespräch mit dem Autor, Computer History Museum, Mountain View, Kalif. (11. Juli 2011)

[10] Es gab offenkundig auch wichtige Ausnahmen; viele gingen auf das Konto von Olivetti, z. B. das von Sottsass 1959 designte Computersystem Elea und der von Bellini 1973 gestaltete Tischrechner Divisumma. Mitte der 1970er-Jahre arbeiteten viele europäische Designfirmen im Grenzbereich von Computer- und Telekommunikationsindustrie.

[11] Bill Moggridge Associates Industrial Designers, Promotionbroschüre (o. D., aber 1979), aus der Sammlung des Autors

[12] Bill Moggridge, „The Lessons of Silicon Valley", in: Design 371 (November 1979), S. 50–52

[13] Bill Moggridge, zit. in: „The Compass Computer: The Design Challenges Behind the Innovation", in: Innovation: The Journal of the Industrial Designers Society of America (Winter 1983), S. 4–8

[14] John Ellenby, zit. in: „The Compass Computer: The Design Challenges Behind the Innovation", in: Innovation: The Journal of the Industrial Designers Society of America (Winter 1983), S. 4–8

[15] Steve Jobs, Interview mit dem Autor, Cupertino, Kalif. (11. November 1998)

[16] Product Development: A Designer's Viewpoint, Apple Product Design Guild, hg. v. Jerry Manock (17. März 1983); Unterlagen von Jerrold C. Manock, dem Autor dankenswerterweise zur Verfügung gestellt

[17] Hartmut Esslinger, Inside frog design, unpubl. Manuskript, zitiert mit Genehmigung des Autors

[18] Peter Lowe, Interview mit dem Autor, Healdsburg, Kalif. (15 Dezember 2010)

[19] Mike Nuttall, in Bezug auf seine Arbeit am GRiD Compass mit Bill Moggridge, im Gespräch mit dem Autor, Portola Valley, Kalif. (13. März 2011)

[20] Bill Moggridge, Einreichung für den Prince Philip Designers Prize, mit freundlicher Genehmigung von Bill Moggridge

[21] Terry Winograd (Hg.), Bringing Design to Software, New York 1996

[22] Lucy Suchman, „Work Practice and Technology: A Retrospective", in: Margaret Szymanski u. Jack Whalen, (Hg.), Making Work Visible: Ethnographically Grounded Case Studies of Work Practice, Cambridge 2011, S. 27

[23] John J. Rheinfrank, William R. Hartman, Arnold Wasserman, „Design for Usability: Crafting a Strategy for the Design of a New Generation of Xerox Copiers", in: Paul S. Adler, Terry A. Winograd (Hg.), Usability: Turning Technology into Tools, Oxford–New York 1992, S. 35

[24] Alan Kay, „Computer Software", in: Scientific American, 251/3 (September 1984), S. 59

[25] Jane Fulton Suri, Interview mit dem Autor, Palo Alto, Kalif. (23. Januar 2012)

MADE 4 YOU

Mobilität / Mobility

Wie bewegen wir uns in Zukunft fort?

MADE 4 YOU

Weitgehende Mobilität ist – zumindest im wohlhabenden Norden – zu etwas Selbstverständlichem geworden: Wir fliegen in den Urlaub, fahren mit der U-Bahn zur Arbeit, mit dem Motorrad in die Natur und mit dem Auto sowieso überall hin. Dass wir uns dabei allzu lang auf fossile Brennstoffe und Verbrennungsmotoren verlassen haben, hat alarmierende Auswirkungen: globale Erwärmung mit verheerenden Folgen, Smog in den Metropolen, um nur die wichtigsten zu nennen. Geht es darum, zukünftige Mobilität zu gestalten, muss der Fokus auf der Nutzung erneuerbarer Energien sowie der Entwicklung emissionsarmer Antriebsformen liegen, Stichwort: E-Mobility. Auch den Individualverkehr gilt es zu überdenken, denn noch mehr Autos werden die Metropolen kaum bewältigen können. Kleinere, sparsame Fahrzeuge und ein effektiver Ausbau öffentlicher Verkehrsnetze sowie neue Mobilitätskonzepte sind die Lösungsansätze. Im Konkreten gehört auch der demografische Wandel berücksichtigt: Mobilität muss etwa den Bedürfnissen der wachsenden Zahl älterer Menschen entsprechen. Da wir uns letztlich aber auch daran gewöhnt haben, dass Mobilität Spaß macht, sind Gestaltungsziele wie Komfort, das Erleben von Schnelligkeit und das Repräsentieren von Lifestyle beim Design für die Konsumdemokratie nach wie vor essenziell.

How will we
move from place to place
in the future?

Extensive mobility has become self-evident—at least in the wealthy North: We fly to our vacation site, ride a subway to work and on a motorcycle out in the countryside, and drive our cars everywhere. The fact that we have relied on fossil fuels and internal combustion engines for much too long has brought alarming consequences: global warming with devastating results and city smog, to name but a few. The design of future mobility must focus on the use of renewable energy as well as the development of low-emission engines; keyword: e-mobility. Private transport should also be rethought, as metropolises are in no position to deal with greater automobile traffic. Smaller, more economical vehicles and a more effective development of public transportation networks, as well as new mobility concepts are approaches for solving the problem. Concretely, demographic change must also be taken into consideration: mobility has to comply with the needs of a growing number of senior citizens. Since we have, ultimately, become accustomed to the fact that mobility is fun, design goals such as comfort, a sense of speed, and expressing lifestyle via design remain essential within consumer democracy.

MADE 4 YOU

Katja Schechtner
AIT Austrian Institute of Technology & MIT Media Lab

Sichtbare/unsichtbare Mobilität

Mobility – Visible/ Invisible

Fahrräder, U-Bahnen, Autos, Motorräder, Fußgänger – immer dichtere Verkehrsströme fließen durch die Städte, die als attraktives Lebens- und Arbeitsumfeld zunehmend wachsen: 2050 sollen, so die Prognose, mehr als 75 Prozent der Menschen weltweit, in Österreich 82 Prozent der Bevölkerung in Städten leben. Auch deren Einzugsgebiete werden stärker genützt. In Kombination mit den Veränderungen im Lebensstil, der Flexibilisierung von Arbeitszeit, dem Trend zu Ein-Generationen-Haushalten und den Möglichkeiten aktiver Freizeitgestaltung führt dies dazu, dass in und um unsere Städte mehr Bewegung ist. Um den Bedürfnissen der Menschen nach Mobilität entgegenzukommen, aber auch die Städte lebenswerter zu gestalten – etwa durch Senkung der Kohlendioxidemissionen, Verminderung des Feinstaubs und Schaffung von Zonen lebendigen Austausches –, arbeiten ForscherInnen international an neuen Technologien sowohl auf Komponenten- als auch auf Verkehrssystemebene.

Fahrräder, U-Bahnen, Autos und Motorräder sind die sicht- und greifbaren Komponenten der Mobilität. Fahrzeuge so zu gestalten, dass sie leiser, sicherer und nachhaltiger werden, stellt einen Schwerpunkt der Technologieentwicklung dar. Im Mittelpunkt stehen hier einerseits alternative Antriebe von Hybridmotoren bis zu reinen elektrischen Motoren, um die Abhängigkeit von fossilen Brennstoffen zu reduzieren. Andererseits arbeitet man an der Entwicklung autonomer Fahrzeuge, die in ständiger Kommunikation mit ihrer Umwelt die Menschen von A nach B bringen sollen.

Forschung und Technologieentwicklung stehen vor großen Herausforderungen: Die komplexen Wechselwirkungen zwischen den Fahrzeugteilen und dem gesamten Fahrzeug gilt es zunächst in Simulationsmodellen möglichst realitätsnah abzubilden, um sie dann weiterentwickeln und optimieren zu können. So werden beispielsweise multiphysikalische Modelle, die alle relevanten elektrischen, magnetischen, mechanischen und thermischen Aspekte berücksichtigen, anfangs virtuell erstellt. Elektrische Maschinen samt Regelung, Leistungselektronik und elektrischen Energiespeichersystemen lassen sich auf Basis dieser Modelle effizient weiterentwickeln, analysieren und erproben.

Erforscht werden weiters sichere und effiziente Kommunikationstechnologien, die einen ständigen Austausch an Informationen zwischen Autos, Infrastruktur und Verkehrsteilnehmern erlauben und etwa mittels revolutionären Fahrzeugdesigns ermöglichen, dass Menschen und Fahrzeugen ganz „instinktiv" aufeinander reagieren. So entwickelt Nicholas Pennycooke am MIT Media Lab in Boston Methoden, wie ein fahrerloses Fahrzeug, das bei-

Bicycles, subways, cars, motorcycles, pedestrians: ever-denser flows of traffic can be observed in cities, which, thanks to their attractive living and working conditions, are constantly growing: in 2050, according to one projection, over 75 percent of the world's population—and 82 percent of Austrians—will live in cities. The metropolitan areas surrounding them are also being increasingly utilized. This development, in combination with lifestyle changes, more flexible working hours, the trend toward one-generation households, and the increasing number of opportunities to actively spend leisure time, is leading to more movement both in and around our cities. In order to meet people's mobility-related needs and to make cities more livable—for example by lowering CO_2 emissions, reducing particulate matter in the air, and creating zones of lively exchange—researchers worldwide are working on new technologies for both the overall traffic system and its individual components.

Bicycles, subways, cars, and motorcycles are the visible and tangible components of mobility. Designing new vehicles that are quieter, safer, and more sustainable is a major emphasis of technological development efforts. A central focus here is on alternative forms of motorization ranging from hybrid technologies to purely electric motors, all of which are intended to reduce dependence on fossil fuels. Another main element is the development of autonomous vehicles that constantly communicate with the surrounding environment while bringing their passengers from point A to point B.

Research and technological development are both faced with major challenges: complex interactions between vehicle parts and the entire vehicle must first be modeled as realistically as possible, as part of simulations within which they can be further developed and optimized. Preliminary multiphysics simulations, for instance, take into consideration all relevant electrical, magnetic, mechanical, and thermal aspects and are carried out in the virtual realm. Such models make it possible to efficiently develop, analyze, and test things like electrical machines with their control systems, power electronics, and systems for storing electrical energy.

Research is also being conducted on revolutionary vehicle designs featuring secure and efficient communication technologies that permit the constant exchange of information between cars, infrastructure, and traffic participants, thereby making it possible for human beings and vehicles to react to one another "instinctively". Nicholas Pennycooke of the MIT Media Lab in Boston, for example, is developing methods by which a driverless vehicle that might be

Mobilität /
Mobility

© Nicholas Pennycooke / MIT Media Lab

MADE 4 YOU

spielsweise unterwegs ist, um einen neuen Passagier abzu-
holen, anderen VerkehrsteilnehmerInnen mitteilen kann,
dass es sie wahrnimmt und auf sie reagieren wird. Die
Scheinwerfer des Fahrzeuges nehmen gleichsam als Augen
Blickkontakt mit FußgängerInnen auf und versichern ihnen
so, dass sie die Straße gefahrlos überqueren können.
Außerdem zeigt Nicholas Pennycookes Auto, derzeit noch
ein roher Forschungsprototyp im Labor, Verfügbarkeit und
Ladestatus anhand von Farbveränderungen der Räder und
Scheinwerfer an.

traveling in order to pick up a new passenger can tell other
traffic participants that it sees them and will react to them.
The vehicle's headlights act like eyes to establish visual
contact with pedestrians, reassuring them that they can
cross the street safely. Pennycooke's car, which is currently
still a laboratory research prototype, also indicates availability and battery status via color changes in its wheels and
headlights.

← ÆVITA – Emotional Car
Design: Nicholas Pennycook / MIT Media Lab

Unsichtbare Steuerungsalgorithmen lenken die Verkehrsströme von Fahrzeugen und FußgängerInnen. Um das
Bewegungsmuster einer Stadt zu verstehen, werden Daten
erfasst und analysiert, darauf aufbauend dann Progno-
sen und Simulationsmodelle entwickelt und damit die
Grundlage für Planung und Leitung der Verkehrsströme
geschaffen. Dieser Teil der Mobilitätsforschung gewinnt
zunehmend an Bedeutung. Intelligente Verkehrsmanage-
mentsysteme sichern die Mobilität jedes einzelnen Bürgers
und halten sie in Balance mit den Gesamtverkehrsströmen
einer Stadt. Die Herausforderung für die Forschung liegt
hier vor allem darin, alle Verkehrsmodi zu berücksichtigen
und ein ausgewogenes Zusammenspiel zu gewährleisten:
So arbeiten WissenschaftlerInnen an der Entwicklung von
Sensoren, die die Charakteristika diverser Verkehrsmodi
erfassen können, wie auch daran, die solcherart erfassten
Daten automatisiert und in Echtzeit zu analysieren. Flexible
Personenzählmatten sollen beispielsweise den Verkehrsbe-
treibern punktgenaue Informationen über das Fahrgastauf-
kommen an hochfrequentierten Durchgängen liefern, um
nicht zuletzt sicherere, automatische Zugangsregelungen
zu Bahnhöfen und U-Bahn-Stationen bei Großveranstal-
tungen zu schaffen. Andererseits werden die beliebtesten
Fahrrad- oder Laufstrecken erfasst, um neue Routen angepasst planen zu können.

Invisible traffic control algorithms are used to regulate
flows of both vehicles and pedestrians. To understand the
movement patterns in a given city, data is collected and anal-
yzed in order to develop projections and simulation models
that can provide a basis for the planning and regulation
of traffic flows. This particular area of mobility research is
gaining increasing importance. Intelligent traffic management systems ensure the mobility of each individual citizen
and keep this individual mobility in balance with a city's
overall flow of traffic. Here, the challenge for research lies,
above all, in considering every mode of transport and ensuring balanced interaction. To this end, scientists are working
on the development of sensors that can discern the characteristics of various ways of moving from place to place,
as well as on the automated and real-time analysis of data
thus collected. Flexible sensor mats for counting people, for
instance, provide transportation system operators with precise information on passenger figures at highly frequented
locations, not least in order to create automated access
points for train and subway stations that are safer in cases of
large events. Other studies look at the most popular cycling
and jogging routes in order to plan suitable new routes.

© Anita Graser / AIT

↑ Eine „Taxistunde" in Wien:
eine Sekunde, eine Minute, fünf Minuten, eine Stunde
nach dem Start der Aufzeichnung
Forschung: Anita Graser / Mobility Department, AIT

„One Hour of Fleet":
after one second, one minute, five minutes and
one hour have elapsed
Research: Anita Graser / Mobility Department, AIT

Mobilität /
Mobility

Mittels Erfassung der GPS-Positionsmeldungen von Taxi-
flotten lässt sich beispielsweise innerhalb weniger Stunden
die „Karte" des Straßensystems einer Stadt zeichnen; der
kontinuierliche Abgleich historischer mit aktuellen Daten
zeigt auf, wo es zu Auffälligkeiten im Verkehrsfluss, etwa
durch einen Unfall, kommt; und Prognosealgorithmen be-
rechnen, wo es dadurch Staus zu erwarten gibt und welche
Maßnahmen zu ergreifen sind, um den Verkehr möglichst
flüssig zu halten. Die Informationen werden dann über
Smartphone-Apps wie beispielsweise Qando, das über die
Ankunftszeiten der nächsten Straßenbahnen informiert,
oder Navigationssysteme weitergegeben.

Bis zum Jahr 2100 stehen wir vor der Herausforderung,
jährlich das Äquivalent von fünf Megacitys für jeweils zehn
Millionen BürgerInnen oder an jedem einzelnen Tag eine
Stadt etwa in der Größe von Linz zu bauen. Täglich werden
sich mehr als acht Milliarden Menschen durch diese Städte
bewegen. Die ForscherInnen, die daran arbeiten, neue Fahr-
zeugkonzepte und Verkehrsinformations- sowie Leitplatt-
formen zu einem funktionierenden Gesamtverkehrssystem
zusammenzuführen, haben ein Ziel: dass sich die Menschen
auch in Zukunft gerne und mit hoher Lebensqualität in
Städten bewegen können.

One of the things that can be accomplished by recording
taxi fleets' GPS signals is the creation of a "map" of a city's
system of streets—using just a few hours' worth of data.
Continuous comparison of historical data with current data,
on the other hand, can reveal anomalies in traffic flows such
as those that occur in connection with accidents; predictive
algorithms can then calculate where such anomalies could
produce traffic jams and what measures could be taken in
order to keep traffic flowing as smoothly as possible.
Pertinent information is then passed on via navigation
systems and/or smartphone applications such as Qando
(a Viennese mobile app that indicates when the next tram
will be arriving).

Between now and 2100, we will be facing the challenge of
building the equivalent of five megacities for ten million
citizens each and every year, or building a city approximately
the size of Linz each and every day. More than eight billion
people will move through these cities on a daily basis. The
researchers who are working on bringing together new
vehicle concepts with traffic information and regulation
platforms to form a functioning overall traffic system all
have one goal: that in the future, people will still be able to
move around cities in ways that are enjoyable and commen-
surate with a high quality of life.

E1 – eone

Konzept für ein elektrisches Motorrad	Concept for an electric motorcycle
Design **Lukas Dönz**	Design Lukas Dönz
Entstehungsjahr **2011**	Year of origin 2010

E1 ist ein von Audi mitbetreutes Studienkonzept für ein elektrisches Motorrad, das eine Reihe bestehender Probleme von Motorrädern und elektrischen Fahrzeugen auf dem Markt gleichermaßen anspricht: schwierige Bedienung, Unfallanfälligkeit, fehlende oder unzureichende Ladestationen, lange Ladezeiten und mangelhafte Ergonomie, um nur einige zu nennen.

Das einschalig konstruierte E-Motorrad verfügt über ein Hub- wie auch ein digitales Steuersystem, einen extra tief liegenden Fahrzeugschwerpunkt, Allradantrieb und zwei Airbags. Austauschbare Batteriesets erleichtern das Aufladen, um durchgehende Fahrbereitschaft zu gewährleisten. Durch seine verstellbare Geometrie unterstützt E1 verschiedene Sitzpositionen; mitgeführtes Kleingepäck findet in der Schalenkonstruktion des Motorrads Platz.

E1 is a study concept supervised by Audi for an electric motorcycle that addresses a series of existing problems of currently available motorcycles and electrical vehicles: difficult to operate, accident-prone, lacking or insufficient charging stations, long charging times, and low ergonomic efficiency, to name but a few.

The single-valve engineered E-motorcycle has stroke and digital control systems, an extra, low-lying vehicle center, all-wheel drive, and two airbags. Replaceable battery sets make it easier to charge, assuring that the vehicle is always ready to drive. Through its adjustable geometry, E1 supports various seating positions; small luggage items can be stored in the motorcycle's shell construction.

© Lukas Dönz

Labor / Laboratory

Mobilität / Mobility

ZEVS

Konzept für ein elektrisches Motorrad	Concept for an electric motorcycle
Design **Bernhard Ranner, Rudolf Stefanich, Anders August Kittelsen**	Design Bernhard Ranner, Rudolf Stefanich, Anders August Kittelsen
Entstehungsjahr **2010**	Year of origin 2010

Wie kann man Nachhaltigkeit und individueller Mobilität einen Coolness-Faktor verleihen? Ziel des ZEVS-Konzeptes ist es, ein Elektromotorrad zu entwerfen, das einerseits Technik inszeniert und andererseits ein echtes „Raw Biker"-Image transportiert. Mit so wenig Verkleidung wie möglich will man einen Kontrapunkt zur üblichen Praxis, Verbrennungsmotoren zu simulieren, setzen und im Gegenteil den Elektromotor durch Sichtbarkeit der Kupferwicklungen und Magneten betonen. Ein explizit eigenes Image anstelle eines Imitats wird, so die Idee, der neuen Technik zu Akzeptanz verhelfen.

Der Sound eines E-Motorrads soll nach Strom und nicht nach einer Harley-Davidson-Imitation klingen. Typisches Elektro-Brummen, Knistern und Funkensprühen kreieren eine neue Brandstrategie. Nicht die urbanen „Hipster" und Öko-Freaks sind also primäre Zielgruppe von ZEVS – für das E-Bike sollen jene begeistert werden, die immer schon Motorrad gefahren sind: harte Jungs mit Route-66-Romantik im Kopf.

How can a coolness factor be added to sustainability and individual mobility? Goal of the ZEVS concept is to design an electric motorcycle that, on the one hand, is technologically staged, and on the other, transports the image of a true "raw biker." By using as little housing as possible, the aim is to set a counterpoint to the usual practice of simulating internal combustion engines, and instead, emphasize the electric motor by exposing its copper coils and magnets. An explicitly individual image rather than imitation is meant to promote acceptance of the new technology.

An e-motorcycle should make electricity sounds rather than posing as Harley Davidson imposter. Typical electric buzzing, rustling, and sparks are part of a new brand strategy. Urban hipsters and eco freaks are not ZEVS's main target group, instead, the aim is to stir interest in the e-bike among those who have always driven motorcycles: tough guys who dream of riding route 66.

© Bernhard Ranner, Rudolf Stefanich, Anders August Kittelsen

Mobilität / Mobility

Labor / Laboratory

Automotive Cockpit

Studie einer Cockpit-Konsole für Autos	Study for a cockpit console for cars
Design **Marko Doblanovic**	Design Marko Doblanovic
Entstehungsjahr **2008**	Year of origin 2008

Das Automotive Cockpit verfolgt die Idee, Automobildesign im Blick auf Erfahrungswelt und Konsumgewohnheiten der 16- bis 21-Jährigen – insbesondere auf die Computerspiele- und Musikkultur – zu überdenken. Die Steuerung des Fahrzeugs basiert auf der Logik der <u>Konsole</u>: Hier wird kein Lenkrad gekurbelt, sondern „Shortcut"-erfahrene Fingerfertigkeit angesprochen. Mit reduzierten Gesten lassen sich alle Funktionen über das vom Flugzeugsteuer inspirierte „Quickwheel" bedienen.

Neuere Konventionen der Massenkonsumkultur wie Digital Customization und einfachste Bedienung sind hier integriert: Display-Styles können ausgewählt werden, ein Musikinterface mit Gestensteuerung ermöglicht Musikkonsum in aller Coolness, Fahrmodi werden je nach Fahrstil eingestellt, eine Skype-Funktion steht bereit. Um das Sicherheitsbewusstsein zu schärfen – schließlich befinden wir uns auf der Straße –, sanktioniert das Soundsystem Fahrfehler: Fährt man zu nah auf, ertönt volkstümliche Schlagermusik, beim Kreuzen einer roten Ampel gar David Hasselhoff ...

The Automotive Cockpit pursues the idea of rethinking automobile design in view of the experiences and consumer behavior of 16 to 21 year-olds—particularly in terms of their computer games and music. The vehicle's control panel is based on the logic of the <u>console</u>: the steering wheel is not cranked, but instead, "shortcut"-proficient dexterity is required. Using minimum gestures, all functions can be accessed via the airplane-control inspired "quickwheel."

The latest conventions of mass consumer culture are integrated here; such as, digital customization and simple operation. Display styles can be self-chosen, and a gesture-controlled music interface makes it possible to listen to music with maximum coolness. Driving modes are set according to driving style, a Skype function is ready to go. In order to activate an awareness of safety—after all, we are out on the road—the sound system imposes sanctions for driving errors. For tailgating, traditional umpah pah Schlager music plays, while running a red light sets off David Hasselhoff ...

Mobilität / Mobility

Labor / Laboratory

© Marko Doblanovic

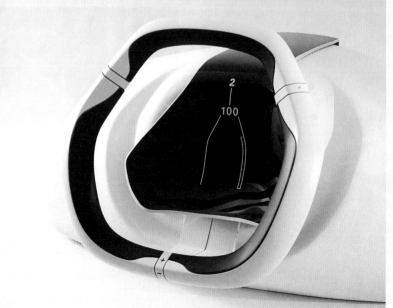

Leonardo

Konzept für ein solarbetriebenes Flugzeug	Concept for a solar-powered airplane
Design **Jupin Ghanbari**	Design Jupin Ghanbari
Entstehungsjahr **2011**	Year of origin 2011

Designprobleme einmal mit den Augen und mit der Semantik der Ingenieurskunst des 15. Jahrhunderts zu betrachten kann sinnvoll und lehrreich sein. Dem Flugobjekt Leonardo dienten die Ornithopter aus Leonardo da Vincis „Codex Atlanticus" als Inspirationsquelle – da Vincis detailgetreuen Schematisierungen der Vogelanatomie merkt man sein Ansinnen, dereinst Flugobjekte zu konstruieren, bereits an.

Technologisch übersetzt ins Heute könnte auf dieser Basis etwa ein solarbetriebenes Elektroflugzeug entstehen. Die Idee, große Tragflächen mit Solarelementen zu bestücken, klingt nahezu logisch; durch bionische Muskeln wird ein Flügelschlag simuliert – etwas, was Flugzeuge, anders als Vögel, letztlich nie zustande brachten. Formale Anleihen wurden konkret bei Storch und Albatros genommen – zwei Königen unter den Flugvögeln.

Taking a look at design problems with the eyes and semantics of fifteenth-century engineering makes sense and can also be very informative. The Leonardo flying object is inspired by the Ornithopter from Leonardo da Vinci's "Codex Atlanticus"—in da Vinci's true-to-detail schematization of a bird's anatomy, one already notices his intentions to design flying objects.

Translated to the present day in terms of technology, this could be used as a basis for producing solar-powered electrical flying objects. The idea of furnishing large carrying surfaces with solar elements sounds almost logical, bionic muscles simulate a wing stroke—something that airplanes, in contrast to birds, have ultimately never been capable of. Formally, concrete references are made to storks and albatrosses—two kings among flying birds.

© Jupin Ghanbari

Mobilität / Mobility

Labor / Laboratory

Human Drive (HD2.0)

Konzept eines Fahrzeugs für Zugpassagiere	Concept of a vehicle for train passengers
Design **Tamas Nyilanszky, Erol Kursani, Christoph Döttelmayer, Jilu Chen**	Design Tamas Nyilanszky, Erol Kursani, Christoph Döttelmayer, Jilu Chen
Redesign **Martin Strohmeier, Boris Stanimirovic, Christian Polonyi, Madeleine Plass**	Redesign Martin Strohmeier, Boris Stanimirovic, Christian Polonyi, Madeleine Plass
Entstehungsjahr **2010**	Year of origin 2010

© Christian Polonyi

Der Personenzug wird ein wichtiges Fortbewegungsmittel bleiben, insbesondere in Zeiten hoher Spritpreise und angesichts der Infragestellung des motorisierten Individualverkehrs als Norm. Der Human Drive will das Reisen mit dem Zug leichter und vor allem stressfreier machen. Das zierliche <u>Fahrzeug</u> transportiert Gepäck und Passagiere bis zum Zugabteil, übernimmt aber auch wichtige Informationsfunktionen während des Aufenthalts im Bahnhof.

Am Vehikel selbst, das an den Eingängen und Gleisen zur Verfügung steht, wird zunächst das Zugticket gescannt. Daraufhin weist ein integriertes Display mit GPS-Navigation den Weg zum Waggon und zeigt alle wichtigen Informationen zur bevorstehenden Zugfahrt sowie zur Infrastruktur vor Ort an. Das Gepäck wird auf einer höhenverstellbaren Ablage transportiert, die bei Bedarf auch beim Einladen und Ausladen dienlich ist. Fortbewegt wird der Human Drive über ein unterstütztes Stepper-System, also über die eigene Körperbewegung.

The passenger train remains a key means of transportation, especially in times of high gasoline prices, and particularly in the face of questioning individual motorized traffic as norm. Human Drive aims to facilitate train travel and, mainly, ease the stress factor. The petite <u>vehicle</u> transports luggage and passengers to the train compartment, and also takes on all of the important informational functions while at the train station.

First, the vehicle, which is available at the entries and tracks, scans the train ticket. Then an integrated display with GPS navigation shows the way to the train and all-important information for the upcoming train journey, as well as the on-site infrastructure. Luggage is transported on an adjustable rack, which if requested, can load and unload it as well. Human Drive is powered by a supported stepper system, that is, through the passenger's body movement.

Mobilität /
Mobility

Labor /
Laboratory

© Kristina Chudikova, Shirin Fani, Erol Kursani, Alexander Wurnig

Smart Traffic Signs

Konzept für eine computergestützte Windschutzscheibe	Concept for a computer-aided windshield
Design	Design
Kristina Chudikova, Shirin Fani, Erol Kursani, Alexander Wurnig	Kristina Chudikova, Shirin Fani, Erol Kursani, Alexander Wurnig
Entstehungsjahr	Year of origin
2008	2008
Staatspreis Verkehr (Sonderpreis)	State Prize Transport (Special Award)

Die computergestützte Erweiterung der Realitätswahrnehmung (engl. „Augmented Reality") durch Einblendung bzw. Überlagerung von Zusatzinformation über Bilder und Videos hat bereits ihren Weg in die Anwendung gefunden, so etwa bei Fußballübertragungen oder digitalen Reiseführern auf Mobilgeräten. Die Smart Traffic Signs machen sich diese Technik zunutze, um BenutzerInnen auf Gefahrenpotenziale im Verkehr hinzuweisen und sie für eine umsichtigere Fahrweise zu sensibilisieren.

Alle für den Verkehr relevanten Informationen finden die BenutzerInnen auf einer Augmented-Reality-<u>Windschutzscheibe</u> angezeigt. Straßenmarkierungen werden in verschiedenen Farben und Farbintensitäten überlagert und verstärkt, um die Unterscheidung zwischen riskanten und sicheren Situationen zu erleichtern, FußgängerInnen und Objekte auf der Straße oder am Straßenrand ebenso hervorgehoben. Da sich die Farbmarkierungen auch relativ zur Fahrgeschwindigkeit verändern, geben die Smart Traffic Signs gleichsam direktes Feedback … und funktionieren als Werkzeug, um das eigene Fahrverhalten zu kontrollieren.

The computer-aided extension of the perception of reality, or „augmented reality," through the masking or superimposition of additional information onto images and videos has already found its way into application, for example, in the broadcasting of soccer matches and in digital travel guides on mobile devices. Smart Traffic Signs make use of this technology to advise users of potential traffic dangers, and sensitize them to more judicious ways of driving.

Users find all traffic-relevant information displayed on an augmented reality <u>windshield</u>. Street markings are superimosed in various colors and color intensities and highlighted to make it easy to distinguish between riskier and safer situations. Pedestrians and objects on the street or by the side of the road are likewise highlighted. Since the color markings change in relation to driving speed, the Smart Traffic Signs offer direct feedback, as it were and function as tools for controlling one's own road behavior.

Mobilität / Mobility

Labor / Laboratory

Rondo

Konzept für ein SeniorInnen-Fahrzeug	Concept for a senior citizen vehicle
Design **Maria Gartner**	Design Maria Gartner
Entstehungsjahr **2011**	Year of origin 2011

Der Anteil von älteren Menschen an der Bevölkerung steigt. Immer mehr von ihnen sind alleinstehend, das heißt weitgehend auf sich gestellt. Senioren die nötige Mobilität im Alltag zu sichern wird daher zu einem dringlichen Erfordernis. Da, wo Menschen nicht mehr imstande sind, alleine Auto zu fahren oder den öffentlichen Verkehr zu nutzen, könnten sogenannte Senior Scooter eine bedeutende Rolle einnehmen. Rondo ist der Entwurf für ein wendiges Fahrzeug für den Außen- und Innenraum, für Supermarkt und Wohnung, das auf E-Mobility setzt.

Mit sicherem, ergonomischem Design, einfacher Bedienung und optimaler Wendigkeit dank spezieller Kugelräder lassen sich die täglichen Wege bei 15 km/h Maximalgeschwindigkeit mit Rondo rasch, aber ohne Unfallgefahr zurücklegen. Konzipiert nach Befragung von NutzerInnen bereits existierender Mobile und Recherchen in deren Lebensumfeld kommt das Design von Rondo den Bedürfnissen älterer Menschen unmittelbar entgegen.

The share of elderly in the population is growing steadily. An increasing number are on their own, which means that they are largely reliant on themselves. Assuring seniors the necessary mobility in their everyday lives has thus become an urgent demand. In situations where people are no longer capable of driving a car or using public transportation, the so-called Senior Scooter can take on an important role. Rondo is a design for an E-mobility-based, agile vehicle for inside and outside, for supermarkets and apartments.

With a safe, ergonomic design, simple operation, and optimal flexibility due to special ball casters, Rondo makes it possible to travel daily routes quickly, at a maximum speed of 15 km per hour, without danger of accidents. Designed based on a survey of users of already existing mobility devices and research into their living environments, Rondo's design directly fulfills the needs of the elderly.

Mobilität / Mobility

Labor / Laboratory

© Maria Gartner

Mercedes-Benz Future

Form- und Technologie-studien für Automobile	Form and technology studies for automobiles
Design **Mercedes-Benz Design**	Design Mercedes-Benz Design
Hersteller **Daimler AG**	Manufacturer Daimler AG
Entstehungsjahre **2010/2011**	Years of origin 2010/2011

Wie wird nachhaltiger Individualverkehr ohne Verbrennungsmotoren in der Oberklasse aussehen? Heißt es ein für alle Mal Abschied nehmen von Fahrkomfort und Ausstattung? Nicht unbedingt. Die mit „F" codierten Forschungsfahrzeuge und Ästhetik-Modelle von Mercedes-Benz führen eine Vision gediegener emissionsfreier Fortbewegung vor: Hochwertig, in einer fließenden, klaren und in die Zukunft weisenden Formensprache werden hier alle wichtigen Eigenschaften der Premiumklasse – zunächst experimentell – in die Zukunft des Elektroautos gedacht, bevor man später auch mit erschwinglicheren Modellen in Serie geht.

Die Studie für den F125 kombiniert effektive Technologien für Gepäckraum, Fahrwerk und Karosserie mit neuartigen Kontroll- und Display-Konzepten im Inneren. F800 bringt „grüne" Technologie mit stilvollem, sportlichem Design zusammen und schafft damit eine Harmonie zwischen automobiler Faszination und den Anforderungen, die aus dem globalen Technikwandel erwachsen – wahlweise als Brennstoffzellenfahrzeug oder mit Plug-in-Hybridantrieb.

What will upper-class, sustainable, individual transportation without internal-combustion engines look like? Will it mean a final adieu to driving comfort and furnishing? Not necessarily. The "F"-code research vehicles and aesthetic models from Mercedes-Benz present a vision of solid, non-emission propulsion. High quality in a fluid, clear, and future-oriented formal language, important premium-class characteristics, are included in the electric car of the future—at first, experimentally—before serial production of more affordable models begins later on.

The study for the F125 combines effective technologies for luggage space, undercarriage, and body with novel control and display concepts in the interior. F800 combines "green" technology with a stylish, sporty design thus developing a harmony between a fascination with cars and the demands evolving from global, technological change—alternatively as fuel-cell vehicle or with plug-in hybrid engine.

© Mercedes-Benz

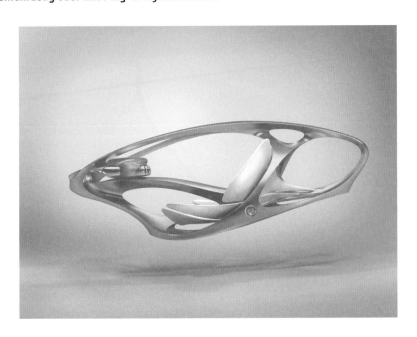

← **Studie Aesthetics No.2**

Study Aesthetics No.2

Mobilität / Mobility

Fabrik / Factory

→ **F 125 Innenraum**
F 125 interior

↓ **F 125 Türdetail**
F 125 door detail

← F 800

→ F 125 Showcar

© Mercedes-Benz

Mobilität /
Mobility

Fabrik /
Factory

Audi A1

Kleinwagen	Compact automobile
Design **Audi Design Team**	Design Audi Design Team
Hersteller **Audi AG**	Manufacturer Audi AG
Entstehungsjahr **2010**	Year of origin 2010

Das Bedürfnis nach Individualität und Wertigkeit steigt bei einer jungen, urbanen und lifestyle-orientierten Käufergruppe. Diesem Trend folgend schlägt Audi einen <u>Kleinwagen</u> vor, der aufgrund seiner hochwertigen Ausstattung unter den Kleinen, Kompakten ein Premium-Auto ist; viele Details sind der Oberklasse entnommen. Der Audi A1 zeigt in diesem Segment progressives Design und spricht mit seiner stadtverkehrsfreundlichen Größe insbesondere auch junge Erstkäufer an.

Der Wagen verströmt sportliches Appeal und verblüfft vor allem mit seinen Möglichkeiten zur Individualisierung: Ganze 800 Konfigurationen des Exterieurs sind möglich – zum Beispiel ein farbig abgesetztes Dach oder Variationsmöglichkeiten bei den Anbauteilen. Weiteren Spielraum bietet das von Flugzeug- und Leichtbau inspirierte Wageninnere: vom farbigen Luftausströmer im Turbinenlayout bis hin zum „media style Paket" mit Fokus auf Infotainment und Interieurdesign. Das in der Ausstellung gezeigte Claymodell zum extrovertiert sportlichen Showcar Audi A1 clubsport quattro ist Beispiel dafür, wie heute über Designoptionen Individualität ausgedrückt wird.

The need for individuality and valence is rising among a young, urban, lifestyle-oriented consumer group. Pursuing this trend, Audi offers a <u>compact car</u> whose high-quality furnishings make it a premium auto among the small compacts, whereby several details are taken from the luxury class. Audi A1 reveals progressive design in this segment, and with its urban-traffic- friendly size, particularly addresses also young, first-time buyers.

The car exudes sporty appeal, and particularly astonishing are the many ways it can be individualized. A total of 800 exterior configurations are possible—for example, a color-offset roof or variations in the extension parts. Additional leeway is offered in the interior, inspired by airplane and lightweight construction: from colorful, turbine-layout air dischargers through to a "media style package" with a focus on infotainment and interior design. The clay model shown in the exhibition of the extroverted, sporty, show car Audi A1 clubsport quattro is an example of how today, individuality is expressed through design options.

© Audi AG

← **Jürgen Löffler**
Audi Exterior Designer

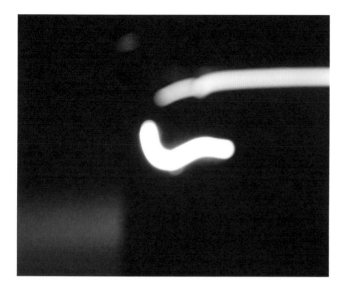

© Audi AG

Mobilität /
Mobility

Fabrik /
Factory

Ford SmartGauge & EcoGuide

**Energieeffizienz-Anzeige
für Hybridautos**

Energy efficiency for
hybrid automobiles

Design
**Smart Design /
IDEO**

Design
Smart Design /
IDEO

Hersteller
Ford Motor Company

Manufacturer
Ford Motor Company

Entstehungsjahr
2010

Year of origin
2010

Die ökologische und ökonomische Effektivität der neuen Hybridfahrzeuge mit Verbrennungs- und Elektromotor verlangt einen umsichtigen Fahrstil: Wann ist welche Energieressource die bessere? Wie fahre ich am schonendsten? Die Ford-SmartGauge-Anzeige liefert FahrerInnen erstmals unmittelbares Feedback zu ihrem Fahrverhalten. Zwei hochauflösende LCD-Farbdisplays geben Auskunft über Benzin- und Batteriestand, den durchschnittlichen und aktuellen Kraftstoffverbrauch, den Energieverbrauch des technischen Equipments (Sound-System, Klimaanlage), das Zusammenwirken von Elektro- und Verbrennungsmotor u. v. m.

Mit vier Anzeigestufen – Inform, Enlighten, Engage und Empower – schafft SmartGauge allmählich ein Bewusstsein für Energieeffizienz. In der Stufe Empower werden FahrerInnen schließlich über alle Funktionen informiert, die sich auf die Effizienz auswirken. Wie schonend man dann tatsächlich gefahren ist, lässt sich am Efficiency Leaves-Display ablesen: Je geringer der Verbrauch, desto mehr grünt es dort!

The ecological and economical effectiveness of the new hybrid vehicles with internal combustion and electric motors calls for a prudent driving style: when is an energy resource the better choice? How can I drive most energy-efficiently? The Ford SmartGauge display offers drivers the first direct feedback on their driving behavior. Two high-resolution full-color liquid crystal (LCD) screens provide information about fuel and battery power, average and instant miles per gallon, power consumption of accessories (sound system, air-conditioning), the combination of electric and internal combustion engines, and much more.

The SmartGauge's four information levels—Inform, Enlighten, Engage, and Empower—coach drivers to an awareness of energy efficiency. At the "Empower" level, drivers are ultimately informed about all functions that effect efficiency. How carefully one has actually driven can be read on the Efficiency Leaves display, which turns greener in response to improved efficiency!

→ Ford Fusion Hybrid

Mobilität /
Mobility

Fabrik /
Factory

© Ford Motor Company

© Ford Motor Company

Mobilität /
Mobility

Fabrik /
Factory

smart eMobility

Elektrokleinwagen-Studien und Elektrofahrrad	Electric compact car studies and electric bicycle
Design **Mercedes-Benz Design**	Design Mercedes-Benz Design
Hersteller **Daimler AG**	Manufacturer Daimler AG
Entstehungsjahre **2011/2012**	Years of origin 2011/2012

Der zweisitzige Kleinstwagen smart gilt seit seiner Einführung 1998 als minimalistischste Alternative im automobilen Stadtverkehr, seine „Elektrifizierung" war nur eine Frage der Zeit. Der smart forvision bietet neben dem neuen Energiekonzept auch den Energieverbrauch reduzierende Materialinnovationen von BASF: transparente, organische Solarzellen, durchsichtige, organische Leuchtdioden, Vollkunststoff-Felgen, besonders leichte Karosseriekomponenten sowie infrarotreflektierende Beschichtungen.

Dass ein Kleinstwagen mehr sein kann als pure Vernunft, zeigen die Concept Cars für das 21. Jahrhundert: Freizeitmobil und Lastesel ist der smart for-us; mit dem aggressiven Image der Mega-Pick-ups bewusst spielend, bietet er mehr Transportfläche, als seine Größe vermuten lässt. Mit dem smart parkour liegt das visionäre Konzept für einen Allrounder vor, der nicht nur auf der Straße fährt, sondern auch Hauswände hochklettern und sogar fliegen kann! Bereits auf dem Markt erhältliche Realität und Ergänzung im smart Mobilitätskonzept ist das smart ebike, das klar mit konventionellem Fahrraddesign bricht.

The two-seater, ultra-compact smart has offered a minimalist alternative for urban driving since its introduction in 1998. It was just a matter of time before it went "electric." In addition to the new energy concept, smartforvision also offers energy saving material innovations by BASF: transparent, organic solar cells, transparent, organic LEDs, all-plastic wheels, especially light bodywork components, and infrared-reflective coatings.

The concept cars for the twenty-first century prove that an ultra-compact car can be more than simply sensible: the smart for-us is leisure mobility and beast of burden; playing consciously with the aggressive image of aggressive pick-ups, it offers more cargo space than one would suspect from its size. smart parkour presents the visionary concept for an all-rounder that not only drives on the street, but can also climb building walls and even fly! A reality and supplement to the smart mobility concept, which is already available on the market, is the smart ebike, which breaks clearly from conventional bicycle design.

→ smart forvision

© Daimler AG

Mobilität / Mobility

Fabrik / Factory

Mobilität /
Mobility

Fabrik /
Factory

↓ **smart for-us**

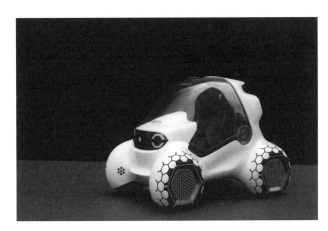

Daimler AG

→ **smart parkour**

Mobilität /
Mobility

Fabrik /
Factory

Renault Twizy

Elektrofahrzeug für den urbanen Raum	Electric vehicle for urban areas
Design **Renault Sport Technologies**	Design Renault Sport Technologies
Hersteller **Renault**	Manufacturer Renault
Entstehungsjahr **2012**	Year of origin 2012

© Denis Meunier

Seit Langem wird gefordert, Automobilität müsse stärker auf die brennenden Anliegen der modernen Gesellschaft – Umweltschutz, Entlastung des urbanen Raums durch weniger oder neuartigen Individualverkehr – eingehen. Der Renault Twizy, ein elektrischer Kleinstwagen für zwei Personen, ist eine klare Reaktion auf diese Forderung. Sein Wendekreis von 3,4 Metern macht ihn im Stadtverkehr extrem wendig; mit 2,34 Metern Länge und 1,24 Metern Breite findet er auch in kleinen Parklücken Platz und hat dennoch genügend Stauraum für den täglichen Einkauf. Trotz seiner geringen Größe strahlt das Fahrzeug Robustheit aus und genügt hohen Sicherheitsstandards.

Neuartige Proportionen – Twizy gleicht einer Zelle oder Wabe auf Rädern – sowie optionale Flügeltüren geben dem Gefährt eine kompakte, freundliche Erscheinung. Der 18 PS starke Elektromotor bringt gute Beschleunigungswerte und ermöglicht hohe Agilität im urbanen Raum. Neben einem Modell mit 80 km/h Höchstgeschwindigkeit ist auch eine auf 45 km/h gedrosselte Variante auf dem Markt, die mit Mopedausweis gelenkt werden kann.

For quite some time now, automobility has been challenged to deal more intensely with modern society's urgent issues—environmental protection, and easing the burdens on urban space through less or new forms of individualized transportation. Renault Twizy, an electric ultra-compact car for two is a clear reaction to this demand. Its turning circle of 3.4 meters (11.15 feet) makes it extremely agile in city traffic; with a length of 2.34 meters (7.68 feet) and width of 1.24 meters (4.07 feet), it also finds room in narrow parking gaps and still has enough stowage for the daily shopping. Despite its small size, the vehicle radiates ruggedness and satisfies high safety standards.

Novel proportions—Twizy looks like a cell or cubicle on wheels—as well as optional gull-wing doors give the vehicle a compact, friendly appearance. The 18 hp electric motor has good acceleration times and enables great agility in the urban space. In addition to a model with a top speed of 80 km/h (49 mph), there is also a version restricted to 45 km/h (28 mph) on the market, which can be driven with a moped license.

Mobilität /
Mobility

→ Studio Renault Sport Technologies

Fabrik /
Factory

Mobilität /
Mobility

Fabrik /
Factory

© Renault Marketing 3D-Commerce

Mobilität /
Mobility

Fabrik /
Factory

Opel Rak e

Studie für ein Leichtbau-Elektrofahrzeug	Study for a lightweight electric vehicle
Design **Adam Opel AG /** **Kiska**	Design Adam Opel AG / Kiska
Entstehungsjahr **2011**	Year of origin 2011

Der Opel Rak e ist eine visionäre Interpretation dessen, wie urbane Mobilität in Zukunft aussehen könnte. Im Leichtbau-Elektrofahrzeug laufen traditionelle Entwicklungsstränge von Automobil und Motorrad zusammen. Das Konzept erinnert an die Kabinenroller der Nachkriegsjahre; damals eine preisgünstige Alternative zum Auto, gilt das Kleinformat heute vor allem als clever, umwelt- und stadtverkehrsfreundlich. Bei rund einem Drittel des Gewichts eines modernen Kleinwagens und 1,3 Metern Breite bietet es zwei hintereinander sitzenden Personen Platz.

Die Pilotenkanzel des batteriebetriebenen Experimentalfahrzeugs dient gleichermaßen als Dach und Windschutzscheibe, sie gewährt eine 270-Grad-Sicht ohne tote Winkel. Türe und Lenkrad fahren automatisch nach oben, wenn sich die Kanzel öffnet. Bei minimalen Energiekosten – etwa einem Euro auf 100 Kilometer Fahrstrecke – leistet das Gefährt autobahntaugliche 120 km/h. Angedacht ist auch eine auf maximal 45 km/h reduzierte Variante, die schon von 16-Jährigen gefahren werden kann.

The Opel Rak e is a visionary interpretation of how urban mobility may look in the future. Traditional lines of development from cars and motorcycles flow together in a lightweight electric vehicle. The concept is reminiscent of the post-war cabin scooters; back then, an inexpensive alternative to a car, while today, the small format is considered clever, environmentally-friendly, and particularly suitable for urban traffic. At around one-third of the weight of a modern compact automobile, and 1.3 meters (4.26 feet) wide, it offers room for two people to sit one behind the other.

The cockpit of the battery-operated experimental vehicle serves as both roof and windshield; it offers a 270-degree view with no blind spots. Doors and steering wheel lift automatically when the cockpit opens. With minimal energy costs—roughly one euro (approx. $1.35) per 100 kilometers (ca. 62 miles)—the vehicle achieves a highway-suitable 120 km/h (75 mph). Also under consideration is a variant reduced to a maximum 45 km/h (28 mph), which can be driven already by 16 year-olds.

© KISKA

© KISKA

Mobilität /
Mobility

Fabrik /
Factory

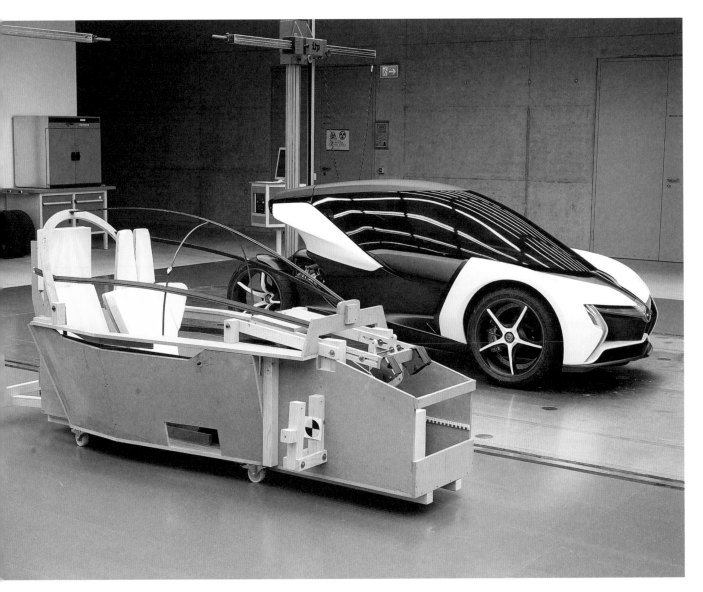

← Clay Model   ↑ Rak e Showcar & Seat Buck

Mobilität /
Mobility

Fabrik /
Factory

KTM Freeride E

Elektro-Crossbike

Electro-Crossbike

Design
Kiska

Design
Kiska

Hersteller
KTM-Sportmotorcycle AG

Manufacturer
KTM-Sportmotorcycle AG

Entstehungsjahr
2011

Year of origin
2011

Der Offroad-Sport gerät zunehmend unter Druck: Steigende Treibstoffpreise, umweltpolitische Bedenken und Lärmbelastung führen dazu, dass Rennstrecken aus dem Umfeld von Siedlungsgebieten verschwinden. Das KTM Freeride E will den <u>Offroad-Motorradsport</u> wieder attraktiver machen, ihn näher an die Städte heranrücken und eine junge Zielgruppe, die sich nicht zuletzt aus Mountainbikern rekrutiert, dafür begeistern. Und das nicht nur mittels alternativer Antriebsquelle, sondern auch durch eine neue Fahrerfahrung, die den Leerraum zwischen Fahrrad und Motorrad füllt.

Bei nur 100 Kilogramm Gewicht birgt die Karosserie einen starken Elektromotor, der die Leistung eines 125cc-Zweigang-Motorrades erzielt. Ein aggressives Design transportiert die Philosophie des Herstellers KTM – „Ready to Race" – und macht erkennbar, dass insbesondere ein junges Publikum angesprochen ist. Die Zukunft „grüner Mobilität", so die Botschaft, hängt vor allem vom Spaß an deren Anwendung ab.

The sport of offroad is subject to increasing pressures: rising fuel costs, ecological considerations, and noise pollution have led to the disappearance of race courses in the immediate environs of settlement areas. The KTM Freeride E aims to make <u>offroad motorcycling</u> attractive again, shifting it closer to cities, and inspiring a young target group who, no least, are recruited from mountain bikers. And this, not only through an alternative power source, but also a new driving experience that fills the gap between bicycle and motorcycle.

Weighing only 100 kilograms (ca. 220.5 lbs), the body conceals an electric motor that achieves the output of a 125cc-two-speed motorcycle. An aggressive design transports the "Ready to Race" philosophy of the manufacturer, KTM, and makes it clear that they are addressing, in particular, a young audience. The future of "green mobility," as the message goes, depends on how much fun it is to use.

Mobilität /
Mobility

Fabrik /
Factory

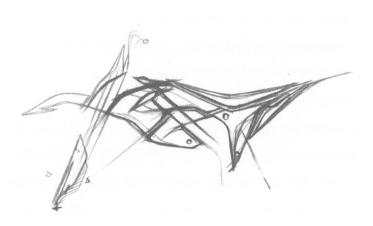

© KISKA

Mobilität /
Mobility

Fabrik /
Factory

Blink Pedestal Charger

Sockel-Ladestation für Elektrofahrzeuge	Platform charging station for electric vehicles
Design **frog design /** **ECOtality**	Design frog design / ECOtality
Hersteller **ECOtality**	Manufacturer ECOtality
Entstehungsjahr **2011**	Year of origin 2011

Schnellladestationen für Elektrofahrzeuge werden das Stadtbild zunehmend prägen, ist doch die Steckdose in der Garage den leistungsstärkeren Elektroautos nicht mehr gewachsen. Bereits heute werden daher in den USA Geräte wie der Blink Pedestal Charger auf öffentlichen Parkplätzen installiert. Lange Kabelreichweite, eine intelligent gestaltete Vorrichtung, die gleichzeitig das Kabel aufnimmt und Platz für den Ladekonnektor bietet, sowie ein webbasiertes Touchscreen-Interface zur Bedienung untermauern die Benutzerfreundlichkeit der Ladestation.

Der standardisierte Ladekonnektor ist robust, wasserfest und für 10.000 Ladezyklen entwickelt, diverse Funktionen – wie etwa ein automatischer Fahrstopp, sobald Strom fließt – erhöhen die Sicherheit. BenutzerInnen, die mehrere bargeldlose Zahlungsoptionen haben, können Ladevorgang und -status über den Screen mitverfolgen. Zusätzliche Anwendungen stehen für die LAN- und Wi-Fi-fähigen Ladestationen zur Verfügung: So lässt sich etwa per GPS am Handy stets die nächstgelegene Stromtankstelle orten.

Fast-charge stations for electric vehicles will increasingly shape the city image, as the electrical outlet in the garage is no match for the more powerful electric cars. Thus, already today, devices such as the Blink Pedestal Charger are being installed in public parking spots in the U.S. Long cables, an intelligently-designed mechanism, which simultaneously takes in the cable and offers room for the charge connector, as well as a web-based touchscreen interface for operation, substantiate the charging station's user-friendliness.

The standardized charge connector is robust, waterproof, and developed for 10,000 charging cycles, as well as offering various safety functions—such as an automatic brake as soon as electricity is flowing. Users have a variety of cash-free payment options and can follow the charging process and status onscreen. Additional applications are also available for the LAN and WiFi capable charging stations: for example, it is possible to search for the next available charging station per GPS on one's cell phone.

Mobilität /
Mobility

Fabrik /
Factory

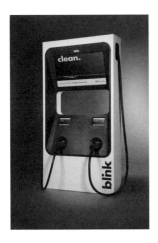

↑ DC Fast Charger

→ L2 Home Charger

© Mark Serr

Mobilität /
Mobility

Fabrik /
Factory

ULF

Niederstflur-Straßenbahn	Ultra low-floor street car
Design **Porsche Design**	Design Porsche Design
Hersteller **Siemens AG**	Manufacturer Siemens AG
Entstehungsjahr **1993**	Year of origin 1993

Je niedriger der Boden einer Straßenbahn, desto einfacher der Ein- und Ausstieg, und desto reibungsloser funktioniert auch der öffentliche Verkehr. Das gilt insbesondere für den Transport älterer Personen, Menschen mit Behinderung, aber auch Reisender mit Gepäck und Eltern mit Kinderwagen. Mit der ULF – Ultra Low Floor Tram – wurde eine Niederstflur-Bahn entwickelt, deren Boden nur 15 Zentimeter über Straßenniveau liegt.

Um die notwendige größere Beweglichkeit zu gewährleisten, besteht ULF aus kleineren Abschnitten als die alte Waggon-Tram. Auch für das Erscheinungsbild war ausschlaggebend, Beweglichkeit und Gelenkigkeit zu vermitteln, was man insbesondere durch Betonung der Gelenkportale erzielte. Die Durchgängigkeit des Innenbereichs erlaubt eine gute Verteilung der Fahrgäste, freie Türbereiche machen einen raschen Fahrgastwechsel möglich. Über funktionales Design gelang es hier, eine Stadt-Ikone zu schaffen, die der alten Tram-Garnitur in puncto Beliebtheit um nichts nachsteht – einen Porsche für jedermann.

The lower the floor of a streetcar, the easier it is to get in and out, thus allowing public transportation to function more smoothly. This applies especially to the transportation of the elderly, people with handicaps, travelers with luggage, and parents pushing strollers. With the ULF – Ultra Low Floor Tram –, a low-floor train has been developed whose floor is only fifteen centimeters above the street level.

In order to assure the necessitated greater flexibility, ULF is composed of smaller sections than the old wagon trams. Mediating flexibility and agility were also decisive in the appearance, which was achieved especially by emphasizing the articulated passages. The pervasiveness of the interior space enables a good distribution of passengers and free door areas make possible a rapid change of passengers. An urban icon, which is no less popular than the old tram, and in no way inferior, has been created here through functional design – a Porsche for everyone.

Mobilität /
Mobility

Fabrik /
Factory

© Porsche Design

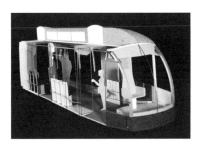

Mobilität /
Mobility

Fabrik /
Factory

Viaggio Comfort

Hochgeschwindigkeitszug	High-speed train
Design **Spirit Design**	Design Spirit Design
Hersteller **Siemens AG**	Manufacturer Siemens AG
Entstehungsjahr **2008**	Year of origin 2008

Die Strecke von Wien nach Salzburg legt er mit 250 km/h in nur 2,75 Stunden zurück. Höchstgeschwindigkeit kommuniziert bereits das Exterieur des Schnellreisezugs Viaggio Comfort, wenngleich seine schnittige Form nicht nur optische Gründe hat, sondern auch der Aerodynamik geschuldet ist. Je optimaler diese nämlich gestaltet, desto ressourcenschonender ist der Betrieb eines Zuges: Gegen Luftwiderstand anzufahren kostet neben Zeit vor allem Energie.

Das Innere beherbergt drei Reise- und Preisklassen: Die Executive Class bietet geräumige Einzel-Liegesitze in hochwertigen Materialien und eine warme, entspannende, indirekte Beleuchtung. Die Business Class verlagert mit größeren Tischen, vielen Steckdosen und bläulich-kühler Beleuchtung das Büro in den Zug. Die Economy Class schließlich schafft mit grünlicher Beleuchtung ein angenehmes Raumklima für das Reisen – trotz geringeren Platzes pro Fahrgast. Dank eines Rollstuhlbereichs mit Hublift, eines Spielabteils für Familien sowie Ruhezonen wird der Reisezug vielfältigen Bedürfnissen gerecht!

It can travel the route from Vienna to Salzburg in only 2 hours, 45 minutes at a speed of 250 km/h (155 mph). The exterior of the high-speed train Viaggio Comfort already communicates maximum speed. However, its streamlined form is not for optics alone, but, instead, also has aerodynamic purposes. The more optimal its design, the greater the train's efficiency: driving against air resistance costs not only time, but also energy.

The interior houses three travel and price classes: Executive Class offers spacious, single reclining seats made of high-quality materials and a warm, relaxing, indirect lighting. Business Class moves the office into the train, with large tables, sufficient electrical outlets, and bluish, cooler lighting. And finally, Economy Class, with its green-hued lighting creates a comfortable traveling environment—despite tighter seating for the passengers. Thanks to a wheelchair area with hub lift, a play compartment for families, as well as quiet areas, the passenger train is able to fulfill diverse needs!

Mobilität /
Mobility

Fabrik /
Factory

© Siemens / Spirit Design

Mobilität /
Mobility

Fabrik /
Factory

Westbahn

Reisezug	Passenger train
Design **Spirit Design**	Design Spirit Design
Hersteller **Stadler Altenrhein AG**	Manufacturer Stadler Altenrhein AG
Entstehungsjahr **2011**	Year of origin 2011

Die Vorzüge des Schienenverkehrs gegenüber der Automobilität wie Entspannung oder auch der Gewinn wertvoller Arbeitszeit machen diesen immer mehr für unterschiedliche Fahrgäste attraktiv. Vom Design des <u>Reisezugs</u> für den privaten Intercity-Betreiber Westbahn auf der Strecke Wien–Salzburg sollten daher alle gleichermaßen angesprochen werden: Reisende mit Laptop oder schwerem Gepäck, Eltern mit Kleinkind oder mobilitätseingeschränkte Personen.

Alle Sitzplätze sind mit großen Klapptischen, Stromanschluss und Zugang zum Internet ausgestattet. Die Sitze gewähren ausreichend Beinfreiheit und sind voll verstellbar, ohne dass sich die Rückenschale im Winkel verändert, das bedeutet: Niemand hat mehr die Lehne vor ihm sitzender Fahrgäste im Gesicht! Auch in puncto Service-Design sticht die Westbahn heraus: Mit einem Steward in jedem Waggon, vier Cafés pro Zug, durchgehender ergonomisch geformter Lederbestuhlung – Erste-Klasse-Komfort im ganzen Zug also – sowie verschiedenen Sitz-, Lounge- und Lehnzonen werden hier neue Maßstäbe für die Mobilität auf Schienen gesetzt.

The advantages of rail traffic as opposed to automobile traffic, such as relaxation, or even the gained valuable working time, even more make it attractive for various passengers. The design of the <u>passenger train</u> for the private Intercity operator Westbahn on the route Vienna–Salzburg, is meant to address everyone equally: travelers with laptops, or heavy luggage, parents with small children, as well as people with limited mobility.

All seats are equipped with large folding tables, electrical outlets, and internet access. The seats offer enough legroom and are entirely adjustable, without changing the angle of the backrest, which means: no one has the backrest of the passenger sitting in front of him or her in their face! The Westbahn also shines in terms of service design, setting new standards for mobility on the rails with a steward in every wagon, four cafés per train, ergonomically shaped leather seating throughout—that is, first-class comfort in the entire train—as well as various seating, lounging, and reclining zones.

Mobilität /
Mobility

Fabrik /
Factory

Mobilität /
Mobility

Fabrik /
Factory

Embraer Legacy 500 Intérieur

Interieur für ein Geschäftsreiseflugzeug	Interior of a business jet
Design BMW Group DesignworksUSA	Design BMW Group DesignworksUSA
Hersteller Embraer	Manufacturer Embraer
Entstehungsjahre 2007–2013	Years of origin 2007–2013

Die optimale Gestaltung des Innenraums eines <u>Business-Jets</u> der Premiumklasse für maximal acht Personen setzt neben der Berücksichtigung wichtiger Prinzipien des Flugzeugbaus und Kenntnissen des Ablaufs von Langstreckenflügen vor allem Gespür für das Schaffen von größtmöglichem Komfort auf kleinem Raum voraus. Das Innere des Embraer 500 wirkt mit seiner durchgehenden Stehhöhe, vergrößerten Fenstern und locker platziertem Mobiliar eher wie ein Wohnraum denn wie eine Flugzeugkabine. Die nahtlose Abfolge von Versorgungsbereich, Kabine, Gepäckraum und Nassraum vermittelt ein offenes Wohngefühl.

Die ergonomischen Sitze lassen sich für ein Nickerchen in Liegeposition bringen oder für eine echte Runde Schlaf mit dem gegenüberliegenden Sitz zum Bett umfunktionieren. Für den Fall, dass man sich umziehen möchte, bietet der Nassraum Zugang zum inneren Gepäckraum. Besonderes Augenmerk wurde auf eine sorgfältige Abstimmung von Farben, Materialien und Texturen der Oberflächen gelegt – letztlich geht es darum, ein Ambiente der Wertigkeit und Exklusivität zu schaffen, eine Luxussuite im Campingbus-Format.

The optimal design of the interior space of a premium-class <u>business jet</u> for maximum eight passengers, demands a sense for creating the greatest possible comfort in a small space in addition to consideration of the principles of airplane construction and knowledge of the process of long-distance flights. The interior of the Embraer 500, with standing height throughout, enlarged windows, and casually placed furniture, seems more like a living room than the cabin of an airplane. The seamless succession of service area, cabin, luggage space, and wet room mediate an open atmosphere.

The ergonomic seats can be reclined for a nap or combined with the seat opposite to make a bed for a good, solid sleep. Should one want to change clothes, the wet room offers access to the interior luggage space. Special attention is given to a careful coordination of the surfaces' colors, materials, and textures—ultimately, the idea is to create an ambiance of high quality and exclusivity, a luxury suite in camping bus format.

Mobilität / Mobility

Fabrik / Factory

© BMW Group DesignworksUSA

Mobilität /
Mobility

Fabrik /
Factory

MADE 4 YOU

Digitale Konvergenz / Digital Convergence

Wie smart sind Technologien von morgen?

Wie tiefgreifend das World Wide Web mit all seinen Möglichkeiten in gerade einmal 20 Jahren unser Leben, Arbeiten und Lernen, die Art, wie wir kommunizieren, konsumieren und sozial agieren, verändert hat, ist schier unfassbar. Mit der Digitalisierung und Vernetzung wurden viele analoge Speicher- und Trägermedien wie Papier und Buch, Tonträger oder analoges Fernsehen entweder obsolet oder bekamen zumindest harte digitale Konkurrenz. Die von uns benutzten Endgeräte – Smartphone, Tablet-Computer etc. – werden dabei immer unspezifischer: Sie öffnen jedes File und jeden Link, können alles wiedergeben und bedienen jede Kommunikationsschnittstelle. Der digitale Code, mit dem sie operieren, ist nun Universalsprache für alle Inhalte, ob Bild, Sound oder Text. Die „Digitale Konvergenz" – das Zusammenfließen all dieser Funktionen und Formate – zu gestalten ist zunehmend die Aufgabe von DesignerInnen, müssen Benutzeroberflächen und Schnittstellen (Interfaces) bei aller Multifunktionalität und Multimedialität doch sinnvoll und verständlich bleiben. Nicht zuletzt wird ein Gerät auf lange Sicht nur am Markt bestehen, wenn seine Benutzung nicht allein zielführend ist, sondern auch Freude macht.

How smart are the technologies of tomorrow?

The profound extent to which the World Wide Web, with all of its possibilities has changed our life, work, and learning, the way we communicate, consume, and interact socially in just barely twenty years is practically unbelievable. With digitization and networking, many analogue storage and carrying media, such as paper and books, sound storage media, and analogue television have become obsolete or have, at least, met with tough digital competition. The end products that we use—smartphone, tablet PC, etc.—are becoming increasingly less specific: they open every file and link, can play everything and use all communication interfaces. The digital code with which they operate is now a universal language for all content, whether image, sound, or text. Designers are increasingly confronted with the challenge of shaping this "digital convergence," this merging of diverse functions and formats. User surfaces and interfaces must remain sensible and understandable despite all of their multi-functionality and multimedia capabilities. And, last but not least, for long-term survival on the market, devices must remain both goal-oriented and a pleasure to use.

MADE 4 YOU

104

Caroline Seifert
Product Design Deutsche Telekom

Unzufriedenheit ist der Antrieb des Wandels

Dissatisfaction Is the Motor of Change

Von IPTV, Konvergenz und Avataren über 3-D, Holografie, soziale Netzwerke, Semantik und künstliche Intelligenz bis hin zu Nano-Robotik und Singularität: Das Internet macht zunehmend transparent, was auf der Welt geschieht. Wird wirklich alles schneller und komplexer? Die gute Antwort: Nein. Alles bleibt einfach, weil die Bedürfnisse des Menschen sich nicht ändern. Streamen wir heute Musik, war es gestern das gute Vinyl, und morgen erkennen intelligente Systeme unsere Identität und bieten uns Musik je nach Stimmung und Situation an.

Design gewinnt in einer Zeit von Kontextualität und technischen Möglichkeiten, Emotion zu gestalten, zunehmend an Bedeutung. Beginnend mit der industriellen Revolution und der einsetzenden Massenproduktion wurde eine wachsende Anzahl von Produkten gestaltet, die auf dem Prinzip „form follows function" beruhen. Dieses Prinzip rückte vom Bauhaus über die Ulmer Hochschule bis zu vielen anderen für Generationen ins Zentrum der Gestaltung. Nicht zuletzt Dieter Rams perfektionierte es als Stilmittel in seinen Entwicklungen für Braun. In den Jahren danach ging es um die Frage, welche Rolle das Design in der sozialen Interaktion spielt. Drei Streifen, Stern und transluzente Computergehäuse wurden zur Projektionsfläche für den Nutzer, Design wurde zum identitätsstiftenden Faktor.

Digitalisierung und Konvergenz. Die technologischen Entwicklungen der Digitalisierung, Miniaturisierung und Mobilisierung stellen das Design vor neue Herausforderungen – und vor neue Chancen. Mit der Verbreitung des mobilen Internets und der Cloud haben sich die Konvergenz-Theorien der 1990er-Jahre teilweise bewahrheitet. Von vielen Endgeräten aus lässt sich kommunizieren, sind Mediendistribution und das Internet erreichbar. Die Post-PC-Ära hat begonnen, analoge und digitale Welt verschmelzen.

Täglich stehen neue Anwendungen und Endgeräte zur Verfügung, die Kommunikation vervielfacht sich drastisch: In jeder Minute werden mehr als 120.000 Twitter-Nachrichten geschrieben, 130.000 Fotos auf Facebook geladen, fast 700.000 Suchanfragen bei Google eingegeben. Nahezu jeder Inhalt existiert bereits in digitaler Form: Musik, Text, Bilder, Spiele und Filme. Durch das Internet und vor allem seine zunehmende mobile Nutzung entstehen Tag für Tag unvorstellbare Mengen digitaler Inhalte, die an fast jedem Ort zu jeder Zeit verfügbar sind. Daten und Inhalte lassen sich auf der ganzen Welt mit einem Klick erreichen und in beliebiger Menge duplizieren.

From IPTV, convergence, and avatars to 3D, holography, social networks, semantics, and artificial intelligence through to nanorobotics and singularity: the Internet is making what's happening in the world increasingly transparent. Is everything really faster and more complex? The positive answer: no. Everything remains simple, because people's needs do not change. Today we stream music whereas yesterday we spun good old vinyl lps and tomorrow intelligent systems will recognize our identity and offer us music to match the mood and situation.

In an era of contextuality and technological possibilities to shape emotion, design becomes ever more important. Starting with the industrial revolution and the onset of mass production, a growing number of products were designed based on the principle "form follows function." This principle shifted to the center of design for generations, from Bauhaus to the Ulmer Hochschule, through to many others. Dieter Rams, no least, perfected it as a stylistic means in his developments for Braun. In the years that followed, at issue was design's role in social interaction. Three stripes, Stern, and translucent computer housing became projection surfaces for the user, design became a factor fostering identity.

Digitization and convergence. The technological developments of digitization, miniaturization, and mobilization present design with new challenges—and new opportunities. With the spread of mobile Internet and cloud technologies, the 1990s' convergence theories have, in part, proven true. A wealth of end devices allow for communication and also access to media distribution and the Internet. The post-PC era is here; analogue and digital worlds are merging.

New applications and end devices are available every day. Communication is multiplying in leaps and bounds: every minute, more than 120,000 Tweets are written, 130,000 photos are uploaded onto Facebook, and nearly 700,000 search terms entered on Google. Almost all content is already available in digital form: music, text, images, games, and films. Through the Internet and, mainly, its increasingly mobile use, every day, an incredible amount of digital content is created, which is accessible almost everywhere at any time. With just a click, data and contents can be accessed anywhere in the world; and can be duplicated as often as desired.

Digitale Konvergenz /
Digital Convergence

MADE 4 YOU

© Deutsche Telekom

Kontext-sensitive Gestaltung. Kontext-sensitives Design erlaubt es dem Menschen, Produkte situationsgebunden zu nutzen. Das Interface, die Funktionen und Anzeichen eines Produktes können sich fundamental ändern, sofern sie in einem anderen Kontext eingesetzt werden. Die Intelligenz der Netze lässt dies bereits heute zu. Zu Hause brauchen wir nicht unbedingt ein Navigationssystem auf unserem Smartphone, aber vielleicht die Steuerung der Fußbodenheizung. Ein anderes Beispiel ist die multimodale Nutzung von Diensten, die es erlauben, im Auto Texte per Sprache abzurufen, oder im Bus auf dem Tablet-PC per Touch.

Aus kontext-sensitiver Gestaltung resultiert das Gefühl von Einfachheit, Leichtigkeit und Intuition. Design reduziert die Komplexität, weil alles personalisiert je nach Situation zur Verfügung steht. Die beste Gestaltung ist die, die man nicht wahrnimmt. Das gilt für das Zusammenspiel aller Dimensionen, in denen der Kunde mit Produkten interagiert: von Form, Material und visuellem Eindruck über Interaktion und Töne bis zum Umgang mit Sprache bei der Bedienung.

Form and Function follow Context and Emotion. Damit ist eine Frage für das Design entscheidend: Was braucht der Mensch? Trotz der rasanten technologischen und gesellschaftlichen Entwicklungen bleiben unsere menschlichen Bedürfnisse konstant. Wir suchen Nähe. Wir wollen kommunizieren und suchen Unterhaltung. Wir hören, schauen, spielen, arbeiten, pflegen die Gesundheit. Wir lernen jeden Tag Neues. Dies bedeutet, dass dem Design in Zukunft die Aufgabe zukommt, Emotion in Kontext zu transformieren und die Funktion und die Form daraus abzuleiten.

DesignerInnen sind deshalb heute viel mehr als Gestalter: Sie sind DenkerInnen, StrategInnen, NetzwerkerInnen, InformationsarchitektInnen und vor allen Dingen eins: Menschen, die „unzufrieden sind". Denn genau das ist der Antrieb zum Wandel.

Context-sensitive design. Context-sensitive design lets people use products in situation-related ways. The interface, functions, and manifestation of a product can change fundamentally, provided they are used in a different context. The net's intelligence already allows for that today. At home, we do not necessarily need a navigation system on our smartphone, but perhaps a way to control the floor heating system. Another example is the multimode use of services, which allow calling up a text by voice in the car, and by touch on the tablet PC while riding on the bus.

A sense of simplicity, lightness, and intuitiveness results from context-sensitive design. Design reduces complexity because everything is available personalized, depending on the situation. The best design is the design we are not aware of. This applies to the interplay of all dimensions in which the customer interacts with products: from form, material, and visual impression through to interaction and sounds, to how language is dealt with in their operation.

Form and function follow context and emotion. In this, one question remains decisive for design: what do people need? Despite rapid technological and social developments, human needs remain the same. We seek closeness. We want to communicate and look for entertainment. We hear, look, play, work, and take care of our health. We learn new things every day. This means that in the future, the task of design will be to translate emotion into context, and will derive its function and form from this.

Designers today are therefore much more than "creators": they are thinkers, strategists, networkers, information architects, and one thing above all: people who "are dissatisfied." After all, that, precisely, is the motor of change.

← T- Gallery, das Zukunftsforum der
Deutschen Telekom, 2012

T- Gallery, the Deutsche Telekom
future forum, 2012

Digitale Konvergenz /
Digital Convergence

Gravity Phone

Konzept für ein Smartphone   Concept for a Smartphone

Design
**Maximilian Salesse, Lukas
Dönz, Joachim Kornauth,
Anton Weichselbraun**

Design
Maximilian Salesse, Lukas
Dönz, Joachim Kornauth,
Anton Weichselbraun

Entstehungsjahr
2010

Year of origin
2010

**Die Geschwindigkeit, mit der Mobiltelefone technisch
„veralten" und strategisch zu Elektroschrott erklärt werden,
scheint weiter zuzunehmen. Das erhöht zwar Umsatzzahlen,
ist aber kaum nachhaltig. Das Gravity Phone-Konzept sieht
vor, den Produktlebenszyklus des <u>Smartphones</u> markant
zu verlängern: mittels eines „Core Device", auf dem alle
Software inklusive Betriebssystem gespeichert ist. Es ist
austauschbar und lässt sich laufend auf neue Versionen hin
aktualisieren. Das robuste Endgerät kann länger benutzt
werden.**

**Neben allen Eigenschaften eines aktuellen Smartphones
verfügt das Gravity Phone auch über die Möglichkeit, beispielsweise ein Gaming-, ein medizinisches oder auch ein
Add-on für Blinde hinzuzufügen. Letzteres stattet das Gerät
etwa mit einem Annäherungssensor aus, der es Blinden ermöglicht, sich in ihrer Umgebung zu orientieren, und macht
die Benutzung eines volumetrischen, haptischen Displays
für die Übersetzung in Brailleschrift möglich.**

Cell phones seem to be technically "obsolete" and strategically declared "electronic scrap" ever more rapidly. This might
boost sales figures, but is hardly sustainable. The Gravity
Phone concept intends to extend the product lifecycle of the
<u>Smartphone</u> in a distinctive way: by means of a "core device"
capable of storing all software, including the operating system.
This device is exchangeable and new versions can be updated
constantly. The robust end product is thus usable for a longer
time.

Along with all of the qualities of current Smartphones, the
Gravity Phone also has possible add-ons for gaming, a medical
app, and one for the blind. The latter equips the device with
an approach sensor enabling blind people to orient in their
surroundings. It also allows for the use of a volumetric, tactile
display for translation into Braille.

© Maximilian Salesse, Lukas Dönz, Joachim Kornauth, Anton Weichselbraun

Digitale Konvergenz /
Digital Convergence

Labor /
Laboratory

Mariposa

Konzept eines digitalen robotischen Begleiters für Kinder	Concept for a digital, robotic companion for children
Design **Florian Wille**	Design Florian Wille
Entstehungsjahr **2011**	Year of origin 2011

Kinder wachsen heute digital vernetzt auf. Schon die Kleinsten machen erste Computererfahrungen; immer mehr Produkte – zum Lernen, Kommunizieren oder Spielen – werden speziell für sie konzipiert. Mariposa löst das Paradigma Tastatur und Bildschirm auf und ersetzt es durch ein robotisches Interface: In genauer Kenntnis des Umfeldes und der Bedürfnisse des Kindes bespielt der „mechatronische Freund" mit seinem Projektor die kindliche Umgebung mit Information.

Mariposa könnte zum Beispiel den Nachhauseweg weisen oder mit auf den Gehsteig projizierten Hinweisen auf Gefahren im Straßenverkehr aufmerksam machen, ebenso Lieblingsfilme, Computer- und Lernspiele auf jede Wand projizieren. Diese Roboter-Vision ist nur ein Beispiel für die Verschmelzung von realer und digitaler Sphäre. Sie regt zum Nachdenken darüber an, wie es sein wird, wenn ein immer größerer Teil der gebauten Umwelt zum digitalen Interface mutiert.

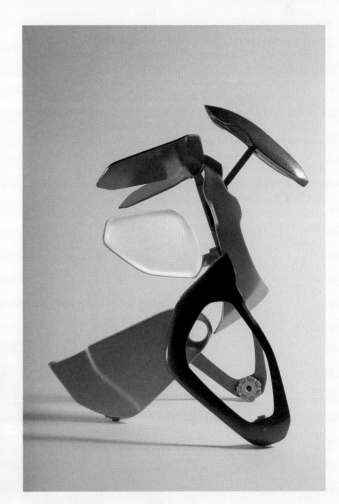

Today's children are growing up in a digitally networked world. Even very young children have already had their first experiences with computers as ever more products are specially conceived for them—for learning, communicating, and playing. Mariposa dissolves the paradigm of keyboard and screen, replacing it with a robotic interface. The „mechatronic friend," with precise knowledge of the child's environment and needs, projects a wealth of information into the child's surroundings.

Mariposa might, for instance, show the way home or point out traffic dangers by projecting information onto the sidewalk; it could project a child's favorite films, computer games, or educational games on any available wall. This vision of a robot is but one example of the merger of real and digital spheres. Mariposa inspires us to think about a future when an ever-increasing share of our built environment will have mutated to digital interface.

© Florian Wille

Digitale Konvergenz / Digital Convergence

Labor / Laboratory

EDGE Mediaspace

Konzept für einen integrierten Multimediaraum	Concept for an integrated multimedia space
Design	Design
Rudolph Stefanich, Erol Kursani, David Pfluegl	Rudolph Stefanich, Erol Kursani, David Pfluegl
Entstehungsjahr	Year of origin
2010	2010

Möglicherweise wird unser Medienkonsum in Zukunft so aussehen: Wir sitzen auf einer bequemen Couch, aber nicht vor dem Fernseher, sondern in einem <u>hypermedialen Raum</u>. Er erlaubt uns die integrierte Nutzung sämtlicher uns zur Verfügung stehender medialer digitaler Anwendungen über ein integriertes Interface – vom Livechat über das 3-D-Heimkino bis hin zur gesamten privaten und geschäftlichen Administration.

Der EDGE Mediaspace ist solch ein Raum. In ihm macht sich die Hardware unsichtbar – wodurch der Nutzer bzw. die Nutzerin den Eindruck bekommt, sich inmitten des medialen Geschehens zu befinden. Papierdünne Lautsprecher, integrierte Kameras, die gesamte Wand einnehmende 3-D-Flatscreens und eine Fernbedienung, mit der über einen einzigen Funktionsknopf ein benutzerfreundliches visuelles 3-D-Interface in Würfelgestalt bedient wird, zeichnen ihn aus. EDGE Mediaspace inszeniert totale mediale Verfügbarkeit im Wohnzimmerambiente.

Although in the future we might consume our media sitting on a comfortable couch, it will be in a <u>hyper media space</u>, rather than in front of a television. By means of a built-in interface, such a space allows for the integrated use of all available existing digital media applications—from live chat to 3-D home cinema, through to all private and business administration.

The EDGE Mediaspace is one such example. The hardware remains invisible within, giving users the impression of being in the midst of media happenings. The space features paper-thin loudspeakers, integrated cameras, a flat screen covering the entire wall, and a remote control with a single functional button for operating the cubic, user-friendly, visual, 3-D interface. EDGE Mediaspace stages total media availability in living-room ambiance.

 © Rudolph Stefanich

Caluma

Konzept für **Message-Schmuck**	Concept for message jewelry
Design **Jessica Covi**	Design Jessica Covi
Entstehungsjahr **2009**	Year of origin 2009

Einst war Körperschmuck Informationsträger expliziter kultureller Botschaften. Er gab Auskunft über die soziale und ökonomische Position des Trägers oder der Trägerin, stand in Verbindung mit Bräuchen und bediente sich einer vielfältigen Symbolik. Diese Funktionen gingen – außer beim Ehering – weitgehend verloren. Caluma, ein Konzept für <u>Statement-Schmuck</u>, geht der Frage nach, wie Schmuck heute wieder kulturelle Bedeutung erlangen könnte.

Kleine digitale Displays, beliebig programmierbar, ornamental angeordnet und direkt auf der Haut getragen – so könnte dieser neue Schmuck aussehen. Ultradünne Hightech-Silikonelemente, so die Idee von Caluma, werden zum individuellen temporären Medien-Tattoo. Gespeist mit digitalen Inhalten nach Wunsch können sie gleichermaßen zum Modeaccessoire werden wie provokantes Statement abgeben.

Body art once functioned as information carrier for explicit cultural messages. It provided information about the bearer's social and economic position, was connected with customs, and made use of complex symbolism. Other than in the case of the wedding ring, these functions have been largely lost. Caluma, a concept for <u>statement-jewelry</u>, pursues the question of how jewelry could again gain cultural significance.

A vision of what this jewelry might look like reveals little digital displays, which can be programmed as desired, ornamentally arranged, and worn directly against the skin. In the Caluma concept, ultra-thin, high-tech silicone elements turn into individual, temporary tattoos. Loaded with customized digital content, the tattoo becomes a fashion accessory, and likewise, delivers a provocative statement.

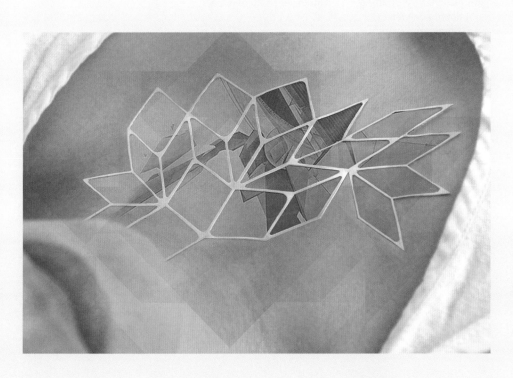

© Jessica Covi

Digitale Konvergenz /
Digital Convergence

Labor /
Laboratory

Dorian Gray Book

Softwarekonzept für Social Networking	Software concept for social networking
Design **Alexander Wurnig, Nadine von Seelen, Harald Tremmel**	Design Alexander Wurnig, Nadine von Seelen, Harald Tremmel
Entstehungsjahr **2010**	Year of origin 2010

© Alexander Wurnig

Obgleich die Industrie der Social Networks so monopolisiert ist wie kaum eine andere, denken DesignerInnen über neue Kommunikationstools nach. Das Dorian Gray Book – benannt nach Oscar Wildes Erzählung, in der das Bildnis des Protagonisten altert, er selbst aber jung bleibt – setzt einerseits bei vermehrter Kontrolle seitens der NutzerInnen an: Wer auf der Benutzeroberfläche was sehen kann, lässt sich genau konfigurieren. Dass jede neue Information ein Ablaufdatum erhält, löst das Problem der bis in alle Ewigkeit gespeicherten Daten.

Andererseits soll Networking möglichst unmittelbar sein: Kontakte werden nach Häufigkeit der Kommunikation gereiht, „Beziehungen" auf einer Timeline angezeigt, auf Wunsch erhält man eine Prognose über deren Zukunft und exakte topografische Daten, die das spontane Zusammentreffen mit Freunden vereinfachen. Zudem können die Lieblingsmarken der NutzerInnen mit diesen in Verbindung treten. Das Dorian Gray Book schreibt damit auch die Entwicklung hin zum individualisierten E-Commerce weiter.

Although social networking is one of the most highly monopolized industries, designers still dream up new communication tools. The Dorian Gray Book—named after Oscar Wilde's story in which the portrait of the protagonist ages while he remains ever young—begins, on the one hand, with increased control on the part of users: it is possible to precisely configure who can see what on the user interface. All new information has an expiration date, which solves the problem of eternally stored data.

On the other hand, networking should be as direct as possible: contacts are arranged according to the frequency of communication and „relationships" are displayed on a timeline. Upon request, future prognoses and precise topographical data can be provided, making it easier to get together with friends. In addition, users can be associated with their favorite brands. The Dorian Gray Book thus furthers development toward individualized, e-commerce.

Kindle eReader

E-Book-Lesegerät

Design
Amazon

Hersteller
Amazon

Entstehungsjahr
2011

E-reader

Design
Amazon

Manufacturer
Amazon

Year of origin
2011

Der Amazon Kindle ist ein <u>E-Book-Lesegerät</u>, mit dem elektronische Bücher und Zeitschriften heruntergeladen und am Display gelesen werden können. War der Kindle bei seiner Produkteinführung 2007 noch zwei Zentimeter stark und hatte eine physische Tastatur, wurden die Folgemodelle – mittlerweile verzeichnet man vier Generationen – immer leistungsfähiger, günstiger, dünner und leichter: Heute wiegt der Kindle eReader nur 170 Gramm und speichert bis zu 3.500 Bücher!

Die Entwicklung des Kindle veränderte die Lesegewohnheiten zahlloser Menschen und macht den Trend zur „Digital Convergence" augenfällig: Heute verkauft Amazon in den USA mehr E-Books als gedruckte Bücher. Auch seine Funktionen wurden ständig erweitert, so ist die vierte Generation – Kindle, Kindle Touch und Kindle Fire – mit virtueller Tastatur ausgestattet. Der bislang erst in den USA erhältliche Kindle Fire bietet ein Farbdisplay, das auch die Wiedergabe von Musik und Film sowie Surfen und Spielen ermöglicht. Er macht den Schritt hin zu den klassischen Tablet-PCs.

Amazon's Kindle is an <u>e-reader</u> with which electronic books and magazines can be downloaded and read. Although the first Kindle was still two centimeters thick and had a physical keyboard when introduced to the market in 2007, subsequent models—the product is meanwhile in the fourth generation—were increasingly more capable, less expensive, thinner, and lighter. Today, a Kindle weighs only 170 grams and can store up to 3,500 books!

Kindle's development changed the reading habits of countless people and made visible the trend to "digital convergence." Nowadays, Amazon sells more ebooks in the U.S. than printed books. Kindle's functions are also constantly expanding, for example, the fourth generation—Kindle, Kindle Touch, and Kindle Fire—are equipped with virtual keyboards. The new Kindle Fire, until now, available in the U.S. only, offers a color display that makes it possible to play music, films, and games as well as surf. It takes the step toward classical Tablet PCs.

© Amazon

Digitale Konvergenz /
Digital Convergence

Fabrik /
Factory

↑ <u>Kindle 1</u>

↑ <u>Kindle 2</u>

↑ <u>Kindle Keyboard</u>

© Amazon

Digitale Konvergenz /
Digital Convergence

Fabrik /
Factory

Echo Smart Pen

Computer-Schreibgerät	Pen computer
Design **Whipsaw**	Design Whipsaw
Hersteller **Livescribe**	Manufacturer Livescribe
Entstehungsjahr **2010**	Year of origin 2010

Echo Smart Pen ist ein <u>Computer-Schreibgerät</u>, der das Lernen erleichtern soll. Mit einer Kamera an seiner Spitze zeichnet er auf spezielles „Dot-Papier" geschriebene Notizen auf und erstellt gleichzeitig Audio-Aufnahmen, etwa von einer Vorlesung oder einem Meeting. Tippt man in den handschriftlichen Notizen eine Passage an, gelangt man zur entsprechenden Stelle des Audio-Files. Standardausgänge für Kopfhörer und Headset, umfangreicher Speicherplatz (4 beziehungsweise 8 GB), eine USB-Schnittstelle zum Computer und leichtes Wechseln der Mine zeichnen den Echo Smart Pen aus.

In der Verwendung mutet das Gerät wie ein ergonomisch gestalteter konventioneller Tintenschreiber an. Die Aufnahmefunktion wird über Antippen der entsprechenden Icons auf dem Dot-Papier gestartet und gestoppt. Mittels Software, die so wie das für den Echo Smart Pen nötige Spezialpapier zusätzlich zu erwerben ist, lassen sich die handschriftlichen Notizen auch in Computerschrift umwandeln oder in 26 Sprachen übersetzen.

Echo Smart Pen is a <u>pen computer</u> that intends to make learning easier. With a camera at its tip, it jots down written notes on special "dot paper" and at the same time creates audio recordings, for example of a lecture or meeting. By tapping on a passage in the handwritten notes, one arrives at the appropriate position in the audio file. The Echo Smart Pen's outstanding features include standard jacks for earphones or headset, extensive storage capacity (4 or 8 GB), a USB computer interface, and easily replaceable ink cartridges.

When in use, the device seems like an ergonomically designed conventional ink pen. The recording function is activated and deactivated by tapping on the appropriate icon on the dot paper. With software, which can be purchased separately, as can the necessary special paper, handwritten notes can be transferred into computer text, or translated into twenty-six languages.

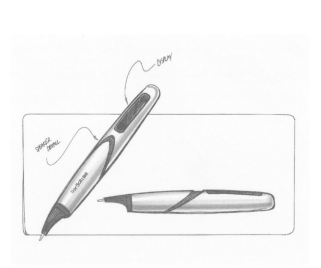

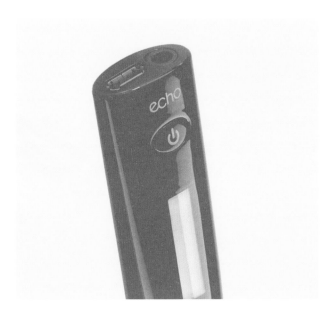

© Whipsaw, Inc.

Digitale Konvergenz /
Digital Convergence

Fabrik /
Factory

© Whipsaw, Inc.

Digitale Konvergenz /
Digital Convergence

Fabrik /
Factory

P'9981

Smartphone	Smartphone
Design **Porsche Design**	Design Porsche Design
Hersteller **Blackberry**	Manufacturer Blackberry
Entstehungsjahr **2011**	Year of origin 2011

Mit der Wahl des richtigen <u>Smart Device</u> lässt sich heute nicht nur kommunizieren, dass man ein echter „Digital Native" ist, sondern auch Prestige- und Qualitätsbewusstsein demonstrieren. Das Blackberry Smartphone P'9981 setzt alles daran, seinen BesitzerInnen über das Design Geschmacksintelligenz zu vermitteln: Schon die strategische Zusammenarbeit mit Porsche Design und die materielle Beschaffenheit des P'9981 – wie etwa sein geschmiedeter Edelstahlrahmen und die von Hand mit Leder ummantelte Rückseite des Gerätes – legen nahe, dass hier kein Wegwerfprodukt entwickelt wurde.

Das nur in limitierter Zahl erhältliche Gerät vereint Blackberry-Technologie und cutting-edge Smartphone-Funktionen. Digitale Konvergenz erscheint hier nicht als Angebot für die breite Masse, sondern als wertiges Nischenangebot. Das manifestiert sich nicht zuletzt in einer PIN-Edition – die Eingabe eines zusätzlichen ID-Codes macht den Kreis seiner BenutzerInnen noch exklusiver – sowie in einer ausschließlich auf diesem Produkt installierten Browser-Anwendung, mit der man etwa Testberichte über Restaurants sowie Kultur- und VIP-Events in der Nähe findet.

Nowadays, the selection of the proper <u>Smart Device</u> not only communicates one's status as a true "digital native," but also demonstrates an awareness of prestige and quality. The Blackberry Smartphone P'9981 puts all its cards on mediating its owners' taste intelligence through its design: already the strategic collaboration with Porsche Design and the material qualities of the P'9981—for example, its stainless steel forged frame and the back of the device, hand encased in leather—make it obvious that here, no disposable product has been developed.

The device, available in limited numbers only, unites Blackberry technology and cutting-edge, Smartphone functions. Digital convergence appears here as a niche offer, rather than something for the broad masses. This becomes clear, no least, in a PIN edition—the entry of an additional ID code makes its circle of users even more exclusive—as well as a browser application installed exclusively on this product, with which one can find test reviews of restaurants, and cultural and VIP events in the vicinity.

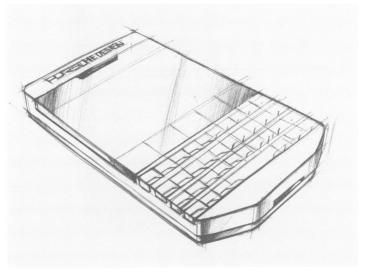

© Porsche Design

Digitale Konvergenz / Digital Convergence

Fabrik / Factory

© Porsche Design

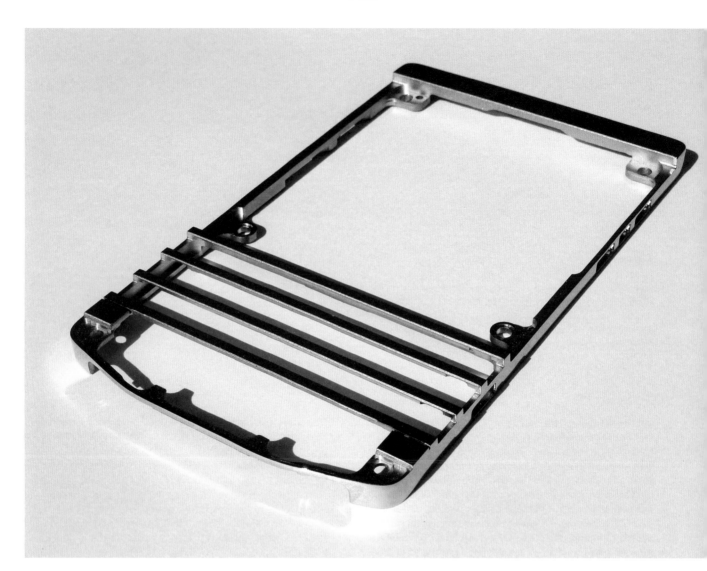

Digitale Konvergenz /
Digital Convergence

Fabrik /
Factory

RWE SmartHome

Integrierte Haussteuerung	Integrated home control
Design **designaffairs**	Design designaffairs
Hersteller **RWE**	Manufacturer RWE
Entstehungsjahr **2010**	Year of origin 2010

Seit der zweiten Hälfte des 20. Jahrhunderts ein Thema, ist die Automatisierung des Heims bis heute kaum über den sensorischen Heizungsthermostat hinausgegangen. RWE SmartHome bringt eine modular aufgebaute und flexibel nachrüstbare Produktfamilie von intelligenten Geräten wie Thermostaten, Bewegungsmeldern, Wandsendern oder Rollladensteuerungen in den Wohnraum. Ein hausinternes Funknetzwerk verbindet diverse Haushaltsgeräte mit einer zentralen Steuereinheit – der SmartHome-Zentrale – und ermöglicht auch die Heizungssteuerung.

Über PC, Internet oder Smartphone kann jedes Element der integrierten Haussteuerung auch aus der Ferne bedient werden. Vieles wird so möglich: etwa übers Wochenende zu verreisen und das Haus bewohnt aussehen zu lassen oder durch bedarfsgerechten Betrieb der Anlage Heizenergie zu sparen. SmartHome ist ein Schritt hin zur Idee des „Internets der Dinge" – es soll die Informationslücke zwischen realer und virtueller Welt allmählich schließen.

Since the second half of the twentieth century, automation of the home has been a topic, yet until today has gone hardly beyond the sensory thermostat. RWE SmartHome brings to the living room a modularly constructed and flexible, upgrade-capable product family of intelligent devices, such as thermostats, motion detectors, wall transmitters, and shutter controls. An internal radio network connects diverse household devices with a central control unit—the SmartHome control center—and also enables heating control.

All elements of the integrated home control can be operated remotely via PC, internet, or Smartphone. This enables quite a lot: for example, going away for the weekend and leaving the house looking as though it is occupied, or saving energy by heating only when necessary. SmartHome is a step toward the idea of an "internet of things"—with the intention of gradually closing the information gap between real and virtual worlds.

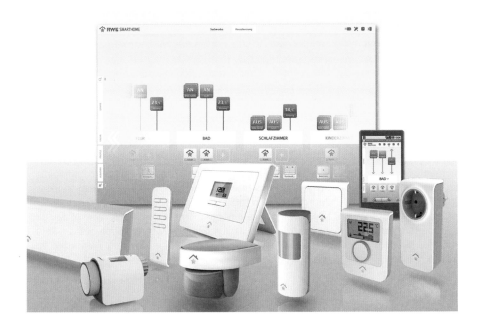

Digitale Konvergenz / Digital Convergence

© designaffairs

Fabrik / Factory

Deutsche Telekom Entertain

Digitale Konvergenz /
Digital Convergence

Digitales Fernsehen	Digital television
Design **Product Design** **Deutsche Telekom**	Design Product Design Deutsche Telekom
Hersteller **Deutsche Telekom AG**	Manufacturer Deutsche Telekom AG
Entstehungsjahre **2008–2012**	Years of origin 2008–2012

Fabrik /
Factory

Technologische Entwicklungen wie Digitalisierung und weltweite Vernetzung stellen das Design vor neue Herausforderungen – und vor neue Chancen. Der Wandel verlangt nach Lösungen, die Komplexität reduzieren, nach Produkten mit verständlichen Bedienkonzepten, benutzerfreundlichen Interfaces und klar strukturierten Informationsarchitekturen – Produkten, die den Menschen durch den Tag begleiten und das Leben und Arbeiten vereinfachen. Im Fokus steht dabei nicht das technisch Machbare, sondern der Mensch mit seinen Bedürfnissen.

Entertain, das digitale Fernsehen der Deutschen Telekom, ist ein gutes Beispiel: Was mit einer Set-Top-Box und Software begann, ist heute eine gesamtheitliche „User Experience", die interaktive Unterhaltung und Mediennutzung auf verschiedenen Endgeräten ermöglicht. Das Smartphone wird zum Programm-Manager, der Tablet-PC zur Fernsehzeitung, der Fernseher zur Videothek. Nutzer können etwa mit dem Smartphone von unterwegs die Aufnahme von Sendungen programmieren und diese jederzeit auf dem Fernseher zu Hause ansehen. Morgen wird der Mensch Dienste und Inhalte nutzen können, ohne dabei auf das Endgerät zu achten.

Technological developments, such as digitization and worldwide networking, present design with new challenges—and new chances. This change calls for solutions that reduce complexity, products with understandable operating concepts, user-friendly interfaces, and clearly structured information architecture. In short, products that accompany people throughout the day and simplify their life and work. Focus in this is not on what is technologically possible, but instead, people and their needs.

Entertain, the digital television of the Deutsche Telekom, is a good example: what began with a set-top box and software, has now become an all-encompassing "user experience" that enables interactive entertainment and media use on various end devices. The Smartphone becomes a program manager; the Tablet PC, a television magazine; the television, a video library. While on the go, consumers can use their Smartphones to program the recording of shows and watch them at any time on the television at home. In the future, people will be able to use services and content without paying any regard to the end device.

© Deutsche Telekom AG

Digitale Konvergenz /
Digital Convergence

Fabrik /
Factory

MADE 4 YOU

Leben und Freizeit / Life and Fun

Was bereitet uns weiterhin Freude?

Macht der Alltag Spaß, so liegt das nicht selten an seiner Produktkultur. Vor allem die Digitale Revolution hat uns mittlerweile Unterhaltungselektronik beschert, die so klein, handlich und mobil ist, dass wir unsere Lieblingsmusik überall hören oder Lieblingsmedien jederzeit konsumieren können – in der U-Bahn, beim Sport, auf der Reise. Manchmal werden die KonsumentInnen sogar in eine virtuelle Realität entführt, wie es bei vielen Computerspielen der Fall ist. Beim Design für die Freizeit ist zudem die Ergonomie unerlässlich: Der Sportschuh muss die Bewegung optimal unterstützen und gleichzeitig Halt geben, beim Tragen eines Ohrhörers sollte der Sound im Vordergrund stehen und das Gerät kaum mehr zu spüren sein. Ob ein Produkt über die richtige Haptik verfügt, sich also richtig angreift und anfühlt, entscheiden schon Babys intuitiv – ein weiterer wichtiger Aspekt bei der Gestaltung, der psychologisches Gespür der DesignerInnen voraussetzt und den Erfolg eines Produktes mitbestimmt. Da wir mit den Dingen des Alltags – über ihre Farbe, Form, Funktion, ihren Preis, die Marke etc. – auch Identität und Lebensstil konstruieren, erhält Design eine machtvolle Funktion im individuellen und kollektiven Streben nach Glück und Zufriedenheit.

What will we continue to enjoy?

When everyday life provides enjoyment, it often has to do with its products. The digital revolution has mainly led to entertainment electronics that are meanwhile so small, handy, and mobile, that we can listen to our favorite music everywhere, and consume our favorite media at any time—in the subway, while playing sports, or traveling. Consumers are sometimes even enticed into a virtual world, such as in many computer games. In addition, ergonometrics are essential in leisure design: sports shoes must allow for optimal movement and at the same time offer support; when wearing earphones, sound should be at the forefront and the device should be as inconspicuous as possible. Babies already intuitively decide whether a product has the right haptics, that is, if it has the right hold and feel—a further important aspect of design, which presumes a designer's psychological intuition, and plays a role in a product's success. Since we also construct our identity and lifestyle through everyday things—their color, form, function, price, and brand name, etc.—design has a powerful function in individual and collective aspirations of happiness and satisfaction.

MADE 4 YOU

Sonia Laszlo
Institut für Europäische Glücksforschung (IFEG), Wien
Institute for European Research of Happiness, Vienna

Das unwandelbare Glück

Immutable Happiness

Glück war, ist und wird auch in Zukunft eine individuelle Resultierende sein. Und es ist multifaktoriell, auf mehreren Umständen und Einflüssen basierend. Stimmt man diese erfolgreich ab, kann man sich selbst und andere im dynamischen Optimum halten. Sich so oft wie möglich ins Optimum zu bringen – das ist die wahre Lebenskunst.

Empfinden wir Menschen dieses Gefühl, das gemeinhin als Glück bekannt ist, möchten wir, dass es andauert. Da dies bei einem Prozess, der per definitionem abläuft und dann von Neuem gestartet werden muss, nicht möglich ist, streben wir danach, dass es wiederkommt. Glück eignet sich daher ideal als Richtungsweiser der Schöpfung: Damit das, was sich gut anfühlt, wiederkehrt, handeln wir entsprechend; schon die Erwartung kann Glücksgefühle hervorrufen. Fühlte sich beispielsweise Geschlechtsverkehr nicht gut an, die Menschheit wäre längst ausgestorben. Wären wir nicht neugierig und würde nicht Neues mit Glücksgefühlen belohnt, die Evolution wäre längst steckengeblieben. Glück ist seit Anbeginn die Antriebsfeder von Lebewesen, speziell und in dieser Stimulierungsvielfalt aber die unserer Spezies, des Homo Sapiens.

Durch den jüngsten Teil unseres Gehirns, den vorderen Schläfenlappen, machen uns Menschen gewisse Dinge – abgesehen von den Urimpulsen, die in älteren Teilen des Gehirns verankert sind – glücklich. Dies ist auch jener Teil, in dem, so es ihn überhaupt gibt, der freie Wille liegt. Dort sollten wir ansetzen, wenn wir etwas über die Zukunft wissen möchten. Denn solange sich der Mensch nicht zu einer anderen Spezies weiterentwickelt, die vielleicht keine Glücksgefühle braucht, werden sich diese nicht ändern. Was wir als Glück empfinden, ist ein biochemischer Prozess, der von unserer Sichtweise der Welt beeinflusst wird und den wir wiederum interpretieren.

Diese Interpretation ist vom Zeitgeist geprägt. Wir sind auch glücklich, wenn wir aus der Sicht des gerade gängigen Gesellschaftsmodels Erfolg haben, nach der gerade herrschenden Moral leben oder gegen sie revoltieren. Glück ist durch reflexive Gesamtlebensbetrachtungen in einen Kontext gesetzt. Daher hängt das, was uns auch in Zukunft glücklich macht, davon ab, wohin sich unsere Gesellschaft entwickelt. Was sich ändert, ist die Gesellschaft und wie diese Dinge bewertet.

Gutes Design versteht die Prinzipien, nach denen der Mensch seit jeher glücklich gemacht werden kann. Und kombiniert sie mit dem, was der Zeitgeist als Trend vorgibt. So wie heute waren wir auch vor weniger als einem Jahrzehnt unglücklich, wenn uns jemand das Herz gebrochen hat – nicht aber darüber, keines der begehrten Mobilfunkprodukte von Apple zu besitzen oder sich nicht via Berührungsschirm mit Menschen zu unterhalten, mit denen man in sozialen Medien befreundet ist. Es gab keine „schlauen"

Happiness has always been and will always be something that is arrived at on an individual basis. And this basis consists of multiple factors, of numerous circumstances and influences. Success in balancing these requires the ability to keep oneself and others within a dynamic optimum. Attaining that optimum state as often as possible—this is the true art of living.

Whenever we human beings feel the emotion commonly referred to as happiness, we want it to last. And since this is impossible for a process that by definition ends and must then be restarted, we strive to make it recur. Happiness is therefore ideally suited for giving direction to creativity: in order to make something that feels good recur, we behave accordingly, and even the mere expectation of happiness can give rise to feelings of happiness. If sexual intercourse, for example, were not pleasurable, humankind would have long since become extinct. And if we were incurious, if novelty were not rewarded by feelings of satisfaction, evolution would have long since stalled. Since the very beginning, happiness has been the driving force within living beings and, considering the diverse array of factors by which our species can be stimulated, within Homo Sapiens in particular.

The youngest part of our brain, the anterior temporal lobe, causes us human beings to find certain things pleasurable above and beyond satisfaction of the basic instincts that reside in the brain's older regions. This is also the home of free will, insofar as free will exists at all. And it is here that we should start if we desire to know something about the future. For as long as human beings do not develop into some other species that perhaps has no need of happiness, these things will not change. What we experience as happiness is a biochemical process influenced by our perspective on the world and, in turn, interpreted by us.

This interpretation is zeitgeist-influenced—a product of our times. One thing that makes us happy is being successful according to the societal model in effect at the moment; and happiness can also result from living according to—or revolting against—currently prevailing morals. Happiness is put in context by the reflexive observation of life in general. For this reason, what makes us happy in the future will be a result of how our society develops. What changes is society and its way of evaluating things.

Good design understands the principles according to which it has always been possible to make human beings happy. And it combines these with what the zeitgeist determines to be the trend. Less than ten years ago, just like today, we were unhappy if someone broke our hearts—but we were not unhappy about not owning one of the coveted mobile devices made by Apple, or about not communicating via touchscreen with somebody whom we know via social networks. "Smart" phones had yet to appear on the market, the iPhone had not

Leben und Freizeit /
Life and Fun

Telefone auf dem Markt, das iPhone war noch nicht erfunden, soziale Medien nahmen nicht in jenem Ausmaß
wie heute Teil unserer Kultur ein. Der Bedarf war noch
nicht geweckt.

© Sonia Laszlo

MADE 4 YOU

Nun leben wir mit unserem Steinzeitmenschengehirn in
einer Gesellschaft, die sich so rasch weiterentwickelt hat,
dass wir mit der Anpassung nicht nachkommen. In den
Ländern des Nordens sind die Menschen reicher als je zuvor,
haben mehr Auswahl denn je. Zu viel Auswahl macht aber
nicht glücklich, wie jeder beobachten kann, der vor die Qual
der Wahl gestellt ist. Einer der Gründe hierfür liegt darin,
dass der „Arbeitsspeicher" des menschlichen Gehirns nur
ungefähr sieben Sachen zeitgleich im Gedächtnis behalten
kann. Sich zwischen mehr als sieben Sachen zu entscheiden
fordert daher extreme Denkarbeit.

Ein weiterer Aspekt: Jede Entscheidung hat den Verlust
einer anderen Sache zur Folge. Zu viel Auswahl macht
bereits im Kindesalter unglücklich, wie Versuche gezeigt
haben. Kluge Eltern entscheiden für ihre Kinder, geben
ihnen dann die Illusion der Auswahl und damit Kontrolle
in einem begrenzten Rahmen. Kleinen Kindern werden viel
öfter Ja- oder Nein-Fragen gestellt. Frage ich mein Kind:
„Willst du Schokoladeeis?", lautet die Antwort „Ja" oder
„Nein, habe keine Lust". Wird das Kind hingegen vor die
Entscheidung gestellt, ob es Schokolade-, Vanille- oder
Erdbeereis möchte, überlegt es eine Weile, schaut, was die
anderen Kinder wählen, und ist dann mit seiner Auswahl
vielleicht gar nicht so glücklich. Es hätte, denkt es, doch
besser Vanille nehmen sollen, so wie seine Schwester.

yet been invented, and social media did not yet play as large
a role in our culture as they do today. The need had not yet
been created.

Our stone-age brains now see us through life in a society
that has developed so rapidly that we are unable to adapt
fast enough to keep up. In the Global North, people are
wealthier—and have more choices—than ever before. But
an excess of choices does not result in happiness, as anyone
can observe when faced with a difficult decision. One of the
reasons for this lies in the fact that the human brain's "RAM"
can only keep around seven things in memory simultaneously. Deciding among more than seven things, therefore,
requires an extreme degree of mental effort.

A further aspect is that every decision brings with it the loss
of something else. Experiments have shown that even children are made unhappy by too much choice. Wise parents
make decisions for their children but then give them the
illusion of choice and thus a limited degree of control. Small
children are far more often asked yes-or-no questions. If I
ask my child: "Do you want chocolate ice cream?" the answer
will be "Yes" or "No, don't feel like it." But a child faced with
the decision between chocolate, vanilla or strawberry ice
cream will think for a while, look to see what the other children are choosing, and then perhaps not be so happy with
his choice after all. I should have taken vanilla like my sister,
he might say to himself.

← Dinge, die jetzt und auch in Zukunft
glücklich machen

Things that make happy, now and in
the future

Jedes Mal, wenn wir auswählen müssen, strengen wir unser Gehirn an. Zu viel Auswahl, die in sich die Gefahr von Verlusten birgt, macht daher unglücklich. Eine Marke, die dieses Prinzip des Glücks perfekt verstanden hat und erfolgreich umsetzt, ist Apple. Die Produktpalette deckt alle Wünsche mit relativ wenig Auswahl ab. Ist die grundsätzliche Entscheidung für ein Produkt gefallen, stehen noch einzelne Preiskategorien und Abstufungen, etwa hinsichtlich des Speicherplatzes, als Möglichkeiten offen. Darüber hinaus lassen sich die Produkte durch Schutzhüllen in allen erdenklichen Farben und Gestaltungen individualisieren. Dies kommt einem weiteren Prinzip entgegen: dass wir uns alle gerne als einzigartig sehen. Wenn wir diesen Glauben bestätigt sehen und unsere Individualität ausleben können, sind wir individuell glücklich.[1]

Every time we are faced with a choice, we must make our brain work. And too much choice, which entails the risk of losses, thus makes one unhappy. A brand that has perfectly understood and successfully acted upon this principle of happiness is Apple. The company's product range caters to all desires while offering a relatively narrow selection of choices. Once the basic decision in favor of a product has been made, one can still choose between individual price categories and performance options such as drive capacity. Furthermore, Apple's products can be individualized with protective covers bearing all manner of colors and designs. This appeals to a further principle: we all like to think of ourselves as being unique. And if we see this belief confirmed and can live out our individuality, then we are indeed individually happy.[1]

[1] Mehr zu Glücksforschung und wirtschaftlichen Zusammenhängen in: Herbert Laszlo, Glück und Wirtschaft (Happiness Economics): Was Wirtschaftstreibende und Führungskräfte über die Glücksforschung wissen müssen, Wien 2008

[1] More on happiness research and economic aspects thereof in: Herbert Laszlo, Glück und Wirtschaft (Happiness Economics): Was Wirtschaftstreibende und Führungskräfte über die Glücksforschung wissen müssen, Vienna 2008

← ... bloß keine Qual der Wahl!

... No spoiling us for choice, please!

Leben und Freizeit /
Life and Fun

Robo Hero Bugs

Konzept für ein Spiel mit autonomen Agenten	Concept for a game with autonomous agents
Design **Benjamin Cselley**	Design Benjamin Cselley
Entstehungsjahr **2011**	Year of origin 2011
Anerkennungspreis der Stadt Wien, verliehen durch die Universität für angewandte Kunst Wien	City of Vienna Merit Prize, awarded by the University of Applied Arts Vienna

Helden und Heldinnen der Bildschirm-, insbesondere der Gamer-Kultur, als real im Raum agierende Roboter neu zu denken ist eine alte Fiktion, aber nicht mehr unmöglich. Das Design der Robo Hero Bugs orientiert sich weitgehend an der japanischen Anime-Tradition und führt eine den Pokémon vergleichbare Typologie ein: Die Helden-Insekten – Kolo, Sho, Aku, Nomia und Twin – haben nicht nur ein individuelles Aussehen, sondern verfügen auch über programmierte individuelle Eigenschaften.

Der Rest ist Training. Die Robo Bugs werden nicht ferngesteuert, sie sind <u>quasiautonome Agenten</u>, die ihr Besitzer zunächst anlernen und „abrichten" muss – es geht bei diesem im Zuge einer Diplomarbeit entwickelten Projekt also auch grundlegend um die Interaktion Mensch–Maschine. Erst danach können die Robo Bugs in den Disziplinen Sumo, Parcour und Harvest gegeneinander antreten und einer eher maskulinen Projektion folgend zu Robo Hero Bugs werden.

Rethinking onscreen heroes, especially those in gamer culture, is an old fiction, which has now become a possibility. The Robo Hero Bugs' design orients for the most part on Japanese Anime tradition, introducing a typology comparable to the Pokémon: the hero-insects—Kolo, Sho, Aku, Nomia, and Twin—not only have their own individual look, but also programmed, personal qualities.

The rest is training. The Robo Bugs are not remotely controlled, they are <u>quasi-autonomous agents</u> who first get to know their owners, and have to be "trued"—this project, developed mainly in the course of a diploma project, is also fundamentally about the interaction of human and machine. Only then can Robo Bugs compete with one another in the disciplines Sumo, Parcour, and Harvest; and following a rather masculine projection, become Robo Hero Bugs.

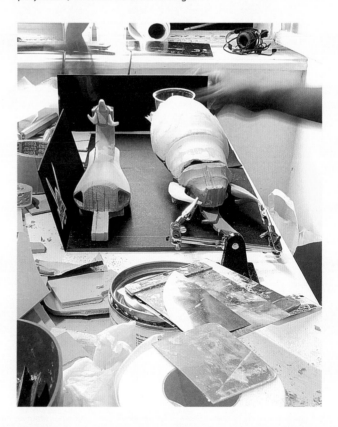

Leben und Freizeit /
Life and Fun

Labor /
Laboratory

© Benjamin Cselley

Gavari

Konzept für eine semiakustische Geige	Concept for a semi-acoustic violin
Design **Gerda Hopfgartner**	Design Gerda Hopfgartner
Entstehungsjahr **2007**	Year of origin 2007

Nur wenige Formen sind im Laufe der Geschichte Veränderungen gegenüber so resistent gewesen wie jene klassischer Instrumente. Nach über 400 Jahren Barockstil wurden in jüngster Zeit nun auch einmal Geigen – vor allem elektrische und elektroakustische – designt, die von der traditionellen Form abweichen. Bei Gavari, einem Kooperationsprojekt mit zwei Wiener Geigenbauern, handelt es sich um einen Entwurf für eine semiakustische Geige.

Inspiriert von „weiblichen Kurven", modernen Jachten sowie Korsetts aus dem Barock, dem Biedermeier und dem Rokoko wurde die typische Geigengestalt zwar beibehalten, aber eben doch abstrahiert und minimalisiert. Alle für den Klang bedeutsamen Kriterien – wie bestimmte geometrische Kurvaturen oder die Stärke des Klangkörpers – wurden jedoch ebenso beibehalten wie die entscheidenden Orientierungspunkte für gute Spielbarkeit (Haptik, konventionelles Größenschema für Geigen etc.). Veränderungswürdig schien der Designerin schließlich die Form, nicht der Klang.

Over the course of history, only very few forms have been so resistant to change as these classical instruments. After more than 400 years of baroque style, violins—mainly electric and electro-acoustic—are also being designed that deviate from traditional forms. Gavari, a collaborative project involving two Viennese violin makers, deals with such a design for a semiacoustic violin.

Inspired by "female curves," modern yachts, as well as corsets from the baroque, bourgeois, and rococo, the typical violin shape is retained, but abstracted and minimized. All criteria crucial to the sound, such as particular geometric curves or the strength of the sound body, are, however, maintained as are the crucial points of orientation for good playability (tactile, conventional general scheme for a violin, etc.). After all, the designers targeted only the form as worthy of change, not the sound.

Leben und Freizeit / Life and Fun

Labor / Laboratory

© GAVARI/Maurizio Maier

131

Urban Performance

Konzept für eine interaktive virtuelle Umgebung	Concept for an interactive virtual environment
Design **Jessica Covi, Christoph Döttelmayer, Tamas Nyilanszky**	Design Jessica Covi, Christoph Döttelmayer, Tamas Nyilanszky
Entstehungsjahr **2010**	Year of origin 2010

Ungebrochen streben Forschung und Entwicklung danach, das Erleben der virtuellen Welt etwa über Datenhandschuhe unmittelbarer zu machen und von der eher passiven Bildschirmrezeption zu befreien. Das Ziel heißt „Immersion": die Identifikation mit dem „Ich" in der virtuellen Welt, die dann als real erlebt wird. Während dies beispielsweise in der militärischen Ausbildung (Flugsimulation) längst angewandt wird, erhofft man sich davon auch in der Unterhaltungselektronik und der Gaming-Industrie Erfolge.

Das Konzept Urban Performance ist ein Beispiel hierfür: Es simuliert die unmittelbare Teilnahme an Sportevents und Turnieren. Über Sensoren an den Händen und Schuhen greifen die SpielerInnen mit ihren Bewegungen interaktiv ins Geschehen ein, eine Datenbrille sorgt für möglichst unmittelbare Teilnahme an der virtuellen Szenerie. Gesteuert wird Urban Performance über Smartphone-Technologie; auch FreundInnen können jederzeit zum Mitzuspielen eingeladen werden.

Research and development have uninterruptedly aimed at making the virtual world accessible though data gloves in an effort to free users from passive screen reception. The goal is "immersion": identification with the "I" in the virtual world, which is then experienced as the real world. While this has long been applied in military training (flight simulation), successful applications are still anticipated in entertainment electronics and the gaming industry.

The Urban Performance concept is an example of this, simulating direct participation in sporting events and tournaments. Through hand and shoe sensors, players use their movements to intervene in what is going on, while data glasses offer the most direct possible participation in the virtual scenery. Urban Performance is controlled via Smartphone technology; friends can be invited to join in the action at any time.

Leben und Freizeit / Life and Fun

Labor / Laboratory

© Jessica Covi, Christoph Döttelmayer, Tamas Nyilanszky

Dynamic Footwear HX1

Studie für einen Hightech-Sportschuh	Study for a high-tech sports shoe
Design **Christoph Döttelmayer**	Design Christoph Döttelmayer
Entstehungsjahr **2010**	Year of origin 2010

Der Mensch verfügt über 200.000 Nervenenden in den Füßen, die alle direkt mit dem Gehirn und, so sagt die Reflexologie, auch mit verschiedenen Körperarealen in Verbindung stehen. Ihre Aktivierung – oder auch Schmerzstillung – ist über gezielte Stimulation der Fußreflexzonen möglich.

Der Laufschuh Dynamic Footwear stimuliert die Fußsohlen durch einen komplexen Sohlenaufbau, für den der piezoelektrische Effekt genutzt wird – das Auftreten von elektrischer Spannung an nichtleitenden Festkörpern, wenn sie elastisch verformt werden. Die 526 Speichereinheiten in der Schuhsohle, die durch die ständige Bewegung beim Laufen elektrische Spannung erzeugen, lassen sich auch individuell per Smartphone-Applikation programmieren – je nachdem, „wo der Schuh drückt"!

The human has more than 200,000 nerve endings in the foot, which are all directly connected with the brain, and as reflexology teaches, also with various body regions. The activation of these regions—or also soothing pain in them—is possible via targeted stimulation of foot reflex zones.

The Dynamic Footwear running shoe stimulates the soles of the feet by means of a complex sole construction that makes use of the piezoelectric effect—the occurrence of electrical tension in non-conducting solid materials when stressed. The 526 storage units that generate electrical tension through the steady movement of running can be programmed individually by means of a Smartphone application—depending on "where the shoe pinches"!

© Christoph Döttelmayer

Leben und Freizeit / Life and Fun

Labor / Laboratory

DiGuitar

Konzept für eine digitale Gitarre	Concept for a digital guitar
Design **Anton Weichselbraun**	Design Anton Weichselbraun
Entstehungsjahr **2009**	Year of origin 2009
MSN Tech & Gadgets **(Top 20 Gadgets)**	MSN Tech & Gadgets (Top 20 Gadgets)

Fühlt sich an wie eine Gitarre, klingt wie eine Gitarre, ist aber keine! Die Vision der DiGuitar kombiniert analoge Spielbarkeit mit vollständig digitalisierter Technik. Diese „Gitarre" hat keine Saiten, stattdessen ist ihr Griffbrett mit einer berührungsempfindlichen Multi-Touch-Oberfläche ausgestattet, die Fingerpositionen und Schlagmuster analysiert. Diese kann sie über MIDI (Musical Instrument Digital Interface) in einen Akkord umwandeln.

Die Bünde der Gitarre sind nicht fixiert, sondern werden flexibel mittels Liquid-Microchannel-Technologie festgelegt, wie sie etwa bei Blindenschrift-Displays Verwendung findet. Das macht DiGuitar wahlweise zur Gitarre oder zum Bass, deren Griffbretter sich unterscheiden. Bei Berührung des Griffbrettes erzeugen piezoelektrische Wandler Vibrationen in der Frequenz der jeweiligen Tonhöhe. Die Rezeptoren in den Fingern lassen den Spieler oder die Spielerin diese Vibrationen wiederum – eine echte Sinnestäuschung – als physische Saite wahrnehmen.

Feels like a guitar, sounds like a guitar, but it isn't one! The visionary DiGuitar combines analogue playability with completely digitized technology. This "guitar" has no strings, instead, its fretboard is equipped with a touch-sensitive, Multi-Touch surface, which analyzes finger position and strumming pattern. It can then convert this through a MIDI (Musical Instrument Digital Interface) into a chord.

The guitar's waistband is not permanent, but instead, is determined flexibly by means of liquid micro-channel technology, similar, for example, to that used for Braille displays. This makes DiGuitar alternately a guitar or bass guitar, which have different fretboards. By touching the fretboard, piezoelectric transformers generate vibrations in the frequency of the appropriate pitch. The finger receptors let the players then perceive these vibrations, for their part, as physical strings— a true sense deception.

© Anton Weichselbraun

Jelly Web

Konzept für einen Internet-Port	Concept for an internet port
Design **Conrad Kroencke**	Design Conrad Kroencke
Entstehungsjahr **2007**	Year of origin 2007
CAT-iq Design Competition 2008 **(1. Preis)**	CAT-iq Design Competition 2008 (1st prize)

Dass wir zunehmend online sind, macht neuartige Interfacelösungen zum dynamischen Innovationsfeld. Beim <u>Interfacekonzept</u> Jelly Web soll das Endgerät zum engen persönlichen Begleiter werden. So kommt es äußerlich als rundes Objekt in Gestalt einer Qualle (engl.: jelly fish) daher und nicht einfach nur als Bildschirmoberfläche. Die Interaktion passiert taktil durch Berühren der „Haut" des Objekts, auf der die grafische Repräsentation der Inhalte angezeigt wird. Externe Sound-/Kamera-Einheiten und ein LCD-Projektor sorgen bei Bedarf für großformatige Wiedergabe.

Jelly Web befriedigt alle Informations- und Kommunikationsbedürfnisse in einem Gerät – vom Browsen über e-Commerce bis zur Unterhaltung. Es ist nicht als Speichermedium gedacht; große Datenmengen, etwa von Digitalfilmen, liegen nach diesem Designkonzept auf den Servern der Anbieter und werden von allen NutzerInnen geteilt. Der Fokus liegt auf schnellem Datentransfer und der intuitiven Nutzung des Interface. Das Konzept der Prothese wie auch jenes des Körperorgans klingen gleichsam an.

The fact that we are increasingly online makes novel interface solutions a dynamic field of innovation. The <u>interface concept</u> Jelly Web aims to make the consumer device a close, personal companion. It thus takes an external appearance as a round object in the shape of a jellyfish, and not simply as a screen surface. The interaction is tactile through touching the „skin" of the object, which displays the graphic representation of the contents. External sound/camera units and an LCD projector provide large-format playback when required.

Jelly Web satisfies all information and communication needs in one single device – from browsing through e-commerce, to entertainment. It is not conceived as a storage medium. This design foresees storage of large amounts of data, for example, from digital films, on suppliers' servers, to be shared by all users. Focus is on rapid data transfer and intuitive use of the interface. It brings to mind both the concept of the prosthesis as well as an organ of the body.

© Conrad Kroencke

135

Labor /
Laboratory

Leben und Freizeit /
Life and Fun

Jambox

Kabelloser Lautsprecher mit Freisprecheinrichtung	Wireless loudspeaker with speaker phone function
Design **Yves Béhar, fuseproject**	Design Yves Béhar, fuseproject
Hersteller **Jawbone**	Manufacturer Jawbone
Entstehungsjahr **2010**	Year of origin 2010

Der Name der Jambox, eines kabellosen <u>Lautsprecher-Speakerphones</u>, erinnert nicht zufällig an die „Boombox" der 1980er-Jahre – einen Kassettenrekorder mit großen Lautsprechern, mit dem die Jugend gern im öffentlichen Raum ihren Musikgeschmack und ihre Identität demonstrierte. Die zeitgenössische Version ist digital und multimedial: Mit Mobiltelefonen, MP3-Playern oder Computern via Bluetooth drahtlos verbunden, gibt die Jambox Musik, Film- und Videospiele-Sound, Telefonate oder auch Gespräche über Konferenzschaltung in hoher Qualität wieder.

Das Gerät ist minimalistisch aus wenigen Gehäuseteilen gestaltet. Zwischen Boden und Abdeckung aus Gummi verläuft rundum eine Lautsprecherfläche aus perforiertem Edelstahl mit Reliefmuster, die aus einem einzigen Blech geformt ist. Dass die Jambox in vier Farben mit vier verschiedenen Mustern zu haben ist, unterstreicht ihre über das Akustische hinausreichende Funktionalität: nämlich Lifestyle und Stilpräferenzen auszudrücken.

The name of the Jambox, a wireless <u>loudspeaker-speaker phone</u>, quite consciously recalls the "boomboxes" of the 1980s—cassette recorders with huge loudspeakers that young people liked to use in public areas to demonstrate their taste in music, and their identity. The contemporary version is digital and multimedial: connected wirelessly with mobile telephones, MP3 players, and computers via Bluetooth, in conference mode, the Jambox plays music, film and video game sounds, telephone conversations, or even regular conversations in high quality.

The device is minimalist, with casing designed from just a few parts. A loudspeaker surface of perforated stainless steel with a relief pattern runs between the bottom and the rubber cover. The surface is shaped from a single piece of sheet metal. The fact that the Jambox is available in four colors with four different patters highlights its functionality, which goes beyond mere acoustics: namely, to express one's preferences in terms of lifestyle and style.

Leben und Freizeit / Life and Fun

Fabrik / Factory

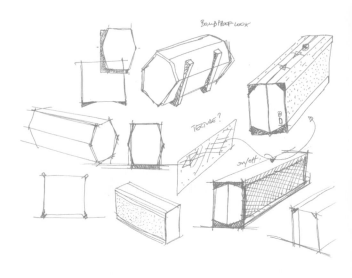

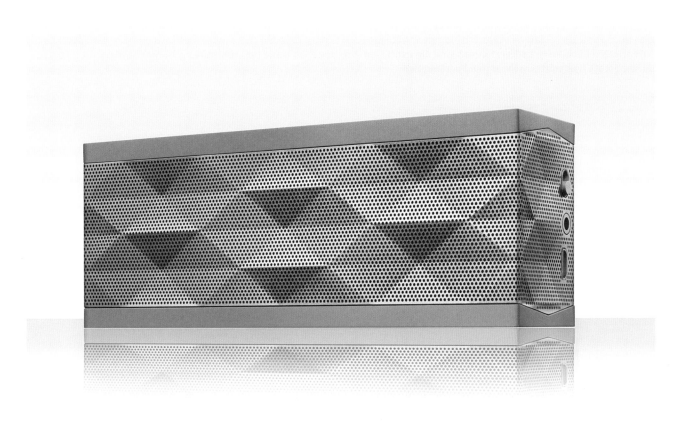

© fuseproject

Leben und Freizeit /
Life and Fun

Fabrik /
Factory

Pleasure-to-People
FORM 2, 3, 4 & 6

Vibratoren	Vibrators
Design (FORM 6) **Ethan Imboden**	Design (FORM 6) Ethan Imboden
Design (FORM 2, 3 & 4) **Ethan Imboden / Yves Béhar, fuseproject**	Design (FORM 2, 3 & 4) Ethan Imboden / Yves Béhar, fuseproject
Hersteller **Jimmyjane**	Manufacturer Jimmyjane
Entstehungsjahre **2006–2011**	Years of origin 2006–2011

Auf dem Markt für Sex-Spielzeug hat Design erst vor einigen Jahren Einzug gehalten, zeitgleich mit dessen teilweiser Neuausrichtung hin zu Wellness („Sexual Wellbeing") und weg aus der Schmuddelecke. Das Label Jimmyjane steht für diese Neubewertung und ist das erste Unternehmen, das für seine Vibratoren internationale Designpreise erhielt.

Die Vibratoren der Pleasure-to-People-Serie schaffen über Form, Beschaffenheit und Vibration Möglichkeiten für sexuelle Stimulation, ohne – wie andere Geräte dieser Art – Geschlechtsorgane nachzuahmen. FORM 2 etwa besitzt zwei einzeln steuerbare Vibrationspunkte, funktioniert sozusagen „stereo". Beim Bestseller FORM 3 wird die Vibration über eine dehnbare Membran mit den Fingerspitzen gesteuert. FORM 4 und 6 sind Varianten mit starkem Motor, die sich auch für die vaginale Stimulation eignen. Dank eines patentierten kabellosen Ladeverfahrens sind die nahtlosen Silikongeräte komplett waschbar und badetauglich.

Design first found its way into the sex-toy market just a few years ago, at the same time as this market's reorientation towards wellness (sexual wellbeing) and away from "the closet." The label Jimmyjane, the first firm to receive international design prizes for its vibrators, represents this revaluation.

The vibrators of the Pleasure-to-People series create opportunities for sexual stimulation through their form, material qualities, and vibration; without imitating sexual organs, which is common among other devices of this type. FORM 2, for example, has two individually controllable vibration points and works in "stereo" as it were. With the bestseller FORM 3, the fingertips control vibration through a ductile membrane. FORM 4 and 6 are varieties with strong motors suitable also for vaginal stimulation. A patented, wireless charging process makes the nearly seamlessly silicone device completely washable and bathtub-safe.

Leben und Freizeit / Life and Fun

Fabrik / Factory

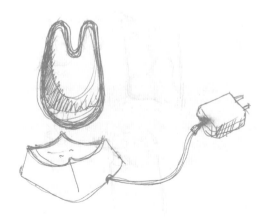

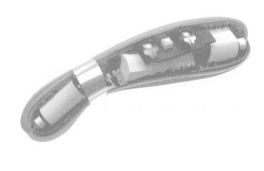

© Jimmyjane

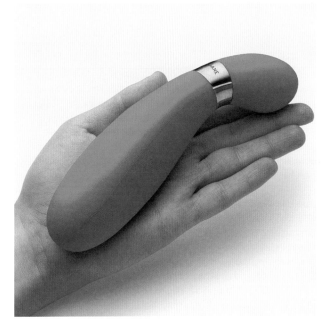

↑ **Form 2, 3, 4 & 6**

Leben und Freizeit /
Life and Fun

Fabrik /
Factory

MAM Perfect

Babyschnuller	Pacifier
Design **Ernst Beranek Design**	Design Ernst Beranek Design
Hersteller **MAM Babyartikel**	Manufacturer MAM Babyproducts
Entstehungsjahr **2010**	Year of origin 2010

Ob sich die Verwendung von Schnullern empfiehlt oder nicht, ist Gegenstand vieler Diskussionen. Insbesondere das Risiko späterer Fehlstellungen des Kindergebisses ist wissenschaftlich belegt. Mit dem MAM Perfect-Schnuller soll dieses Risiko so weit wie möglich minimiert werden. Sein Silikonsauger ist im Schnitt um 60 Prozent schmäler und auch weicher als der anderer Schnuller. Das bedeutet, dass weniger Druck auf Kiefer und Zähne ausgeübt wird; die beruhigende Wirkung des Saugers bleibt jedoch erhalten.

Auch der Schild des gemeinsam mit Kieferorthopäden und pädiatrischen Zahnärzten entwickelten MAM Perfect ist gestaltet: Wichtig waren dabei die richtige Form für das Babygesicht sowie genügend Löcher für die Hautatmung. Um eine optimale Passform zu gewährleisten, gibt es den Schnuller in drei Größen: für die ersten sechs Lebensmonate, ab sechs Monaten und ab 16 Monaten. Auch Farbgebung und Dekor sind nach kinderpsychologischen Kriterien der jeweiligen Altersgruppe angepasst.

Whether the use of pacifiers is recommended or not is the subject of many a discussion. The risk of a later false positioning of the deciduous teeth, in particular, is scientifically verified. The MAM Perfect-pacifier intends to reduce this risk as greatly as possible. Its silicone nipple is, on average, 60 percent smaller and also softer than that of other pacifiers. That means that less pressure is exerted on the jaws and teeth; the comforting effect of the nipple, however, remains the same.

The mouth shield of the MAM Perfect, which was designed together with orthodontists and pediatric dentists, is also carefully designed: important here is the correct form for a baby's face as well as enough holes to allow the skin to breathe. In order to achieve an optimally fitting form, the pacifier is available in three sizes: for babies up to six months, older than six months, and older than sixteen months. The color and pattern are also customized according to child psychology criteria applicable to each age group.

© MAM Babyartikel

Leben und Freizeit /
Life and Fun

Fabrik /
Factory

Pato

Zahnungshilfe für Babys und Kleinkinder	Tooth aid for babies and infants
Design **taliaYsebastian**	Design taliaYsebastian
Hersteller **Mapa / NUK**	Manufacturer Mapa / NUK
Entstehungsjahr **2012**	Year of origin 2012

Die Zeit des Zahnens stellt für Babys und Kleinkinder ebenso wie für deren Eltern eine Herausforderung dar. Da Schmerzstillung mittels Medikamenten bei den Kleinen ein sensibles Thema ist, bietet sich als beste Alternative noch immer das Kauen auf Gegenständen an – etwas, was Kinder ohnehin von sich aus tun, um die Schmerzen zu lindern. Pato ist ein speziell hierfür entwickeltes <u>Mund-Spielzeug</u>, das nicht nur den Druck auf Zahnfleisch und Gaumen reduziert, sondern Kinder auf positive Weise an die regelmäßige, selbstbestimmte Mundhygiene heranführt.

Das Design von Pato soll durch seine Farbgebung und Geometrie einerseits positive Emotionen bei Kindern wecken. Andererseits weist es bewusst Analogien zu Mundhygieneartikeln auf, wie Kinder sie bei Erwachsenen sehen. Das Projekt, das die jungen Designer noch in der Studienzeit entwickelt haben, wurde gemeinsam mit der deutschen Firma Mapa unter der Marke NUK entwickelt.

Teething time is a challenge for babies and infants, as well as their parents. Since relieving children's pain by means of medication is a sensitive theme, the best alternative remains gnawing on objects—which children do on their own, anyway, to ease the pain. Pato is a <u>tooth toy</u> specially developed for this, which not only reduces pressure on gums and palate, but also introduces children in a positive way to regular, autonomous oral hygiene.

Pato's design should, on the one hand, awake positive emotions in children with its color and geometry. On the other hand, it also has conscious analogies to articles for oral hygiene that children see adults using. The project, which the young designers already devised during their student days, was developed together with the German firm Map and the brand NUK.

© Mapa GmbH, Germany

Natural Nurser

Babyflasche	Baby bottle
Design **Whipsaw**	Design Whipsaw
Hersteller **Adiri**	Manufacturer Adiri
Entstehungsjahr **2007**	Year of origin 2007

War vielleicht Prüderie der Grund dafür, dass <u>Baby-flaschen</u> nicht schon früher das Aussehen und die Haptik der weiblichen Brust simulierten? Der Natural Nurser hat damit jedenfalls kein Problem, wie an seinem patentierten „Nipple"-Design zu sehen ist. Als wirklich innovativ gilt das „Fill, Twist and Feed"-System der Flasche: Sie wird über die breite Bodenöffnung befüllt und mit einer Schraubkappe geschlossen, während der weiche Sauger und der Behälter aus einem Guss sind.

Die Praxis hat gezeigt, dass dieses System einfacher zu bedienen ist als konventionelle Flaschen mit Plastikeinsätzen und kleineren Öffnungen am Flaschenhals. Ein spezielles Ventil am Boden des Natural Nurser lässt beim Trinken die Luft entweichen. In drei Größen mit unterschiedlich großen Öffnungen am Sauger erhältlich, ist die Flasche spülmaschinenfest und kam bereits bei der Markteinführung 2007 ohne die Verwendung von Bisphenol-A enthaltenden Polycarbonaten aus, die mittlerweile für Babyflaschen EU-weit verboten sind.

Was it perhaps because of prudery that <u>baby bottles</u> have not hitherto simulated the appearance and feel of the female breast? The Natural Nurser, in any case, has no problem with that, as can be seen by its patented "Nipple" design. A true innovation is the bottle's "fill, twist and feed" system: it is filled through the wide bottom opening, and closed with a twist cap, while the soft nipple and holder are from a single mold.

Practice has proven this system simpler to use than conventional bottles with plastic inserts and small openings at the bottle neck. A special valve on the bottom of the Natural Nurser lets air escape while the baby is drinking. Available in three sizes with different size openings on the nipple, the bottle is dishwasher-safe, and was introduced into the market in 2007 already free of Bisphenol-A (BPA) polycarbonates, which are meanwhile banned throughout the EU.

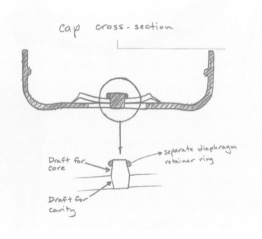

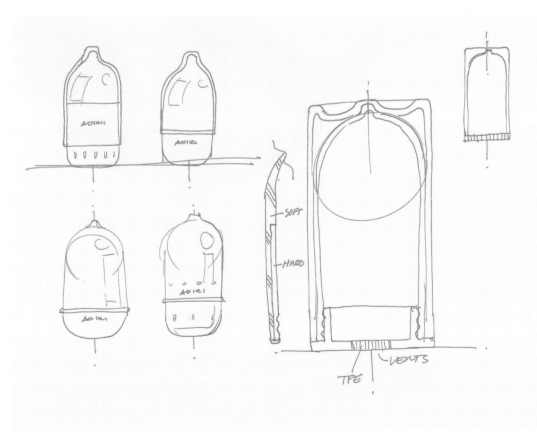

© Whipsaw, Inc.

Powered Voice

Ergonomisches Mikrofon-/Lautsprecher-Set	Ergonomic microphone-loudspeaker set
Design **GK Design Group**	Design GK Design Group
Hersteller **Molten**	Manufacturer Molten
Entstehungsjahr **2008**	Year of origin 2008

Wer sich auf offener Flur Gehör verschaffen will, die Hände aber nicht frei hat, um etwa ein Megaphon zu halten, dem wird Powered Voice gute Dienste leisten. Diese Neuheit aus dem Bereich der <u>Wearable Electronics</u> besteht aus einem Headset-Mikrofon und einem leichten, ergonomisch gestalteten Lautsprecher, der in einer Art Holster direkt am Körper getragen wird. Powered Voice unterstützt beispielsweise TrainerInnen, die gleichzeitig sprechen und sich bewegen müssen, denkbar ist aber auch die Verwendung bei Produktvorführungen, auf Demonstrationen und nicht zuletzt in der militärischen Ausbildung.

Das Lautsprecherteil lässt sich in zwei Positionen am Körper tragen: Dank seines ergonomischen Designs schmiegt es sich – je nach Gebrauch – wahlweise seitlich an die Rippen oder um die Hüfte. Ein AUX-Eingang für externe Geräte dient dazu, einen MP3-Player anzuschließen und zusätzlich Musik zu spielen – für die passende Untermalung beim Aerobictraining oder vielleicht ja auch als Marschmusikbegleitung.

Powered Voice offers a valuable service for those who want to make themselves heard out in the open, but have no hand free for holding something, such as a megaphone. This novelty in the <u>wearable electronics</u> field is a headset microphone and light, ergonomically designed loudspeaker worn directly on the body in a type of holster. Powered Voice supports coaches, for example, who have to speak and move at the same time; while its use is also imaginable in product presentations, at demonstrations, and, last but not least, in military training.

The loudspeaker part can be carried on the body in two positions: due to its ergonomic design it can nestle sideways on the ribs or a hip—depending on use. An AUX input for external devices can also be used to connect an MP3 player to also play music—providing the appropriate background music for aerobics, or maybe even an accompaniment of marching music.

© GK Design Group

Leben und Freizeit / Life and Fun

Fabrik / Factory

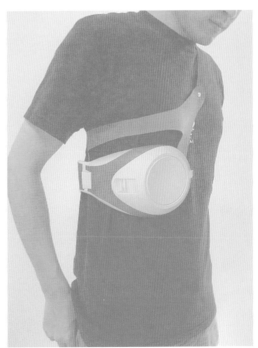

Fidelio SoundSphere

© Philips

Drahtlose Lautsprecher	Wireless loudspeaker
Design **Philips Design**	Design Philips Design
Hersteller **Philips**	Manufacturer Philips
Entstehungsjahr **2011**	Year of origin 2011

Die persönliche Musik-Playlist auf Smartphone oder MP3-Player scheint vor allem für die jüngere Generation mittlerweile unerlässlich. Musik hört man längst nicht mehr nur zu Hause über die HiFi-Anlage, sondern wo man geht und steht, „gestreamt" oder „downgeloadet" via Mobilgerät und Earphones. Die Fidelio SoundSphere verbindet beide Hör-Philosophien miteinander: Sie fungiert als Docking-Lautsprechersystem für iPod, iPhone und iPad – das aber mit dem Anspruch, die Soundqualität einer hochqualitativen Heim-Stereoanlage zu liefern.

Ausgestattet mit AirPlay von Apple, funktioniert die SoundSphere drahtlos. Die Lautsprecher können in mehreren Zimmern platziert werden, sie müssen lediglich mit dem Drahtlosnetzwerk verbunden sein. Der aus Holz handgefertigte Korpus der Lautsprecher hat eine speziell auf Soundqualität hin berechnete Wölbung. Die teleskopartigen zusätzlichen „Tweeter" – das sind Lautsprecher für hohe Frequenzen – sollen eine noch bessere Klangerfahrung bewirken.

It seems that the personal music play list on Smartphones and MP3 players has meanwhile become indispensable, especially for the younger generation. For quite some time now, one no longer listens to music only at home on the hi-fi system, but wherever one is; "streamed," or "downloaded" via mobile devices and earphones. Fidelio SoundSphere combines both listening philosophies: it functions as a docking-loudspeaker system for iPod, iPhone, and iPad—but with the claim of delivering the sound of a high-quality stereo system.

Equipped with Apple's AirPlay, SoundSphere works wirelessly. The loudspeakers can be placed in different rooms; they simply have to be connected to the wireless network. The loudspeakers' handmade wooden bodies have a special curvature calculated for sound quality. The telescope-like additional "tweeter"—loudspeakers for high frequencies—are meant to deliver an even better sound experience.

CX 980, MX 980 & OMX 980

Kopf- und Ohrhörer-Serie	Series of headphones and earphones
Design **BMW Group DesignworksUSA**	Design BMW Group DesignworksUSA
Hersteller **Sennheiser**	Manufacturer Sennheiser
Entstehungsjahr **2010**	Year of origin 2010

Seit es zum Alltag gehört, überall Musik zu hören und viele Stunden des Tages mit <u>Kopf- oder Ohrhörern</u> zu verbringen, ist der Markt für diese stetigen Begleiter gewachsen. Gleichzeitig stieg der Druck auf die Hersteller, unverwechselbares Design und Qualität zu erschwinglichen Preisen anzubieten. Um diesen Anspruch zu erfüllen, werden Kooperationen geschlossen – in diesem Fall zwischen dem namhaften Audiospezialisten Sennheiser und der Designagentur BMW Group DesignworksUSA.

Die drei Produkte der Serie „Expression" sind leicht, in ihrer asymmetrischen Gestaltung ergonomisch und zeichnen sich durch eine zierliche, facettierte Formgebung aus. Sie sind für jeweils unterschiedliche Bedürfnisse konzipiert: Der OMX 980 in „Y"-Form mit Ohrbügeln eignet sich vor allem für sportliche Betätigung. Der MX 980 mutet mit seinem eleganten, durchbrochenen Metallteil fast wie ein Schmuckstück an. Und der in sehr schlichtem Design gehaltene CX 980 ist der einzige Ohrkanalhörer der Serie für unterwegs.

Ever since it has become part of everyday life to listen to music everywhere and spend numerous hours every day with <u>headphones or earphones</u>, the market for these constant companions has grown. At the same time, manufacturers have been pressured to offer distinctive design and quality at affordable prices. In order to meet this demand, collaborations have taken place—in this case, between renowned audio specialist Sennheiser and the design agency BMW Group DesignworksUSA.

The three products in the "Expression" series are light, ergonomically asymmetrical, and distinguished by their delicate, faceted design. Each is conceived for a different purpose: The "Y"-shaped OMX 980 with ear clip is suited mainly for sports. The MX 980, with its elegant, open-work metal section seems almost like a piece of jewelry. And the CX 980, whose design is kept very simple, is the only in-ear phone of the series for on the go.

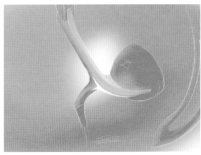

← CX 980, MX 980 & OMX 980

© BMW Group DesignworksUSA

Leben und Freizeit / Life and Fun

Fabrik / Factory

MADE 4 YOU

Leben und Arbeit / Life and Work

Was erleichtert uns Arbeit und Alltag?

MADE 4 YOU

Zwar unterliegt auch unsere Freizeit heute zunehmend der Gestaltung und Optimierung, nach wie vor ist es aber der Bereich der Arbeit, in dem Effektivität, Schnelligkeit und reibungslose Abläufe im Vordergrund stehen. Sicheres, funktionales Werkzeug, optimale Arbeitsorganisation oder auch Maschinen, die menschliche Arbeit ersetzen, sorgen für eine Steigerung der Produktivität. In der postfordistischen Arbeitswelt wird immer weniger körperlich gearbeitet, stattdessen sind wir immer mehr an Schreibtisch und Computer gebunden – die Gestaltung von Büroarbeitsplätzen, ihre Ergonomie und Beleuchtung spielen daher eine große Rolle. Da wir uns mit unserer Arbeit ein Stück weit verwirklichen, geht es aber auch im Arbeitsumfeld nicht nur um streng funktionale, sondern ebenso um emotionale Aspekte, um Stimmungen. So steigert ein freundlich gestaltetes Arbeitsumfeld, das etwa Farbigkeit, intelligente Raumgestaltung und Arbeitswerkzeuge einführt, deren Bedienung Freude macht, die Arbeitszufriedenheit. Zufriedenheit aber hält die Menschen erwiesenermaßen nicht nur gesund, sondern steigert über diesen positiven Weg wieder die Produktivität – was selbstredend auch für Arbeiten im Haushalt gilt!

What can make
work and everyday
life easier for us?

While today's leisure time is, indeed, increasingly subjected to design and optimization, the work area continues to be where efficiency, speed, and smooth processes are foregrounded. Safe, functional tools, optimal work organization, and labor-saving machines lead to an increase in productivity. In the post-Fordian working world, ever less physical labor is performed; instead, we are increasingly bound to our desks and computers. The design of office spaces, their ergonometrics and lighting, thus play a major role. Since we realize our personalities, to a certain extent, through our work, the working environment is not restricted to purely functional aspects, but also includes emotional ones, and atmospheres. A working environment with a friendly design, introducing coloring, intelligent interior architecture and equipment, which is thereby enjoyable to work in, increases work satisfaction. And it has been shown that satisfaction not only keeps people healthy, but is also a positive way to increase productivity—which, of course, also applies to work done at home!

MADE 4 YOU

152

Jeremy Myerson
Helen Hamlyn Centre for Design, Royal Collage of Art,
London (RCA)

Raum zum Denken – Design für Wissensarbeiter

Mit „Leben und Arbeit" ist jene Art von praxisbezogener Forschung, wie sie das 1991 gegründete Helen Hamlyn Centre for Design am Royal College of Art (RCA) in London betreibt, treffend betitelt. Wir beschäftigen uns mit Designforschung und realisieren Projekte mit der Wirtschaft, die dazu beitragen, das Leben der Menschen in gewisser Weise zu verbessern.

In drei Forschungslabors mit den Schwerpunkten Gesundheitsvorsorge, Altern und Arbeitsplatz organisiert, erfolgt unsere Arbeit interdisziplinär und integrativ. Zwar hat jedes Labor seine eigenen Themen und wendet spezifische Methoden an, gemeinsam ist allen jedoch eine designethnografische Herangehensweise an Leben und Arbeit. Unsere WissenschaftlerInnen kommen aus den verschiedensten Bereichen, sind aber – ob als Textil- oder MöbeldesignerInnen, als Designingenieure oder ArchitektInnen – durchwegs gestalterisch tätig. Wir nutzen Visualisierungstechniken als Forschungsinstrument, um Nutzerbedürfnisse sichtbar zu machen. Die Art und Weise, wie das geschieht, erweist sich für das an einem neuen Produkt oder einer neuen Dienstleistung arbeitende Designteam als verbindend und sinnstiftend.

Im „Work & City"-Forschungslabor beispielsweise wird der Frage nachgegangen, wie Arbeitsplätze sich ändern müssen, um den Anforderungen der Wissensökonomie Genüge zu tun. Dass unsere Kooperation mit dem österreichischen Büromöbelhersteller Bene und die Entwicklung der PARCS-Möbelkollektion (Seite 170) parallel liefen, ist für unsere Arbeitsweise charakteristisch.

Die von der Londoner Designfirma PearsonLloyd gestaltete PARCS-Serie gilt als eines des ersten speziell für WissensarbeiterInnen entworfenen modularen Möbelsysteme. Die Kollektion besteht aus Einzelelemente, die sich variabel gruppieren lassen, um je nach Bedarf einen Rahmen für intensive Konzentration, Teamarbeit oder Rückzug und Reflexion – die drei wichtigsten Ausprägungen von Wissensarbeit – zu schaffen.

Nahm das traditionelle Büro noch Anleihen an der Fabrikhalle, spielt die von Zeit und Bewegung bestimmte Überwachungshierarchie bei einem Großteil der Arbeit, die wir heute vollbringen, längst keine Rolle mehr. Wissensarbeit basiert darauf, theoretisches Wissen und Erlerntes in einer Kultur der Kooperation, des Experiments und der Initiative zur Anwendung zu bringen. Damit erfordert sie einen viel flexibleren Ansatz.

Parallel zu Entwicklung und Design der PARCS-Serie führte das Helen Hamlyn Centre for Design im Auftrag von Bene eine Studie über die unterschiedlichen Typen von WissensarbeiterInnen durch, die sich in der aufkommenden Wissensökonomie tummeln. Ziel war es, zu einem besseren Verständnis jener Menschen zu gelangen, die das PARCS-

Space for Thought – Designing for Knowledge Workers

"Life and Work" is an apt title for the type of practice-based research undertaken by the Helen Hamlyn Centre for Design at the Royal College of Art, London. Founded in 1991, we undertake design research and projects with industry that contribute in some way to improving people's lives.

Our work is interdisciplinary and inclusive, and organized in three research labs focusing on healthcare, ageing and the workplace. Each lab has its own particular themes and methods, but what binds the whole together is a design-ethnographic approach to life and work. Our researchers are all designers in various disciplines (from textiles and furniture to design engineers and architects)—and we use visualization techniques as a research tool for capturing user requirements in a way that is engaging and meaningful for any design team working on a new product and service.

Our Work & City research lab, for example, is strongly interested in how the workspace must change to meet the needs of the knowledge economy, and our collaboration with Austrian manufacturer Bene in a parallel project to the development of the PARCS collection (page 170) of workplace furniture is typical of how we work.

PARCS, designed by London design consultants PearsonLloyd, can be described as one of the first modular furniture systems specifically designed for knowledge workers. The range presents elements of furniture that can be configured to accommodate intense concentration, teamwork, or reflection and escape—three of the most important aspects of knowledge work.

The traditional office derived its template from the factory floor, but the time-and-motion supervised hierarchy is no longer relevant for much of the work we do today. Knowledge work depends on applying theoretical knowledge and learning in a culture of collaboration, experiment, and initiative. As such, it requires a much more flexible approach.

In parallel with the design and development of the PARCS system, the Helen Hamlyn Centre for Design at the RCA was commissioned by Bene to conduct a piece of design research to investigate the different types of knowledge workers who inhabit the emerging knowledge economy. The aim was to understand better the people who would use the PARCS system in new and different configurations.

Our study, "Space for Thought" (2009), led by researcher Catherine Greene, presented four "types" of knowledge worker who interact with the office building in a different way: the "Anchor" is almost entirely desk based; the "Connector" moves around a lot within the building; the "Gatherer" makes regular journeys away from the office but always returns; and the "Navigator" is rarely in the office at all, a senior ambassador working for the organization at arm's length.

153

© Helen Hamlyn Centre for Design

MADE 4 YOU

→ Auswahl von Zeichnungen:
**Darstellung der eigenen Mobilität in
Bezug auf das Bürogebäude mittels
eines grafischen Tools**

A selection of drawings created
using a graphical tool to elicit
responses to mobility in relation to
the office building.

System in neuartigen Konstellationen und unter verschiedenen Umständen verwenden würden.

Unsere von Catherine Greene geleitete Studie „Space for Thought" (2009) ermittelte vier „Typen" von WissensarbeiterInnen, die auf unterschiedliche Weise mit dem Bürogebäude interagieren: Der „Anker" arbeitet fast ausschließlich am Schreibtisch, der „Verbinder" ist viel innerhalb des Gebäudes unterwegs, der „Sammler" verlässt das Büro regelmäßig, kehrt aber stets zurück, und der „Navigator" – ein leitender Repräsentant, der seine Tätigkeit außerhalb der Organisation verrichtet – ist kaum je im Büro anzutreffen. Es ist das komplexe Zusammenspiel zwischen diesen vier Typen, das die Vielfalt der Wissensarbeit ausmacht.

Wie kamen wir zu dieser Typologie? In der Studie wurden mehrere qualitative Forschungsmethoden angewandt. Unter anderem befragte man in halbstrukturierten Interviews 20 für unterschiedliche Mobilitäts- und Erfahrungsprofile repräsentative WissensarbeiterInnen, nahm ethnografische Studien in einem Medienunternehmen, einer Immobilien- sowie einer Public-Relations-Firma vor und hielt einen NutzerInnen-Workshop ab.

Um Antworten zu evozieren, kam im Interviewprozess eine neuartige Zeichenübung zur Anwendung. Mittels eines einfachen grafischen Rechercheinstruments sollten die TeilnehmerInnen dazu angeregt werden nachzudenken, wie sie das Bürogebäude nutzen. Jeder Proband bekam ein Blatt Papier vorgelegt, auf dem ein graues Quadrat zu sehen war – es stand für das Büro. Nun sollte der Teilnehmer bzw. die Teilnehmerin die eigene Mobilität in Bezug auf das Büro durch Aufzeichnen der Bewegungen in und um die Schachtel herum darstellen. Diese Zeichentechnik erwies sich als effektiv, ermutigte sie die Interviewten doch dazu, ihre Arbeitsmuster und Gewohnheiten auf eine Art und Weise zu beschreiben, wie dies mit Worten schwer möglich gewesen wäre.

It is the complex interactions between these four types that make up the rich tapestry of knowledge work.

How did we arrive at these typologies? The study was undertaken using a range of qualitative research methods including semi-structured interviews with twenty knowledge workers representing different levels of mobility and experience, ethnographic studies in a media company, real estate business and a public relations firm, and a user workshop.

A novel drawing exercise was introduced to elicit responses during the interview process. In each interview, a simple graphic research tool was introduced to engage participants in thinking about how they use the office building. Each was presented with a grey box on a piece of paper, the box representing the office building, and invited to describe their mobility in relation to the office by drawing their movements in and around the box. This drawing technique proved effective in encouraging participants to describe their working patterns and habits in ways that would be hard to capture in words.

The graphic tool used during the interviews captured how users perceive their work patterns. The resulting drawings could be plotted along a scale of mobility from low to high representing a complete spectrum of knowledge workers.

Mit diesem in den Interviews eingesetzten grafischen Instrument ließ sich erfassen, wie Arbeitsmuster wahrgenommen werden. Die aus den Zeichnungen resultierenden Ergebnisse wurden auf eine das gesamte Spektrum der WissensarbeiterInnen repräsentierende Mobilitätsskala von Hoch bis Niedrig eingetragen.

Die Erkenntnisse aus dieser Studie flossen in die Entwicklung der PARCS-Kollektion ein. Sie lieferten wichtige Informationen darüber, wie das Möbelsystem angelegt und spezifiziert werden sollte.

The findings from our study were fed into the development of PARCS, helping to inform the way the system could be configured and specified.

↓ Icons developed by the researcher from a mapping of the visual data to show the different knowledge worker typologies

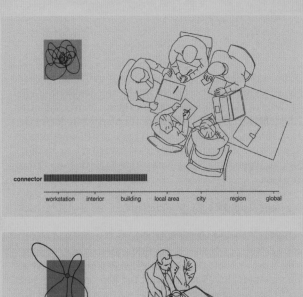

connector

workstation   interior   building   local area   city   region   global

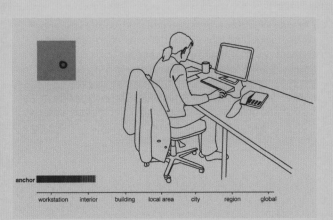

anchor

workstation   interior   building   local area   city   region   global

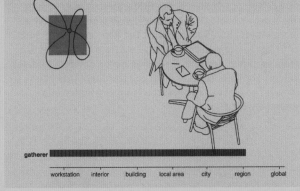

gatherer

workstation   interior   building   local area   city   region   global

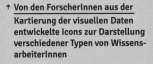

↑ Von den ForscherInnen aus der Kartierung der visuellen Daten entwickelte Icons zur Darstellung verschiedener Typen von WissensarbeiterInnen

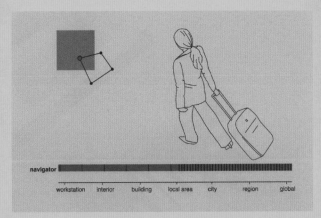

navigator

workstation   interior   building   local area   city   region   global

© Helen Hamlyn Centre for Design

Leben und Arbeit /
Life and Work

Valentine 2.0

Konzept für ein Notebook	Concept for a notebook
Design **Anton Weichselbraun,** **Martin Zopf, Julia Kaisinger,** **Pia Weitgasser**	Design Anton Weichselbraun, Martin Zopf, Julia Kaisinger, Pia Weitgasser
Entstehungsjahr **2007**	Year of origin 2007

„Cultural Recycling", das bewusste Aufgreifen ikonischer historischer Formen, ist nicht zuletzt seit den Retro-Wellen der letzten Jahrzehnte wieder ein Thema. Hinter Valentine 2.0 steht die Idee, ein Notebook für heutige Bedürfnisse zu gestalten, das aber die Anmutung und den emotionalen Appeal einer Designikone der Sixties besitzt – in diesem Fall der legendären Schreibmaschine Valentine von Ettore Sottsass.

Die neue Valentine ist grundlegend an die Vorläufertechnologie Schreibmaschine angelehnt: Wichtigstes formgebendes Element ist die ausziehbare Tastatur und nicht, wie bei Notebooks üblich, der Bildschirm. Dieser kommt – in visueller Analogie zum einstigen Papierblatt – hier als ausziehbarer Flexi-Screen daher. Die Begründung für solch ein Designkonzept lieferte übrigens Ettore Sottsass selbst, indem er darauf drängte, im Design neben den funktionalen auch emotionale Aspekte groß zu schreiben. Und kaum etwas ist so emotional besetzt wie unsere materielle Vergangenheit ...

"Cultural Recycling," the conscious use of iconic historical forms, has again become a theme, no least due to the retro trend in the past several decades. Behind Valentine 2.0 is the idea of designing a notebook for today's needs that has the look, feel, and emotional appeal of a design icon of the 1960s—in this case, Ettore Sottsass's legendary Valentine typewriter.

The new Valentine is based, in principle, on the forerunner technology of the typewriter: the most important formal element is the pull-out keyboard and not, as is common with notebooks, the screen. This is present—in a visual parallel to the sheet of paper—as a pull-out flexi-screen. Ettore Sottsass himself provided the reason for such a design concept in that he insisted on attaching importance to emotional aspects alongside the functional in design. And almost nothing is as emotionally charged as our material past ...

@ Anton Weichselbraun

Model Machine

Konzept einer multifunk-tionalen Werkbank für professionellen Modellbau	Concept for a multifunctional workbench for professional model making
Design **Bernhard Ranner**	Design Bernhard Ranner
Entstehungsjahr **2011**	Year of origin 2011

Neben Skizzieren und Rendern kommt dem Bau eines drei-dimensionalen Modells im Designprozess große Bedeutung für die Beurteilung von Ergonomie, Haptik und Funktionalität eines Objekts zu. Allerdings verfügen meist nur große Firmen über eigene Modellbauwerkstätten – der Rest improvisiert. Model Machine ist der Entwurf für eine kompakte, wenig Platz beanspruchende Werkbank speziell für die Modellher-stellung, die sich auch kleine Büros und Start-ups leisten können.

Alle wichtigen Werkzeuge sind integriert: Band- und Tisch-säge, Bohr- und Schleifvorrichtungen, Drehbank und Fräse sowie automatischer Staubabzug. Durch Rotation der beiden grundlegenden Elemente wird das jeweilige Werkzeug ver-fügbar. Inspiriert von multifunktionalen Produkten, wie sie schon länger für den Hobbybereich angeboten werden, ist diese Werkbank jedoch massiver, etwas größer und explizit auf die Bedürfnisse von DesignerInnen zugeschnitten.

Along with sketching and rendering, the construction of a three-dimensional model is given great importance in the design process for ascertaining an object's ergonometric, tactile, and functional qualities. Nonetheless, usually only large firms have their own model making workshops—the rest improvise. Model Machine is a design for a compact work-bench specially made for creating models, which takes up little room and is affordable by small offices and start-ups.

All important tools are integrated: band saw and table saw, drilling and sanding equipment, lathe and milling machine, as well as an automatic dust buster. Rotating the two basic ele-ments makes available the appropriate tool. Although inspired by multifunctional products, long offered in the hobby area, this workbench is more solid, somewhat larger, and specially customized for designers' needs.

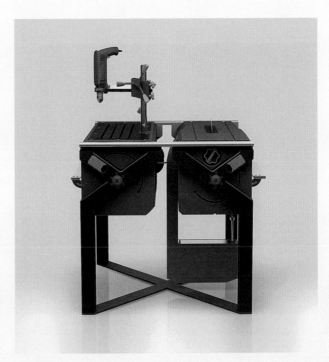

Leben und Arbeit / Life and Work

Labor / Laboratory

© Tobias Schlorhaufer

157

Kaputt.R

Konzept für einen Abrissroboter	Concept for a demolition robot
Design	Design
Florian Wille, Bernhard Ranner, Erol Kursani, Anton Weichselbraun	Florian Wille, Bernhard Ranner, Erol Kursani, Anton Weichselbraun
Entstehungsjahr	Year of origin
2008	2008

Roboter in Arbeitsfeldern einzusetzen, in denen es für den Menschen zu gefährlich oder schwierig wird – etwa, wegen Lärm- und Staubbelastung sowie vieler anderer Gefahren, bei Demolierungsarbeiten – hat eine lange Denktradition. Mit Kaputt.R wurde ein autonomer <u>Abrissroboter</u> konzipiert, der in gefährlichen Bereichen menschliche Arbeit effektiv ersetzt.

Der Roboter verfügt über zwei klappbare Arme, von denen einer stets als Gegengewicht fungiert, und vier Füße mit Raupenantrieb, die der Fortbewegung und Stabilisierung dienen. Ihre breite Verteilung sorgt auch dafür, dass die maximal mögliche Belastung des Bodens nicht erreicht wird. Für Abrissarbeiten kann eine Reihe von Werkzeugen angebracht werden, etwa Kreissäge, Pflug, Schaufel, aber auch Spezialwerkzeuge wie eine Power-Gun. Mit Letzterer lassen sich Druckwellen erzeugen, die das Gemäuer schwächen; es ist dann leicht abzutragen. Dank 3-D-Software und Sensoren navigiert der Roboter ganz ohne menschliche Aufsicht.

Using robots in a work area that is too difficult or dangerous for humans—demolition work, for example, because of noise and dust exposure as well as a number of other dangers—has a long, conceptual tradition. Kaputt.R is a design for an autonomous <u>demolition robot</u> that can effectively replace human labor power in dangerous areas.

The robot has two foldable arms, one of which always works as a counter weight, and four feet with caterpillar drive to provide forward propulsion and stability. The wide spread of the feet also assures that the maximum possible load of the base is not reached. For demolition work, a number of tools can be attached, such as chain saw, plough, shovel, and also special equipment including a power gun. The latter is able to generate pressure waves, which weaken masonry making it easier to carry away. Thanks to 3-D software and sensors, the robot navigates entirely without human control.

© Benjamin Cselley

Fit@work

Konzept für einen Trainings-Bürosessel	Concept for a training office chair
Design **Benjamin Cselley, Daniel Wyrobal, Dietmar Kolar**	Design Benjamin Cselley, Daniel Wyrobal, Dietmar Kolar
Entstehungsjahr **2010**	Year of origin 2010

Das rapide Wachstum des Dienstleistungssektors bei gleichzeitigem Schwund handwerklicher und industrieller Produktion hat die Arbeitswelt in den nördlichen Staaten grundlegend verändert: Wir sitzen, und das heute vorwiegend am Computer – die Digitale Revolution hat die Menschen endgültig an ihre Schreibtische gebunden. Verspannungen, Wirbelsäulenschäden und „Repetitive Strain Injury" sind nur einige bekannte Folgen, die das Individuum, aber auch das Gesundheitssystem belasten.

Der Bürosesselentwurf Fit@work greift diese Problematik auf und bringt das Fitnesscenter ins Büro: Seine Armlehnen lassen sich zum Rudergerät umfunktionieren, in die Lehne sind Expander für das Trainieren der Armmuskeln eingebaut. Ein Mechanismus lockert auf Wunsch die Statik des Sessels: Im „Rodeo"-Sitz muss der oder die Sitzende unter Einsatz von Rücken- und Bauchmuskeln das Gleichgewicht halten. Ein Bürosessel für die postindustrielle Arbeitswelt!

The rapid growth of the service sector with a simultaneous disappearance of handicraft and industrial production has fundamentally changed the working world in the countries of the north: we sit, and do so mainly at the computer—the digital revolution has ultimately tied people to their desks. Tension, spinal damage, and "repetitive strain," are only a few of the known consequences burdening the individual, and also the health system.

The office chair design Fit@work takes up this problem and brings the fitness center to the office: its arm rests can be converted into a rowing machine, and the backrest has built-in expanders for training arm muscles. If desired, there is a mechanism that loosens the chair's balance: in "rodeo" chair, the sitter has to use their back and stomach muscles to maintain balance: An office chair for the post-industrial working world!

Labor /
Laboratory

Leben und Arbeit /
Life and Work

159

Life NAVI

Konzept für Life
Management Software

Design
**Maria Gartner, Alexander
Wurnig, Marko Doblanovic,
Boris Stanimirovic**

Entstehungsjahr
2010

Concept for life
management software

Design
Maria Gartner, Alexander
Wurnig, Marko Doblanovic,
Boris Stanimirovic

Year of origin
2010

Zeitmanagement ist in der Leistungsgesellschaft essenziell. Der Imperativ zur Selbstoptimierung gilt längst nicht mehr nur im Bereich der Erwerbsarbeit, sondern auch in Alltag und Freizeit. Angesichts wachsender To-do-Listen verliert man allerdings leicht den Überblick, verzettelt sich, bleibt in gewohnten Mustern stecken. Live NAVI, eine Life-Management-Software für Mobilgeräte und Computer, will hier Abhilfe schaffen.

Grundlage von Life NAVI ist ein einfaches Interface mit Zeitleiste und klaren Farbcodes, auf dem alle Tätigkeiten und Termine in diversen Kategorien und mit verschiedener Priorität angelegt werden. Über einen regelmäßigen Pop-up-Dialog bewahrt man die Kontrolle, ob die Tagesplanung eingehalten wird; mit wenigen Schritten können Aktivitäten auch umorganisiert und direkt Entschuldigungs-E-Mails gesendet werden. Statistikfunktionen liefern schließlich Feedback darüber, ob und wie man es geschafft hat, sein Zeitmanagement zu verbessern oder auch nicht!

Time management is essential in performance-oriented society. The imperative of self-optimization has long moved beyond the area of gainful employment and become relevant for everyday life and leisure time. Yet faced with growing "to-do" lists, one easily loses sight of the big picture, becomes involved in details, and gets stuck in familiar patterns. Live NAVI, life management software for mobile devices and computers, intends to offer help in this area.

The basis of Life NAVI is a simple interface with a time panel and clear color codes on which all activities and appointments are arranged in diverse categories and with various priorities. Via a steady pop-up dialogue, one maintains control of whether the daily schedule is kept; with just a few steps, activities can be reorganized, and apology mails immediately sent. Statistic functions deliver feedback in the end, of whether and how one has successfully improved his or her time management or not!

© Maria Gartner, Alexander Wurnig, Marko Doblanovic, Boris Stanimirovic

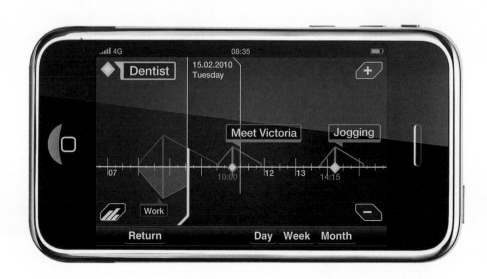

Eneloop Solar Charger

Solar-Ladegerät	Solar charger
Design **GK Design Group**	Design GK Design Group
Hersteller **Sanyo**	Manufacturer Sanyo
Entstehungsjahr **2006**	Year of origin 2006

Angesichts der unzähligen Gadgets in unserer Wohn- und Arbeitswelt sind wiederaufladbare Batterien zum Standard geworden. 2005 kam mit der Eneloop von Sanyo eine Batterie auf den Markt, die sich bis zu tausendmal aufladen lässt. Auch ihre Produktsprache war neu: Statt mit gewohnt maskuliner Power-Hardware-Ästhetik traten die neuen Batterien in Weiß und in Verpackungen auf, die an jene von Hygieneprodukten erinnern.

Mit dem Ladegerät Solar Charger, das wie eine Materialisierung der Idee von „sauberer Energie" anmutet, wird diese Ästhetik weitergeschrieben. Er kann Batterien mit Solarenergie aufladen. Die Form einer asymmetrischen Pyramide erlaubt es, ihn je nach Einfallswinkel der Sonne zu positionieren. Das Produkt, das dem Konsumverständnis der viel zitierten „LoHaS" mit ihrem „Lifestyle of Health and Sustainability" perfekt entspricht, weist einmal mehr darauf hin, dass die Tage der herkömmlichen Batterie, die in Nullkommanichts zu Sondermüll wird, wohl ebenso gezählt sind wie jene der Edison-Glühbirne.

In view of the countless gadgets in our home and working worlds, rechargeable batteries have become the standard. In 2005, Eneloop by Sanyo was brought onto the market, a battery that can be recharged up to 1,000 times. Its product language was also new: rather than masculine, power-hardware aesthetics, the new batteries appeared in white, with packaging that brought to mind hygiene products.

These aesthetics are continued by Solar Charger, which looks like a materialization of the "clean energy" idea. What it does is charge batteries with solar power. Its form, an asymmetrical pyramid, allows it to take its position based on the sun's angle of incidence. The product, which perfectly corresponds with the consumption philosophy of the oft-cited "LoHaS," that is, "Lifestyle of Health and Sustainability," once again shows that similar to the Edison light bulb, the days of the common battery, which becomes hazardous waste in less than a second, are numbered.

© GK Design Group

Leben und Arbeit / Life and Work

Fabrik / Factory

Tunable White LED

Steuerbares LED-Licht	Tunable LED light
Design **Zumtobel Lighting**	Design Zumtobel Lighting
Hersteller **Zumtobel Licht GmbH**	Manufacturer Zumtobel Licht GmbH
Entstehungsjahr **2012**	Year of origin 2012

Auch wenn es uns kaum bewusst ist: Im Verlauf eines Tages verändert sich nicht nur der Helligkeitsgrad von Licht, sondern auch der Farbeindruck, den es erzeugt. Das Warmweiß eines Sonnenaufgangs in freier Natur sorgt für angenehme Stimmung, intensives Tageslichtweiß macht wach und erhöht die Aufmerksamkeit. Tunable White ist eine Lösung für LED (light-emitting diodes – Leuchtdioden), mit der sich auf Knopfdruck unterschiedliche <u>Lichtfarben und -intensitäten</u> erzeugen lassen.

In Verkauf und Präsentation können damit beispielsweise bestimmte Materialien, Farben und Oberflächen zu optimaler Wirkung gebracht werden. In fensterlosen Besprechungsräumen lässt sich der Ermüdung durch Nachempfindung des natürlichen Tageslichtverlaufs entgegenwirken. Kunstwerke und andere lichtempfindliche Objekte werden schonend beleuchtet, und auch im Privaten kann man je nach Bedürfnis Feierabendstimmung oder Arbeitsatmosphäre herstellen. Tunable White macht Lichtwirkung bewusst und ultimativ verfügbar.

Although we hardly recognize it, over the course of a day, light changes not only its degree of brightness, but also the color impression it creates. The warm white of sunrise in open nature provides an agreeable atmosphere, daylight's intensive white keeps us awake and makes us more attentive. Tunable White is a solution for LED (light-emitting diodes), enabling the generation of different <u>light colors and intensities</u> at the touch of a button.

For sales and presentation, for instance, the optimal effect can be generated by certain materials, colors, and surfaces. In windowless conference rooms, fatigue can be counteracted by recreating natural daylight. Artworks and other light-sensitive objects can be illuminated without damage, and in private, one can produce a relaxing mood or work atmosphere, as desired. Tunable White makes the effect of light deliberate, and provides ultimate availability.

Leben und Arbeit /
Life and Work

Fabrik /
Factory

© Zumtobel

WMF 1

Kaffeepadmaschine	Coffee pad machine
Design **designaffairs**	Design designaffairs
Hersteller **WMF**	Manufacturer WMF
Entstehungsjahr **2007**	Year of origin 2007

Als kleinste Kaffeepadmaschine der Welt ist die WMF 1 für exakt eine Tasse gemacht – und zwar für eine ganz spezielle: Der zugehörige Henkelbecher dient nicht nur als Trinkgeschirr, sondern ist fester Bestandteil der Funktion wie auch des Designs. Die passgenaue Aussparung für den Becher an der Front des Geräts wirkt wie ein großformatiges Icon, das „Kaffeepause!" ruft.

Das Bedienkonzept der WMF 1 ist radikal reduziert: Eine Tasse Wasser und ein Kaffeepad ergeben per Knopfdruck eine Tasse Kaffee. Mit der Mini-Maschine ist ein schlichtes, funktionales Produkt gelungen, das auf dem besten Weg ist, zur Design-Ikone zu werden. Das ultimative Gerät für Singles – eine stark anwachsende Bevölkerungsgruppe – folgt darüber hinaus dem Prinzip des „Inclusive Design", des Designs für alle: Ob zu Hause oder im Büro, ob von Jung oder Alt lässt sich die WMF 1 überall betreiben, wo es Wasser und eine Steckdose gibt.

The WMF 1 is the world's smallest coffee pad machine, made for exactly one cup—but one very special cup indeed: the accompanying mug serves not only as drink ware, but is also an integrated component of function and design. The customized gap for the cup at the front of the device looks like a large-format icon calling out „coffee break!"

WMF 1's operating concept is radically minimized: one cup of water and a coffee pad produce a cup of coffee at the press of a button. The mini machine has had great success as a simple, functional product and is on the best course to becoming a design icon. The ultimate device for singles—a quickly growing population group—also follows the principle of "inclusive design," the design for all: whether at home or in the office, young or old, the WMF 1 can be operated anywhere where there's water and somewhere to plug in.

Leben und Arbeit / Life and Work

Fabrik / Factory

© WMF

OXO Good Grips

Ergonomische Hand-Küchengeräte	Ergonomic kitchen utensils
Design **Smart Design**	Design Smart Design
Hersteller **OXO International**	Manufacturer OXO International
Entstehungsjahre **1990–2012**	Years of origin 1990–2012

Bei den täglichen Arbeiten in Küche und Haushalt ist ergonomisch gestaltetes funktionales Werkzeug ein Segen – und nicht zuletzt ein Beitrag zur Gesundheitsvorsorge. Das dachte sich auch der Haushaltswarenfabrikant Sam Farber, der nicht einsah, warum seine Frau von der Benutzung einfacher <u>Hand-Küchengeräte</u> Schmerzen in den Händen erleiden sollte. Also wandte er sich an eine Designagentur, eine Gerontologin wurde hinzugezogen, und nach eingehender Forschung und Entwicklung kamen 1990 schließlich die ersten OXO-Küchengeräte auf den US-Markt.

Ihr Griff aus Santopren – einem dem Naturgummi sehr ähnlichen Material – ist so gegossen, dass er an bestimmten Stellen stärker nachgibt und damit Ermüdungserscheinungen und Druckstellen deutlich entgegenwirkt. Die Serie OXO Good Grips basiert auf der Idee des „Inclusive Design", das Produkte für eine möglichst weit gefächerte Gruppe von NutzerInnen entwickelt: für Jung wie Alt, Männer wie Frauen, Rechts- wie LinkshänderInnen, Gesunde wie Menschen mit speziellen Bedürfnissen, etwa ArthritispatientInnen. Auf dieser Grundlage entsteht größtmöglicher Gebrauchskomfort für alle.

For daily work in the kitchen, ergonomically designed, functional tools are a blessing—and, no least, a preventative health measure. The household goods producer Sam Farber, who did not understand why his wife should suffer pain in her hands from the use of simple <u>kitchen utensils</u>, thought this, too. So he turned to a design agency, a gerontologist was brought in, and after intense research and development, the first OXO kitchen products were ultimately introduced to the U.S. market in 1990.

Their grips of santoprene—a material quite similar to natural rubber—are produced in such a way that they stretch more in certain places and thereby clearly counteract signs of fatigue and pressure points. The OXO Good Grips series is based on the idea of "inclusive design," which develops products for an extremely widespread group of users: for young and old, men and women, right-handed and left-handed people, healthy people, as well as those with special needs, such as arthritis patients. This provides a basis for the greatest possible use-comfort for all.

Leben und Arbeit / Life and Work

Fabrik / Factory

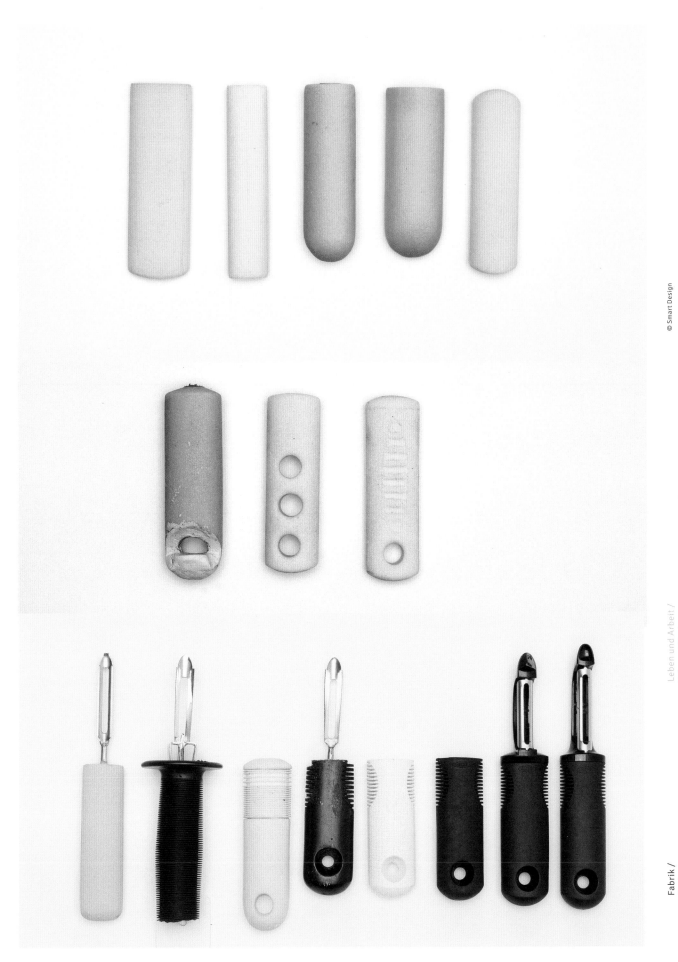

© Smart Design

Leben und Arbeit /
Life and Work

Fabrik /
Factory

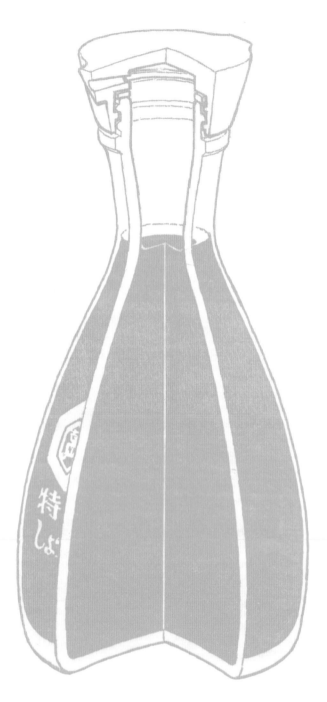

Kikkoman Dispenser

Tischflasche **für Sojasauce**	Dispenser for soy sauce
Design **Kenji Ekuan,** **GK Design Group**	Design Kenji Ekuan, GK Design Group
Hersteller **Kikkoman**	Manufacturer Kikkoman
Entstehungsjahr **1961**	Year of origin 1961

Hierzulande erst durch den Boom asiatischer Gastronomie bekannt geworden, feierte sie im vergangenen Jahr bereits ihren Fünfziger: die Tischflasche für Sojasauce von Kikkoman des Designers Kenji Ekuan von 1961, die weltweit als beispielgebend für gutes Design gilt. Mit ihr kam das Grundnahrungsmittel Sojasauce in einer modernen, benutzerfreundlichen und vor allem „gebrandeten" Flasche direkt auf den Tisch. Sie wurde ein Markterfolg sondergleichen – und nicht zuletzt eine Ikone, die dem Design mit Ablaufdatum bis heute beharrlich trotzt.

Die schlichte, geschwungene Form orientiert sich bei aller Modernität an archetypischen, kulturell verinnerlichten Vorbildern – sie ist an traditionelle Karaffen für Sake angelehnt. Insbesondere auf die funktionale Gestaltung des Ausgusses wurde viel Sorgfalt verwendet: Bis das Ausgießen optimal funktionierte und der Spender nicht mehr nachtropfte, wurden hunderte Arbeitsmodelle hergestellt. So entstand eine formvollendete Verpackung, die für ein „Refill" konzipiert wurde.

Although it first became well known in these parts through the boom of Asian restaurants, it already celebrated its fiftieth anniversary last year: Kikkoman's soy sauce dispenser designed by Kenji Ekuan in 1961, considered exemplary for good design worldwide. It brought soy sauce, a basic food item, from the producer directly onto the table—in a modern, user-friendly and, most importantly, „branded" bottle. The Kikkoman bottle also represents market success beyond compare and an icon that persistently defies design with a "sell-by" date.

Despite all of its modern attributes, the simple, curved form is oriented on archetypical, culturally internalized role models—it borrows from traditional cruets for Sake. Particular care was taken in the functional design of the spout: hundreds of working models were made until the pouring was optimized and the dispenser no longer dripped. In this way, created was a perfect packaging form that is also suitable for refilling.

© GK Design Group

Leben und Arbeit /
Life and Work

Fabrik /
Factory

Dyson Ball DC36

Staubsauger	Vacuum cleaner
Design	Design
James Dyson	James Dyson
Hersteller	Manufacturer
Dyson	Dyson
Entstehungsjahr	Year of origin
2012	2012

Bald 20 Jahre ist es nun her, dass James Dyson mit der Erfindung der Cyclone-Technologie die Funktionsweise und das Aussehen von <u>Staubsaugern</u> revolutionierte: Die Dyson-Geräte arbeiteten seither ohne Staubbeutel und nahmen mit konstanter Saugkraft sogar kleinste Staubpartikel und Allergene auf. Formgebung und Design folgten dem Prinzip der transparenten Inszenierung von Technik und nicht, wie üblich, ihrem Verbergen in einem Gehäuse.

Für die neueste Dyson-Staubsaugergeneration, „Ball" genannt, setzte man sich vor allem mit der Manövrierbarkeit auseinander: Bis er seine präzise Lenkbarkeit gefunden hatte, wurden mehr als 500 Prototypen entwickelt. Dank seines niedrigen Schwerpunkts und des namensgebenden Balles anstelle von Rädern lässt sich das Gerät einfach um enge Kurven und Möbel lenken. Darüber hinaus erleichtert sein zentraler Lenkmechanismus das Nachziehen erheblich. Der kleine, kompakte und im Verbrauch sparsame Ball DC36 wurde explizit für Kleinwohnungen und ältere Menschen entwickelt – er reagiert damit auf die Transformation urbanen Wohnens ebenso wie auf die Bedürfnisse einer immer älter werdenden Bevölkerung.

It was almost twenty years ago that James Dyson revolutionized the functional principle and appearance of <u>vacuum cleaners</u> with the invention of Cyclone technology: until now, Dyson devices have worked without dust bags and have gathered even the smallest dust particles and allergens with their constant sucking power. Their form and design pursued the principle of transparent staging of technology and not, as usual, concealing it in casing.

In the latest generation of Dyson vacuum cleaners, "Ball," maneuverability becomes the key feature: more than 500 prototypes were created until precise tractability was achieved. Thanks to its low center of gravity and a ball, which gave it its name, rather than wheels, the device can steer easily around narrow curves and furniture. In addition, its central steering mechanism makes it a lot simpler to pull. The small, compact, and efficient Ball DC36 was developed explicitly for small apartments and the elderly—thus reacting to the transformation in urban living as well as the needs of an aging population.

Leben und Arbeit /
Life and Work

Fabrik /
Factory

© Dyson

Leben und Arbeit /
Life and Work

Fabrik /
Factory

© Bene AG

Leben und Arbeit /
Life and Work

Fabrik /
Factory

PARCS

Büromöbel	Office furniture
Design **PearsonLloyd**	Design PearsonLloyd
Hersteller **Bene**	Manufacturer Bene
Entstehungsjahr **2009**	Year of origin 2009

In unserer wissensbasierten Gesellschaft (Knowledge Economy) arbeiten wir zusehends in einem Umfeld, in dem wir flexibel denken und agieren, dabei kommunikativ und teamfähig sein müssen. Zurückgezogenes konzentriertes Arbeiten ist ebenso erforderlich wie fluider kommunikativer Austausch. Den Rahmen hierfür kann herkömmliche Büroinnenarchitektur oftmals nicht bieten. Die modularen und offenen PARCS <u>Büromöbel</u> wurde nach einem umfassenden Research unter WissensarbeiterInnen speziell für die Anforderungen ihres Arbeitsalltags gestaltet.

Die PARCS Causeways beispielsweise animieren zu legeren Meetings im Sitzen, Stehen oder Lehnen, der „Ohrensessel" Wing Chair schirmt akustisch und visuell ab und erleichtert dadurch fokussiertes Arbeiten. Ein markantes Möbel ist die Toguna – ein Mini-Besprechungsraum für kurze Meetings, dessen Name einem westafrikanischen Versammlungsort entlehnt wurde. Die Idea Wall dient als Medienwand für Präsentationen und zugleich als „Raumteiler".

In our knowledge economy, we work increasingly in an environment in which we think and act flexibly, and in this, must be communicative and team players. Secluded, concentrated work is demanded just as much as fluid, communicative exchange. Standard interior office design is often unable to offer a framework for this. The modular and open PARCS <u>office furniture</u> has been designed based on comprehensive research on knowledge workers, especially for the demands of their everyday work.

PARCS Causeways, for example, encourage casual meetings while sitting, standing, or leaning. The "Ohrensessel" Wing Chair provides a shield, visually and acoustically, and thereby facilitates concentrated work. Toguna is a remarkable piece of furniture, a mini conference space for short meetings whose name was borrowed from a West African meeting place. The Idea Wall serves as a media wall for presentations and, at the same time, as a partition.

Leben und Arbeit / Life and Work

Fabrik / Factory

Sayl Chair

Bürostuhl	Office chair
Design	Design
Yves Béhar, fuseproject	Yves Béhar, fuseproject
Hersteller	Manufacturer
Herman Miller	Herman Miller
Entstehungsjahr	Year of origin
2010	2010

Bei der Konstruktion des Sayl-Bürostuhls stand das Prinzip der Hängebrücke Pate. Die Kunststofflehne kommt ohne Rahmen aus; als Segel zwischen den Sitz und eine Y-förmige Mastkonstruktion gespannt, gibt sie Halt, ist aber gleichzeitig flexibel und sorgt dank ihrer netzartigen Textur für Belüftung.

Die Designaufgabe für den Sayl lautete, einen leistbaren Bürostuhl zu entwerfen, der in Sachen Qualität jedoch den hohen Anforderungen des als Ergonomie-Spezialist bekannten Herstellers entspricht. Durch einen Entwurf, der nicht nur mit wenigen Materialien – und damit einer geringen Zahl an separat zu produzierenden Teilen –, sondern auch einer kleinen Menge derselben auskommt, ließen sich die Produktionskosten ebenso wie die CO$_2$-Bilanz gering halten. Bemerkenswert sind die zahlreichen Möglichkeiten der Individualisierung, die Sayl mit verstellbarer Sitzneigung, Sitztiefe und Sitzhöhe bietet. Selten hat ein ergonomisch gestalteter Arbeitsstuhl so viel Spaß gemacht!

Construction of the Sayl office was inspired by the suspension bridge. The plastic back is frameless; stretched as a sail between seat and Y-shaped mast construction, it provides support but at the same time is flexible and thanks to its net-like texture, offers ventilation.

The challenge presented by Sayl was to draft an affordable office chair that nonetheless meets with the high quality demands of the manufacturer, highly regarded as an ergonomics specialist. By means of a design that makes do with little material, a low number of separately produced parts, as well as a low amount of the same, it was possible to keep both production costs and carbon-dioxide emissions to a minimum. Remarkable are the numerous possibilities for individualization offered by Sayl with its adjustable seating angle, depth, and height. Ergonomically-designed office chairs are rarely so much fun!

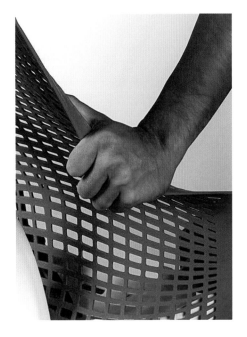

© fuseproject

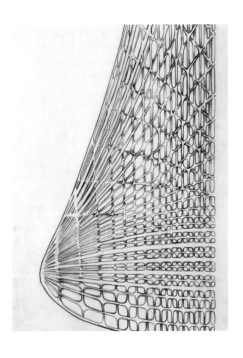

Yves Béhar mit Funktionsmodell

Yves Béhar with functional model

Leben und Arbeit /
Life and Work

Fabrik /
Factory

173

Staxo 40

Gerüstsystem	Shoring system
Design **Doka**	Design Doka
Hersteller **Doka**	Manufacturer Doka
Entstehungsjahr **2010**	Year of origin 2010

Die Bauindustrie steht unter großem Zeit- und Kostendruck, angesichts komplexer werdender Baukörper aber auch vor der Herausforderung, entsprechende Traggerüste zu entwickeln. Mit Staxo 40 liegt ein leichtes Traggerüst zur Unterstellung von Betonschalungen für den Hochbau vor. Patentiertes Kernelement des innovativen Industrieprodukts sind H-Rahmen aus Stahl, die mit Diagonalkreuzen ausgesteift und mit Kupplungsstücken sowie Rohrsteckern erweitert werden. Die durchdachte Konstruktion macht eine Reduktion der Einzelteile gegenüber herkömmlichen Systemen um 40 Prozent möglich. Daraus resultieren entsprechende Gewichts- und Ressourceneinsparungen sowie vereinfachte Montage.

Bei dem Gerüstsystem, das auch auf Basis einer eingehenden Analyse der Abläufe und Erfordernisse auf der Baustelle entwickelt wurde, legte man besonderes Augenmerk auf die Sicherheit. Vollflächige und durchgängige Montageebenen, stabile Leiteraufstiege und Konsolen gewährleisten sicheres Arbeiten; mit 40 Anschlagpunkten für Schutzausrüstungen und Geländer lassen sich zusätzliche Vorkehrungen gegen Absturz treffen.

The construction industry is under extreme time and cost pressure in the face of ever more complex building volumes, but also the challenge of developing corresponding shoring towers. Staxo 40 presents a lightweight shoring tower for bracing concrete formwork for high rise construction. Patented core element of this innovative industrial product are steel H-frames, reinforced with diagonal cross braces and expanded by coupling pieces and pipe fittings. The carefully conceived construction enables a 40 percent reduction of individual parts as compared with conventional systems. This leads to savings in terms of weight and resources, and simplified assembly.

The shoring system, which was developed based on a detailed analysis of events and demands on the construction site, pays special attention to safety. Safe working conditions are guaranteed by gapless and continuous assembly decks and sturdy ladderways and consoles; forty anchorage points for safety equipment and railings also make it possible to take additional precautions against accidents.

Leben und Arbeit /
Life and Work

Fabrik /
Factory

© Doka

Leben und Arbeit /
Life and Work

Fabrik /
Factory

MADE 4 YOU

Gesundheit / Health

Wie schaffen wir Gesundheitssysteme für alle?

Medizinische Wissenschaft und Forschung haben in Verbindung mit neuen Technologien die Produkte im Gesundheitswesen revolutioniert. So führte die Computersimulation bionischer Prinzipien zur Entwicklung neuartiger Prothesen; mobile, digitale und mit Sensorik ausgestattete Geräte erlauben die Therapie zu Hause und emanzipieren PatientInnen von der Klinik; Avatare (virtuelle Personen) leiten per Bildschirm bei der Rehabilitation oder bei Fitnessübungen an. Neben der Verbesserung der medizinischen Versorgung stehen bei der Entwicklung neuer Produkte zusehends die ökonomischen, ökologischen und sozialen Komponenten des Gesundheitssystems im Blick. Im Sinne einer patientenzentrierten Medizin haben technische und Design-Innovationen daher zum Ziel, den spezifischen Bedürfnissen unterschiedlicher Gruppen – sei es die rapide steigende Zahl älterer Menschen, seien es Menschen mit Behinderungen verschiedenster Art – gerecht zu werden. Das bedeutet für DesignerInnen, dass sie sich mit diesen Bedürfnissen intensiv auseinandersetzen müssen. Bei der Gestaltung der Produkte stehen aber auch Prävention, Vorsorge und nicht zuletzt der Erhalt von möglichst viel Lebensqualität, auch in der Krankheit, im Fokus.

How can we create
health care systems
for all?

In connection with new technologies, medical science and research have revolutionized products in the healthcare field. Computer simulation of bionic principles, for example, has led to the development of new types of prostheses; mobile, digital devices furnished with sensorics that allow therapy at home, thereby liberating patients from the clinic. Avatars (virtual people) provide onscreen instructions for rehab and fitness exercises. The development of new products increasingly has in view economic, ecological, and social components of the health system, in addition to improvements in medical care. In line with patient-centered medicine, technological and design innovations thereby aim to cope with the specific needs of various groups—whether the rapidly growing number of senior citizens or people with various types of handicaps. The consequence for designers is that they must grapple intensely with these needs. But in the design of products, focus is also on prevention, care, and no least, the preservation of the best quality of life possible, even when ill.

MADE 4 YOU

Hans Prihoda
Geschäftsführer der Lasergruppe Material-
bearbeitungsges.m.b.H. /
CEO of Lasergruppe Materialbearbeitungsges.m.b.H.

3-D-Rapid Prototyping – Technik im Dienste des Patienten

3-D Rapid Prototyping – Technology in the Service of the Patient

Zufälligkeiten sind unberechenbare Größen, die in der Wissenschaft nicht selten zu Entdeckungen und neuen Erkenntnissen führen. Wie sich aus der Begegnung eines Physikers und eines Mediziners zeit- und kosteneffiziente Wege für die Diagnostik und Vorbereitung plastisch-chirurgischer Operationen ergaben, zeigt ein Gespräch von Thomas Geisler, MAK-Kustode Design, mit Hans Prihoda, Geschäftsführer der Lasergruppe Materialbearbeitungsges.m.b.H.

M 4 Y: Womit beschäftigt sich die Lasergruppe?
Hans Prihoda: Seit mehr als 40 Jahren ist die Firma Lasergruppe Materialbearbeitungsges.m.b.H. im Bereich Modellbau und Rapid Prototyping tätig. In Weiterentwicklung unserer Produkte stießen wir vor zwei Jahrzehnten auf die Lasertechnik und begannen, mit dem gebündelten Laserlicht Materialien zu bearbeiten. Die mehr als fünfjährige Entwicklungsarbeit brachte uns zur Bearbeitung von Kunststoffen mittels Lasertechnik. Eine eigens entwickelte Lasermaschine machte es möglich, Kunststoffteile im Zehntel-Millimeter-Bereich hochpräzise zu fertigen und damit eine neue Qualitätsära im technischen Rapid Prototyping einzuleiten.

Wie kam es zur Anwendung Ihrer Technologie im medizinischen Bereich?
Anlässlich eines Besuches in unserer Fertigungstechnik erwähnte ein befreundeter Arzt, wie hilfreich eine hochpräzise Rapid-Prototyping-Darstellung des Knochenskeletts für Medizindiagnostik und Operationsvorbereitung wäre. Dies gab den Ausschlag, sich intensiver mit der Datenstruktur von Röntgenbildern zu befassen. Rasch stellte sich heraus, dass mit den Daten von 2-D-Röntgenbildern keine 3-D-Darstellung möglich ist. Damals, im Jahr 1992, kamen gerade die ersten medizinischen Computertomografen im Wiener Allgemeinen Krankenhaus (AKH) zum Einsatz. Die 3-D-Daten, die sie lieferten, waren für uns jedoch vorerst nicht lesbar.

Coincidences are unknown quantities, which, in science, frequently lead to discoveries and new knowledge. How an encounter between a physicist and a physician led to cost-efficient methods of diagnosis and of preparation for plastic surgery procedures was the topic of a discussion between Thomas Geisler, MAK Curator, Design, and Hans Prihoda, CEO of Lasergruppe Materialbearbeitungsges.m.b.H.

M 4 Y: What is Lasergruppe's field of activity?
Hans Prihoda: Lasergruppe Materialbearbeitungsges.m.b.H. has been working in model construction and rapid prototyping for over 40 years now. Two decades ago, in the context of our own product development activities, we came across laser technology and began working on materials using beams of concentrated laser light. Subsequent research and development lasting over five years brought us to the point where we were using laser technologies to process plastics. A laser unit developed specifically for this purpose gave us the ability to produce plastic parts with a precision of a tenth of a millimeter, and this ushered in a new era of quality in technical rapid prototyping.

How did your technology find its way into the medical field?
On a visit to our production engineering department, a doctor friend of mine mentioned how helpful he thought highly precise 3-D prints of the human skeleton could be in medical diagnosis and surgery preparation. His comment was the impetus for us to begin looking more closely at the data structure of X-ray images. It instantly became evident to us that we could not do 3-D printing based on the data contained in 2-dimensional X-ray images. At that time, in 1992, Vienna General Hospital had just begun using its first medical computed tomography (CT) scanners. At first, however, we were unable to read the 3-D data that they provided.

What was new about what you developed?
Many years of experimentation and analysis conducted together with CT engineers eventually led to success in finding an interface on the unit which, in combination with implementation software that we then developed, was able to

181

Was war an Ihrer Entwicklung neuartig?

In langjährigen Versuchen und Analysen mit den Technikern der Computertomografen fanden wir gemeinsam eine Schnittstelle am Gerät, die mittels eines von uns entwickelten Umsetzungsprogrammes erstmals für uns lesbare 3-D-Medizindaten lieferte. Um menschliche Skelettteile in 3-D-Modellen darzustellen, mussten wir aber noch Bearbeitungsprogramme für diese Daten entwerfen. Allerdings lieferten die Computertomografen damals noch Bilder in groben Auflösungen (fünf Millimeter Schichtabstand) – trotz des hohen Interpolieraufwandes war daher nur eine sehr ungenaue 3-D-Darstellung möglich.

Wie entwickelte sich Ihre Forschungsarbeit angesichts der Fortschritte in der Medizin?

Die nächsten Generationen der Computertomografen mit einer Auflösung von weniger als einem Millimeter gaben uns die Möglichkeit, Knochendarstellungen mit einer Genauigkeit im Zehntel-Millimeter-Bereich durchzuführen. Die Universitätsklinik für Mund-, Kiefer- und Gesichtschirurgie sowie die Abteilung für Osteologie an der Universitätsklinik für Radiodiagnostik haben während der gesamten Entwicklungsphase sehr eng mit uns zusammengearbeitet: In beiden Instituten hatte man erkannt, welche wesentlichen Vorteile sich aus der Fertigung von begreifbaren und präzisen medizinischen 3-D-Modellen ergaben.

Wo findet Ihre Technologie praktische Anwendung, und welchen Nutzen haben Patienten und Gesundheitswesen?

Diese Modelle eignen sich hervorragend zur Unterstützung der Diagnostik, zur Operationsplanung und insbesondere für das Einpassen notwendiger Implantate: Da das vorhandene chirurgische Instrumentarium voll einsetzbar ist, wird hier zunächst das Modell „operiert"; speziell bei Tumorerkrankungen werden notwendige Knochenentfernungen durchgeführt und Metallimplantate im Modell eingesetzt. Damit lässt sich jeder Schritt ohne Beanspruchung des Patienten im voraus durchführen und die Operationstechnik festlegen. Bei der Operation am Patienten dient das Modell als wichtige Informationsquelle, es verkürzt die Operationszeit um bis zu 50 Prozent. Dadurch reduzieren sich auch die Kosten für den Leistungsträger.

In welche Richtung geht Ihre angewandte Forschungsarbeit zurzeit?

Diese Technik hat sich in der klinischen Anwendung sehr bewährt, und es wurde rasch der Ruf nach einer Darstellung der Gefäße laut. Nach einer entsprechenden Entwicklungsphase war es uns möglich, kontrastierte Gefäße über den Computertomografen darzustellen und auch hier die mathematischen Werte in 3-D-Modelle umzusetzen. Um bessere Information zu liefern, entwickelten wir ein Verfahren, das es erlaubt, eine zweite Kontrastfarbe für die Darstellung zu wählen. Damit können am Modell entweder der Tumor oder die Gefäße in dieser zweiten Farbe sichtbar gemacht werden. In einem nächsten Entwicklungsschritt nahmen wir die Weichteildarstellung über dem Knochenskelett in Angriff. Dies bringt sowohl dem Arzt als auch dem Patienten große Vorteile: Durch „Überstülpen" der Weichteilmaske über das vorhandene Knochenskelett kann man bereits vor der Operation erkennen, wie sich das Aussehen verändern wird. Nötigenfalls lassen sich entsprechende Anpassungsmaßnahmen vornehmen.

give us our first-ever readable 3-D medical data. But in order to show parts of the human skeleton as 3-D models, we first had to write other software that would process this data. The CT scanners available at the time were still putting out fairly low-resolution images (as in: five-millimeter slice intervals), so it was only possible to produce a very imprecise 3-D print even after having done a lot of interpolation.

How has your research work progressed in the context of medical advances since then?

The next generation of CT scanners featured sub-millimeter measurement resolutions, and that gave us the ability to image bones with tolerances down to tenths of millimeters. Both the Department of Cranio-Maxillofacial and Oral Surgery and the Osteology Division of the Department of Radiology at Vienna General Hospital worked together with us very closely during the entire development process—both institutions recognized the substantial advantages to be had from the ability to produce comprehensible and precise medical 3-D models.

What are the practical applications of your technology, and what benefits does it provide to patients and to the healthcare system in general?

These models are ideally suited to playing a supporting role in the diagnostic process and in the planning of surgical procedures, especially in cases where necessary implants need to be fitted: since the complete range of existing surgical instruments can be fully employed, the entire "surgery" is first done on the model; in cases where tumors are involved, the necessary removal of bone tissue is done and metal implants are fitted. This allows every single step to be performed ahead of time and the surgical technique to be determined, all without causing stress to the patient. And when it comes time to operate on the patient, the model serves as an important source of information, thanks to which the length of the procedure can be reduced by up to 50 percent. This also reduces the cost to the insurer.

What direction is your applied research work currently taking?

Since this technology proved itself very well in clinical applications, there were soon calls for a way to image arteries. Consequently, following a corresponding development phase, we were able to image contrast-enhanced arteries using a CT scanner—and here, as well, to translate the mathematical values thus collected into 3-D models. In order to provide better information, we developed a process that allows a second contrasting color to be chosen and used in the image. This second color can be used to make either the tumor or the arteries more clearly visible. In the next stage of development, we set about finding a way to image the soft tissue overlying the skeleton. This provides great advantages for both doctors and patients: by "sliding" the soft tissue mask over the preexisting skeleton, it is possible to see how the outward appearance will change, prior to actually doing the surgery. As a result, any necessary adaptations can be made ahead of time.

Wie sehen Sie Ihre Arbeit im Kontext dieser Ausstellung?
**Diese Entwicklung bietet ein sehr gelungenes Beispiel
dafür, wie sich Technik zum Wohle des Menschen einsetzen
lässt. Insbesondere bei schweren Erkrankungen werden
Diagnostik, Operationsvorbereitung und Anpassung eines
Implantats deutlich erleichtert. Und das 3-D-Modell macht
es möglich, das Aussehen bereits vor der Operation zu
bestimmen.**

How do you view your work in the context of this exhibition?
Our development represents a highly successful example of
how technology can be used to the benefit of human beings.
Especially in cases of serious illness, it makes diagnosis, surgery prep and implant adaptation considerably easier. And
the 3-D model also makes it possible to determine how the
patient will look afterwards before the surgery takes place.

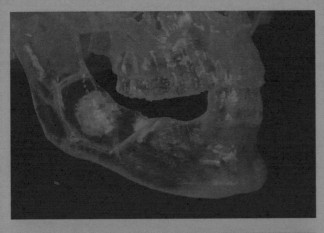

← Ein vom Tumor zersetzter
menschlicher Unterkiefer

A human mandible (lower jaw)
disintegrated by a tumor

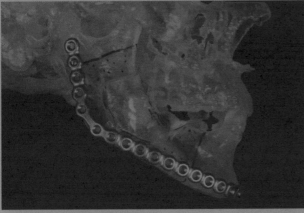

← Anpassung der vorübergehenden
Fixierung des Kiefers zur Einheilung

Adjustment of the temporary jaw
restraint for healing

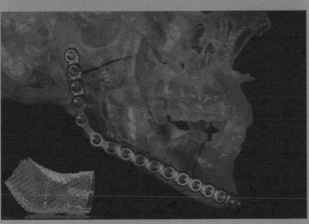

← Der Kiefer mit Eigenknochen-
formtäschchen und Anpassung der
vorübergehenden Fixierung zur
Einheilung

Jaw with autologous bone graft cage,
adjustment of temporary restraint for
the healing phase

© Lasergruppe GmbH

Gesundheit /
Health

Mobilysis

© Maria Gartner, Dimitar Genov, Stefan Silberfeld, Nico Strobl

Konzept für ein mobiles Dialysegerät	Concept for a mobile dialysis device
Design **Maria Gartner, Dimitar Genov, Stefan Silberfeld, Nico Strobl**	Design Maria Gartner, Dimitar Genov, Stefan Silberfeld, Nico Strobl
Entstehungsjahr **2011**	Year of origin 2011
Österreichischer Staatspreis Design 2011 (Sonderpreis Design Concepts)	Austrian National Design Award 2011 (Special prize, Design Concepts)

DialysepatientInnen verbringen viele Stunden ihres Lebens in Krankenhäusern und Gesundheitseinrichtungen, die nicht selten überlastet sind. Mobilysis ist der Entwurf für ein mobiles System zur Bauchfelldialyse, das es Menschen mit Nierenversagen erlaubt, die notwendige Blutreinigung zu Hause oder an jedem anderen Ort vorzunehmen. Vereinfacht gesagt wird bei der Dialyse eine Reinigungsflüssigkeit in die Bauchhöhle eingeführt, sie bindet vor allem schädlichen Harnstoff und wird dann außerhalb für den nächsten Zyklus gereinigt.

Mobilysis ist gegenüber stationären Geräten verblüffend handlich konzipiert: Die Reinigungsflüssigkeit wird im Gürtel gleichmäßig gespeichert, alle Technikkomponenten sind in vorderseitigen Kunststoffkapseln untergebracht. Bedient wird Mobilysis entweder durch ein Smartphone oder alternativ direkt am Gerät. Bei breitem Einsatz könnten solche mobilen Geräte nicht nur die Autonomie von PatientInnen erhöhen, sondern auch Gesundheitseinrichtungen entlasten.

Dialysis patients spend many hours of their lives in frequently overburdened hospitals and health facilities. Mobilysis is a design for a portable system for peritoneal dialysis, which allows a person with kidney failure to perform vital blood cleansing at home or elsewhere. Put simply, in dialysis, a dialyzing liquid is introduced into the abdominal cavity, which captures lethal urea and then removes it outside of the body for the next cycle.

In contrast to stationary devices, Mobilysis is conceived in an amazingly manageable way: the cleansing liquid is stored evenly along the belt, all technical components are housed in plastic capsules in the front. Mobilysis is operated either by a Smartphone or, alternatively, directly on the device. Widespread use of such mobile devices would not only increase patients' autonomy, but also provide relief for health facilities.

Labor / Laboratory   Gesundheit / Health

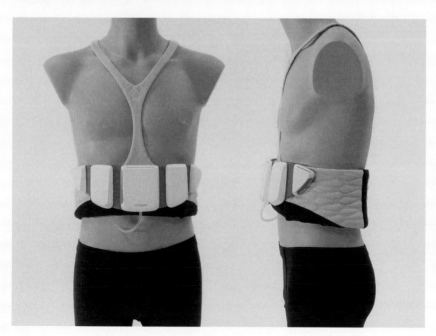

Business Arm Prosthesis

Konzept für einen **Internet-Port**	Study for an arm prosthesis
Design **Helene Steiner, Nico Strobl, Lukas Pressler, Ania Pawlowska**	Design Helene Steiner, Nico Strobl, Lukas Pressler, Ania Pawlowska
Entstehungsjahr **2010**	Year of origin 2010

Die Prothetik hat sich bis dato meist darauf konzentriert, nicht nur die Funktion natürlicher Gliedmaßen zu ersetzen, sondern meist auch deren Aussehen zu simulieren. Das Ziel: für die Betroffenen so viel „Normalität" wie möglich herzustellen. Prothesen darüber hinausgehende, technisch durchaus mögliche Funktionen zu implementieren blieb zumeist dem Science-Fiction-Genre vorbehalten.

Die Idee der Business Arm Prosthesis geht nun diesen entscheidenden Schritt weiter und der Frage nach, ob nicht gerade die vielfältigen technischen Möglichkeiten einer Prothese PatientInnen neues Selbstvertrauen und ein positives Verständnis ihrer Einzigartigkeit bringen könnten. Inspiriert vom Begriff des Cyborgs (Cybernetic Organism – ein Mischwesen aus lebendem Organismus und Maschine) integriert die Prothese alltägliche Geräte wie Smartphone, Schraubenzieher, USB-Stick und Kamera. Neue Konzepte von Lebensqualität werden damit zumindest denkbar.

Until now, prosthetics has concentrated mainly on not only replacing the function of natural limbs, but also simulating their appearance. The goal being to produce as much "normality" as possible for those affected. Implementing prostheses beyond that with entirely feasible functions usually remained reserved for science fiction.

The idea of the Business Arm Prosthesis now takes the next, decisive step and asks whether precisely these diverse, technical possibilities might give prosthetics patients renewed self-confidence and a positive understanding of their uniqueness. Inspired by the Cyborg concept (Cybernetic Organism—a hybrid of living organism and machine), the prosthesis includes integrated devices, such as a Smartphone, screwdriver, USB stick, and camera. At the least, it allows us to imagine new concepts of the quality of life.

© Helene Steiner, Nico Strobl, Lukas Pressler, Ania Pawlowska

Gesundheit /
Health

Labor /
Laboratory

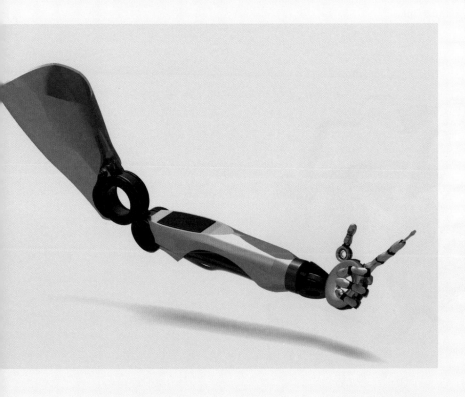

Carrier

© Julia Kaisinger, Mathias Mayrhofer, Bilge Demirci, Xiulian Benesch, Niki Iranmanesh

Konzept für einen robotischen Rollstuhl	Concept for a robotic wheelchair
Design **Julia Kaisinger, Mathias Mayrhofer, Bilge Demirci, Xiulian Benesch, Niki Iranmanesh**	Design Julia Kaisinger, Mathias Mayrhofer, Bilge Demirci, Xiulian Benesch, Niki Iranmanesh
Entstehungsjahr **2009**	Year of origin 2009
Österreichischer Staatspreis Design 2009 (Förderungspreis für Experimentelles Design)	Austrian National Design Award 2009 (Sponsorship prize for experimental design)

Welche sind die größten Probleme, mit denen sich Menschen im Rollstuhl tagtäglich konfrontiert sehen? Der Gang zur Toilette etwa, der auch zur Herausforderung werden kann, wenn Behindertentoiletten vorhanden sind. Mit einer eingehenden Analyse und Interviews mit Betroffenen gingen fünf Studierende nahezu anthropologisch an ihr Design eines verbesserten Rollstuhls heran.

Ihre Lösung für das genannte Problem: Rückwärts gefahren lässt sich der Carrier über jeder Standardtoilette platzieren, mittels Senkung der Lehnenkonstruktion wird der Sitzwechsel erleichtert. Durch Kombination von gewöhnlichem Rad und Riemenantrieb können Treppen und Hindernisse überwunden werden. Zudem ist Carrier in der Lage, die Person in eine stabile stehende Position zu heben, was nicht nur dem besseren Erreichen von Gegenständen, sondern etwa auch dem Gespräch mit Stehenden auf Augenhöhe dient. Gesellschaftliche Integration und mehr Autonomie für RollstuhlfahrerInnen sind wichtige Ziele des Projekts.

What major problems do people in wheelchairs deal with on a daily basis? Going to the toilet, for example, can be a challenge even when handicapped toilets are available. Carrying out in-depth analysis and interviews with persons concerned, five students took an almost anthropological approach to their design of an improved wheelchair.

Their solution for the cited problem is the Carrier: driven in reverse, it can be placed over almost any standard toilet; sinking the backrest makes the change of seats easier. A combination of common wheels and a belt drive makes it possible to overcome stairs and obstacles. In addition, Carrier is capable of lifting a person into a stable, standing position, which not only makes it easier to reach objects, but also to carry on a conversation at eye-level with people who are standing. The project's key goals are social integration and increased autonomy for wheelchair riders.

Portable Lifesupport (COPD Relief)

Konzept für ein mobiles interaktives Therapiegerät

Concept for a mobile, interactive therapy device

Design
Oskar von Hanstein, Benjamin Cselley, Lukas Pressler, Niklas Wagner

Design
Oskar von Hanstein, Benjamin Cselley, Lukas Pressler, Niklas Wagner

Entstehungsjahr
2009

Year of origin
2009

Angesichts überlasteter Gesundheitseinrichtungen und Rationalisierungsdrucks wird darüber diskutiert, Rehabilitations- und Therapiemaßnahmen, wo es machbar ist, an Computertechnik zu delegieren. Portable Lifesupport ist eine _interaktive mobile Einheit_ für PatientInnen mit COPD, Chronisch-obstruktiver Lungenerkrankung. Mithilfe von Avataren – künstlichen Personen in der virtuellen Welt – werden Erkrankte, zumeist ehemalige RaucherInnen, therapeutisch begleitet.

Ziel des Portable Lifesupport ist es, bewusstes Atmen zu trainieren und das Lungenvolumen zu erhöhen. Schritt für Schritt führt der persönliche Avatar an die Therapien heran und animiert dazu, sich mit der persönlichen Leistungsfähigkeit auseinanderzusetzen. Übungen und „Atemspiele" stehen zum Download bereit. Das Gerät begleitet die medikamentöse Behandlung und löst im Notfall auch einen Alarm aus. Informationen gehen online direkt an den behandelnden Arzt.

Faced with over-taxed health facilities and pressure to rationalize, there is discussion of delegating rehabilitation and therapy measures, when feasible, to computer technology. Portable Lifesupport is an _interactive mobile unit_ for patients with COPD, chronic-obstructive lung disease. With the help of avatars—characters in the virtual world—sufferers, mainly former smokers are accompanied through their therapy.

The goal of the Portable Lifesupport is to train conscious breathing and increase lung volume. The personal avatar introduces the therapy step by step, and encourages patients to grapple with their individual abilities. Exercises and "breathing games" are available for download. The device is an accompaniment to medication, and in an emergency, it sets off an alarm. Information is sent online directly to the attending physician.

Labor /
Laboratory

Gesundheit /
Health

Pablo & Timo System

Computergestützte Rehabilitationsgeräte	Computer-aided rehabilitation devices
Design (Pablo System) **David Rahm, Maik Hartnig, Johannes Knafl**	Design (Pablo System) David Rahm, Maik Hartnig, Johannes Knafl
Design (Timo System) **David Rahm**	Design (Timo System) David Rahm
Hersteller **tyromotion**	Manufacturer tyromotion
Entstehungsjahre **2011/2012**	Years of origin 2011/2012

Physiotherapie und Rehabilitation bei motorischen Störungen sind zeit- und kostenaufwendige Leistungen. Beim Wiedererlernen motorischer Funktionen, etwa nach Schlaganfällen, können repetitive Bewegungsabläufe eine große Rolle spielen; für die Anleitung der PatientInnen eignen sich hier auch computergestützte <u>Reha-Geräte</u>, die zudem wichtige Daten liefern.

Die modular aufgebauten Systeme Pablo und Timo sind für das Training der oberen Extremitäten bzw. von Gleichgewicht und Balance gedacht. Die sensorischen Übungsgeräte messen Kraftanstrengungen und -verlagerungen, zeichnen die Daten auf und werten sie für die weitere Behandlung aus. Über interaktive Trainingssoftware werden PatientInnen via Computerbildschirm bei ihren Übungen spielerisch angeleitet und motiviert. Dabei liefert explizites Design stets eine Gebrauchsanweisung mit: Auf den ersten Blick lässt sich erkennen, welche Bereiche sensorisch aktiv sind; die an Fahrradlenker angelehnte Form des Pablo-Gerätes leitet intuitiv zur richtigen Benutzung an.

Physiotherapy and rehabilitation in cases of motor skill disorders can be time and cost intensive services. In relearning motor skill functions, after a stroke, for example, repetitive movement sequences can play a major role; computer-aided <u>rehab devices</u> are also well-suited for instructing patients, and additionally deliver important data.

The modular systems Pablo and Timo are intended for training the upper extremities, for example, for poise and balance. The sensory training devices measure strenght efforts and shifts, record the data, and evaluate them for further treatment. Interactive software playfully instructs and motivates patients in their exercises via computer screen. The explicit design offers constant instructions for use: the sensory activated areas are immediately recognizable; Pablo's form, borrowed from a bicycle's handlebars, intuitively instructs one to use it correctly.

→ Timo System

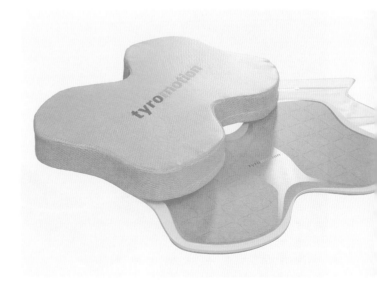

Gesundheit / Health

Fabrik / Factory

↓ **Pablo System**

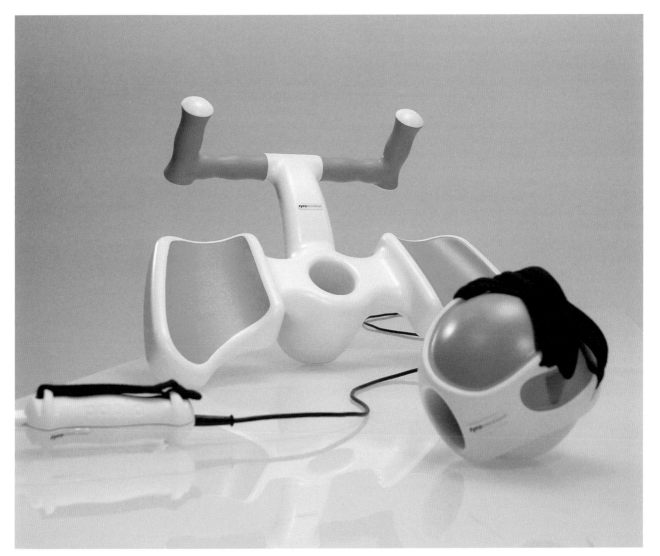

© tyromotion GmbH

Gesundheit /
Health

Fabrik /
Factory

Ganymed

Gehhilfe	Walking aid
Design **Ganymed**	Design Ganymed
Hersteller **Ganymed**	Manufacturer Ganymed
Entstehungsjahr **2012**	Year of origin 2012

Unfälle, Krankheit oder das Alter können <u>Gehhilfen</u> notwendig machen. Da Krücken die Belastung von Beinen und Wirbelsäule auf Schultern und Arme verlagern, kommt es dort nicht selten zur Überbeanspruchung. Die Gehhilfe Ganymed will Mobilität und optimalen Gebrauch gleichermaßen gewährleisten. Ihr nach vorne versetzter S-förmiger Stützpunkt bietet eine Entlastung und bewirkt, dass der Griffbereich nicht umklammert werden muss. Sowohl Kraftaufwand als auch beschriebener Radius fallen damit beim Vorschwingen viel kleiner aus als bei herkömmlichen Gehhilfen.

Der bis zur Transparenz durchbrochene, haptisch aber wie ein geschlossener Körper anmutende biomimetisch konstruierte Griff verringert das Gewicht des Geräts und belüftet die Hand. Die ovalen Füße am Ende des Teleskoprohrs ermöglichen bei Drehung weicheres oder härteres Aufsetzen. Sowohl die Füße als auch die ergonomischen Griffschalen sind in verschiedenen Qualitäten bzw. Härtegraden erhältlich und austauschbar.

Accidents, illness, and age can make <u>walking aids</u> necessary. Crutches shift the burden from legs and spine to shoulders and arms, frequently leading to overstraining these areas. The Ganymed walking aid aims to guarantee both mobility and optimal use. Its forward-mounted, S-shaped base relieves strain, and hands no longer have to clasp the grip. Both exertion and described radius when swinging the device forward are thus reduced in comparison to standard walking aids.

The biomimetic-seeming grip, which is constructed in nearly transparent open-work, haptic but like a closed body, lowers the device's weight and provides ventilation for the hand. The oval feet at the end of the telescopic cylinder can be twisted to enable a softer or harder touch on the ground. Both the feet, as well as the ergonomic molded recess are available in various qualities and degrees of hardness, and are replaceable.

Gesundheit / Health

Fabrik / Factory

© ganymed

Gesundheit /
Health

Fabrik /
Factory

Gait Solution

Unterschenkel-Orthese	Lower leg orthosis
Design **GK Design Group**	Design GK Design Group
Hersteller **Kawamura Gishi**	Manufacturer Kawamura Gishi
Entstehungsjahr **2005**	Year of origin 2005

Orthesen sind medizinische Hilfsmittel zur Stabilisierung, Entlastung, Führung oder Korrektur von Gliedmaßen. Die Gait Solution, eine Unterschenkel-Orthese, verwendet hierfür komplexe Öldruck-Scharniere. Der hydraulische Effekt wie auch die Schmierfunktion des Öls erleichtern die Bewegung; dadurch wird eine weiche Gehbewegung ermöglicht und ein – etwa durch halbseitige Lähmung hervorgerufener – schwerfälliger Gang korrigiert.

Für das Anlegen der Orthese ist es nicht notwendig, das Bein anzuheben – eine große Erleichterung für Menschen mit Lähmungen. Gait Solution wird wie ein Pantoffel angezogen und mit Klettverschlüssen fixiert. Die Gestaltung zielt auf Unauffälligkeit und darauf ab, weitgehende Normalität zu ermöglichen. Das kommt etwa im radikal reduzierten Volumen und in hautfarbenen Gurten zum Ausdruck. Anders als die meisten Orthesen erlaubt Gait Solution auch das Tragen normaler Schuhe in der gewohnten Größe.

Orthoses are medical aids for stabilizing, relieving, guiding, and correcting limbs. Gait Solution, a lower leg orthosis employs complex oil-pressure hinges for this purpose. The hydraulic effect, and the oil's lubrication function, eases movement: this enables a smooth stride and corrects a cumbersome gait caused, for example, by partial paralysis.

It is not necessary to lift one's leg to put on the orthosis—a major relief for people with paralysis. Gait Solution is put on like a slipper and fastened with Velcro fasteners. The shape aims at being discrete and enabling as much normality as possible. This is expressed by the radically reduced volume and skin-colored belt. Unlike most orthoses, with Gait Solution, it is possible to wear regular shoe in one's usual size.

Gesundheit /
Health

Fabrik /
Factory

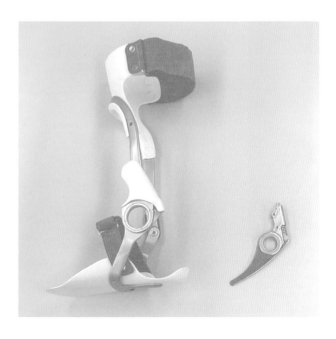

© GK Design Group

Gesundheit /
Health

Fabrik /
Factory

Color-Changing Splint

Armschiene für Kinder	Arm splint for children

Design	Design
Wei Hung Chen, Ta Yo Chen, Taiwan Textile Research Institute / TTRI	Wei Hung Chen, Ta Yo Chen, Taiwan Textile Research Institute / TTRI

Entstehungsjahr	Year of origin
2011	2011

Im Sinne der patientenzentrierten Medizin sollen Methoden und Produkte nicht nur therapeutische Wirkung entfalten, sondern auch im Hinblick auf unterschiedliche emotionale Bedürfnisse gestaltet werden. In der Kinder- und Jugendmedizin kommt diesem Zugang große Bedeutung zu: Kinder haben oft noch keine rationale Einstellung zu Krankheit und Schmerz entwickelt, auf Arzt oder Krankenhaus reagieren sie mit Angst und Verstörung.

Die Farbeffekt-Armschiene bringt Spiel und Ablenkung in die Behandlung kleiner PatientInnen. Aus thermoplastischem Material gefertigt, lässt sie sich durch Erhitzen verformen und nimmt innerhalb von drei Minuten eine passgenaue, stabile Form am Kinderarm an – damit wird die Behandlungszeit um die Hälfte reduziert. Mit dem Erhitzen ändern sich neben der Form auch Farbgebung und Muster der bunten Schiene – ein überraschender visueller Effekt, der die Kinder für die Dauer der Prozedur von ihren Schmerzen und Ängsten abzulenken hilft!

In line with patient-centered medicine, methods and products should not only display therapeutic effects, but also be designed with various emotional needs in mind. In pediatrics and medical care for adolescents, this approach is extremely important: often, children have not yet developed a rational attitude to illness and pain, and react to doctors and hospitals with fear and distress.

The color-changing arm splint brings a bit of playfulness and distraction in the treatment of young patients. Produced from thermoplastic materials, it can be molded when heated, taking on a customized, stable form on the child's arm. The treatment time is hereby cut in half. Heating changes not only the form, but also the coloring and pattern of the colorful splint—a surprising visual effect, which helps distract children from their pain and fear during the procedure!

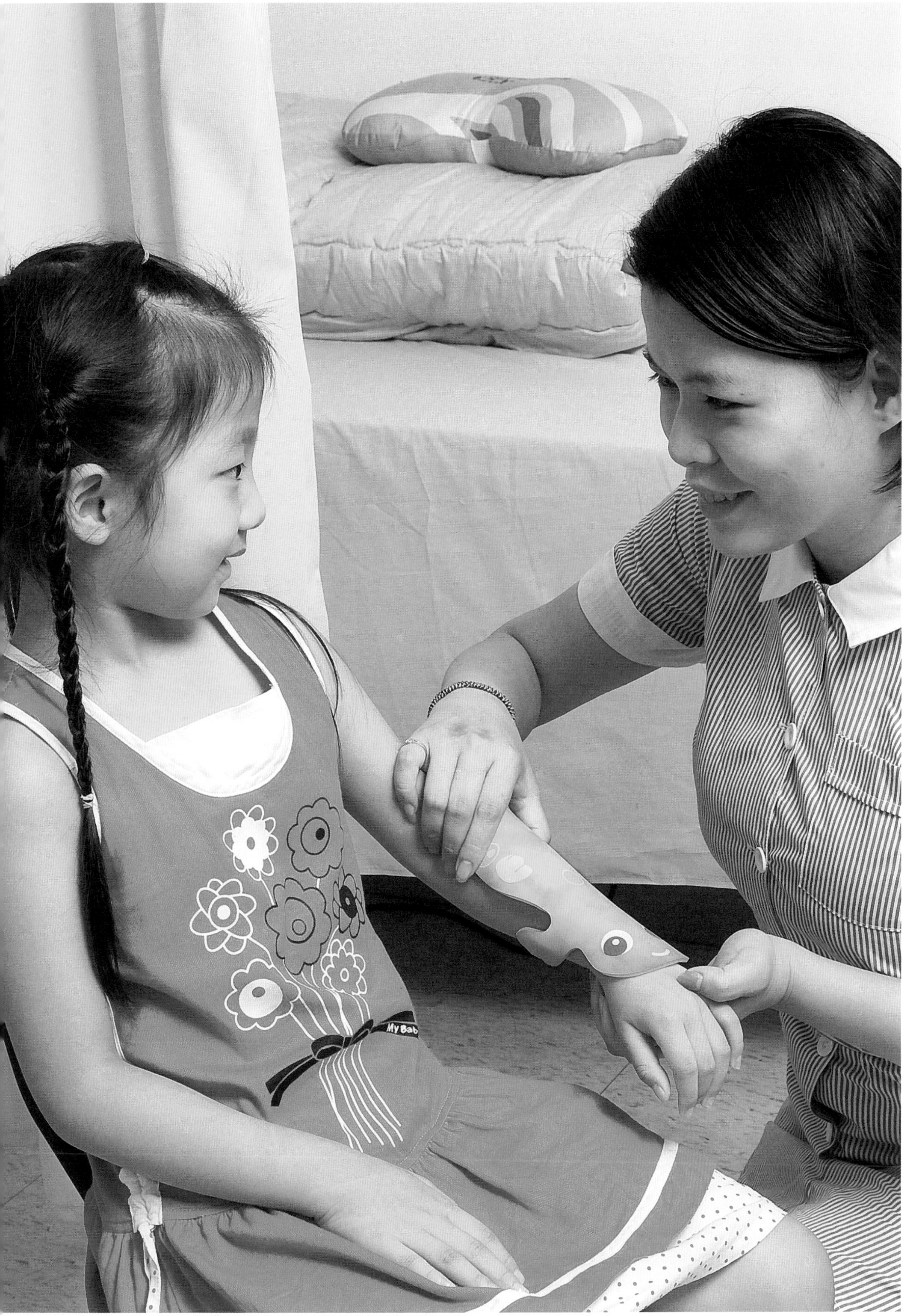

© Taiwan Textile Research Institute (TTRI)

Gesundheit /
Health

Fabrik /
Factory

© Whipsaw Inc.

Gesundheit /
Health

Fabrik /
Factory

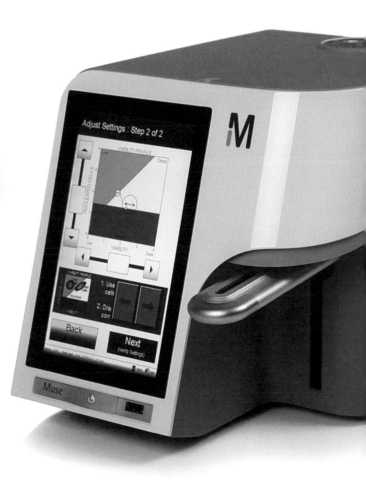

Muse Cell Analyzer

Zellanalysator	Cell analyzer
Design **Whipsaw**	Design Whipsaw
Hersteller **Millipore**	Manufacturer Millipore
Entstehungsjahr **2012**	Year of origin 2012

Der Muse Cell Analyzer ist ein automatischer Zellanalysator für medizinische Labors, der Zelltypen identifiziert und deren Anzahl, Dichte sowie Status bestimmt. Avancierte Technik (miniaturisierter Laser und Kapillar-Technologie) macht ihn gegenüber anderen Analysatoren bedeutend kleiner und damit auch mobiler. Die Bedienung ist simpel: Ein Hebearm nimmt die Zellprobe auf; über Touch-Screen und einfache Anweisungen werden BenutzerInnen automatisch durch den Analyseprozess geführt. Für die tägliche Wartung gilt es lediglich die beiden oberen Behälter – einen für frische, einen für verschmutzte Spülflüssigkeit – auszutauschen.

Das kleine, hochautomatisierte Gerät etabliert das nahtlose Ineinandergreifen von Funktionen auf dem Touchscreen, Lade- und Spülmechanismus. Dieser kompakte „Task-Flow" wird auch gestalterisch suggeriert – durch die Grundform zweier ineinandergreifender Bänder, das eine weiß, das andere hellgrün. Deren Farbigkeit bringt Abwechslung ins Laborambiente.

The Muse Cell Analyzer is an automatic cell analyzer for medical laboratories. It identifies cell types and ascertains their number, concentration, and viability. Sophisticated technologies (miniaturized laser and capillary technology) make it smaller and thus also more mobile than other analyzers. Operation is simple: a lever arm takes in the cell sample; via touch-screen and simple instructions, users are led automatically through the analysis process. In terms of daily care, only the two top containers have to be exchanged—one for fresh cleaning solution and one for used solution.

The small, highly-automated device establishes a seamless meshing of functions on the touch screen, and mechanisms for filling and cleaning. This compact "task flow" is also suggested by the design—through the basic form of two intermeshed bands, one white, the other light-green. Their coloring brings a dash of variety into the laboratory ambiance.

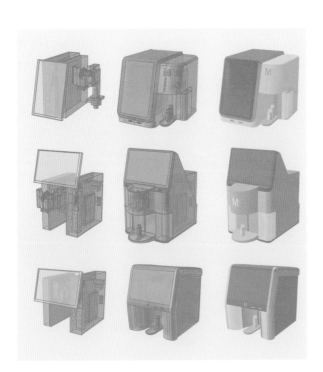

Kiss Series

Universalverschluss für Trinkgefäße	Universal drinking cup caps
Design **I.C.I. Design Institute**	Design I.C.I. Design Institute
Hersteller **I.C.I. Design Institute**	Manufacturer I.C.I. Design Institute
Entstehungsjahr **2009**	Year of origin 2009

Wie das Angebot an neuartigen Verschlusskappen für Flaschen und vielfältige Becherdesigns für Coffee-to-Go belegen, ist die wachsende Mobilität auch bei der Flüssigkeitsaufnahme ein Thema. Die Kiss Series reiht sich in diesen Trend ein. In zwei Größen – für Tassen und Becher oder für PET-Flaschen – erhältlich, verfügen die Silikondeckel über einen neuartigen Trinkschlitz, der erst durch sanftes Draufbeißen geöffnet wird und Flüssigkeit durchlässt. Der Effekt: kein Verschütten mehr.

Die Universalverschlüsse der Kiss Series sind weich, aber dennoch so widerstandsfähig, dass auch bei umgestürztem Becher keine Flüssigkeit ausläuft. Sie kommen nicht nur unterwegs oder im Büro zum Einsatz, sondern eignen sich insbesondere auch für Kinder und kranke, ältere oder pflegebedürftige Personen. Die wiederverwendbaren Aufsätze können sterilisiert und zur einfachen Reinigung umgestülpt werden. In Gestaltung und Farbgebung wurde die Balance zwischen freundlichem Alltagsprodukt und ergonomischem Hygieneartikel gefunden.

As evident by the offer of novel caps for bottles and diverse cup designs for coffee-to-go, mobility has also become a theme in the area of liquid refreshment. The Kiss Series is part of this trend. Available in two sizes—for cups and mugs or PET bottles, the silicon caps have a novel drinking slit that is opened by a gentle bite, thus allowing liquid to pass through. The effect: no more spillage.

The universal drinking cup caps of the Kiss Series are soft while remaining resistant enough to prevent liquid from leaking, even with a toppled cup. They are useful not only when on the go or in the office, but are also especially suitable for children and the ill, elderly, and infirm. The reusable covers can be sterilized and turned inside out for easy cleaning. Their design strikes a balance between friendly everyday product and ergonomic hygiene article.

Gesundheit / Health

Fabrik / Factory

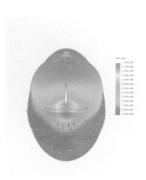

© I.C.I Design Institute Inc

Gesundheit /
Health

Fabrik /
Factory

Endura Scrubs

OP-Bekleidung	OP clothing
Design **Smart Design**	Design Smart Design
Hersteller **Cardinal Health**	Manufacturer Cardinal Health
Entstehungsjahr **2009**	Year of origin 2009

Dass im Operationssaal eines Krankenhauses alles top funktionieren muss, um reibungsloses Arbeiten zu gewährleisten, gilt auch für die Bekleidung des Personals. Endura ist eine gemeinsam mit ÄrztInnen und Pflegepersonal entwickelte Bekleidung für OPs und Notfallambulanzen. Gegenüber der traditionellen Baumwoll-OP-Kleidung, die sich seit den 1960er-Jahren nicht wesentlich verändert hat, wurden hier zahlreiche Verbesserungen vorgenommen.

Aus leichtem, synthetischem, flusenfreiem und reißfestem Material gefertigt, das sich auf der Haut gut anfühlt, bieten Endura-Teile als weitere Neuerungen maximale Bewegungsfreiheit, Lüftung durch Netzeinsätze, funktionale Taschen sowie Stretch-V-Ausschnitt (keine Knöpfe mehr). In jeder der fünf Unisex-Größen sind die Hosen am Bund und am Saum zusätzlich individuell anpassbar. Auch die allgemeine Bilanz ist beachtlich: Die Zweiteiler sind günstig in der Herstellung und dennoch – sie halten mehr als 90 Waschzyklen aus – beständiger als herkömmliche Modelle. Auch dass sie nicht so heiß gewaschen werden müssen und schneller trocknen, wirkt sich positiv auf die Ökobilanz aus.

The need for everything in an operating room of a hospital to function perfectly in order to guarantee that work goes smoothly, applies also to the staff's clothing. Endura is a line of clothing for OPs and emergency rooms developed together with doctors and nursing staff. In contrast to traditional cotton OP clothing, which has not changed much since the 1960s, numerous improvements have been made.

Manufactured from light, synthetic, lint-free, and tear-proof material, which feels good on the skin, Endura items offer, as a further innovation, maximum freedom of movement, ventilation by means of net inserts, functional pockets, as well as stretch v-necks (no more buttons). In each of the five unisex sizes, the pants can be individually fitted at the waist and seam. The overall balance sheet is also remarkable: the two-piece outfits are inexpensive to produce, yet more durable than traditional models—they can withstand more than ninety wash cycles. The fact that the clothes can be washed at lower temperatures and dry faster, also has a positive effect on the environment.

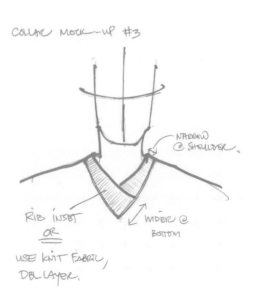

© Smart Design

Gesundheit /
Health

Fabrik /
Factory

Tango!

Sprachgenerator und Kommunikationshilfe	Speech generator and communication aid
Design **Howard Nuk, Richard Ellenson / frog design**	Design Howard Nuk, Richard Ellenson / frog design
Hersteller **DynaVox**	Manufacturer DynaVox
Entstehungsjahr **2007**	Year of origin 2007

Tango! ist ein <u>Sprachgenerator</u> und eine Kommunikationshilfe für Kinder und Jugendliche mit schwersten Sprach- oder Lernbehinderungen, verursacht etwa durch Zerebralparese oder Autismus. BenutzerInnen wählen aus tausenden Wörtern und rund 2.500 individuell abänderbaren Phrasen rasch aus und verwandeln das, was sie sagen wollen, in gesprochene Sprache. Dabei offeriert das System einfachen Zugang zu Themen samt relevantem Vokabular, unter anderem über Icons und selbstgemachte Fotos, sowie eine schnell verfügbare Vorauswahl der am häufigsten benutzten Bausteine.

Für Aufnahme und Stimmwiedergabe nahm man Anleihen bei der Audiotechnik: So lässt sich etwa die Stimme eines Erwachsenen zu der eines Kindes verfremden (Voice Morphing). Zudem vermag Tango! Emotionen zu transportieren, denn die Stimme kann auf Wunsch flüstern, jammern oder laut rufen. Da bei Zerebralparese auch die manuelle Motorik reduziert ist, ermöglicht das einfache Layout mit sechs versenkten Auswahlfeldern und wenigen Funktionsknöpfen zielgerichtete Kommunikation; die geringe Größe und das ergonomische Design sorgen dafür, dass die Nutzung und nicht die Technik im Vordergrund steht.

Tango! is a <u>speech generator</u> and communication aid for children and young people with severe speech impediments or learning disabilities caused, for example, by cerebral palsy or autism. Users can choose quickly from thousands of words and around 2,500 individually modifiable phrases to transform what they want to say into spoken language. In this, the system offers easy access to topics including relevant vocabulary, for example, by means of icons and self-made photos, as well as an easily accessible pre-selection of the most commonly used building blocks.

Recording and voice reproduction borrow from audio technologies: for example, the voice of an adult can be morphed to one of a child (Voice Morphing). Tango! is also able to transport emotions. On request, the voice can whisper, whine, or shout loudly. Since manual motor skills are also reduced with cerebral palsy, the simple layout allows for targeted communication with six sunken selection fields and just a few function buttons; the small size and ergonomic design likewise assure that use and not technology are at the forefront.

Gesundheit /
Health

Fabrik /
Factory

© DynaVox Systems LLC

Sonicare DiamondClean

Elektrische Zahnbürste	Electric toothbrush
Design **Philips Design**	Design Philips Design
Hersteller **Philips**	Manufacturer Philips
Entstehungsjahr **2011**	Year of origin 2011

Beim Design von Produkten für die tägliche Körperpflege gilt es Funktionalität und Leistung ebenso in Betracht zu ziehen wie jeweils geltende Vorstellungen von Schönheit und Hygieneritualen. Mit einer Oberfläche, die an Porzellan erinnert, einem einzigen Funktionsknopf und einem nur bei Betrieb sichtbaren Leuchtdisplay repräsentiert die elektrische Zahnbürste Sonicare DiamondClean gleichermaßen Schlichtheit in der Anmutung und im Gebrauch wie technische Reife. Ihr Name korrespondiert mit dem diamantförmigen Bürstenkopf ebenso wie mit der Vorstellung von makelloser Reinheit.

Ein Metallring etabliert eine sinnfällige Grenze zwischen dem Bürstenaufsatz und jenem Teil, den man in der Hand hält. Das Handstück hat einen quadratischen Querschnitt mit abgerundeten Kanten, wodurch es gut zu manövrieren ist. Zum Aufladen stellt man die Bürste einfach in das Mundspülglas – sie wird per Induktion über den Metallboden des Glases aufgeladen. So bleibt ein altes Ritual trotz neuester Technik erhalten.

In designing products for personal hygiene, functionality and performance must be taken into consideration along with currently valid ideas of beauty and hygiene rituals. With a surface that brings to mind porcelain, a single operating button, and a light display visible only when in use, the Sonicare DiamondClean electronic toothbrush presents both simplicity in appearance and technical sophistication in use. Its name refers to both the diamond-shaped brush head and the idea of flawless purity.

A metal ring sets a sensible border between the brush top and the part held in the hand. The handle has a square cross section with rounded edges offering good maneuverability. To charge the brush, one simply places it in the rinsing glass—charging takes place by induction through the metal floor of the glass. Thus, despite cutting-edge technology, an old ritual remains intact.

© Philips

Gesundheit /
Health

Fabrik /
Factory

Leveraged Freedom Chair

Rollstuhl für unwegsames Gelände	Wheelchair for rough terrain
Design **Continuum**	Design Continuum
Entstehungsjahr **2010**	Year of origin 2010

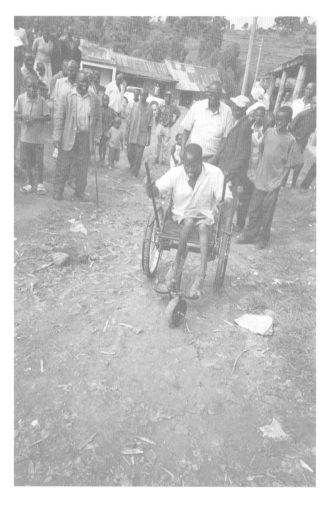

↑ **LFC in Kenia**
Design: Amos Winter, Jake Childs / Continuum & Jung Geun Tak / MIT Mobility Lab

Bei steinigem Untergrund oder Steigungen sind der Mobilität von RollstuhlfahrerInnen bald Grenzen gesetzt. Der Leveraged Freedom Chair – ursprünglich ein Projekt des MIT (Massachusetts Institute of Technology) zur Gestaltung eines Rollstuhls für den Einsatz in Entwicklungsländern – erwarb sich allerdings schnell den Ruf des „Mountainbikes unter den Rollstühlen". Die Schlüsseltechnik ist – neben dem dritten Rad – sein Hebelantrieb: Fasst man die Hebel weit unten, so wird ein hoher Gang eingestellt, der schnelles Fahren in der Ebene oder bergab ermöglicht. Bedient man sie an ihrem oberen Ende, ermöglichen niedrige Gänge die Fortbewegung auch bergauf und auf unwegsamem Gelände.

Auf diese Weise ermöglicht es der LFC, sich auf rauem Terrain mit 53 Prozent weniger Kraftanstrengung und auf der Ebene um 80 Prozent schneller fortzubewegen als ein konventioneller Rollstuhl. Alu- und Carbonfaserteile sorgen für Leichtigkeit bei gleichzeitiger Stabilität, die Verwendung handelsüblicher Fahrradteile vereinfacht die Wartung. Das Produkt verspricht einen sprunghaften Anstieg der Mobilität und Autonomie von RollstuhlfahrerInnen.

On rocky ground and on slopes, wheelchair riders soon meet the limits of their mobility. The Leveraged Freedom Chair was originally an MIT (Massachusetts Institute of Technology) project aiming at the design of a wheelchair for use in developing countries, however it soon acquired the reputation of "mountain bike among wheelchairs." The key technology, along with the third wheel, is its lever drive: by grabbing the lever far down, a higher gear is set allowing for higher speeds on level ground or downhill. By operating the lever higher up, lower gears allow for propulsion uphill and in rough terrain.

In this way, the LFC makes it possible to move in rough terrain with the exertion of 53 percent less energy, and ride 80 percent faster on level ground than with a conventional wheelchair. Aluminum and carbon fiber parts provide lightness and, at the same time, stability, while the use of standard bicycle parts simplifies maintenance. The product promises a sudden increase in the mobility and autonomy of wheelchair riders.

© MIT Mobility Lab

Gesundheit /
Health

Fabrik /
Factory

MADE 4 YOU

Überleben / Survival

Was
sichert unser
(Über)leben?

Effektive Lawinensuchgeräte und taugliche Werkzeuge für den Erste-Hilfe-Koffer können sich im Notfall für Einzelne als lebensrettend erweisen – sie sind aber auch „Design fürs Überleben". Bezogen auf die gesamte Weltbevölkerung hat das Thema Überleben noch größere und vor allem längerfristige Dimensionen: 8,1 Milliarden Menschen werden laut Club of Rome im Jahr 2040 auf der Erde leben, und das bei knapper werdenden Ressourcen. Da diese Ressourcen ungleich verteilt sind, muss technische und Design-Innovation immer wieder dort ansetzen, wo es tatsächlich ums nackte Überleben geht: in Entwicklungs- und Schwellenländern. Wollen DesignerInnen passende Produkte und Strategien für die Linderung von Not entwickeln, ist vor allem die Betrachtung spezifischer Lebensumstände und lokaler Bedingungen von Bedeutung. Für die wohlhabenden Länder wiederum gilt es, rasch effektive Konzepte für nachhaltiges, ressourcenschonendes Leben und Wirtschaften zu erarbeiten – wie etwa jenes der „Smart City". Nicht zuletzt muss es aber auch um eine globale Umverteilung gehen: Die gegenwärtigen Hungersnöte und die Klimakatastrophe betreffen uns alle, auch wenn andere sie zuerst zu spüren bekommen.

What guarantees our existence and survival?

In an emergency, effective avalanche beacons and capable tools in the first-aid bag can prove lifesaving for individuals—and they, too, are "designs for survival." With regard to the overall world population, however, the theme of survival has even greater, and, mainly, more long-term dimensions: 8.1 billion people will live on earth in 2040 according to the Club of Rome, and will do so with diminishing resources. Since there is an unequal distribution of these resources, techno-logical- and design-innovation must consistently be applied in situations that are truly about pure survival: in developing and newly industrialized countries. When designers aim to develop appropriate products and strategies for the alleviation of need, important first and foremost is the consideration of specific living situations and local conditions. For wealthy countries, on the other hand, necessary is the rapid development of ef-fective concepts for sustainable, resource-friendly living and commerce—the "Smart City," for instance. In the end, however, the issue is global redistribution: current famines and climate catastrophes affect us all, even when it is others who feel the affects first.

→ Hippo Water Roller, 1991
Design: Pettie Petzer, Johan Jonker

Friedrich von Borries
Hochschule für Bildende Künste Hamburg (HFBK)
University of Fine Arts Hamburg

Zwischen Notwendigkeit und Lifestyle

Between Necessity and Lifestyle

Entwerfen, so Vilém Flusser, ist der Gegensatz zu Unterwerfen.[1] Sich vor Bedrohungen der Natur zu schützen und so die Chancen auf ein Überleben zu steigern war schon immer eines der wesentlichen Ausgangsmomente von Gestaltung – ob es um den Entwurf eines Hauses, eines Kleidungsstückes oder die Entwicklung von Werkzeugen ging. Doch auch heute ist das Überleben in vielen Lebenssituationen gefährdet, und Design versucht hier, Lösungsansätze zu entwickeln.

Im Kontext der Entwicklungshilfe finden sich eindrucksvolle Beispiele dafür: etwa der sogenannte Hippo-Roller[2], mit dem Wasser auf einfache Weise von entfernten Brunnen nach Hause transportiert werden kann, oder der LifeStraw[3], eine Art Strohhalm mit eingebautem Wasserfilter, der verschmutztes Wasser unmittelbar vor dem Trinken reinigt. So wird Menschen das Überleben ermöglicht, die keinen Zugriff auf sauberes Trinkwasser haben.

Designing, writes Vilém Flusser, is the opposite of resigning.[1] Protecting oneself from the threats of nature and thereby increasing one's chance of survival has always provided a central impetus for design—be it the design of a house or of a garment, or the development of tools. And even today, many situations in which people live harbor threats to survival, and the field of design attempts to develop approaches by which to respond.

International development efforts provide impressive cases in point: these include the so-called Hippo water roller[2], which provides an easy way of taking home water from distant wells, or the LifeStraw[3], a type of straw with a built-in water filter that purifies dirty water immediately before it is drunk. Such innovations facilitate the survival of people who lack access to clean drinking water.

Überleben /
Survival

© Grant Gibbs, hipporoller.org

211

Aber auch in reicheren Regionen der Erde kommt es, insbesondere nach Natur- und Umweltkatastrophen, immer wieder zu krisenhaften Situationen, zu deren Bewältigung Design einen entscheidenden Beitrag leistet. So entwickelt beispielsweise der japanische Architekt Shingeru Ban seit den 1990er-Jahren „Disaster Relief Projects"⁴, auf Pappe und Textilien basierende Strukturen für Notunterkünfte, wie sie unter anderem nach Erdbeben in der Türkei oder nach dem Atomunfall in Fukushima zum Einsatz kamen. „Survival through design"⁵ ist die mit den Mitteln der Gestaltung formulierte Antwort auf überraschende, lebensgefährdende Ereignisse, der jedoch eine Widersprüchlichkeit innewohnt: Denn die Produkte lösen nicht die eigentlichen Probleme, sondern wirken lediglich an der Oberfläche der unmittelbaren Not- oder Krisensituation.

But even in the world's wealthier regions, crisis-like situations repeatedly arise—particularly in the wake of natural and environmental disasters—which design makes a decisive contribution toward resolving. The Japanese architect Shingeru Ban, for example, has been designing "Disaster Relief Projects"⁴ since the 1990s. These are cardboard and textile-based structures for emergency shelters, which have been used following earthquakes in Turkey and the nuclear accident in Fukushima. But "survival through design,"⁵ the response to unexpected, life-threatening events formulated by creative means, features an innate contradiction: the resulting products do not solve the underlying problems; all they do is superficially ameliorate the emergency or crisis at hand.

© Voluntary Architects' Network + Shigeru Ban

→ **Paper Partition System 4**
Raumteiler aus Kartonrollen für Notunterkünfte, 2006
Design: Shigeru Ban Architects

Paper Partition System 4
for evacuation facilities, 2006
Design: Shigeru Ban Architects

MADE 4 YOU

Setzt man sich mit derartigen Not- und Krisensituationen auseinander, so fällt ins Auge, dass ihnen in unserer von Angst und Katastrophismus geprägten Gesellschaft eine Funktion zukommt: Jedes noch so ferne Unglück dringt über die Medien in unsere Köpfe, und eine eingespielte Bildpolitik verfestigt den Eindruck einer sich rasant wandelnden und dabei immer gefährlicher werdenden Welt. Dabei sind viele Katastrophen, die sich heute zutragen, keineswegs überraschende Ereignisse, sondern das Ergebnis bewusst eingegangener Risiken, dies gilt für die Überschwemmung von New Orleans ebenso wie für Fukushima. Die Künstlerin und Kulturwissenschaftler Yana Milev erkennt darin ein gezieltes „Emergency Design"⁶.

Diese Form der Weltgestaltung, die Katastrophen bewusst produziert oder zumindest in Kauf nimmt, ist zudem ökonomisch attraktiv. Zum einen vergrößert die Risiko-Erhöhung die Gewinnspannen, zum anderen bringen Katastrophen neue Wirtschaftszweige hervor. Schon in der Frühzeit des Kapitalismus entstand die Idee der Versicherung, die darauf fußt, dass ein Kollektiv gemeinsam Risiken trägt und damit den Einzelnen entlastet. Inzwischen ist ein umfassender Katastrophenmarkt entstanden, der von Rückversicherungen über Präventionen bis zu Krisenreaktionskräften alles Mögliche abdeckt. Für die herbeigeführten Krisen und Katastrophen müssen Schutzmechanismen und Überlebensstrategien entwickelt werden – und diese lassen sich wieder gut vermarkten. Selbst die Politik profitiert von diesem Emergency Design; sie nutzt die Schreckstarre nach

When pondering such emergency and crisis situations, one notices that they in fact have a function to perform in our fearful and catastrophe-obsessed society: even the most distant adverse event is hammered into our minds by the media, and a well-oiled apparatus of image production reinforces the impression of a rapidly transforming and ever-more-dangerous world. Even so, many of the catastrophes that occur today are by no means surprising events, but result from consciously taken risks. This holds just as true for the flooding of New Orleans as it does for Fukushima. It is in this sense that the artist and cultural scholar Yana Milev discerns a deliberate "Emergency Design."⁶

This way of shaping the world, deliberately producing catastrophes or at least taking them for granted, is attractive from an economic standpoint. For one thing, increased risk means increased profit margins, in addition to which catastrophes even give rise to new types of economic activity. Back in the early days of capitalism, the concept of insurance came about based on the idea of collectivizing risk and thereby easing the burden on individuals. Since that time, human society has witnessed the advent of a full-blown catastrophe market covering all manner of things from reinsurance to preventive measures and crisis response personnel. For all the self-inflicted crises and catastrophes, protective mechanisms and survival strategies must be developed—and these can, in turn, be easily marketed. Even politics profits from such Emergency Design; political actors take advantage of the panicked states of collective

Katastrophen, um weitgehend unbemerkt unpopuläre politische Maßnahmen durchzusetzen.[7] Dieser Mechanismus lässt sich im Zuge der Finanzkrise ebenso beobachten, wie dies nach 9/11 in Form der sogenannten Antiterrorgesetze der Fall war.

Die umfassende Durchdringung der Gesellschaft von den Sachzwängen, die aus Not- und Krisensituationen resultieren, findet im Privaten ihre Fortsetzung. Denn das Individuum will sich in einer konkurrenzorientierten Gesellschaft, die das Darwin'sche „Survival of the fittest" zum Credo erhoben hat, bewähren; es sucht die Gefahr, um sich selbst zu beweisen. Beim Streben nach dem ultimativen Kick verwandelt sich dann ein sinnvolles Instrument wie ein Lawinensuchgerät in ein Lifestyle-Gadget, dessen ursprüngliche Funktion ad absurdum geführt ist.

So bewegt sich Design, das sich mit Fragen des Überlebens auseinandersetzt, in einem Feld spannungsvoller Ambivalenzen. Überleben zu ermöglichen und auf Extremsituationen zu reagieren ist grundlegende Aufgabe aller Gestaltung. Überlebenssichernde Produkte zu entwickeln gehört zu den sinnvollsten Tätigkeiten, die ein Designer heute erfüllen kann.[8] Heute ist Überlebensdesign jedoch auch Sinnbild und Spiegel einer Gesellschaft, die permanent Gefahrensituationen herstellt, weil die Maximierung von Risiko ihre ökonomische Grundlage ist ... und das Erlebnis des Überlebens konstitutiver Bestandteil ihrer Selbstvergewisserung.

paralysis following catastrophes to introduce unpopular political measures with minimal public scrutiny.[7] This mechanism is just as evident in the context of the financial crisis as it was in the case of the so-called anti-terror legislation passed following 9/11.

The comprehensive pervasion of society by practical constraints arising from emergencies and crises also extends to the private sphere. Individuals desire to prove themselves in a competition-oriented society that has elevated Darwin's "survival of the fittest" to a statement of faith; they seek out danger in order to prove themselves. It is thus that, in striving for the ultimate thrill, a sensible device such as an avalanche transceiver can be transformed into a lifestyle gadget—making a mockery of its original function.

And it is thus that design oriented toward issues of survival now exists within a field of tense ambivalences. Facilitating survival and reacting to extreme situations is the fundamental task of all design. Developing survival-ensuring products numbers among the most meaningful activities that a designer can engage in today.[8] But today's survival-related design has also come to be a metaphor and mirror for a society that unceasingly produces dangerous situations because its economy feeds upon the maximization of risk ... and because the experience of survival is an essential component of its self-assurance.

Überleben /
Survival

[1] Vilém Flusser, „Abbild – Vorbild", in: Schriften, Band I, Lob der Oberflächlichkeit. Für eine Phänomenologie der Medien, Mannheim 1995

[2] Entworfen von Pettie Petzer und Johan Jonker, siehe auch: www.hipporoller.org

[3] Hergestellt und entwickelt von Vestergaard Frandsen, siehe auch: www.vestergaard-frandsen.com/lifestraw

[4] Matilda McQuaid, Shigeru Ban, London 2006

[5] Vgl. hierzu Richard Neutra, Survival Through Design, New York 1954. Neutra befasste sich bereits Jahre vor dem Entstehen der Ökobewegung mit Fragen der Umweltzerstörung.

[6] Vgl. Yana Milev, Emergency Design. Anthropotechniken des Über/Lebens, Berlin 2011

[7] Naomi Klein, Die Schock-Strategie: Der Aufstieg des Katastrophen-Kapitalismus, Frankfurt am Main 2007

[8] Vgl. hierzu auch Victor Papanek, Design for the Real World, New York 1984, insbesondere das Kapitel „Design for Survival and Survival through Design", S. 322

[1] Vilém Flusser, „Abbild – Vorbild," in: Schriften, Band I, Lob der Oberflächlichkeit. Für eine Phänomenologie der Medien, Mannheim 1995

[2] Designed by Pettie Petzer and Johan Jonker, see also: hipporoller.org

[3] Developed and produced by Vestergaard Frandsen, see also: vestergaard-frandsen.com/lifestraw

[4] Matilda McQuaid, Shigeru Ban, London 2006

[5] See Richard Neutra, Survival Through Design, New York 1954. Neutra dealt with issues of environmental destruction years before the environmental movement was born.

[6] See Yana Milev, Emergency Design. Anthropotechniken des Über/Lebens, Berlin 2011

[7] Naomi Klein, The Shock Doctrine: The Rise of Disaster Capitalism, New York 2007

[8] See also Victor Papanek, Design for the Real World, New York 1984, particularly the chapter „Design for Survival and Survival through Design," pp. 322–347

Aqualris

Konzept für einen Wasserfilter	Concept for a water filter
Design **Talia Radford**	Design Talia Radford
Entstehungsjahr **2011**	Year of origin 2011
Victor J. Papanek Social Design Award (Finalist), BIO – Biennale of Industrial Design 2011 (Österreich-Beitrag)	Victor J. Papanek Social Design Award (finalist), BIO – Biennial of Industrial Design 2011 (Austrian contribution)

Der Zugang zu sauberem Trinkwasser stellt in vielen Regionen der Erde ein großes Problem dar. Natur- oder auf den Menschen zurückzuführende Katastrophen (Krieg, Umweltverschmutzung etc.), vor allem aber auch Armut behindern den Bau und Erhalt der zur Wasserversorgung nötigen Infrastruktur. Mit Aqualris wurde ein Konzept für einen tragbaren optischen Wasserfilter entwickelt, der es seinen BenutzerInnen erlaubt, unabhängig von Energie und Infrastruktur sauberes Trinkwasser zu gewinnen.

Das handliche Gerät, das mit einem Gurt am Körper getragen werden kann, sammelt, filtert und neutralisiert Wasser. Dieses wird im Filter an einer Schicht mit Konverter-Kristallen vorbeigeschleust, die das Sonnenlicht in keimtötende UV-C-Strahlung umwandeln. Würde man Menschen in kritischen Regionen mit diesem erstaunlich einfachen Lowtech-Gerät ausstatten, ließe sich wohl so manche Cholera-Epidemie eindämmen.

Access to clean drinking water presents a problem in many regions of the world. Natural and manmade catastrophes (war, pollution, etc.) and primarily poverty interfere with the construction and maintenance of the necessary infrastructure for water supply. Aqualris is a concept for a portable, optical water filter that allows its users to obtain clean drinking water independent of energy or infrastructure.

The portable device, which can be carried on the body by means of a belt, gathers, filters, and neutralizes water. In the filter, the water passes through a lever with converter crystals that transfer sunlight into germicidal UV-C rays. Equipping people in critical regions with this amazingly simple, low-tech device could curtail many a cholera epidemic.

© Maurizio Maier

Überleben / Survival

Labor / Laboratory

S-Quip

Konzept für eine Rettungsdrohne	Concept for an emergency rescue drone
Design	Design
Lukas Pressler, Johannes Müller, Lukas Vejnik, Joachim Kornauth	Lukas Pressler, Johannes Müller, Lukas Vejnik, Joachim Kornauthr
Entstehungsjahr	Year of origin
2011	2011

Mit mehr als 20.000 Fällen jährlich allein in Europa nimmt das Ertrinken bei den nicht natürlichen Todesursachen die dritte Stelle ein. Bei Rettungsaktionen kommt es auf jede Sekunde an. S-Quip ist eine sogenannte Drohne, ein unbemanntes Luftfahrzeug, das automatisch Strände und Uferbereiche, Hafenregionen oder die Bereiche um Schiffe beobachtet. Drohen Personen zu ertrinken, agiert die Drohne autonom und leistet schnell erste Soforthilfe.

Wird eine Person in Not ausgemacht, löst sich die Drohne von ihrer Basisstation und fliegt zur hilfesuchenden Person. Noch bevor sie deren Position an die Rettungseinheiten übermittelt, wirft sie einen Rettungsring ab, der sich selbsttätig aufbläst. Damit ist die kritische Phase überbrückt, bis die Hilfsmannschaften am Ort des Geschehens eintreffen und die in Not geratene Person aus dem Wasser holen können.

With 20,000 cases every year in Europe alone, drowning takes third place among the natural causes of death. In rescue actions, every second counts. S-Quip is a so-called drone, an unmanned aircraft that mechanically guards over beaches and shores, harbor regions, and the area around ships. When someone is in danger of drowning, the drone reacts on its own and immediately offers first-response emergency aid.

Should a person in distress be spotted, the drone separates from its base station and flies to the individual in need of help. Even before communicating its position to the rescue unit, S-Quip throws out an automatically inflating life ring. The critical phase is thus bridged until the rescue squad can arrive at the site of the incident and pull the person in need out of the water.

© Joachim Kornauth

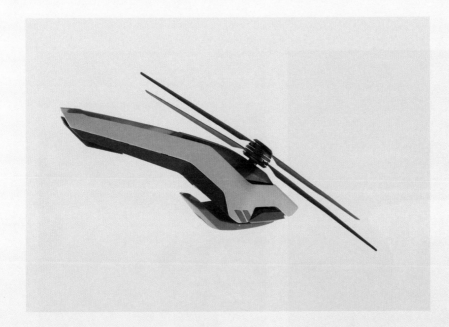

Guardian Angel

Konzept für ein fliegendes Überwachungsgerät	Concept for a flying surveillance device
Design **Theresa Lobkowicz**	Design Theresa Lobkowicz
Entstehungsjahr **2009**	Year of origin 2009

In Zeiten einer zunehmenden Privatisierung von Risiken passt sich der Guardian Angel dem gestiegenen gesellschaftlichen Angstpegel optimal an, denn mit dem jackentaschengroßen <u>Mini-Helikopter</u> mit Überwachungskamera wird Überwachungstechnik personalisiert: Wer in seinem Besitz steht, hätte die Möglichkeit, sein Umfeld stets auf Gefahren hin zu kontrollieren. Das Gerät überblickt die Szenerie, nimmt Bild, Sound und geografische Informationen auf und kann diese prinzipiell auch direkt per Video-Livestream an Überwachungsfirmen, Polizei oder Nothilfe übermitteln.

Neben der Kriminalitätsbekämpfung ließe sich der Guardian Angel aber auch zugunsten der Sicherheit kranker oder alter Menschen einsetzen – dort, wo schnelle Hilfe lebensrettend sein kann. Tatsächlich lassen sich viele Situationen ausmalen, in denen sich die persönliche, interaktive Form der Überwachung als hilfreich erweisen würde!

In an era of increasing risk privatization, Guardian Angel is a perfect match for the heightened fear level; the jacket-pocket-size <u>mini helicopter</u>, with surveillance camera, personalizes surveillance technology: those who have one are able to constantly control their environment for dangers. The device looks over the scenery, records images, sounds, and geographic information and, principally, is able to transfer these directly, per live stream video, to surveillance firms, police, or emergency assistance.

Along with fighting crime, Guardian Angel can also be used for the safety of ill or elderly people—there, where immediate help can be life saving. In fact, many situations can be imagined in which this personal, interactive form of surveillance would prove helpful!

Überleben / Survival

Labor / Laboratory

© Theresa Lobkowicz

216

Safe Food Project

Konzept eines Küchengeräts für Fleischerzeugung	Concept for a kitchen instrument for making meat
Design **Oskar von Hanstein**	Design Oskar von Hanstein
Entstehungsjahr **2011**	Year of origin 2011

ExpertInnen vertreten zunehmend die Meinung, dass die konventionelle Produktion von Fleisch vor allem aufgrund ihrer katastrophalen ökologischen Auswirkungen nicht mehr lange aufrechtzuerhalten ist. Schon gar nicht könne die gesamte Weltbevölkerung auf diese Weise versorgt werden. Möglicherweise liegt im <u>Züchten von Muskelzellen „in vitro"</u>, wie es in Labors weltweit erprobt wird, die Lösung für eine nachhaltige Versorgung der Menschheit mit tierischem Protein.

Das Safe Food Project dreht die Uhr noch ein wenig weiter vor und entwirft die Vision der Fleischzucht durch die VerbraucherInnen zu Hause: mit einem Gerät, das Muskelzellen – nach Wunsch vom Rind, Schwein, Lamm etc. – unter Zugabe von Nährlösung, Mineralstoffen und Vitaminen wachsen lässt, zeitlich abgestimmt auf das nächste Dinner mit Familie oder Freunden. Da damit auch das Fleisch alter und seltener Nutztierrassen einfach gezüchtet werden könnte, würde das Safe Food Project neben nachhaltiger Fleischwirtschaft sogar die Artenvielfalt fördern.

Experts increasingly voice the opinion that conventional meat production cannot be maintained for much longer, mainly due to the catastrophic ecological effects. It is already not possible to supply the world's population in this way. The solution for a sustainable <u>supply of animal protein</u> for humanity might possibly be found in the cultivation of muscle cells "in vitro," as has been tested out in labs throughout the world.

The Safe Food Project turns the clock a bit further ahead and designs a vision whereby meat is cultivated by users at home: with a device that allows the muscle cells—of beef, pork, lamb, etc.—to grow in perfect timing for the next dinner with family or friends, through the addition of a nutrient solution, minerals, and vitamins. Since the meat of older and also rare breeds of animals could be cultivated with ease, the Safe Food Project would foster species diversity along with a sustainable meat industry.

Überleben / Survival

Labor / Laboratory

© Oskar von Hanstein

217

Chulha

Lowtech-Herd	Low-tech stove
Design **Philips Design**	Design Philips Design
Hersteller **Dezentral mit lokalen Produzenten**	Manufacturer Decentralized with local producers
Entstehungsjahr **2008**	Year of origin 2008

In vielen Regionen Indiens, Afrikas und Lateinamerikas wird vor allem im ländlichen Gebiet nach wie vor in kleinen Innenräumen ohne Rauchabzug geheizt und gekocht. Die daraus resultierende Vergiftung der Raumluft hat teils dramatische Auswirkungen auf die Gesundheit: Laut WHO sterben rund 800.000 Kinder weltweit jährlich an Folgeerkrankungen. Besonders betroffen sind auch Frauen, die zumeist noch als für Haus und Herd allein zuständig gelten.

Chulha (indisch für „Herd") schafft hier Abhilfe. Der Lowtech-Herd aus Lehm mit Rauchabzug und besonders geringer Rauchentwicklung wurde in Zusammenarbeit mit NGOs, lokalen DesignerInnen und BenutzerInnen entwickelt. Chulha ist relativ günstig aus vor Ort verfügbarem Material herzustellen und leicht zu installieren. Das Design zielt auf effiziente Energienutzung, gesundheitsschonende Anwendung sowie dezentrale und individuelle Herstellungsmöglichkeit ab. Einem Open-Design-Ansatz folgend ist der Entwurf über www.lowsmokechulha.com frei verfügbar.

In many regions of India, Africa, and Latin America, particularly in rural areas, heating and cooking still takes place in small, indoor spaces without smoke outlets. The pollution of indoor air that results from this can have dramatic health effects: according to WHO, approximately 800,000 children die every year from related illnesses. Particularly affected are women, as they are still seen as holding sole responsibility for house and hearth.

Chulha (Indian for "stove") offers help here. The clay, low-smoke and low-tech stove was developed in collaboration with NGOs, local designers, and end users. Chulha is relatively inexpensive to manufacture from materials available on site, and is easy to install. The design aims at efficient energy consumption, healthy operation, as well as the possibility for decentralized and individual manufacture. Based on an open design approach, the design is available at no cost: www.lowsmokechulha.com.

Überleben /
Survival

Fabrik /
Factory

© Philips Design

Überleben /
Survival

Fabrik /
Factory

Ox

Studie eines Leichttraktors für Entwicklungsländer

Study for a lightweight tractor for developing countries

Design
Spirit Design / Technische Universität Wien / Universität für Bodenkultur Wien

Design
Spirit Design / Vienna University of Technology / University of Natural Resources and Life Sciences Vienna

Entstehungsjahr
2010

Year of origin
2010

Überleben / Survival

85 Prozent der landwirtschaftlichen Arbeitskräfte in Entwicklungs- und Schwellenländern sind Kleinbauern, die gerade einmal das Notwendigste, insbesondere für den eigenen und regionalen Bedarf, produzieren. Für sie ist eine – angesichts der wachsenden Bevölkerung unumgängliche – Produktivitätssteigerung durch Maschineneinsatz meist nicht möglich: Die Anschaffungs- und Betriebskosten sind zu hoch. Ox will das Segment des Leichttraktors für einen von großen Erntemaschinen dominierten Markt erschließen und die lokale, autarke Landwirtschaft fördern.

Das kostengünstige Arbeits- und Transportfahrzeug für Kleinbauern soll mit Biogas betrieben werden, das in dezentralen Anlagen der dörflichen Gemeinschaften selbst hergestellt wird. Auch aus Wind- und Solarstrom produziertes Methan kommt für den Betrieb des Ox infrage. Die Designstudie setzt auf einen interdisziplinären Designprozess und ist ein Förderprojekt des „Automotive Design Center" in Wien.

Eighty-five percent of the rural labor force in developing and newly industrialized countries comprise small farmers who just barely manage to produce the bare essentials for their own and regional demands. Increasing productivity by using machinery—an absolute necessity in light of growing populations—is not possible for them, in most cases: the purchase and operating costs are too high. Ox aims to develop the lightweight tractor segment in a market dominated by large harvesting machinery, thereby supporting local, independent agriculture.

The inexpensive work and transport vehicle for small farmers is planned to run on biogas that can be self-manufactured in decentralized facilities in village communities. Also methane, produced by hydroelectricity and solar power, can be used to operate the Ox. The design study relies on an interdisciplinary design process and is a granted program by the „Automotive Design Center" in Vienna.

Fabrik / Factory

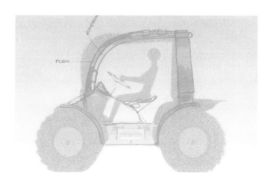

220

© Spirit Design

Überleben /
Survival

Fabrik /
Factory

Rosenbauer Panther

Flughafenlöschfahrzeug	Airport firefighting vehicle
Design **Spirit Design**	Design Spirit Design
Hersteller **Rosenbauer International AG**	Manufacturer Rosenbauer International AG
Entstehungsjahr **2005**	Year of origin 2005

Ein <u>Flughafenlöschfahrzeug</u> ist kein alltägliches Gerät, sondern kommt in speziellen Notsituationen an speziellen Orten zum Einsatz. Das sollte sich auch im Design des Rosenbauer Panther widerspiegeln – er ist das Flaggschiff des oberösterreichischen Unternehmens Rosenbauer, des Weltmarktführers bei Flughafenlöschfahrzeugen.

Der Fahrzeugaufbau wurde nach technologischen, ergonomischen und Kostenkriterien neu überdacht. Durch Verbesserungen am Aufbau ließ sich beispielsweise die Produktionsplanung ökonomisch optimieren – in der Industrie ein wichtiger Faktor. Wesentlich waren auch intuitive Bedienbarkeit und Ergonomie des Cockpits sowie die gute Sicht des Fahrers: Große Scheiben gewähren freien Blick auf die Umgebung und den Wasserwerfer, den er zu bedienen hat. Die Formensprache des Panther, der in Feuerrot gehalten ist, soll schließlich auch die emotionalen Attribute unterstreichen, die der Hersteller kommunizieren will: Verlässlichkeit, Sicherheit, Kraft und Dynamik.

An <u>airport firefighting</u> vehicle is no common piece of equipment; it is deployed in special emergency situations at special places. Rosenbauer's Panther also reflects that in its design, and is the flagship of the Upper Austrian firm Rosenbauer, the world's leader in airport firefighting vehicles.

The vehicle's construction was newly conceived based on technological, ergonomic, and cost criteria. Through improvements in construction, the production planning, for example, could be optimized—a key factor in the industry. Also essential were intuitive operation and ergonomics of the cockpit, as well as good vision for the driver: large windshields provide a free view of surroundings and the water-cannons to be operated. The formal language of Panther, which is painted fire-red, should ultimately highlight the emotional aspects that the manufacturer intends to communicate: reliability, safety, power, and dynamics.

Überleben /
Survival

Fabrik /
Factory

© Rosenbauer

Überleben /
Survival

Fabrik /
Factory

Eton TurboDyne

Notfallgeräte	Emergency devices
Design **Whipsaw**	Design Whipsaw
Hersteller **Eton Corporation**	Manufacturer Eton Corporation
Entstehungsjahr **2011**	Year of origin 2011

Unter dem Namen „TurboDyne" entstand in Kooperation mit dem Amerikanischen Roten Kreuz eine Serie von <u>Notfallgeräten</u> für den Endverbraucher. Die drei Nothelfer versorgen im Ernstfall mit Licht und Information, liefern außerdem Strom für andere elektrische Geräte. Road Torq ist ein leistungsfähiger Spot und Warnblinker, Rover ein Notfallradio mit direkter Verbindung zum Wetterdienst, Blitzlicht und Handy-Ladegerät. Axis schließlich kombiniert als Sicherheits-Tool Breitband-Empfang, AM-/FM-/NOAA-Empfang und Ladegerät.

Alle drei Produkte lassen sich mittels eines Handkurbel-Dynamos betreiben – die Energie wird also direkt vor Ort erzeugt. Die TurboDyne-Geräte mit ihren zahlreichen Reflektoren und einer einheitlichen Farbkombination aus Rot, Weiß und Silber zeichnen sich durch radikale Notfall-Ästhetik aus und kommunizieren damit sofort ihre Bestimmung. Die klare, geradezu kindgerechte Formgebung wirkt vertrauenserweckend und ist auch ein wenig retro angelegt.

In cooperation with the American Red Cross, a series of <u>emergency devices</u> for the end user were created under the name "TurboDyne." The three TurboDyne devices provide light and information in a real emergency, and also deliver electricity for other electrical devices. Road Torq is an efficient spot and hazard warning light; Rover is an emergency radio with direct connection to weather services, a flashlight, and cell-phone charger. Finally, as a safety tool, Axis combines broadband and AM-/FM-/NOAA reception, and is a charger.

All three products can be operated by means of a hand-crank dynamo—their power is thus produced directly, on site. The TurboDyne devices are distinguished by their radical emergency aesthetics, with numerous reflectors and a uniform color combination of red, white, and silver, communicating their purpose directly. The clear, practically child-operable form inspires trust, and even has something retro about it.

Überleben /
Survival

Fabrik /
Factory

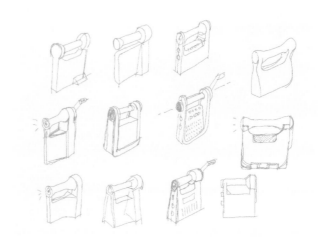

PIEPS Vector

Lawinenverschütteten-suchgerät	Avalanche transceiver
Design **PIEPS /** **Nussbaumer Design SAS**	Design PIEPS / Nussbaumer Design SAS
Hersteller **Seidel Elektronik**	Manufacturer Seidel Electronics
Entstehungsjahr **2012**	Year of origin 2012

Mit einem <u>Lawinenverschüttetensuchgerät</u>, kurz: LVS-Gerät, lassen sich Lawinenopfer, die ebenfalls damit ausgestattet sind, per Antenne anpeilen, orten und bergen. Da deren Überlebenschancen bereits nach 15 Minuten drastisch sinken, zählt hier jede Sekunde. Das österreichische Unternehmen PIEPS, das seit 1972 Sicherheitsgeräte für Eis und Schnee entwickelt, gilt als weltweiter Technologieführer bei der Herstellung von digitalen LVS-Geräten.

Sein neues Produkt, der PIEPS Vector, verfügt über vier Antennen mit einer Reichweite von bis zu 80 Metern. Da die beiden Hauptantennen gleichzeitig messen, sind eine Verdoppelung der Empfindlichkeit, eine größere Suchstreifenbreite und schnellster Erstempfang gegeben. Zusätzlich unterstützt durch GPS (Global Positioning System), können Suchende schneller geortet und die exakten Koordinaten des Fundortes direkt an die Suchmannschaften übermittelt werden. Das GPS prüft auch, ob kein Suchbereich ausgelassen wurde.

An <u>avalanche transceiver</u> makes it possible to narrow the search, locate, and rescue an avalanche victim who is likewise equipped with such a device. Since survival chances sink drastically already after fifteen minutes, every second counts. The Austrian firm PIEPS, which has developed safety devices for ice and snow since 1972, is the world's technological leader in the manufacture of digital avalanche transceivers.

Their new product, the PIEPS Vector, has four antennas with a range of up to 80 meters (262.4 feet). The two main antennas measure simultaneously, thus doubling the sensitivity, and providing a greater search strip width and the fastest possible first reception. Additionally supported by GPS (Global Positioning System), searchers can locate the victim faster and mediate the exact coordinates of the site directly to the search team. The GPS also checks that none of the search area has been left out.

© PIEPS GmbH

Überleben /
Survival

Fabrik /
Factory

Smart City Wien

Konzept für nachhaltige Stadtentwicklung und -planung	Concept for sustainable urban development and planning
Design **Stadt Wien (MA 18) / Institutionen und Initiativen aus Wien**	Design The City of Vienna (municipal department 18) / local stakeholders
Entstehungsjahr **2011**	Year of origin 2011

Seit Jahren führt Wien die internationalen Rankings in Sachen Umwelt- und Lebensqualität an. Mit der Initiative Smart City hat die Stadt in den letzten Jahren eine Vision für ihre längerfristige Zukunft erarbeitet – ein Modell für die <u>energieeffiziente und klimaschonende Entwicklung Wiens</u> bis 2020 sowie einen entsprechenden Aktionsplan für die nächsten drei bis fünf Jahre.

Die wichtigsten Inhalte des Konzepts sind neben dem Ausbau der spezifischen Stärken Wiens als Standort für Forschung und Technologieentwicklung vor allem die Bündelung und Vernetzung der städtischen Funktionsbereiche und – Stichwort: Partizipation – die Beteiligung der Bürger-Innen an den Planungsprozessen. Das Leben und Arbeiten ökologisch und sozial nachhaltig zu gestalten erweist sich für die wachsenden Städte, auch global gesehen, auf lange Sicht überlebenswichtig. Eines jener Wiener Pilotprojekte, bei dem zukünftige Urbanität in diesem Sinne schon bald erprobt werden wird, ist die Seestadt Aspern. 2011 wurde Smart City Wien bei den ersten World Smart City Awards mit Platz 1 ausgezeichnet.

For years now, Vienna has gained top international rankings in matters of environmental quality and quality of life. With the Smart City initiative, over the past few years the city has worked out a vision for its longer-term future—a model for <u>Vienna's energy-efficient and climate-friendly development</u> until 2020, as well as a corresponding action plan for the next three to five years.

The most important content of the concept are, along with the expansion of Vienna's specific strengths as a location for research and technology development, mainly the integration and networking of urban functional areas, and—key term: participation—citizen involvement in the planning process. Designing life and work in an ecologically and socially sustainable way has proven necessary for the long-term survival of growing cities, also from a global perspective. One of the Viennese pilot projects in which future urbanity will soon be tested out already, is Seestadt Aspern. In 2011, Smart City Wien was awarded first prize at the inaugural World Smart City Awards.

© TINA VIENNA

Überleben / Survival

Fabrik / Factory

MADE 4 YOU

Werkzeuge / Tools

Das L a b o r der Ausstellung „MADE 4 YOU. Design für den Wandel" bildet neben der Präsentation von Zukunftskonzepten den räumlichen Hintergrund für fachübergreifend angelegte Workshops, die im Rahmen der Kooperation „design⟩ neue strategien" von MAK und departure, der Kreativagentur der Stadt Wien, umgesetzt werden. Ziel der Workshops ist das Erproben und die Erarbeitung einer für den zeitgemäßen Designprozess hilfreichen „Toolbox" an Methoden und praktischen Herangehensweisen.

Besides presenting concepts for the future the L a b o r a t o r y of the exhibition "MADE 4 YOU. Design for Change" provides the spatial environment for interdisciplinary workshops, organised within the program "design⟩ new strategies", a cooperation of MAK and departure, the creative agency of the City of Vienna. The goal of the workshops will be the testing and development of a "toolbox" of methods and practical approaches to help the topical design process.

Harald Gründl
Institute of Design Research Vienna (IDRV)

d'lab.01:
Werkzeuge für die Design-Revolution

d'lab.01:
Tools for the Design Revolution

Um einen Wandel herbeizuführen, braucht es eine Design-Revolution, nach der sich DesignerInnen nicht mehr mit der Gestaltung von immer neuen Variationen von Produkten, sondern mit der Frage befassen, wie Bestehendes weiter- oder umdefiniert bzw. radikal verbessert werden kann. Die Design-Revolution wird auch unseren technologisch geprägten Innovationsbegriff von heute stürzen. Wir beginnen damit, uns von tradierten Produkt- oder Designvorstellungen zu lösen, setzen auf das Experiment, auf Solidarität statt Wettbewerb. Im Vordergrund steht die soziale Relevanz von Design. Soziale Innovation, Informiertheit statt Naivität, Austausch und Vernetzung, offene Weitergabe vom Wissensressourcen und Querdenken – das ist eine gute Grundhaltung für den Start.

Global Tools. 1973 konstituierte sich Global Tools als loser Zusammenschluss von Protagonisten der radikalen italienischen Architektur- und Designszene. Ziel war es, Themen der Kommunikation, Konstruktion, des Überlebens und aller mit dem Körper verbundenen Artikulationen von Design und Architektur in Laboratorien experimentell weiterzuentwickeln. In den 1970er-Jahren lag der Fokus auf der Weisheit und Veränderungskraft des Archaischen und Handwerklichen. ABB. 1 In der Reaktion auf die prekäre Umweltsituation unseres Planeten, Folge einer nicht nachhaltigen Entwicklung der westlichen Konsumkultur, wird die Aktualität dieses Ansatzes erkennbar. Unser Workshop „Werkzeuge für die Design-Revolution", Beitrag zur Ausstellung „MADE 4 YOU. Design für den Wandel", ist das Ergebnis einer intensiven Recherche von Strategien aus dem Bereich des dienstleistungsorientierten kommerziellen Designs, aber auch von Gegen- und Alternativkonzepten. Nicht-Intellektualität und alte Weisheiten, die Innovationsparadigmen der 1970er, müssen mit Informiertheit und technologischem Verständnis erweitert werden. Die vom Philosophen Frithjof Bergmann formulierte doppelte Infragestellung unserer Rolle im Universum – „was wir wirklich wirklich brauchen"[1] – wird für zukunftsweisendes Design zentral sein. Das „Raumschiff Erde" (Richard Buckminster Fuller, 1969) muss für die gesamte Weltbevölkerung funktionieren.[2] Die Gebrauchsanleitungen dafür sind größtenteils schon geschrieben!

Dekonstruktion. Industrialisierte Produkte bestehen aus einer Vielzahl von technologischen Werkstoffen. Der Weg aus der Wegwerfgesellschaft führt hin zu einer Kreislaufwirtschaft. Designprozesse müssen auf den gesamten Lebenszyklus des Produktes oder der Dienstleistung ausgeweitet werden und die Frage der Herkunft der Materialien ebenso berücksichtigen wie jene eines funktionierenden Sammelsystems. ABB. 2 Wir dürfen nicht nur das Produkt, sondern müssen auch Fabriken der Zukunft entwerfen.

For change to come about, a design revolution is necessary after which designers attend to further defining or redefining what exists, that is, radically improving it, rather than designing a steady stream of new variations of products. The design revolution will also topple the current technologically-shaped concept of innovation. We hereby begin to disconnect from traditional ideas of products and design; to rely on experiment, on solidarity rather than competition. The social relevance of design shifts to the forefront. Social innovation, being well-informed rather than naïve, exchange and networking, openly passing on knowledge resources, and lateral thinking—that's a good basic position for the start.

Global Tools. In 1973, Global Tools came together as a loosely knit group of protagonists from the radical Italian architecture and design scene. The goal was to further develop the themes of communication, construction, survival, and all articulations of design and architecture tied to the body—experimentally, in laboratories. In the 1970s, focus was on the wisdom and transformative power of the archaic and crafts-based. FIG. 1 The topicality of this approach becomes clear in reaction to our planet's precarious environmental situation, the result of Western consumer culture's non-sustainable development. Our workshop, "Werkzeuge für die Design-Revolution," (Tools for the Design Revolution), a contribution to the "MADE 4 YOU. Design for Change" exhibition, is the result of intensive research into strategies found in the area of service-oriented, commercial design, but also counter concepts and alternatives. Non-intellectuality and old wisdom, innovation paradigms of the 1970s, must be expanded to include being well-informed and an understanding of technology. The double questioning of our role in the universe as formulated by Frithjof Bergmann "what we really really want"[1]—will be central for future- oriented design. The "Spaceship Earth" (Richard Buckminster Fuller, 1969) must work for all of the world's population.[2] The operating manual is, in large part, already written!

Deconstruction. Industrialized products are compiled from a multitude of technological materials. The path out of a disposable society leads to a circulation society. Design processes must be expanded to include a product's or service's entire life cycle, and the origins of the material must be taken into account, as must a functioning collection system. FIG. 2 We cannot simply design products of the future, but must also design their factories. Technological tools help in precisely defining the lifecycle and environmental impact of design, and offer the opportunity to make decisions based on more than gut feelings.

Werkzeuge /
Tools

© Edizioni L'uomo e l'arte – giugno 1974 – stampato in proprio

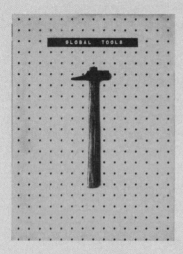

↑ ABB. 1
Cover „Global Tools", 1974

FIG. 1
Cover, "Global Tools", 1974

MADE 4 YOU

Technologische Werkzeuge helfen, den Lebenszyklus und die Umweltauswirkungen von Design genau zu bestimmen, und geben uns die Möglichkeit, Entscheidungen nicht nur aus dem Bauch zu treffen.

Kommunikation. Der Weg unserer industriellen Produktion in eine nachhaltige Richtung wird durch das „Grünwaschen" von Produkten in Aufmachung und Bewerbung konterkariert. Ein grüner Mantel aus Behauptungen, die entweder falsch oder irrelevant sind, legt sich über Produkte, die Mensch und Umwelt schädigen. Ökolabels versuchen die Komplexität der Umweltauswirkungen auf einfache Weise darzustellen. Deren Glaubwürdigkeit und Unabhängigkeit sind Voraussetzungen für die Orientierung an einer nachhaltigen Zukunft. Ein „Greenwashing Lab" stellt im Workshop Werkzeuge vor, mit denen sich sowohl Konsumenten als auch Designer vor grünen Lügen schützen können. ABB. 3

Kollaboration. Design als Wettbewerbsfaktor – so lautete der Slogan von Marketing und Design in der Vergangenheit. Dieser Wettbewerb berücksichtigte allerdings nicht die wahren Kosten[3] des Designs. Den Preis für die Gewinne zahlen die Umwelt und der Mensch. Daher muss die Politik, müssen alle aktiv werden und sich für neue Spielregeln einsetzen. Die Werkzeuge, die es braucht, um Design nachhaltiger zu denken, müssen frei verfügbar, der Umgang mit ihnen Teil der Ausbildung sein. Die Designausbildung ist heute von falschen Rollenbildern geprägt. DesignerInnen müssen neue Aufgabenfelder definieren, innerhalb derer sie partnerschaftlich interagieren und partizipative Designszenarien steuern. Wir alle sind DesignerInnen. Nicht die individuelle Kreativität macht jemanden zum Designer, sondern die Fähigkeit, mittels designimmanenter Werkzeuge die Resultate eines kollaborativen Designprozesses als wünschenswerte Zukunft darzustellen und umzusetzen.

Communication. The path of industrial production towards sustainability is thwarted by the "greenwashing" of products in their format and presentation. A green cloak of claims that are either false or irrelevant hangs over products that damage people and the environment. Eco-labels try to offer simple presentations of complex environmental consequences. Their credibility and autonomy are necessary for orientation toward a sustainable future. A "Greenwashing Lab" in the workshop presents tools with which both consumers as well as designers can protect themselves from green lies. FIG. 3

Collaboration. The erstwhile slogan of marketing and design declared design as competition factor. This competition, however, did not consider the true costs of design.[3] The price of profits is paid by the environment and people. Therefore, politics and everyone must become involved and advocate for new game rules. The necessary tools for making design more sustainable must be freely available, and working with them should be included in design curriculums. Education in the area of design is currently shaped by false role models. Designers must define new task areas within which they act in partnerships and manage participatory design scenarios. We are all designers. Individual creativity does not make someone a designer, but rather, the ability to use tools inherent to design to present and implement the result of a collaborative design process as a desirable future.

© IDRV, 2012

← ABB. 2
Mistplatz

FIG. 2
Garbage transfer station

↑ ABB. 3
Stifte

FIG. 3
Pens

Theorie. Ästhetische, gesellschaftliche und technologische Innovationen sind das Ergebnis von Experimenten und von in Laboratorien unterschiedlichster Disziplinen entstandenen Theorien. Nun ist die Zeit gekommen, die relevanten Ansätze auszuwählen und das Design zu revolutionieren. Zwischen Hausverstand und Quantentheorie bildet sich ein Kosmos neuen Wissens. Das Lokale und das Globale werden zu Innovationslaboratorien einer informierten Designhaltung. Das „unsichtbare Design", wie es Lucius Burckhardt nannte[4], wird neue „konviviale Werkzeuge" (Ivan Illich) für die Gesellschaft bereitstellen.[5]

Theory. Aesthetic, social, and technological innovations are the result of experiments and theories arising in the laboratories of diverse disciplines. The time has now come to select relevant approaches and revolutionize design. A cosmos of new knowledge is forming between common sense and quantum theory. The local and global become innovation laboratories of an informed attitude to design. "Invisible design," as Lucius Burckhardt called it,[4] will furnish society with new "tools for conviviality" (Ivan Illich[5]).

Werkzeuge /
Tools

[1] Frithjof Bergmann, Neue Arbeit, Neue Kultur, Freiburg 2004

[2] Richard Buckminster Fuller, Bedienungsanleitung für das Raumschiff Erde und andere Schriften, hg. v. Joachim Krausse, Dresden 1998

[3] True Cost Design von John Thackara, http://www.doorsofperception.com/learning-institutions/true-cost-design-in-three-steps/ (23.5.2012)

[4] Lucius Burckhardt, „Design ist unsichtbar" (1980), in: ders., Wer plant die Planung? Architektur, Politik und Mensch, Berlin 2004, S. 187–199

[5] Ivan Illich, Selbstbegrenzung. Eine politische Kritik der Technik, München, 1998

[1] Frithjof Bergmann, Neue Arbeit, Neue Kultur, Freiburg 2004

[2] Richard Buckminster Fuller, Operating Manual for Spaceship Earth, ed. Jaime Snyder, Basel 2008

[3] True Cost Design by John Thackara, http://www.doorsofperception.com/learning-institutions/true-cost-design-in-three-steps/ (23 May 2012)

[4] Lucius Burckhardt, "Design ist unsichtbar" (1980), in: ibid., Wer plant die Planung? Architektur, Politik und Mensch, Berlin 2004, pp. 187–199

[5] Ivan Illich, Tools for Conviviality, London 1973

MADE 4 YOU

234

Susanne Roiser, Ilse Klanner
Institut für Entrepreneurship und Innovation, WU Wien
Institute for Entrepreneurship and Innovation, Vienna University
of Economics and Business

d›lab.02:
Design Thinking –
Interdisziplinäre
Lösungsansätze

d›lab.02:
Design Thinking –
An Interdisciplinary
Approach to Solutions

Aus dem Blickwinkel neuer Technologien sowie geänderter Gesellschaftsstrukturen und -normen betrachtet, bergen bestehende Produkt- und Servicelösungen häufig ungenutztes Innovationspotenzial. Funktionale Fixierung[1], gelerntes (und selten hinterfragtes) Verhalten sowie gewohnte Lösungen verhindern oftmals, dass nicht mehr zeitgemäße Lösungen und Optimierungspotenziale erkannt werden. Da der traditionelle herstellergetriebene Produktentwicklungsprozess den Kunden nicht als Innovator, sondern als Käufer interpretiert, werden zudem viele Lösungen am Kunden vorbeientwickelt. Flop-Raten von bis zu 90 Prozent bei Neuprodukteinführungen haben ein Umdenken und die verstärkten Integration von Kunden in den Innovationsprozess zur Folge.[2]

Im Innovationsprozess stehen Unternehmen häufig auch vor der Herausforderung bereichsübergreifender und interdisziplinärer Zusammenarbeit. Ein wesentliches Element für erfolgreiche Innovationen stellt hier das Entwickeln von Schnittstellenkompetenzen, auf Organisationsebene die Implementierung bereichsübergreifender Strukturen zur Zusammenarbeit dar.

Die Methode Design Thinking[3] ist ein anwenderzentrierter Ansatz, um Innovationen zu generieren – von der Neuprodukt- und Serviceentwicklung bis hin zu neuen Geschäftsmodellen. Als empathische Identifikation ungedeckter Kundenbedürfnisse und Problemlösung in interdisziplinärer Zusammenarbeit gewährleistet die Methode, dass funktionale Fixierung überwunden und der Fokus auf die wesentlichsten Kundenanforderungen gerichtet wird. Ihr Grundprinzip ist das „Erfahrbarmachen" von „Customer Pain": impliziten, ungedeckten, schwer identifizierbaren Kundenanforderungen. Die Anwendung von Design Thinking macht Sinn, wenn implizite Kundenbedürfnisse schwer aufzudecken sind und heutige Lösungen oder Produkte nicht mehr zufriedenstellen. Das Ergebnis solcher Projekte sind kreative Ideen, gepaart mit „angreifbaren" Lösungen[4], etwa Funktionsmodellen, Visualisierungen oder Prototypen.

Angewandtes Design Thinking. Im InnoLAB am Institut für Entrepreneurship und Innovation arbeiten Designer, Künstler, Techniker, Natur-, Wirtschafts- und Humanwissenschaftler in interdisziplinären Teams an realen Themenstellungen, um systematisch innovative Ideen,

Existing product and service solutions often bear within them untapped innovative potential when viewed in light of both new technologies and changing social structures and norms. An obsession with functionality[1], learned (and seldom questioned) behaviors, and habitual choices of familiar solutions often combine to prevent recognition of solutions' obsolescence or optimization potentials. Since the product development process—which has traditionally been producer-driven—perceives the customer not as an innovator but as a buyer, many solutions are developed without really having taken the customer into account. However, product launch flop rates of up to 90 percent are encouraging reconsideration of this model, with the customer being accorded a larger role than before in the process of innovation.[2]

In the innovation process, companies are often faced with the additional challenge of multi-area and multidisciplinary collaboration. Here, an important element of successful innovation is the development of interfacing competencies, as well as the implementation of structures covering multiple areas at the organizational level.

The method called "Design Thinking"[3] is a user-oriented approach to generating innovation—from the development of new products and services all the way to new business models. By virtue of its empathy-based identification of unfulfilled customer needs and its strategy of problem solving via interdisciplinary collaboration, this method ensures that the usual obsession with functionality is overcome, with the focus being shifted to the most important customer requirements. Its fundamental principle consists in facilitating the experience of something known as "customer pain": this term denotes implicit, unfulfilled and hard-to-identify customer requirements. The employment of Design Thinking makes sense wherever implicit customer needs are difficult to identify and present-day solutions or products no longer produce satisfaction. The results of such projects are creative ideas paired with "palpable" solutions[4] such as functional models, visualizations or prototypes.

Applied Design Thinking. At InnoLAB, run by the Institute for Entrepreneurship and Innovation, designers, artists, engineers, natural scientists, economists, and social scientists work in interdisciplinary teams focused on real

Werkzeuge /
Tools

235

Lösungsansätze und Funktionsmodelle zu entwickeln, die mehrfach mit Anwendern getestet werden. Kernelement der Lernerfahrung ist neben dem methodischen Wissen die bereichsübergreifende Zusammenarbeit – der Wissens- und Erfahrungstransfer über Fachrichtungen hinweg und das Kennenlernen neuer Herangehensweisen.

Inhaltlich gliedern sich die Projekte in zwei Phasen ABB. 1: In einer intensiven Recherchephase gilt es konkrete Themenstellungen zunächst zu analysieren und Innovationspotenziale zu identifizieren, bevor in einer Ideen- und Konzeptentwicklungsphase Lösungsansätze erarbeitet, visualisiert sowie Funktionsmodelle erstellt und im Feld getestet werden.

topics in order to develop innovative ideas, problem-solving approaches, and functional models; these are then subjected to repeated tests involving users. In addition to methodological knowledge, a core element of the learning experience is multidisciplinary collaboration—the transfer of knowledge and experience across areas of expertise, as well as exchange for the purpose of becoming acquainted with new approaches.

In terms of their content, the projects are grouped into two phases FIG. 1: In an initial phase of intensive research, the task is to first analyze concrete thematic areas and then identify potentials for innovation. This is followed by a phase of idea and concept development that involves the generation and visualization of approaches to solutions and the construction and field-testing of functional models.

© Susanne Roiser, Ilse Klanner

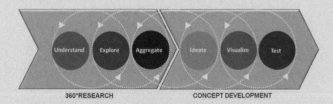

← **ABB. 1**
Methodischer Design-Thinking-Prozess am InnoLAB

FIG. 1
Design Thinking method used at the InnoLAB

MADE 4 YOU

→ **ABB. 2**
Erfahrbahrmachen impliziter und ungedeckter Kundenbedürfnisse im „Elderly Suit"

FIG. 2
Making implicit and undiscovered customer needs perceivable in the „elderly suit"

Das Flugzeug 65+. Ein Beispiel: Vor dem Hintergrund der demografischen Entwicklung – 2030 werden mehr als 40 Prozent der Weltbevölkerung zur Altersgruppe 65+ zählen – wurde nach Verbesserungen in Flugzeugkabinen gesucht, welche die speziellen Bedürfnisse dieser Zielgruppe berücksichtigen. Besonderes Augenmerk lag auf Einschränkungen des Seh- und Hörvermögens sowie der Motorik – dieser „Customer Pain" ließ sich durch das Tragen von „Elderly Suits" realitätsgetreu nachempfinden. ABB. 2

The airplane "65+". An example would be the following project: With demographic developments in mind—by 2030, the 65+ age group will make up over 40 percent of the world's population—an attempt was made to devise possible improvements to airline cabins that take into account the special needs of this target public. Particular attention was paid to limitations on visual and hearing ability and motor skills—this type of "customer pain" was simulated in a realistic manner by fitting participants with "elderly suits." FIG. 2

→ **ABB. 3**
**Prototyping verdeutlicht
Lösungsideen.**

FIG. 3
Prototyping demonstrates
solution ideas.

**Aufbauend auf einer anwenderzentrierten Markt- und
Bedürfnisanalyse, die rund 200 Tiefeninterviews mit
Passagieren und Experten, Beobachtungen und Selbsttests
umfasste, wurden „Key Insights" – konkrete Innovations-
potenziale – identifiziert. Basierend auf diesen Erkennt-
nissen entstanden mittels iterativer Feedback- und
Testschleifen systematisch Lösungskonzepte und Funk-
tionsmodelle. Das Ergebnis waren neuartige Universal-
Designkonzepte für mehr Komfort und Staubereich sowie
Aufstehhilfen und personalisierte Ablagefächer.** ABB. 3

Based on a user-centered market/needs analysis comprised
of around 200 in-depth interviews with passengers and
experts, as well as on observations and self-tests, "key
insights" were identified regarding concrete potentials for
innovation. Based on these findings, systematic solutions
and functional models were conceived by means of iterative
testing and feedback loops. This process resulted in novel
universal design concepts for more comfort and storage
space, as well as for personalized storage bins and devices
to assist passengers in standing up. FIG. 3

Werkzeuge /
Tools

[1] Karl Duncker, „On Problem
Solving", in: Psychological
Monographs 58/5, 1945; Herbert
G. Birch, Herbert S. Rabinowitz,
„The Negative Effect of Previous
Experience on Productive Thin-
king", in: Journal of Experimental
Psychology 4 (1951), S. 121–126

[2] Eric von Hippel, Democratizing
Innovation, Cambridge, Mass.,
1979

[3] Tim Brown, „Design Thinking",
in: Harvard Business Review, Juni
2008, S. 84–92; Jane Fulton Suri,
R. Michael Hendrix, „Developing
Design Sensibilities", in: Rotman
Magazine, Frühjahr 2010, S. 59–63

[4] Tom Kelley, „Prototyping is the
Shorthand of Design", in: Design
Management Journal, 12/3 (2001),
S. 35–42

[1] Karl Duncker, "On Problem Solving", Psychological Monographs
58/5 (1945); Herbert G. Birch,
Herbert S. Rabinowitz, "The Negative Effect of Previous Experience
on Productive Thinking", Journal of
Experimental Psychology 4 (1951),
p. 121–126

[2] Eric von Hippel, Democratizing
Innovation, Cambridge 1979

[3] Tim Brown, "Design Thinking",
Harvard Business Review June
2008, p. 84–92; Jane Fulton Suri,
R. Michael Hendrix, "Developing
Design Sensibilities", in Rotman
Magazine, Spring 2010, p. 59–63

[4] Tom Kelley, "Prototyping is the
Shorthand of Design", Design
Management Journal 12/3
(2001), p. 35–42

AutorInnen /
Authors

Friedrich von Borries ist Architekt, lehrt Designtheorie und kuratorische Praxis an der Hochschule für bildende Künste in Hamburg und leitet das „Projektbüro Friedrich von Borries" in Berlin. 2008 war er Generalkommissar und Kurator des deutschen Beitrages bei der Architekturbiennale von Venedig, 2001 kuratierte Borries im Museum für Kunst und Gewerbe Hamburg die Ausstellung „Klimakapseln. Überlebensbedingungen in der Katastrophe".

Friedrich von Borries is an architect. He teaches design theory and curatorial practice at the Hochschule für bildende Künste in Hamburg and manages the "Projektbüro Friedrich von Borries" in Berlin. In 2008 he was general commissioner and curator of the German contribution to the Architectural Biennale in Venice; 2001 he curated the exhibition "Climate Capsules: Means of Surviving Disaster" at the Museum für Kunst und Gewerbe Hamburg.

Hartmut Esslinger ist Designer. Der Gründer der Design- und Strategieagentur frog design mit Sitz in San Francisco und Büros auf allen Kontinenten arbeitet seit 40 Jahren mit Firmen wie Sony, Apple, Louis Vuitton, SAP, Siemens oder Lufthansa zusammen. Nach seiner Tätigkeit als Professor für Industriedesign (ID2) an der Universität für angewandte Kunst in Wien ist er seit 2011 DeTao Master für Strategisches Design am Shanghai Institute of Visual Art in Shanghai.

Hartmut Esslinger is a designer. He is founder of the design and strategy agency frog design with headquarters in San Francisco and offices on all continents. For the past forty years he has worked together with firms such as Sony, Apple, Louis Vuitton, SAP, Siemens, and Lufthansa. Following his position as Professor of Industrial Design (ID2) at the University of Applied Arts in Vienna, since 2011 he has been DeTao Master for Strategic Design at the Shanghai Institute of Visual Art in Shanghai.

Thomas Geisler ist MAK-Kustode für Design und Mitbegründer der Vienna Design Week. Bis 2010 Lehrender und Senior Scientist an der Abteilung Designtheorie und -geschichte der Universität für angewandte Kunst in Wien, führten seine Forschungen mit Martina Fineder zur Gründung der Victor J. Papanek Foundation. Er ist Mitherausgeber der kommentierten deutschen Ausgabe von „Victor Papanek: Design für die reale Welt. Anleitungen für eine humane Ökologie und sozialen Wandel" (2009).

Thomas Geisler is MAK Curator, Design and Co-founder of the Vienna Design Week. Until 2010, lecturer and Senior Scientist at the Department of Design Theory and History at the University of Applied Arts in Vienna, his research with Martina Fineder led to the founding of the Victor J. Papanek Foundation. He is a co-editor of the annotated German edition of "Victor Papanek: Design für die reale Welt. Anleitungen für eine humane Ökologie und sozialen Wandel" (2009).

Harald Gründl ist Gründer und Leiter des Institute of Design Research Vienna (IDRV) und Partner des international erfolgreichen Designbüros EOOS. 2008 als außeruniversitäres Institut gegründet, um einen unabhängigen, akademischen Beitrag zur sich etablierenden Designwissenschaft zu leisten, erarbeitet das IDRV interdisziplinäre Strategien der Wissensproduktion und -vermittlung und fokussiert auf Forschung in den Bereichen Sustainable Design und Designgeschichte.

Harald Gründl is founder and head of the Institute of Design Research Vienna (IDRV) and a partner in the internationally successful design office EOOS. Founded in 2008 as a non-university institute in order to offer an independent, academic contribution to the emerging science of design, IDRV works out interdisciplinary strategies for knowledge production and mediation and focuses on research in the areas of sustainable design and design history.

Barry M. Katz ist Professor für Design am California College of the Arts und Consulting Professor im Bereich Design und Mechanical Engineering an der Stanford University sowie Forschungsbeauftrager bei der Design- und Innovationsagentur IDEO. Katz ist Koautor der Bücher „Change by Design" (2009, mit Tim Brown) und „NONOBJECT" (2010, mit Branko Lukic). Demnächst erscheint sein neues Buch „Phase Change: The Dynamic History of Silicon Valley Design".

Barry M. Katz is Professor of Design at the California College of the Arts and a consulting professor in the area of design and mechanical engineering at Stanford University as well as research consultant at the design and innovation agency IDEO. Katz is co-author of the books "Change by Design" (2009, with Tim Brown) and "NONOBJECT" (2010, with Branko Lukic). His latest book "Phase Change: The Dynamic History of Silicon Valley Design" will be published shortly.

Sonia Laszlo ist Kommunikationswissenschaftlerin. Die Tochter des Glücksforschers Herbert Laszlo ist an dem von ihm begründeten Institut für Europäische Glücksforschung (IFEG) sowie als Gastvortragende an der Universität Wien tätig und schreibt an ihrer Dissertation über den Themenbereich „Glück und Film". Ihr erstes Buch ist für Herbst 2012 geplant.

Sonia Laszlo is a communication scientist. The daughter of happiness research Herbert Laszlo, she works at his Institut für Europäische Glücksforschung (IFEG) and as a visiting lecturer at the University of Vienna. She is writing her dissertation on "Happiness and Film." Publication of her first book is planned for autumn 2012.

Jeremy Myerson ist Direktor des Helen Hamlyn Centre for Design am Royal College of Art, London, und Helen Hamlyn Professor für Design. Als Wissenschaftler, Autor und Designaktivist richtet er seinen Fokus auf den Einfluss eines menschenzentrierten Gestaltungsansatzes auf die Innovation. Myerson ist Autor zahlreicher Bücher über Arbeitsplatzgestaltung, unter anderem „The 21st Century Office and New Demographics New Workspace", sowie Berater von Designschulen in Hong Kong und Korea.

Jeremy Myerson is Director and Chair of the Helen Hamlyn Centre for Design at the Royal College of Art, London. As an academic, author, and activist in design, a key theme of his work is the impact of a people-centered design approach on innovation. He is the author of a number of influential books on workplace design, including "The 21st Century Office and New Demographics New Workspace" and is an adviser to design schools in Hong Kong and Korea.

Katarina V. Posch ist Professorin für Designgeschichte und -theorie am Pratt Institute in New York, einer der renommiertesten Kunsthochschulen der USA. Auf interkulturelle Themen spezialisiert, lehrt und publiziert sie unter anderem über japanisches, europäisches und amerikanisches Design im gesellschaftlich-historischen Kontext. Dr. Katarina V. Posch war international für zahlreiche Institutionen kuratorisch und beratend tätig, unter anderem für das Museum of Arts and Design in New York, das Vitra Design Museum in Deutschland und das Centre Georges Pompidou in Paris.

Katarina V. Posch is Professor of Design History and Theory at the Pratt Institute in New York, one of the most renowned art academies in the U.S. She specializes in intercultural themes, and, among other topics, teaches and publishes on Japanese, European, and American design in a socio-historical context. Dr. Katarina V. Posch has worked internationally as curator and consultant for numerous institutes, including the Museum of Arts and Design in New York, Vitra Design Museum in Germany, and the Centre Georges Pompidou in Paris.

MADE 4 YOU

Hans Prihoda ist Geschäftsführer der Lasergruppe Materialbearbeitungs-ges.m.b.H, die seit über 40 Jahren in den Bereichen Medizintechnik, Kunststoff- und Lasertechnik führend tätig ist. Der gelernte Techniker – Prihoda studierte nach Pflichtschule und Ausbildung als außerordentlicher Hörer an der TU Wien Physik und Kunststofftechnik – ist Bundesinnungsmeister der Bundesinnung der Kunststoffverarbeiter in der Wirtschaftskammer Österreich und als Kommerzialrat Mitglied zahlreicher Ausschüsse.

Susanne Roiser und Ilse Klanner sind Forschungsmitarbeiterinnen am Institut für Entrepreneurship und Innovation der WU Wien, das unter der Leitung von Nikolaus Franke steht. Roiser und Klanner entwickelten das 2012 mit dem Preis für „Exzellente Lehre" der WU Wien ausgezeichnete interdisziplinäre, universitätsübergreifende Kursformat InnoLAB, in dem umfassende Design-Thinking-Projekte mit Kooperationspartnern aus der Praxis umgesetzt werden.

Katja Schechtner studierte Architektur, Städtebau und Technologiefolgen-forschung an der TU Wien und der Columbia University in New York, arbeitete als Beraterin und Forscherin in Japan, Irland, den Niederlanden, den USA und Portugal. Am AIT Austrian Institute of Technology leitet sie ein Team von 35 WissenschaftlerInnen im Bereich Dynamic Transportation Systems, darüber hinaus ist sie Visiting Scholar am MIT Media Lab in Boston.

Caroline Seifert ist Senior Vice President Product Design der Deutschen Telekom. Zum Product Design gehört auch das Zukunftsforum T-Gallery, in dem das Kundenerlebnis im digitalen Leben von morgen konzipiert und prototypisch entwickelt wird. Caroline Seifert arbeitet seit über 20 Jahren im Bereich der Telekommunikation und entwickelt mit Leidenschaft neue Produkte und Services.

Hans Prihoda is CEO of the Lasergruppe Materialbearbeitungsges.m.b.H., which has been involved as a leading firm in the areas of medical technology, plastics and laser technology for more than forty years. The trained technician—after completing his secondary schooling, Prihoda studied physics and plastics technology as a non-matriculated student at the Vienna University of Technology—is the Federal Guild Master of the Federal Guild of Plastics Manufacturers in the Austrian Economic Chambers and, as Kommerzialrat (Councilor of Commerce), a member of numerous committees.

Susanne Roiser and Ilse Klanner are Teaching Assistants and Researchers at the Vienna University of Economics (WU Wien)'s Institute of Entrepreneurship and Innovation, which is headed by Nikolaus Franke. Roiser and Klanner developed an interdisciplinary, interuniversity course format InnoLAB, in which comprehensive design-thinking projects are realized with cooperation partners involved in practice. The course format was awarded the WU's prize for "excellent teaching" in 2012.

Katja Schechtner studied architecture, urban planning, and technology research at the Vienna University of Technology and Columbia University in New York. She has worked as a consultant and researcher in Japan, Ireland, the Netherlands, the U.S., and Portugal. At AIT Austrian Institute of Technology she heads a team of thirty-five scientists in the area of Dynamic Transportation Systems, and is, in addition, a visiting scholar at the MIT Media Lab in Boston, MA, U.S.A.

Caroline Seifert is Senior Vice President of Product Design at Deutsche Telekom. A division of product design is the future forum T-Gallery, where the customer experience in the digital life of tomorrow is conceived and developed as prototype. Caroline Seifert has worked for more than twenty years in the areas of telecommunications and has a passion for developing new products and services.

Danksagung. Das Zustandekommen einer solch umfangreichen Ausstellung mit Katalog ist nur durch die kollegiale Zusammenarbeit und tatkräftige Mitwirkung vieler Beteiligter im MAK möglich – Danke! Als kuratorisches Team bedanken wir uns insbesondere bei den mit Projekten beteiligten Designagenturen, Studios und Unternehmen, die in ihren Archiven und Projektdokumentationen physisches oder digitales Material recherchiert und für den Katalog sowie für die Ausstellung als Leihgaben zur Verfügung gestellt haben. Die Umsetzung der umfangreichen Ausstellung gelang nur durch die unterstützende Eigenleistung der Leihgeber.

Ebenso gilt unser Dank allen AutorInnen, die sowohl zur Ausstellung als auch zum Katalog wertvolle Beiträge geleistet haben. Ein besonderer Dank gilt dem „ID2 Staff" – Hartmut Esslingers ehemaligen AssistentInnen Martina Fineder, Nikolaus Heep, Peter Knobloch, Norbert Kurz, Matthias Pfeffer und Stefan Zinell an der Universität für angewandte Kunst Wien (dieAngewandte), durch deren kontinuierliche Betreuung und Einsatz die Studienprojekte, die nun im „Labor" mit Stolz gezeigt werden konnten, erst diese Qualität erreicht haben. Martina Gartner war in der Koordinierung der zum Teil in aller Welt verstreuten StudienkollegInnen und AbsolventInnen eine große Hilfe.

Acknowledgements: Producing such a comprehensive exhibition and accompanying catalogue is only possible through the collaboration and resourceful efforts of many at the MAK – thank you to all of you! In particular, the team of curators want to express their gratitude to the design consultancies, studios and corporations who participated in the project, digging up physical or digital material from archives and project documentations and making it available on loan for the exhibition and the catalogue. Getting this large-scale exhibition under way was only possible through the help and generous support of the lenders.

Our thanks also go to all authors who made valuable contributions to the exhibition and the catalogue. Special thanks go to the "ID2 Staff"—Hartmut Esslinger's former assistants at the University of Applied Arts Vienna, Martina Fineder, Nikolaus Heep, Peter Knobloch, Norbert Kurz, Matthias Pfeffer, and Stefan Zinell, whose continuing and selfless tutoring commitment helped the student projects which are now proudly presented in the "Laboratory" section of the show to attain the quality they have. Martina Gartner was a great help in coordinating former fellow students and graduates, many of whom are dispersed all over the world today.

AutorInnen /
Authors

Impressum /
Imprint

Diese Publikation erschien anlässlich der
Ausstellung / This catalogue was published
on the occasion of the exhibition

MADE 4 YOU
Design für den Wandel / Design for Change

6.6.–7.10.2012
MAK Wien / Vienna

Gastkurator / Guest Curator
Hartmut Esslinger

Kurator / Curator
Thomas Geisler, MAK-Kustode Design /
MAK Curator, Design

Kuratorische Assistenz / Curatorial Assistance
Ivana Andrejic-Djukic

Ausstellungsgestaltung, Grafik Design /
Exhibition Design, Graphic Design
Vandasye (Georg Schnitzer, Peter Umgeher)

Ausstellungsorganisation / Exhibition management
Sibylle Kulterer

Registrar
Susanne Schneeweiss

Herausgeber / Editors
Christoph Thun-Hohenstein
Hartmut Esslinger
Thomas Geisler

Katalogredaktion / Catalogue editing
Thomas Geisler

Textredaktion / Text editing
Tina Thiel

Redaktionelle Mitarbeit / Editorial assistance
Ivana Andrejic-Djukic

Lektorat / Copy editing
scriptophil. die textagentur (deutsch / German),
Beverley Blaschke, Anna Mirfattahi, Nadjeschda
Morawec, Lisa Rosenblatt (englisch / English)

Übersetzungen / Translations
ins Englische / into English
Lisa Rosenblatt, Christopher Roth
ins Deutsche / into German
Michael Strand (Esslinger, Katz, Posch)

Grafik / Graphic Design
Vandasye

Schrift / Typeface
Signika

Papier / Paper
SoporSet Premium Offset

Herstellung / Production
Holzhausen Druck, Wien / Vienna

© 2012 Texte und Fotos bei den Autoren und
Fotografen / Texts and photographs by the authors
and photographers

© 2012 für die abgebildeten Werke von /
for the reproduced works by Le Corbusier,
Pierre Jeanneret, Charlotte Perriand (S. / p. 27):
VBK Wien / Vienna und / and VG Bild-Kunst, Bonn

© 2012 MAK Wien / Vienna
Verlag für moderne Kunst Nürnberg

Erschienen im / Published by
Verlag für moderne Kunst Nürnberg GmbH
Königstrasse 73, D-90402 Nürnberg
www.vfmk.de

ISBN 978-3-86984-346-9
Printed in Austria

Bibliografische Information Der Deutschen Nationalbibliothek /
Bibliographic information published by Die Deutsche Nationalbibliothek

Die Deutsche Nationalbibliothek verzeichnet diese Publikation in der
Deutschen Nationalbibliografie; detaillierte bibliografische Daten sind
im Internet über http://dnb.ddb.de abrufbar. / Die Deutsche Nationalbibliothek lists this publication in the Deutsche Nationalbibliografie; detailed bibliographic data is available on the Internet at http://dnb.ddb.de.

Distributed in the United Kingdom: Cornerhouse Publications
Distributed outside Europe: D.A.P. Distributed Art Publishers, Inc.

Wir haben uns bemüht, sämtliche Rechteinhaber ausfindig zu machen.
Sollte dies in Einzelfällen nicht gelungen sein, so bitten wir die
Rechteinhaber, uns darüber in Kenntnis zu setzen. / We have tried to
ascertain all the owners of the rights. If we did not succeed in all cases
to do so, information by the owners of the rights would be appreciated.

MAK
Stubenring 5, 1010 Wien, Austria
T +43 1 711 36-0
F +43 1 713 10 26
E office@MAK.at
MAK.at

MAK Center for Art and Architecture,
Schindler House
835 North Kings Road
West Hollywood, CA 90069, USA

Mackey Apartments
MAK Artists and
Architects in Residence
1137 South Cochran Avenue
Los Angeles, CA 90019, USA

Fitzpatrick-Leland House
MAK UFI – Urban Future Initiative
Mullholland Drive/8078 Woodrow
Los Angeles, CA 90046, USA

T +1 323 651 1510
F +1 323 651 2340
E office@MAKcenter.org
MAKcenter.org

Josef Hoffmann Museum, Brtnice
Eine Expositur der Mährischen Galerie
in Brno und des / A Joint Branch of the Moravian
Gallery in Brno and the / MAK Wien / Vienna

náměstí Svobody 263
58832 Brtnice,
Tschechische Republik / Czech Republic

T +43 1 711 36-258
E josefhoffmannmuseum@MAK.at
MAK.at